COLERIDGE'S POETIC
INTELLIGENCE

COLERIDGE'S POETIC
INTELLIGENCE

JOHN BEER
Fellow of Peterhouse, Cambridge

First published 1977 by
THE MACMILLAN PRESS LTD
London and Basingstoke
Associated companies in New York
Dublin Melbourne Johannesburg and Madras

ISBN 0 333 21312 2

Printed in Great Britain by
WESTERN PRINTING SERVICES LTD
Bristol

Man is so in love with intelligence, that where he is not intelligent enough to discover it, he will impress it.

*Coleridge on the so-called landscape
'improvements' at Highgate*

The definite, the fixed, is death: the principle of life is the indefinite, the growing, the moving, the continuous.

*Coleridge's conversation as recreated by
Hazlitt*

Contents

Preface and Acknowledgements   ix

Abbreviations   xv

1   A Sense of Magic   1

2   At the Springs of Romance   17

3   Shoots and Eddies   41

4   Primary Consciousness   70

5   Riddling Energies   95

6   The Characters of Life   119

7   An Exploring Fiction   147

8   Animated Nature   185

9   Light and Impulse   220

10   Other Relays   260

Notes   288

Index   309

Preface and Acknowledgements

My earlier study, *Coleridge the Visionary*, was written in the excitement of discovering that various key images in the great poems owed their existence not only to their vividness and sensuousness, but also to their association with certain basic patterns of ideas: ideas which could be shown to have been developing in Coleridge's mind for some years and to have re-echoed in his work for the remainder of his life.

The patterns to be discerned hung together coherently and illuminated many of Coleridge's other statements; it was harder to be sure about their status in his own mind, however. The reading of *Kubla Khan* which emerged was at once complex and suggestive, allowing one to read the poem either as a succession of exotic and resonant images, 'to their own music chanted', or to penetrate that surface and glimpse ideas and images concerning the nature of human genius that were moving beneath, to form patterns of their own. In the case of *The Ancient Mariner*, on the other hand, the illumination was less total: while some incidents, such as the 'dawn-vision', were set in context, others, such as the nightmare events, were hardly touched upon. It was not altogether clear to me how sophisticated – or indeed, at times, how conscious – Coleridge's attitude to his own ideas had been.

Some years later, while pursuing a point of scholarly identification, I came across a piece of evidence which helped to open up further prospects. In studying its implications I came to discern a key to Coleridge's original theory of human consciousness, a key which he had evidently been exploring during the years of his greatest poetry and his most intense psychological investigations. Further research in allied areas suggested that his theory of the organic had also evolved at an early period, with certain features which distinguished it from the theories which were being produced simultaneously in Germany. It was the evolution of these twin themes, I came to believe, which helped to explain his interest in comparative mythology, where he must have hoped to trace a primeval recognition of the same ideas. More immediately, however, their interweaving had provided him with instruments of considerable subtlety in exploring the actual phenomena of organic life and of human consciousness, even if it had also led him eventually into areas of self-contradiction from which he found it difficult to extricate himself.

The present study takes the main story up to 1805, before those inherent self-contradictions had caused the extensive fissions sometimes to be detected in the later writings. A further study would call for consideration both of the later ideas and of the ways in which, while reflecting the discontinuity created by Coleridge's predicament in 1805–13, they still harked back to his original preoccupations; it would, I believe, throw additional light on both his achievement and his reputation in his own time.

In judging his influence upon his contemporaries an awareness of the larger development of his thought is in fact very necessary, since various of them encountered him at different periods of his life. The kind of influence exerted differs, according to the stage which Coleridge himself had reached at the time of the first meeting. Unless these various stages are fully understood, therefore, some important elements in nineteenth-century thought become obscured. In the present study I concern myself primarily with those who came upon Coleridge as a young man.

During the period since my earlier study, the publication of Coleridge's work has taken various leaps forward. The *Collected Letters*, which were then just beginning to appear, are now complete. The *Notebooks*, similarly, which I was originally obliged to read in manuscript, are now available up to 1819 with very detailed annotations. The *Collected Coleridge*, gradually assuming substantial form, is another source of growing benefit.

In addition, several substantial critical and scholarly studies have appeared. Walter Jackson Bate's *Coleridge*, despite its unpretentious appearance, is one of the most perceptive accounts of Coleridge's life as a whole, suggesting some good reasons for the bewildering complexity of his achievement. Thomas McFarland's *Coleridge and the Pantheist Tradition*, a massive account of the tradition to which Coleridge was attracted and of his own distinctive contribution to it, has indicated the subtle duality of the resulting philosophical position. Richard Haven's delicate study, *Patterns of Consciousness*, has drawn attention to other distinguishing features of Coleridge's view of the mind; a reader who consults it in conjunction with the present work will find that the two studies run harmoniously together, but with varying emphases, the main difference being that Haven sees the evolution of Coleridge's position as something that belongs primarily to the post-German years, whereas I offer reasons for supposing that it was evolved at an earlier date in relation to particular contemporary books and ideas. Elinor Shaffer's '*Kubla Khan' and the Fall of Jerusalem* has drawn attention to the impact of biblical criticism in England from the 1790s onwards, and its possible relevance to some of Coleridge's poetic enterprises.

Norman Fruman's *Coleridge: the Damaged Archangel*, which deals with the unacknowledged borrowings scattered here and there in Coleridge's writings, is a study of a different kind. In one respect it is a useful *aide-memoire*, bringing together the various evidences of this phenomenon which have come to light (often in widely separated sources) over the years, and which, when viewed together, raise intricate and sometimes disturbing questions about Coleridge's personality and intellectual development. Mr Fruman's stance as prosecuting counsel is less helpful, however, since he is led to generalise a whole interpretation of Coleridge's personality from the instances he has collected, while not seeing that from another, equally selective, range of evidences a totally different picture would emerge. A full understanding of Coleridge requires a complexity of analysis quite beyond the reach of such partial graspings; the attitude of dry cynicism which pervades Mr Fruman's book simply muddies the waters further.

The interested reader who wishes to find further discussion of Mr Fruman's position (including his various errors and omissions) will find it in some of the longer reviews that have appeared since the book came out. Most of the matters in question fall outside the scope of the present volume, since there were comparatively few such borrowings in the early period. If Coleridge had died on his way to Malta in 1804, the instances then in existence could hardly have justified more than a short article. In one important respect, however, what I have to say bears on a basic theme of his book. Coleridge is presented there as an anxious man of limited intellectual powers, driven by an abnormal upbringing to thirst after the security of a reputation which could be won only by appropriating the work of others. The Coleridge who emerges in the following pages is a different kind of figure; basically ebullient and enthusiastic, sometimes over-reaching himself in the eagerness of his own aspirations, sometimes wrong, but continually stimulating himself and others to new acts of self-awareness. Coleridge produced no great system of philosophy, but he had a gift which many philosophers of his time lacked – an extremely delicate and perceptive intelligence. When that intelligence is not confined and stretched on the rack of a criminal indictment but seen flowering in its own original setting, the reasons for Coleridge's extraordinary impact on some of his leading contemporaries become more comprehensible.

I have incurred many debts in writing this study, debts which are in some cases co-extensive with my work on Coleridge as a whole. Mr Hugh Sykes Davies suggested many years ago that I should work on Coleridge's psychological ideas; although the project proved intractable at that time my initial work for the project has since served me in good stead. The late Humphry House, whose early death was a great blow to Coleridge studies in England, gave me much encouragement and help in the earliest stages; Professor Basil Willey has offered constant wisdom and encouragement over the years. I owe a continuing debt to Kathleen Coburn and George Whalley, both as friends and as fellow-editors in the *Collected Coleridge*; I am also deeply grateful to Thomas McFarland for his frequent hospitality and the concomitant exchanges of ideas. The sad death of Earl Leslie Griggs in a motor accident has removed a scholar and friend who had bestowed many kindnesses over the years.

I have gained a great deal from friendship with Coleridgeans in Cambridge, such as Sita Narasimhan, whose conversation sent me back to Boehme yet again, and Elinor Shaffer, who has drawn attention to possible Continental influences and parallels in Coleridge's life. I have learned much from examining the theses of D. M. Robbins, R. H. Wells, H. Yamanouchi and J. D. Gutteridge and from supervising the research of (among others) John Drew and Kathleen Wheeler. Others with whom I have discussed Coleridge's work profitably include Antonia Byatt (who made me conscious of the opposition to 'fixities and definites' in his poetry and philosophy), Frank Kermode (who provided, among other things, an apt quotation from Plotinus), Roy Park, Stephen Prickett, David Newsome, George Watson, Paul Magnuson, Graham Hough, Anthony Harding, John Woolford, Lionel Knights, Ted Kenney and Robert Langbaum. I am also very grateful to Professors R. L. Brett, R. A. Foakes and Asa Briggs for discussing various points by correspondence. One of my themes was first developed in a paper for a meeting of the Wordsworth Society at St John's College, another was presented in a paper to the Conference of University Lecturers for 1974, which was held in Dublin: I am grateful to the organisers for giving me these opportunities. The Coleridge Bicentenary Lectures in Cambridge in 1972, which brought scholars such as M. H. Abrams, Owen Barfield, D. M. MacKinnon and Dorothy Emmet to the platform, in addition to others, mentioned earlier, were a further source of stimulus, as has been the Wordsworth Summer School at Ambleside which, for some years now, has introduced Wordsworthians and Coleridgeans to one another beneath the kindly seigniory of Richard Wordsworth. Some of the final writing was undertaken during the Fall Term of 1975 at the University of Virginia; the graduate seminars on Romantic Poetry there (and an invitation to lecture at Washington and Lee University nearby) proved to be a great stimulus and aid in organising my ideas.

Acknowledgements are due to Victoria University Library at Toronto for permission to quote from an unpublished manuscript letter from W. G. Kirkpatrick; to Messrs Routledge and Kegan Paul and Princeton University Press for permission to quote from the published volumes of Coleridge's *Notebooks* and to Oxford University Press for permission to quote from editions of Coleridge's *Collected Letters* and *Poetical Works*. I am also grateful to the librarians and staff of Cambridge University Library, the British Library, the Bodleian Library, Peterhouse, the Cambridge English Faculty Library and Carlisle Cathedral Library for their many courtesies and help.

My final, and largest debts are to Mrs Hazel Dunn, whose ability to interpret even the roughest page of my manuscript has saved me hours of work, and to my wife, who, as always, has been unfailing in her support and the effects of whose presence in the following pages I can, even now, hardly begin to guess at.

Cambridge, 1976   J. B. B.

Abbreviations

(Place of publication in London unless otherwise stated. Periodicals are abbreviated according to the standard usage adopted in the Cambridge Bibliography of English Literature.)

AR   S. T. Coleridge, *Aids to Reflection*, (1825).

Aurora   Jacob Boehme, *Aurora. That is the Day-springs. Or Dawning of the Day in the Orient Or Morning Rednesse in the rising of the SUN. That is the Root or Mother of Philosophie, Astrologie & theologie from the true Ground*, (etc.) (1656).

BB   G. Whalley, 'The Bristol Library Borrowings of Southey and Coleridge, 1793–8'. *The Library*, 5th Series, IV, 114–32 (Oxford, 1950).

BL   S. T. Coleridge, *Biographia Literaria*, ed. J. Shawcross, 2 vols (Oxford, 1907).

BM   British Museum (the British Library).

Boehme (BM)   *The Works of Jacob Behmen*. With figures, illustrating his principles, left by the Reverend William Law. [Edited by G. Ward and T. Langcake] 4 vols (1764–1781). (Copy in the BM with Coleridge's annotations, pressmark C.126.k.I.)

C & S   S. T. Coleridge, *On the Constitution of the Church and State, According to the Idea of Each*, 2nd ed. (1830).

Carlyle	Thomas Carlyle, *Life of John Sterling* (1851) (chapter 'Coleridge').
Carlyon	Clement Carlyon, *Early Years and Late Reflections*, 4 vols (1836–58).
CL	*Collected Letters of Samuel Taylor Coleridge*, ed. Earl Leslie Griggs, 6 vols (Oxford, 1956–7).
CN	*The Notebooks of Samuel Taylor Coleridge*, ed. Kathleen Coburn (1957–).
C Variety	*Coleridge's Variety: Bicentenary Studies*, ed. J. B. Beer, (1975).
DNB	*Dictionary of National Biography* (1885–).
DQW	*The Collected Works of Thomas de Quincey*, ed. David Masson, 14 vols (Edinburgh, 1889–90).
DW	*Collected Works of Sir Humphry Davy, Bart*, ed. John Davy, 9 vols (1839–40).
DWJ	*Journals of Dorothy Wordsworth*, ed. Ernest de Selincourt, 2 vols (Oxford, 1941).
Friend	S. T. Coleridge, *The Friend*, ed. Barbara Rooke, 2 vols (*Collected Coleridge* IV) (1969).
Gillman	James Gillman, *Life of Samuel Taylor Coleridge*, Vol I (all published) (1838).
HCR	*Henry Crabb Robinson on Books and their Writers*, ed. E. J. Morley, 3 vols (1938).
HW	*The Complete Works of William Hazlitt*, ed. P. P. Howe, 21 vols (1930–4).
IS	*Inquiring Spirit, a New Presentation of Coleridge from His Published and Unpublished Prose Writings*, ed. Kathleen Coburn (1951) (cited by page).
KL	*Letters of John Keats, 1814–21*, ed. H. H. Rollins, 2 vols (Cambridge, Mass., 1958).
Lectures (1795)	*Lectures 1795 On Politics and Religion*, ed. Lewis Patton and Peter Mann (*Collected Coleridge* I) (1971).
LL	*The Letters of Charles Lamb to which are*

added Those of Her Sister Mary Lamb,
ed. E. V. Lucas, 3 vols (1935).

LL (Marrs)
The Letters of Charles and Mary Ann Lamb, ed. E. W. Marrs, Jr. (Ithaca, N.Y., 1975–).

LW
The Works of Charles and Mary Lamb, ed. E. V. Lucas, 7 vols (1903–5).

NB
S. T. Coleridge, Unpublished MS notebooks in the BM.

PL
S. T. Coleridge, *Philosophical Lectures,* ed. Kathleen Coburn (1949).

Poems (Ev.)
S. T. Coleridge, *Poems,* ed. J. B. Beer, Everyman's Library, (1963, rev. 1974).

PW
The Complete Poetical Works of Samuel Taylor Coleridge, ed. E. H. Coleridge, 2 vols (Oxford, 1912).

RX
John Livingston Lowes, *The Road to Xanadu, a Study in the Ways of the Imagination,* (1927, Revised ed. 1930).

Sh C
S. T. Coleridge, *Shakespearean Criticism,* ed. T. M. Raysor, 2 vols (1930).

Sulivan
Sir Richard Joseph Sulivan, *A View of Nature, in letters to a traveller among the Alps. With reflections on atheistical philosophy, now exemplified in France,* 6 vols (1794).

TT
Specimens of the Table Talk of the late S. T. Coleridge, ed. H. N. Coleridge, 2 vols (1835).

Watchman
S. T. Coleridge, *The Watchman,* ed. Lewis Patton, (*Collected Coleridge* I) (1970).

WL (1787–1805)
Letters of William and Dorothy Wordsworth, 1787–1805, ed. E. de Selincourt, 2nd ed. revised C. Shaver (Oxford, 1967).

WL (1806–1817)
Letters of William and Dorothy Wordsworth, 1806–1817, ed. E. de Selincourt, 2nd ed. revised M. Moorman (Oxford, 1969).

WP
The Poetical Works of William Wordsworth, ed. Ernest de Selincourt and

	Helen Darbishire, 5 vols (Oxford, 1940–1949).
W Pr	*The Prose Works of William Wordsworth*, ed. W. J. B. Owen and Jane Worthington Smyser, 3 vols (Oxford, 1974).
W Pr (Gr)	W. Wordsworth, *Prose Works*, ed. A. B. Grosart, 3 vols (1876).
W Prel	W. Wordsworth, *The Prelude*, ed. E. de Selincourt, 2nd ed. revised. H. Darbishire (Oxford, 1959).
W Prel (1805)	1805 version of *The Prelude*, as printed in the preceding.

I

A Sense of Magic

The year 1793 in England was to be remembered later as a time of unusual excitement, when the publication of Godwin's *Political Justice* had set in motion a wave of altruistic thinking among young men of the English middle class. Sympathies with the ideals of the French Revolution which had not previously found a means of expression now found a rallying point in Godwin's rational and benevolent philosophy. Thirty years later, comparing the remembered idealism of those days with current, more cynical attitudes, Hazlitt was to break into impassioned questionings:[1a]

Was it for this that our young gownsmen of the greatest expectation and promise, versed in classic lore, steeped in dialectics, armed at all points for the foe, well read, well nurtured, well provided for, left the University and the prospect of lawn sleeves, tearing asunder the shackles of the freeborn spirit and the cobwebs of school-divinity, to throw themselves at the feet of the new Gamaliel, and learn wisdom from him? Was it for this, that students at the bar, acute, inquisitive, sceptical (here only wild enthusiasts) neglected for a while the paths of preferment and the law as too narrow, tortuous, and unseemly to bear the pure and broad light of reason? Was it for this, that students in medicine missed their way to Lecturerships and the top of their profession, deeming lightly of the health of the body, and dreaming only of the renovation of society and the march of mind? Was it to this that Mr. Southey's *Inscriptions* pointed? to this that Mr. Coleridge's *Religious Musings* tended? Was it for this, that Mr. Godwin himself sat with arms folded, and, 'like Cato, gave his little senate laws'? Or rather, like another Prospero, uttered syllables that with their enchanted breath were to change the world, and might almost stop the stars in their courses?

Oh! and is all forgot? Is this sun of intellect blotted from the sky? Or has it suffered total eclipse? Or is it we who make the fancied gloom, by looking at it through the paltry, broken, stained fragments of our own interests and prejudices?

It is a passage which deserves close attention. A touch of irony may be detected in the very extravagance of the language; it emerges more strongly in Hazlitt's need to cite Pope's satirical portrait of Atticus before allowing himself to compare Godwin with Prospero. Yet neither kind of irony, the inflating or the undercutting, would be there were it not for the concealed strength of feeling which it defends. Rather, it indicates the difficulty which Hazlitt finds, even now, in knowing what status should be given to that remembered afflatus.

It is altogether in keeping with this uncertainty that the two names which most immediately recall the spirit of the time for him are those of Southey and Coleridge. For Coleridge, 1793 itself was in fact a year of disaster, marked by his Cambridge debts and his despairing enlistment as a dragoon. Nevertheless, his collaboration with Southey in plans for an American community in the following year had given vivid expression to the current mood, while the poems which they produced subsequently could be seen as having given a finer tone to Godwinism.

Coleridge remained the most riddling figure. Others, having tasted the treatment meted out to those who stepped out of line with their society, had beaten a quick retreat to the city of security from which they began – or so Hazlitt felt. Coleridge, by contrast, had remained in the wilderness, neither participating in the advance towards a new order nor retreating to the old. To anyone who had participated in the Godwinian dawn and still looked back on it with nostalgia, his behaviour was the hardest to understand.

In other essays, Hazlitt pursued the enigma. He conveyed the excitement of hearing Coleridge's discourse in 1798 and wrote a fascinated itinerary of Coleridge's explorations in the world of books and ideas, moving rapidly and eagerly from one system to another. Yet here too in the imagery there are touches that prepare for an ultimate disillusionment:

> And then he fell plump, ten thousand fathoms down (but his wings saved him harmless) into the *hortus siccus* of Dissent . . .
>
> (HW XI 32)

We are to pick up a firm echo of Satan's flight through Chaos:

> all unawares
> Flutt'ring his pennons vain plumb down he drops
> Ten thousand fadom deep, and to this hour
> Down had been falling, had not by ill chance
> The strong rebuff of some tumultuous cloud
> Instinct with Fire and Nitre hurried him
> As many miles aloft   (PL II 932–8)

The suggestion of vain pursuit, of a mistaken archangel winging his way through Chaos (with Hazlitt's change of 'plumb' into 'plump' momentarily transposing Milton's sardonic humour into a more ridiculing mode) is picked up more bitingly at the end of the essay, when Hazlitt quotes Milton again concerning the effects of Coleridge's more conservative later writings: 'His words were hollow, but they pleased the ear'.

Hazlitt's various reminiscences might stand for many that were produced in Coleridge's lifetime and after his death. These range in attitude from hero-worship to cynicism (Hazlitt ingeniously combines both), but certain common themes come through again and again. Most of his friends agreed that Coleridge was unlike anyone else they had ever met and that to know him was an exciting experience; many also felt at some stage a disturbing sense of betrayal, as if the man had not lived up to all that he had promised them. And most of them found, like Hazlitt, that their writing was raised to a higher pitch as they tried to describe him.

Sometimes the descriptions of Coleridge as an oracular figure had a touch of ritual flattery, as when W. G. Kirkpatrick, seeking a meeting with him in 1827, writes of his diffidence in approaching him and then continues:[2]

> Yet still, as if fascinated in the labyrinth of some enchanted ground, for all the overawing & the drawing back, a stronger

fatality impels me forward. How in the issue of the adventure to fare the hapless Errant knows not, nor yet with what apology to face the Archimage, upon whose privacy he has been intruding at some ill-omened hour, and who in the sanctuary of his own thoughts may at that moment be holding communion with the higher powers, or contemplating the face of nature without her veil . . .

At such moments a salutary counterweight is provided by Carlyle's account of the same period, with its domesticating irony:

> . . . to the rising spirits of the young generation he had this dusky sublime character; and sat there as a kind of *Magus*, girt in mystery and enigma; his Dodona oak-grove (Mr Gilman's house at Highgate) whispering strange things, uncertain whether oracles or jargon.   (Carlyle 70)

Yet even Carlyle does not deny the unusual powers of the man he is describing; he simply makes sure that we recognise him as a fallible human being. He dispels with a few deft touches, for example, the myth of an eternal Highgate audience, hanging breathless on Coleridge's every word, and replaces it with the actuality of a group of people, attracted by Coleridge's reputation, who would, as the monologue got under way, evolve into 'secondary humming groups', but who would fall silent again when he reached one of his 'islets of the blest and intelligible'. Carlyle was torn between admiration for the 'eloquent artistically expressive words' and 'piercing radiances' of the discourse and impatience at its apparent aimlessness.[3] Of one thing he was certain, however: 'No talk, in his century or in any other, could be more surprising.'[4]

In earlier years Coleridge was more consistently compelling as a speaker; we need only turn to Lamb's account of his eloquence at Christ's Hospital or Hazlitt's of his preaching at Shrewsbury. It was those who knew him longest who most retained this sense of excitement, moreover; Lamb wrote of his presence at Highgate in 1816: 'Tis enough to be within the whiff and wind of his genius for us not to possess our souls in quiet',[5] while Wordsworth described him as wonderful – 'wonderful for the originality of his mind, and the power he possessed of throwing out grand central truths from which might be evolved the most comprehensive systems.'[6]

In these and other accounts one notes how readily the imagery of magic comes into play. When he was translating *Wallenstein* in 1800, Lamb described him as having looked like a conjuror;[7] in old age Leigh Hunt could still describe him as 'a good-natured wizard, very fond of earth, and conscious of reposing with weight enough in his easy chair, but able to conjure his æthe-realities about him in the twinkling of an eye.'[8] His ability to conjure ideas into vivid existence was something which many of his friends delighted in – even if they were sometimes taken aback to discover that one or two of the feats of knowledge were performed with the aid of a hidden device behind the conjuror's back. De Quincey was one of the first to comment publicly on Coleridge's tendency to obscure his sources – his 'infirmity' as he called it – which he found exhibited both in conversation and in some of his published works. Other friends were disturbed, puzzled or simply amused by these discoveries; none, however, found their belief in his powers compromised. De Quincey himself was explicit on the paradox involved:

> He spun daily, and at all hours . . . from the loom of his own magical brain, theories more gorgeous by far . . . With the riches of El Dorado lying about him he would condescend to filch a handful of gold from any man whose purse he fancied . . .   (DQW II 146)

Again the word 'magical' appears.

The point which needs to be emphasised, however, is that in the case of Coleridge this element of magic is not simply an epiphenomenon, fittest for rhetorical use – whether as a vehicle for dismissing his larger claims or for embellishing an occasional compliment to his intellectual gifts; it is germane to an understanding of his whole career. He lived at a time when many had thought magic to have finally been banished from the rational world, but when new discoveries in chemistry and electricity – known about, but as yet hardly explained – were opening men's minds again to the mysterious powers of the universe, powers which had been by-passed rather than comprehended in the theories of eighteenth-century science. The young Coleridge, looking at the phenomena involved with fresh eyes, found it natural to ask whether there might not be a more intimate relationship than was normally supposed between the powers traditionally ascribed to magic and the inner powers of nature.

There are signs that at one stage he pursued a strong interest in the literature of magic and read what he could find on the subject. If so, the interest was probably at its height in adolescence, when he had access to the 'great circulating library' in Cheapside;[9] the indications of such interests in his later recorded reading and writing are sporadic, as if he were returning to a long-familiar subject rather than exploring it for the first time. The same is true of his later use of imagery drawn from magic. These are usually produced in some context where he is stressing the pre-eminence of reason or some conventional virtue; it is only when one lingers over the image itself that one sees it to have a strong life of its own. Recalling his early political beliefs and warinesses, for instance, he writes,

> Thanks to the excellent Education which I had received, my reason was too clear not to draw this 'circle of power' round me, and my spirit too honest to attempt to break through it.
>
> (Friend II 146 (I 233))

Later in the same work he writes, of the love of one's country,

> Here, from within this circle defined, as light by shade, or rather as light within light by its intensity, only within these magic circles rise up the awful Spirits, whose words are Oracles for Mankind, whose love embraces all Countries, and whose voice sounds through all Ages!
>
> (Friend II 323 (I 293))

And in the Philosophical Lectures he relates how, during the Enlightenment,

> the subtlest mysteries of life and organization, even of the intellect and moral being, were conjured within the magic circle of mathematical formality.
>
> (PL 342. Cf. ShC II 69, 84)

In the Biographia he draws on another image:

> The magic rod of fanaticism is preserved in the very adyta of

human nature; and needs only the re-exciting warmth of a
master hand to bud forth afresh and produce the old fruits.

(BL I 130)

Once again the vivid and detailed exactness of the imagery
suggests a long-standing depth of attachment in the author's
mind – half-drawing him away momentarily from the main point
at issue, perhaps. When he places such statements against more
explicit uses in the early period, such as the projected delights of
his American community, where

> dancing to the moonlight roundelay
> The wizard Passions weave an holy spell   (PW I 69)

or the circular dance which forms itself round the inspired genius
in the last stanza of *Kubla Khan*, we are justified in suspecting
that the interest in magic lore had long been at work in
Coleridge's imagination, and remained there, ready to offer its
services even when his overt and rhetorical end was of a rather
different kind.[10]

If it were simply the case that Coleridge was haunted by the
imagery of a subject which, as a subject, he had long ago dismissed, the interest of the matter would be strictly limited. We
should be dealing with one facet of a complicated personality
which could be said to enhance his attractiveness while also
exerting a somewhat equivocal effect upon his character. The
matter becomes more complex, however, once it is grasped that
Coleridge was not only fascinated by magic as magic, but that in
later, more sceptical moods he was still asking what Mill was
later to describe as the characteristic Coleridgean question – not
'Is this true?' but 'What is the meaning of it?'[11] The point to
be argued in the present study is that Coleridge, while rejecting
the immediate phenomena of magic, came to believe at an early
stage that certain elements in traditional magical lore were in
fact relevant to an understanding of human nature at its deepest
levels: and that although the forces at those levels, corresponding
to the operation of the power of life itself in the human being,
could not be inspected directly by human consciousness, they
made their presence felt through images normally associated
with certain magical and hermetic beliefs. Through lack of
attention to what they revealed, he felt, his contemporaries were

liable to find themselves betrayed into a totally mechanical universe, where life was no more than an unusual – and ultimately irrelevant – manifestation. On prolonged contemplation, such a universe must inevitably turn into a 'universe of death'. With the aid of the powers revealed in the human consciousness, by contrast, the universe could remain what it had always been for the child: a 'universe of life', its apparent fixities and definites subject to the transforming power of vitalised human perceptions – which in turn corresponded to powers actually at work everywhere in animated nature.

One favourite image of life should be mentioned immediately in this connection: that of the spring, with its never-ending resource of energy. Among other things, it offered a dramatic presentation of a silent work always going on in the universe: it was even a feature of the world of vegetation, where the repeated unfolding of bud and blossom, a slow and silent work of the everyday world, would, if speeded up ten thousandfold, be seen more vividly as a never-failing ebullience. When Coleridge was in his more lofty youthful moods he could picture an exalted Newton in heaven,[12]

> gazing, in the spring
> Ebullient with creative energy

or speak of 'Contemplant Spirits' there, hovering over

> th'immeasurable fount
> Ebullient with creative Deity!   (PW I 124)

In a more chastened frame of mind he might invert its significance, writing of his own speculations as

> Bubbles that glitter as they rise and break
> On vain Philosophy's aye-babbling spring.
>   (PW I 102)

– but the image was still present. In an intermediate mood, at once serious and self-deprecating, he could use the activity of boiling liquid as another version of the phenomenon, referring humorously to his own mind as an 'Idea-pot'[13] and suggesting that a friend should hang his mind 'as a looking-glass'

> over my Idea-pot, so as to image on the said mind all the
> bubbles that boil in the said Idea-pot ...   (CL I 294)

When he tried to come to terms with the strange mixture of truths and delusions that he found in Boehme, some years later, the related image of the magic cauldron came readily to his mind:[14]

> Frequently does he mistake the dreams of his own over excited nerves, the phantoms and witcheries from the cauldron of his own seething Fancy, for parts or symbols of a universal Process . . .

To a congenial young friend, equally, he could write:

> It is a source of strength and comfort to know, that the labors and aspirations and sympathies of the genuine and invisible Humanity exist in a social world of their own, that it's attractions and assimilations are no platonic fable, no dancing flames or luminous bubbles on the magic cauldron of my Wishes; but that there are even in this unkind life spiritual parentages, and filiations of the soul . . .   (CL v 176)

Two other images of magic that worked strongly in Coleridge's mind, if we follow the various hints in his verse and prose, were those of the magician's wand and the magic circle. The one, which also included various images of club and staff, found its extreme in the magic rod that could be made to blossom and grow; the other moved from the 'circle of power' concept to an interest in circling waves, circular dances, children's rounda-bouts, circles round the moon, eddies in water and, in the animal world, eddyings and spirallings of all kinds.

In certain great classical images, the two modes could be seen to run together. One was that of the serpent-entwined tree, familiar both from illustrations of the tree in the Garden of Eden in Genesis and from classical sources such as the serpent-guarded tree of fruit in the Hesperides. Another was that of the winged, serpent-encircled staff or caduceus carried by Hermes. This, one of the most common of traditional mythological symbols, was available to him in the illustration of Mercury in Tooke's *Pantheon*, a book which he pored over at school.[15] (A similarly twined serpent round the staff of Aesculapius in the same volume haunted his memory for years as an image of healing.)[16] In all such emblems a vegetative form was surrounded by circles of power.

In Tooke's *Pantheon* he could also have found it asserted that the Moses of the Old Testament and the Bacchus of ancient mythology were one and the same character.[17] Even if he did not respond immediately to this surprising parallel, with its various resonances, he would be likely to have noticed one feature of the biblical story: that Moses and his brother Aaron are both represented as possessing magical powers involving rod and serpent. Moses casts his rod on the ground and it turns into a serpent; he picks it up again and it turns back into a rod. Later in the wilderness he uses his rod to strike waters from the rock; when his people have been bitten by a serpent he sets up the image of a serpent on a pole which they can look at and be healed. Aaron, also, has the power of turning his rod into a serpent; when he later puts his rod in the temple it buds, blossoms and yields almonds.[18]

There are various indications that Coleridge in youth sometimes saw himself as a new Moses, destined to lead his followers through the wilderness, striking springs from the rocks of their eighteenth-century rationalism and bringing them to a land flowing with milk and honey. We may think, for example, of his later description of the part played by the mystics in his early thinking (where the 'wilderness' is a wilderness of doubt): 'If they were too often a moving cloud of smoke to me by day, yet they were always a pillar of fire throughout the night' – which may be read in conjunction with Lamb's characterisation of him at school: 'with hope like a fiery column before thee – the dark pillar not yet turned'.[19] Lamb's wry comment, 'His face when he repeats his verses hath its ancient glory, an Archangel a little damaged',[20] may similarly be read both against classical accounts of the inspired poet and against the biblical story that when Moses came down from the mount, his face shone so brightly that the people could not look at him without a veil – a set of parallels which Coleridge was to recall and elaborate on in Rome some years later, when he saw the horns of glory on Michelangelo's statue of Moses.[21]

All this may be viewed indulgently as a harmless piece of youthful extravagance, particularly since it was cultivated not with aspirations after personal aggrandisement but rather with a hope of arousing men to new vision and love of one another. There was another side to his personality, of course, as may be seen from his brief period of extravagance and debaucheries at Cambridge, or his occasional displays of youthful arrogance. One suspects that he sometimes relied upon a magical providence to rescue him from the results of irresponsible actions. His friends of the time seem to have regarded him primarily as an enthusiast, however, as when his brother called him a 'hot-headed Moravian',[22] or when Mary Evans, his first sweetheart, wrote, sadly, 'There is an Eagerness in your Nature which is ever hurrying you into the sad Extreme'.[23] On the one hand, we can read his later account of himself during the *Watchman* tour in the *Biographia*:

> O! never can I remember those days with either shame or regret. For I was most sincere, most disinterested! My opinions were indeed in many and most important points erroneous; but my heart was single. Wealth, rank, life itself then seemed cheap to me, compared with the interests of (what I believed to be) the truth, and the will of my maker. I cannot even accuse myself of having been actuated by vanity; for in the expansion of my enthusiasm I did not think of *myself* at all.
>
> (BL I 115)

On the other, we can look at his own, more light-hearted account of the walking-stick which he carried on his tour of North Wales, bearing the head of an eagle (its eyes rising suns, its ears Turkish crescents), a portrait of its owner and, among other things, the 'Line of Beauty' waving down it 'in very ugly Carving'.[24] Comparing this with the staff of Hermes, it is not hard to see why he bought it so eagerly from a countryman whom he found carrying it near Cambridge. (Later he was to suggest that the reason for swinging a stick while walking was to distribute one's animal spirits to as many points of the compass as possible.)[25] Through these various levels of seriousness, there runs a common note of exuberance and eager inquiry.

If we are right to picture the youthful Coleridge as occupying his mind and imagination with images of budding rod, ebullient spring, irradiations of glory from the body and, centrally, the winged, serpent-entwined staff of Mercury as possible interrelated interpretative emblems of the primary nature of life itself, however, we must still enquire what status they have in his thought as a whole.

Although they help to interpret a number of his poems, both major and minor, as we shall see, their presence is by no means evident in the prose works at first sight. More often they are found in isolated images of the kind noticed above, where the imaginative effect seems almost accidental to the main argument. Coleridge seems to have become far more cautious of such theories in later life, using them, when he used them at all, in the service of other beliefs rather than allowing them to flourish in their own right. Even in his early years, moreover, they were – at least after his earliest flush of enthusiasm – explored esoterically alongside sober doctrines more readily acceptable to – and comprehensible in – the society of his time. The general process involved is described in the *Biographia*, when Coleridge says, speaking of his religious beliefs in youth;

> I was at that time and long after, though a Trinitarian (i.e. ad normam Platonis [on the Platonic model]) in philosophy, yet a zealous Unitarian in Religion.   (BL I 114)

This he glosses a few pages later:

> These principles I held, *philosophically*, while in respect of revealed religion I remained a zealous Unitarian. I considered the *idea* of the Trinity a fair scholastic inference from the being of God, as a creative intelligence; and that it was therefore entitled to the rank of an *esoteric* doctrine of natural religion. But seeing in the same no practical or moral bearing, I confined it to the schools of philosophy.   (BL I 136–7)

In spite of a slightly disparaging tone, the importance which Coleridge attaches to his esoteric trinitarianism emerges when he goes on to say that he believes its existence to have been responsible for his eventual rescue from Unitarianism. And the full significance of his phrase 'ad normam Platonis' begins to emerge when one considers the hieroglyphic versions of the Trinity as sun, serpent and wings which were current in the late eighteenth century,[26] and Coleridge's own assertions elsewhere that Plato had taught an esoteric version of the doctrine, as comprising Will, Mind and a wisdom which was also the energy of Love, which he had confided only to a few followers.[27] This, we begin to see, is no orthodox doctrine of Father, Son and Holy Ghost but, literally, a paradigm of creative intelligence – which

Coleridge believes to be hidden within the orthodox doctrine and to be interpretative of the natural world as well as of the human psyche.

While these esoteric concerns help to explain some of the more puzzling images in Coleridge's major poetry, the existence of such an esoteric strain emerges again in a slightly different form, when Coleridge writes to Davy in 1801 about his projected book 'Concerning Poetry & the Nature of the Pleasures derived from it':

> ... if I write what I ought to do on it, the Work would supersede all the Books of Metaphysics hitherto written/and all the books of Morals too.—To whom shall a young man utter *his Pride*, if not to a young man whom he loves?—
>
> (CL II 671)

In another letter a month later he writes of his recent 'intense Study':

> If I do not greatly delude myself, I have not only completely extricated the notions of Time and Space; but have overthrown the doctrine of Association, as taught by Hartley, and with it all the irreligious metaphysics of modern Infidels—especially, the doctrine of Necessity.—This I have *done* ...   (CL II 706)

A week after this he writes:

> Newton was a mere materialist—*Mind* in his system is always passive—a lazy Looker-on on an external World. If the mind be not *passive*, if it be indeed made in God's Image, & that too in the sublimest sense—the Image of the *Creator*—there is ground for suspicion, that any system built on the passiveness of the mind must be false, as a system.   (CL II 709)

Two years later, however, once again reversing the 'ebullience' image (as in *The Eolian Harp*), he refers to 'that Letter which in the ebulliency of indistinct Conceptions I wrote to you respecting Sir Isaac Newton's Optics' and asks for it to be destroyed, as 'a Letter which if I were to die & it should ever see the *Light* would damn me forever, as a man mad with Presumption'; three months later he returns to the request, referring now to his former 'hope of optico-metaphysical discovery'.[28] Whatever it was that he had envisaged, we note that it had had to do, once again, with the active powers of the human mind, seen explicitly as an 'Image of the Creator'. Nor did this esoteric element pass out of his writing. We find him in Malta, for example, writing of the 'Truth that was in him' as something which could not be uttered lightly or in the wrong company – or at least, not until the right moment arrived: 'I cannot, I *may* not bear the reproach of profaning the Truth, which is *my Life*, in moments when all passions heterogeneous to it are eclipsing it to the exclusion of its dimmest ray . . .'[29]

Years later, in a letter of October 1819 for *Blackwood's Magazine* (not published there, and perhaps never despatched) he wrote,

> I cherish, I must confess, a *pet* system, a bye blow of my own Philosophizing; but it is so unlike to all the opinions and modes of reasoning grounded on the atomic, Corpuscular and mechanic Philosophy, which is alone tolerated in the present day, and which since the time of Newton has been universally taken as synonimous with Philosophy itself—that I must content myself with caressing the heretical Brat in private— under the name of the Zoödynamic Method—or the Doctrine of *Life*. (CL IV 956)

There were reasons for his strange evasiveness in these matters. As Walter Jackson Bate and Thomas McFarland have shown, Coleridge developed a curiously strong fear of putting forward any theories which might be construed pantheistically, a fear which only grew with the years.[30] Nevertheless, we hardly begin to understand his intellectual career unless we understand that an esoteric strain, with all its implications, played a central part in his early thinking. For this reason, it is profitable to look at the occasional places where he himself offers an example of interpretations which differ according to whether the same phenomenon is being contemplated by the uninitiated, the novice or the adept as for example in a marginal comment to Herder's *Kalligone*, where he notes that[31]

> [a] Serpent in a wreath of folds basking in the Sun is beautiful to Aspasia, whose attention is confined to the visual impression, but excites an emotion of Sublimity in Plato who contemplates under that Symbol the Idea of Eternity.

In another such comment, this time in the margins of Boehme, he suggests that the myth of the serpent and the tree in Genesis is an allegory, the serpent being a symbol of 'intellective Invention':

> The II Chapter of Genesis appears to be little more than a translation of Sculptured Figures into words—the serpent being the Egyptian Symbol of intellective Invention, idolized by the Descendants of Ham, but the same, taken separately, as the φρονημα σαρκος, the wisdom of the flesh, in St Paul. Distinctive & discursive knowlege was & by the fitness of the symbol remains, represented in the ramifications of a Tree, full of fruit but with the Serpent (which has here a double meaning, as being significant of poison or evil secretly working) wreathing the Boughs—Thus, the Mythos speaks to the Catechumen & to the Adept—To the Catechumen it states the simple Fact, viz. that Man fell & falls thro' the separation, and insubordination of the Fancy, the Appetence, & the discursive Intellect from the Faith or Practical Reason.—To the Adept it conveys the great mystery, that the origin of moral Evil is in the *Timeless*, εν τῳ αχρονῳ—in a spirit, not comprehended within the consciousness—tho revealed in the conscience of Man! (Boehme (BM) III 82–3)

Coleridge's thought here is somewhat obscure at first sight. This is a late and involved elaboration, however, written in years when Coleridge had turned his terminology to the service of a more orthodox faith than he entertained in youth. When we return to the earlier period we can see that the symbols used here darkly (though not, on an assiduous reading, unintelligibly) have their origin in a former, more simple symbolic interpretation which had given him the inspiration for a new view of human nature. In earlier days the emphasis had been not on theology itself, where it was to lead him into involved and even abstruse patterns of thought, but on 'natural religion' and 'creative intelligence': he had sought to understand the nature of life and the workings of the human mind with their aid, involving himself, in the process, with contemporary advances in science and psychology.

Any attempt to educe the nature of Coleridge's esoteric thinking during these years must aim at description rather than at a critical account. The areas of science and psychology in which Coleridge found himself are not in fact those where exact criticism is altogether appropriate: for they are precisely the areas where quantitative measurement and controlled experiment cease to be easily available and where scientists themselves still tread with caution. At the end of the study it will be possible to indicate ways in which some of his themes proved prophetic of later trends; but the main purpose must be to show Coleridge's ideas in the process of their gradual unfolding. For irrespective of the merits of the theories which he evolved, a prime value of the exploration was that it focused his attention in new ways on objects of the natural world and helped to keep his intelligence alive both to new ideas and to its own activity. To follow Coleridge along these paths is to see the processes of organic life and of human intelligence illuminated in new ways.

2

At the Springs of Romance

Although late eighteenth-century England was not in all respects austere, its official face was somewhat forbidding to a sensitive and imaginative child. The demands of expanding Empire favoured public education of boys within a Spartan environment and exposed them to the rough justice of authoritarian schoolmasters. Nor were their glimpses of the larger world reassuring. A ruthless economic system, based on individual enterprise, under a concept of over-riding law which had recently been fortified by the enthronement of law in scientific and mathematical thinking, was little questioned or criticised. Within the bounds established by that domination beautiful houses could be built, gardens planted, social graces cultivated, but these were always sensed as oases of order established against a larger wildness. There was still less scope for the ranging of free imagination – indeed, its unfettered exercise was widely thought to endanger sanity.

In literature, where the imposition of law was more restrictive than in the other arts, scope for a relaxation of the limits was sought by invoking the idea of nature as licensing 'irregularities', provided they were contained within some organic pattern. Nevertheless, it remains generally true that the rôle of imagination was as restricted here as in the world at large. A light indulgence of fancy might be tolerated; it was even fashionable to imagine what it might be like to be a great imaginative poet; but the inhibitions on larger expression were severe.

There was however one area in which imagination could flourish more freely, under a traditional indulgence. The romance form had for centuries been available as a mode by which the uneducated might be entertained and children quietly instructed.

If more sophisticated adults looked over their shoulders and found themselves unexpectedly gripped, that could be regarded, after all, as a traditional rôle of the pastoral.

During the eighteenth century, however, the genre received an unexpected access of strength by the discovery of many such fictions in the cultures of other countries. This fact could not be ignored by those who sought to discover from the general activities of nations the true nature of mankind; particularly when translations of the popular tales that circulated in the Near and Far East, brought back by travellers, achieved wide popular success.

In one respect, moreover, the new imports differed sharply from those already familiar to European readers. Whereas Christian values were naturally taken for granted in the Western variety, characters in the typical Eastern tale inhabited a universe apparently governed by arbitrary law and amoral caprice. The sensual pleasures they enjoyed, moreover, were described with an explicitness and exotic detail that would have been frowned upon in their European counterparts.

Coleridge, who, according to his own account, had by the age of six read not only the commoner chap-books but 'Belisarius, Robinson Crusoe and Philip Quarll', acknowledged his early captivation. His discovery of *The Arabian Nights' Entertainment* was, in fact, fraught with an excitement bordering on terror:

> ... One tale ... (the tale of a man who was compelled to seek for a pure virgin) made so deep an impression on me (I had read it in the evening while my mother was mending stockings) that I was haunted by spectres, whenever I was in the dark—and I distinctly remember the anxious & fearful eagerness, with which I used to watch the window, in which the books lay—& whenever the Sun lay upon them, I would seize it, carry it by the wall, & bask, & read—. My Father found out the effect, which these books had produced—and burnt them.   (CL I 347)

A modern reader may doubt the wisdom of an action which was likely to leave the effects of the books as an unresolved trauma; and indeed the inhibitory pattern of an expansive excitement checked by the chill of rigorous harsh judgement is a familiar and recurring feature of Coleridge's later career. Our main concern, however, is with the content of these tales.

Many collections were available by Coleridge's time: Persian Tales, Turkish Tales, Mogul Tales, Tartar Tales, for example.[1*] One slightly different set was entitled *Tales of the Genii*. Published anonymously, this is now known to have been an entirely fictitious work by James Ridley, but it would have taken a sophisticated reader to tell the difference. Atlhough this well-known work could hardly have escaped him, the main evidence for Coleridge's having read the book is that it looks forward to his later works in an unusually detailed way. As we turn its pages and read the adventures of Abudah the merchant, reading first of the scene produced by the Genius of Riches for his delight ('a vast and expanded dome, which seemed to cover a whole plain, and rose to the clouds'[2]), then of the voyage given to him by the Queen of Pleasures, through 'the meanders of the current', where he sees hanging rocks and woods of spices, and smells perfumes breathing sweetness over the cool stream; as we read of the disaster that befalls him in the temple, where lightning blasts it and the ruins fall in 'huge fragments', leaving him to crawl through a dungeon of lust until he emerges, unexpectedly on top of a high mountain and is acclaimed by a multitude;[3] or of the Caliph of Baghdad who is transported to another ravishing landscape and springs to embrace a beautiful houri only to find the ground moving under their feet, leaving them parted by a 'dismal chasm'; from the bottom of which 'Wild notes of strange uncouth warlike music' arise,[4] we recognise not only the landscape but also, in snatches, the very phrases of *Kubla Khan*. Many literary sources have been proposed for that poem but none, perhaps, touches it so consistently and at so many points. It may well be that Ridley's tales provided the deepest source-layer of all, dating from an early and enthralled reading. It is the kind of book which he would be likely to have found in the Cheapside circulating library if he had not discovered it earlier.

The significance of the apparent influence deepens once it is observed that Ridley's handling of the Eastern tale differed in one important respect from the authentic product. Despite his use of arbitrary transitions and highly sensuous descriptions, Ridley's moral world is recognisably that of eighteenth-century England. The reverses of fortune have a moral effect, the pursuit of luxury is ultimately condemned. *Kubla Khan,* it may be argued, conveys similar hints of Western values within its semi-oriental structure.

Even in his childhood Coleridge became aware of the arbitrary operations of apparently magical connections between events. On the one hand there was the occasion when he ran away from home and was, according to his own account, rescued by the merest chance next morning on the very brink of the River Otter. On this occasion one of the most vivid memories was of his father, whose favourite child he was, at the moment of his restoration:

> I remember, & never shall forget, my father's face as he looked upon me while I lay in the servant's arms—so calm, and the tears stealing down his face: for I was the child of his old age.
>
> (CL I 353–4)

Two years later, this same father, who had removed the *Arabian Nights* but had also tried to teach him about the wonder of the stars, arrived home unexpectedly early from a visit to Plymouth, having had a vision the previous night of Death touching him with his dart, and, after a cheerful supper, died suddenly. The child Coleridge, who did not even know of his father's return, but woke to hear his shriek, said immediately 'Papa is dead!'[5] The event, with its strange operations of chance and preter-natural knowledge, also marked the end of childhood indulgence for Coleridge, who was sent away to Christ's Hospital soon afterwards. The relationship between magic and arbitrary chance that is often embodied in the Eastern tale, plunging a character from great fortune to its opposite at a single stroke, had now intervened devastatingly in his own career.

The ardent imagination which had responded so vehemently to the *Arabian Nights' Entertainments* was still active in Coleridge when he went away to Christ's Hospital. The young-ster who was so busy swimming the Hellespont in a London street as to be mistaken for a pickpocket by a passer-by – who then, realising his mistake, presented him with a ticket for a circulating library, the stock of which he proceeded to devour – was vividly demonstrating the possessive power of his fantasy life.[6] Even when he reached the top of the school a volume of the *Arabian Nights* still stood alongside the classical texts on his

bookshelf.⁷ At fourteen, he tells us, he was in a 'continual low
fever':

> ... My whole being was, with eyes closed to every object of
> present sense, to crumple myself up in a sunny corner and
> read, read, read—fancy myself on Robinson Crusoe's Island,
> finding a mountain of plum-cake, and eating a room for my-
> self, and then eating it into the shapes of tables and chairs—
> hunger and fancy! (Gillman 20)

The association of imagination with hunger is a familiar feature
of ascetic experience;⁸ in addition we may note Lamb's suggestion
that the imaginative life of the schoolboy at Christ's Hospital
was intensified by enclosure and frequent religious observances:

> The Christ's Hospital boy is a religious character. His
> school is eminently a religious foundation; it has its peculiar
> prayers, its services at set times, its graces, hymns and
> anthems, following each other in almost monastic closeness
> of succession. This religious character in him is not always
> untinged with superstition. That is not wonderful, when we
> consider the thousand tales and traditions which must circu-
> late, with undisturbed credulity, amongst so many boys, that
> have so few checks to their belief from any intercourse with
> the world at large ... (LW I 142)

The incubatory atmosphere described by Lamb gives a further
clue to the part played by Coleridge's imagination in his intellectual development. Had he simply been a man who read a
good deal of imaginative literature in his childhood and retained
a taste for it amidst later adult concerns, this would hardly have
been remarkable. What was unusual in his case was the intensity
of his continuing concern and his interest in the transforming
powers involved. A feature of the romance, particularly as encountered in childhood, is that at a certain point it may temporarily initiate the human psyche into a different order of being.
stamping the experience, so long as it lasts, with a strong sense
of reality which is strangely complementary to that surrounding
everyday experience. The sense involved is cognate with that
which operates during the activity of dreaming. The age-old
observation that while we are asleep we have no foolproof means

of ascertaining whether or not we are dreaming is further testimony of this power – a power which may perhaps be latent in all human perception, giving it that 'stamp of the real' which adds an imaginative dimension to the other kind of authenticity that is established by the normal checks of sense-perception.

The appeal of the romance, then, particularly in childhood, is not limited to its power of giving pleasure, even that 'pleasing terror' beloved of the eighteenth century, but to its power of convincing the reader that he or she is actually caught into the world that it has conjured into being. When Alice passes through the looking-glass into a house which seems to have the same shape as the one she has left, yet in which other laws, particularly of space, are found to hold sway, the events are peculiarly appropriate to the effect which romances in general have upon a receptive mind.

Adults learn to treat the phenomenon warily and patronisingly; to a child, on the other hand, it can be bewilderingly strong. It is not difficult, of course, even at that age, to disentangle the world of the romance from the objective world of sense-perception whenever the two are in equal juxtaposition; the problem lies in finding any convincing criterion (other than the conventionally accepted superiority of objective perception) by which it can be established that the one is more *real* than the other, since, as we have seen, it is germane to the 'romance experience' that a crucial element in the 'sense of reality' has already deserted to its side.

Against the tendency of contemporary intellectual life, Coleridge gave serious attention to this phenomenon. He interested himself, throughout his life, not only in romances of all kinds, but in superstitions, the supernatural and everything associated with the phenomenon of faith generally. Why did some human beings persist in believing certain things in the teeth of strong objection to the contrary? Could it be that in some sense the power of imagination spoke *truer* than the cool, perceptual judgement; that it was in fact linked to another order of reality, which it strove to represent and keep alive in its possessor? These were questions which never ceased to haunt him, however many disillusionments and discouragements he might encounter and acknowledge in the process.

Moreover, the intellectual scene during his boyhood and

youth, was unusually propitious for such an investigation. The emergence of new ideas in the natural sciences, the revival of Platonism in philosophy, the awakening of new political aspirations all encouraged the young aspirant to reinterpret all areas of human experience and to look with a new interest at ancient metaphysical traditions. Perhaps, after all, the hidden order of nature was more complex than Newton's mathematical demonstrations had suggested; even Newton, after all, had been drawn to supplement his observations with a certain amount of unverified scientific speculation.[9] When Coleridge speaks of his 'very early Turn to metaphysics and speculative philosophy', and of his 'rage for metaphysics' while still at school,[10] then, his remarks are explicable in terms of the contemporary intellectual scene.

Unfortunately Coleridge has left little record of his early reading in this field, beyond mentioning Voltaire's *Philosophical Dictionary* and the essays on 'Liberty' and 'Necessity' in Cato's *Letters*.[11] There is, however, one small piece of evidence which is suggestively specific. In a letter of July 1817 he mentions that, while still at Christ's Hospital, he 'conjured over' the *Aurora* of Jacob Boehme.[12] This statement, taken in conjunction with tributes to Boehme at various points in his later writings, warrants further investigation, particularly in view of the influence exerted by Boehme over other Romantic writers.

Boehme's works had been known in England since the seventeenth century, but their appeal had been restricted. To those who admired the lucidity of contemporary scientific thought, the style could not but have seemed obscure and turgid, and Samuel Butler's scepticism in *Hudibras* to be totally justified.[13] A century later John Wesley, in spite of his own religious fervour, found them 'most sublime nonsense, inimitable bombast, fustian not to be paralleled',[14] while William Law, their chief champion, converted few to his enthusiasm. The rediscovery of Boehme at the end of the century was in fact a continental, rather than an English phenomenon. Whereas Coleridge and Blake were almost alone among major English intellectual figures in mentioning him with respect, German writers such as Hegel, Schelling, Tieck and Novalis acknowledged a heavy influence.[15]

It is not at first easy to see exactly what they were all responding to in his work. Stoudt's comment that 'While somehow agreeing that Boehme is significant, historians of philosophy read their own systems into him' is shrewd.[16ω] It is only, in fact, when we look at his work against the context of eighteenth-century thought, that the enthusiasm becomes explicable. For the tendency of that thought, as we have seen, had been to stresss the omnipotency of natural law, particularly as revealed in the heavens, and to demand that human nature be reduced to conformity with it. By the end of the century a note of resistance was coming to be heard, an assertion that human nature had claims to be listened to in its own right. Boehme, who had kept alive the old alchemical sense of correspondences between man and nature, was for this reason appealing. Whilst assuming that external nature and human nature were at some level identical in their ordering he had not accepted the dominance of the external but written as if knowledge of each 'nature' could throw light upon the processes of the other. To those who were becoming aware of newly discovered chemical and electrical powers that were as active in human beings as in the external world, the concept of such mutual illumination was ready for fresh exploration.

The idea had a particularly important bearing on the nature of art. The tendency of eighteenth-century aesthetics had been to isolate human 'sensibility', stressing the importance of feeling yet finding for it no secure place within the intellectual scheme of things. The man of sensibility, made automatically aware of his isolation, might feel himself to be in danger of a reputation for madness, like the poet of Gray's Elegy or the young Wordsworth.[17] He could not expect for his poetry the kind of respect that was given to works of science. If thinkers like Boehme were right in affirming the existence of a central correspondence between man and nature, on the other hand, poetry might be restored to an intellectual status as important and potentially revealing as that of any scientific treatise.

That Coleridge was among those excited by this prospect is suggested by his various nostalgic references to Boehme. Although it is in a scientific context that he speaks of his 'conjuring' over *Aurora*, however, there is no need to suppose that he first came to the German writer with such questions as his primary concern. The *Aurora* is not simply Boehme's most pantheist work; it also contains many passages of pure delight in the manifestations of nature and in the pleasures of virtuous love which could be expected to atract the sensibility of an adolescent, before he thought of exploring any underlying metaphysical implications.

I have suggested elsewhere that a favourite illustration of Coleridge's concerning the proper status of imagery in literature and thought had its origin during these years.[18] Against those who insisted on analysing similes closely and destructively, he would argue that for a writer to use figurative language was more like offering a candle, which the recipient was at liberty either to use for his illumination or to snuff out, leaving nothing but the stench. And a likely source for the idea, I have pointed out, is to be found in the following passage of Boehme's *Aurora*, describing the fall of Lucifer:

> As when a man kindleth a Wax *Candle*, it giveth Light, but when it is put out, then is the Snuffe or Candle, darknesse: *Thus* also the light shineth from all the powers of the Father: but when the powers are perished or *corrupted*, then the light is extinguished, and the powers would remain in darknesse, as is apparant by *Lucifer*.

> The Ayr also is not of such a kind *in* God, but is a lovely pleasant still breath or voyce blowing or moving; that is; the *exit* going forth, or moving, of the powers, is the *original* of the Ayr, in which the Holy Ghost riseth up

> Neither is the water of such a kind in God, but it is the *source* or fountain in the powers, *not* of an elementary kind, as in this world; if I should liken it to any thing, I must liken it to the Sap or *Juyce* in an Apple, but very bright and *lightsome* like Heaven, which is the Spirit of all powers.

> It is Lord Lucifer which hath thus *spoiled* it, that it rageth and raveth so in this world, which so runneth and floweth and is so thick and dark, and moreover *if it runneth not*, it becometh stinking . . . (Aurora viii 14–17)

The importance of such a passage extends beyond that of an isolated influence, for it suggests the kind of imagery that appealed to the young Coleridge. The sharp, clear quality of the successive images (the lucency of the candle, the sharp juicy quality of the apple, the light movement of the breeze) all in fact foreshadow a kind of imagery that was to come naturally to him when he wrote his greatest poems.

Boehme's underlying idea that nature itself was fallen had a particular appeal in the late eighteenth century, moreover. In one respect, at least, it could be related to the kind of universal benevolence presupposed in Pope's familiar lines:

> All Nature is but Art, unknown to thee;
> All Chance, Direction, which thou canst not see;
> All Discord, Harmony, not understood;
> All partial Evil, universal Good . . .
>
> (*Essay on Man*, i, 289–92)

William Law, Boehme's chief disciple and expositor in eight-eenth-century England, used his imagery and ideas primarily in a more conventional mode, to arouse the sinner to repentance which absolving the Deity from moral responsibility for the workings of his wrath, for example.[19] There was latent scope, however, even in the accepted beliefs of the time, for a more radical and benevolent development, as some readers would not be slow to see.

The issue which Boehme's enthusiasm left open was the extent to which human beings might hope to regain Paradise during their own mortal lives. Once fallen, it might be thought, nature must remain fallen; yet there were persistent hints in these writings that the fallen human being, if once awakened to an understanding of his own condition, might come to know some-thing of the pleasures that had preceded the Fall. Such hints were, of course, all the more welcome at a time when the new stress on the workings of the human psyche which accompanied the early stirrings of romanticism was setting the concept of the Fall itself under hostile scrutiny. Whether or not Boehme's view of the fall of nature was historically and factually true, it might be psychologically true: perhaps the very appeal of his writings might be due to a conformity with truths which were already known instinctively in the unconscious. But if so, was it not also possible that a renovation of human consciousness might involve, in the psyche at least, restoration to the lost paradise?

Such ideas could readily be assimilated to Rousseau's view of childhood. If it was the case that, by his contact with civilisation,

man inevitably declined from an original virtue, and if (as
followed from this) the mind of the child was nearer the ideal
state than was the mind of the adult, then it became legitimate
to explore the imaginative world of the child in the hope of
discovering lost truths. Such considerations, in their turn, lent
new colour to, say, Boehme's comparison of the unfallen angels
to

> little children, which walk in the fields in *May*, among the
> *flowers*, and pluck them, and make curious Garlands, and
> Poseys, carrying them in their hands rejoycing . . .

These angels, he says,

> rejoyce in the delicious pleasant May of God.

(*Aurora* xii 45; 47)

The possibilities stretched further. To a mind oppressed by the
dreariness of the Newtonian universe in its ultimate implications, Boehme's imagery of nature was restorative. In contrast to
the darkness and cold which must stretch beyond the workings
of Newton's world-machine he offered the sense of a universe
that was ultimately grounded in colour and music:

> This Heavenly Salitter, or powers one in another, generate
> Heavenly joyful fruits and colours; all manner of Trees and
> Plants, on which do *grow* the fair pleasant and lovely fruits of
> *life.*
> There Spring up also in these powers and vertues, all
> manner of Blossoms and *Flowers*, with fair Heavenly colours
> and smells.
> They are of *Several* Tastes, each according to its Quality
> and kind, very *Holy, Divine* and full of joy.

(*Aurora* iv 22–4)

And if these were the true powers in the universe, it followed
that the central Being must share the same qualities. Boehme's
God is not the dark first mover of a Paleyan world-machine but
'an All-mighty, All-wise, All-knowing, All-seeing, All-hearing,
All-smelling, All-feeling, All-tasting God, who in himself is
meek, friendly, gracious, merciful and full of Joy, yea joy it
self'.[20]

Boehme's 'scientific' thinking was equally provocative. As we have seen, he undercut many of the moral presuppositions of the eighteenth-century universe by the very simple strategy of including the whole of nature in the Fall itself. The evil in the world was, he claimed, due to a lapse that was natural as well as supernatural. In an order that was essentially variegated, cyclical and dynamic, Lucifer, turning away, had chosen to cling to a single part of the process; he had elected to dwell in the darkness that subsisted in light and to contract to the hardness that ought to be no more than a single stage in the divine process. As a result this larger process (the 'total God') was thrown into disarray. The 'love-fires' at the centre of the universe were turned into 'wrath-fires' and man, finding himself in Lucifer's condition, lived under a sense of threat in a world that was manifestly defective. Although it was not immediately evident to man, therefore, certain oppressive features of the physical world, such as rocks and ice, acted as necessary and merciful limits to the unbridled expansions and contractions of energy, reflecting limits that had been placed upon the fallen powers of Lucifer himself:

> When *King Lucifer* elevated himself, then he elevated himself in the seven qualifying fountain-spirits, and *kindled them* with his elevation, so that all was wholly *burning*, and the astringent quality was so *hard* and Compact, that it generated stones; and it was so *cold*, that it made the sweet spring or fountain-water turn to *Ice*.   (*Aurora* ix 82)

Despite the occasional vividness of Boehme's imagery and the attractiveness of some of his ideas, however, it is doubtful whether Coleridge would have been drawn so strongly to his pages had they not also, from time to time, thrown up hints of ideas which might mediate in the larger intellectual conflicts already mentioned. It may be suggested, for example, that the linking of mind and imagination which they encouraged was one force which brought Coleridge, even in his schooldays, to study the Neoplatonists. Lamb's picture of him as a 'young Mirandula' in the cloister of Christ's Hospital is well known. The casual passer by was spellbound, he tells us,

> to hear thee unfold, in thy deep and sweet intonations, the mysteries of Jamblichus, or Plotinus (for even in those years

thou waxedst not pale at such philosophical draughts), or reciting Homer in his Greek, or Pindar . . .   (LW II 21)

The writings of the Neoplatonists, which were enjoying a new vogue during Coleridge's schooldays owing to the enthusiasm of Thomas Taylor, whose long series of translations had just begun to appear, are not only in line with the kind of visionary speculations propagated by Boehme but sometimes suggestively close to them; and this is particularly true of the two specifically mentioned by Lamb. The most likely source for a knowledge of Plotinus on Coleridge's part is the small volume of his work which Taylor published in 1787, entitled *Concerning the Beautiful*. This contains the idea of God as the One at the heart of things, of his nature as a central light, which human perception recreates in little in every act of perception, and of the difference between the 'corporeal eye' of normal perception and the 'intellectual eye' which pierces the unity of the universe.[21] Plotinus warns that when the eye too earnestly 'converts itself to the nature of the illuminated objects' it 'perceives less their splendid original.'[22]

Of Iamblichus Coleridge could have learned rather less from Taylor, since the published translations available at that time contain only a short reference to him, in the *Commentary on Proclus*. Even this, however, provides an important summary of his teaching:[23]

. . . This admirable book fully solves all the doubts concerning the impassivity of a divine nature; demonstrates its omnipresence, and never-failing energy; shews that we are continually surrounded with its light; and that all the divinities subsist in indivisible union, and indissoluble consent.

One important theme of Iamblichus, his stress on energy, emerges clearly here. It could be said, indeed, that these two philosophers, respectively, were the Neoplatonists most likely to speak to Coleridge's age, Plotinus expounding a philosophy in which the imagination was paramount and Iamblichus emphasising the importance of 'energy' and 'energising'. Imagination and energy were precisely the two forces that advanced young men could most readily call to their aid as modes of circumventing the cold rationalism of the current intellectual tradition.[24]

So far, however, we have hardly touched on what is perhaps the crucial element in Boehme's thinking, so far as Coleridge was concerned. In the midst of Boehme's strange tissue there may be discerned the materials for a complicated and central nexus of correspondences, all related to the working of the heart.

In nature this correspondence appears as a link between the the rôle of the sun in the universe and the rôle of the heart in the human body:

> First behold the _Sun; It_ is the Heart or _King_ of all Stars, and giveth _light_ to all stars from the East to the West, it enlightneth and warmeth all, all liveth and groweth by its power; besides, the joy of all creatures standeth in its power.

> _The Heart_ in man Signifieth the Heat, or the Element of Fire, and it is also the Heat: for the Heat in the whole Body, hath its Original in the _Heart._ (_Aurora_ ii 13; 40)

When these statements are put together Boehme may be seen as adumbrating a view of nature and of man in which the central force of each corresponds with that of the other. Just as the sun's light may be seen as its 'heart of hearts', the vivifying and enlightening element within an energy that would otherwise be destructive, so, it is being suggested, the heart of man, experienced immediately as a source of warmth, contains an inner core which must be inhabited by light if its human possessor is not to become corrupted or hardened. In Boehme's view, this resource is always available to human beings:

> ... when the flash is caught in the fountain of the Heart, then the Holy Ghost riseth up in the seven qualifying or fountain Spirits, into the Brain like the Day-break, Dawning of the Day, or Morning Rednesse ... (_Aurora_ xi 132)

Boehme's vision of the ideal in physical nature is not restricted to a possible correspondence between the light in the sun and the light in the human heart. The sun is the central light-fountain of the solar system, certainly, but its work is mirrored and miniatured by the equally essential element of water, which could also be seen as furnishing a medium through which the heart of the universe is made manifest:

> ... Heaven is the _Heart_ of the water, as in all creatures, and

in all that, which is in this world, the water is the *Heart* thereof and nothing can Subsist without water, be it in the flesh or out of the flesh, in the Vegetables of the earth, or in Metals and Stones, in every thing the water is the kernel or the Heart of it.   (*Aurora* ii 52)

One's first instinct might be to regard sun and water as natural contraries, the heat of the sun constantly acting to evaporate water from the surfaces of nature and leave them dry. This is to ignore their total process, however, The operation of the sun's heat, more largely considered, does not destroy the earth's moisture but sets it in motion, drawing it off from the earth and sea and raising into the clouds, from which it can eventually return to water the earth on a wider scale. What was at first sight (and actually is, in particular parts of the earth) a destructive work comes to be seen in its general working as a merciful work of circulation, without which physical life could not exist at all.

In the same way, the most characteristic moving of water, as seen in the fountain or spring, bears its own correspondence, this time a very literal one, to the work of the heart in man, where a similar spring keeps in movement a circulation of blood without which the human being would quickly die.

Boehme also traced the process to the deity. Just as he believed light to be the heart of the sun, so the Son was the 'light' in the Father, while the Holy Spirit introduced the sense of outgoing motion:

... the Father is the *power* and Kingdom, and the Sonne is the *Light* and Splendor in the Father, and the Holy Ghost is the *moving* or *exit* out of the powers of the Father and of the Sonne, and formeth figureth *frameth* and Imageth all.

(*Aurora* vii 42)

As has already been suggested, Boehme's work might not have been so appealing had it not been echoed by the convergence of various intellectual traditions within the intellectual scene at the end of the eighteenth century. New work in the physical sciences had drawn attention to the part played by active forces in nature, as opposed to the passive obedience which was a major feature of Newton's world. With the advance of physical knowledge the human body itself could be studied in a similar light.

One could not investigate the nature of air or electricity without being aware of the vital part played by oxygen in maintaining human life, or of the galvanic elements in physical response. This range of new knowledge, coupled with a lack of developed investigation, encouraged largeness of speculation: formerly discredited systems of ideas were now revived and newly examined.

To illustrate the materials available for such syncretic speculation we may return to the image of the fountain. Although the nexus of possible correspondences reaches a new level of intimacy in Boehme's various writings, the individual cross-connections may also be traced elsewhere in writers who were readily available to Coleridge.

The idea that the heart of all things is a fountain, for instance, is voiced by Plotinus in terms as sensuous as any found in Boehme.[25*]

> All flows, so to speak, from one fount not to be thought of as some one breath or warmth but rather as one quality englobing and safeguarding all qualities—sweetness with fragrance, wine-quality, and the savours of everything that may be tasted, all colours seen, everything known to touch, all that ear may hear, all melodies, every rhythm.

Reference to the sun as a fountain is a feature of several earlier writers. Lucretius, for example, spoke of it as 'that large Fountain of liquid light', and many English poets followed the hint, the most memorable example being in Milton's lines describing the original creation of the sun:

> Of light by far the greater part he took,
> Transplanted from her cloudy shrine, and placed
> In the sun's orb, made porous to receive
> And drink the liquid light, firm to retain
> Her gathered beams, great palace now of light.
> Hither as to their fountain other stars
> Repairing, in their golden urns draw light,
> And hence the morning planet gilds her horns . . .
>   (Par. Lost, vii 359–66)

In other mystic writers and religions, a direct connection was presupposed between the sun and harmony. In the Indian and

Greek mythologies, for instance, Krishna and Apollo were alike gods of harmony and of the sun,[26] while the legend of the temple of Memnon in Egypt, where the image of the god was said to send forth a musical sound when it was touched by the beams of the rising sun, was used by several eighteenth-century writers, including Akenside, Darwin and Coleridge himself.[27*]

The idea that the core of the creative process in nature was best imaged as a fountain, similarly, was not confined to the ancients. In his *Disquisition on Matter and Spirit* Joseph Priestley cited Giordano Bruno's belief that[28*]

> as there is no active force in nature, but that of God; this being is the infinite force which unites all the parts of matter, an immense spring which is in continual action.

Various eighteenth-century writers dwelt in a more general manner on the fountainous nature of the human heart. Cowper for example, who wrote[29]

> Your heart shall yield a life-renewing stream

traced a parallel between the operation of the heart and the workings of virtue:[30]

> The stream that feeds the well-spring of the heart
> Not more invigorates life's noblest part,
> Than virtue quickens, with a warmth divine
> The powers that sin has brought to a decline.

This is a fairly straightforward and even predictable simile, perhaps; it is more striking to see the great William Harvey himself, a century earlier, pressing the imagery further in his famous essay *On the Motion of the Heart and Blood in Animals* (1628):[31*]

> The heart, consequently, is the beginning of life; the Sun of the Microcosm, even as the Sun in his turn might well be designated the heart of the World.

So far we have observed a series of ideas, each of which might be linked with one or more of the others:

(1) The sun as the physical source of all harmony
(2) The sun as a fountain of light
(3) Creation as proceeding from a single fountain
(4) The sun as the heart of the universe

(5) The heart as the sun of the body
(6) The heart as a fountain
(7) The existence of a single fountain of the senses in the body.

Any of the ideas might be used to provide an isolated metaphor, obviously; but when several were found working together, as in Boehme, there must have been a strong temptation to explore the possibility that a larger truth was concealed within these correspondences, involving, perhaps, an actual physical connection in nature itself; the sun as heart of the universe and the heart as sun of the body might actually share similar characteristics, so that to study the operation of one was to understand more fully the working of the other. The connecting links suggested by Boehme, based on the idea that each was a fountain, with light, not heat, as its true centre, offered one suggestive pattern.

This nexus of possible links, for understandable reasons, seems to have fascinated Coleridge in his early youth. If one believed that the sun was not just a furnace, but a fountain, in the full sense of the word – that is, that it did not just radiate light continuously but that it also received back power continuously from the universe (as the heart receives back its own blood) the universe could be seen in a different manner from that proposed by the mechanists. The inherent image of the Newtonian universe, that of a giant mechanism running down to decay and death, was considerably modified if one supposed that the sun at its centre was not a mighty fire slowly burning itself out but a perpetually self-renewing fountain of energy and light. At this time, before the formulation of the Laws of Thermodynamics, it was a particularly attractive alternative theory. The sun was thereby transformed from a self-destructive ball of fire into a pulsating fountain, an original source of all creative life, answered to in its turn by the life of every organism on earth. In human terms, such a conception was invigorating. Instead of contemplating the inevitability of death and decay as he looked about him in the universe (in the manner of contemporary graveyard poets), a human being could focus his attention on the sun and on the springs and fountains of water which he saw everywhere in nature around him, organising his conceptions of animated nature around their omnipresent, fountainous life. If he had learned from Sterne and Rousseau to consult the dictates of his heart before taking action, moreover, he need no longer feel himself so readily subject to the charge of sentimentalism. Instead, he might feel himself licensed to sense there a power which corresponded to the power in the sun or the fountain, an ebullient energy which could make all his actions sublime. Instead of simply melting in pity or yearning in sympathy he could find a different and more dynamic centre for his emotions, allowing dilations of energetic impulse to alternate with contractions to pity, and arguing to himself that this process of his sensibility was ratified in the universe at large.

Such a conception could be preserved from the charge of pantheism by making a distinction encouraged in Boehme's writings. While heat was, he declared, a necessary vital force,

> ... the *Light* in the Heat giveth power to all qualities, so that all groweth *pleasant* and joyful. Heat without Light availeth not the other qualities, but is a *perdition* to the Good, an evil source or Spring: for all is spoiled in the fiercenesse or wrath of the Heat. Thus the light in the heat is a quick Spring or living fountain; into which the Holy Ghost entreth, but not into the fiercenesse or wrath.   (*Aurora* i 13)

In Coleridge's time this idea was also playing an important part in the teachings of Swedenborg, who maintained that the visible sun of the universe, a body whose heat was often destructive, was not the true sun; *that* subsisted beyond the physical order in a more humanised form, its heat and light always in perfect balance. The theme was given a certain topicality by current scientific concerns, which included a strong interest in newly discovered forms of energy and illumination. If heat was equated with energy, light with imaginative activity, it became possible to project the idea of a human condition in which energy and imagination would both play their full part – as when Coleridge, having experienced both the cold rationalism of the Unitarians and the fanatical energy of contemporary Methodism, wrote in a notebook 'Socinianism moonlight, Methodism a stove. O for some sun to unite heat and light!'[32]

The ramifications of this larger run of imagery in Coleridge's symbolic writings have been traced elsewhere. It plays its part, I have suggested, in the sun and moon imagery of the supernatural poems, and in the evolution of a philosophy of human sexuality which would see its ideal in an energy tempered and transfigured by love. The possibilities involved seem to have continued working in his mind for a very long time. Annotating Boehme years later, for example, he writes that while Boehme's 'Salitter' is to be equated with gravitation, 'it is gravitation as in the Sun, at once the center of gravity and the fountain of Light'; on another page, he comments:[33]

> That not Heat but Light is the Heart of Nature is one of those truly profound and pregnant Thoughts that ever and anon astonish me in Behmen's writings . . .

At the same time, the fragmentation and guarded use of such ideas in his later life suggests that he was not then using them for the first time, or with total commitment, but looking back to the enthusiasms of an earlier period: that they had first been formulated during his schooldays, in other words, and allowed full and free rein only in the uncritical eagerness of adolescence.

Such an interpretation squares with a reading of his early life which would place the climax of his visionary speculations in the Michaelmas Term of 1793 at Cambridge. It was then that his interest in the esoteric emerged again as he quoted Maximus Tyrius to his friends at an evening gathering[34] and tried to redeem his growing debts by writing for the prize a Greek ode on Astronomy (the set subject) which drew heavily on his visionary ideas. In this poem (which survives in Southey's translation)[35] correspondences between the human mind and the heavens are invoked throughout. The existence of other suns in the universe is related to the relationship between the godlike soul in man and those of others. By contemplating the stars, the soul comes to know itself and spread its wings:

> Soon mingled with thy fathers thou shalt shine
> A star amid the starry throng,
> A God the Gods among.

The boldest stroke in the poem is that by which Newton is viewed not simply as a God (which was allowable poetic licence at that time) but as a God who transcends the mathematician in himself. This Newton is not simply the Newton of eighteenth-century engravings who stretches out his compasses to measure his diagrams of the heavens, but a godlike figure who actually guides the course of the stars and, looking into the very heart of creative energy, recognises there a correspondence with his own powers:

> There, Priest of Nature! dost thou shine
> NEWTON! a King among the Kings divine.
> Whether with harmony's mild force,
> He guides along its course
> The axle of some beauteous star on high,
> Or gazing, in the spring
> Ebullient with creative energy,
> Feels his pure breast with rapturous joy possest,
> Inebriate in the holy ecstasy.

The failure of the Ode to win the prize set in motion a train of events that culminated in Coleridge's enlistment in the army. He acknowledged his defeat with rueful humour: 'it was so *sublime* that nobody could understand it'.[36] He could still say, four years later, however, (consoling another unsuccessful entrant), 'the finest poem, I ever wrote, lost the prize ... an ode may *sometimes* be too bad for the prize; but VERY OFTEN too good.'[37]

The images of the Greek Ode demonstrate that aspiration was mingling with humility in Coleridge's quest for correspondences. Nor can it be pretended that the presence of this strain was wholly beneficial to his development. Many of the lapses and failures in his early career are associated with an over-readiness to trust the dictates of the 'illuminated heart'. A range of speculations which was harmless enough in the cloister of Christ's Hospital proved more dangerous in the less restrictive atmosphere of Cambridge, where it encouraged enthusiasm and a behaviour based on the impulse of the moment. Coleridge's undergraduate career, which began with honest industry, gradually became more and more disastrous as he plunged into debt and indulged in debaucheries. As things got worse, he seems for a time to have lost touch with everyday realities, escaping to London after the failure of his Greek ode, using his last money to buy a lottery ticket[38] and, when that failed to win a prize, enlisting as a dragoon. Only after several months was he discovered and bought out by his brothers.

One result of the debâcle was a growing cautiousness. Never

again would Coleridge indulge his speculations so freely as he
had done in the Ode on Astronomy; there would always be an
instinct towards reserve. Yet the seeds that had been sown during
those early years continued to grow. Coleridge's dream of setting
up a new concordat between energised imagination and reason
was too well-suited to an age which was searching for new more
optimistic modes of behaviour to be lightly set aside, particularly
since there was much in contemporary thought and science that
could provide further materials for such an enterprise. In the
years that followed, therefore, Coleridge was always particularly
attracted by any phenomena which related the workings of the
imagination to the workings of the human heart in a manner
that could claim intellectual respectability.

In the sphere of literature, the enterprise realised itself as an
attempt to provide both new ways of looking at nature and what
might be termed a language for 'the heart's imagination'. With
the new definition given to it by such speculations, that language would no longer be identifiable with the melting accents
of a sentimental heroine, but could draw on images from the
natural world which impress by their freshness and clarity. The
imagery of lucent candle, quiet breeze, clear stream and juicy
apple which we noted in the Aurora passage have precisely this
quality; taken together, they produce an effect in the imagination
which none could work separately, an effect associable, among
other things, with the sharp sensations of childhood.

The attempt to bring imagery of innocent and sensuous vividness into the forefront of poetic vision and to link it with the
sensed workings of the human heart was to be an important
element in the early Romantic enterprise; an enterprise which
Coleridge shared with Blake and to which (it may be claimed)
he introduced Wordsworth. The venture was to achieve its
highest point in the poetry and letters of Keats – to whom we
owe the twin formulation, 'the holiness of the Heart's affections
and the truth of Imagination', along with the famous declaration
that 'what the imagination seizes as beauty must be Truth.'[39]

If, in Coleridge's hands, the enterprise was also to be, at times,
a somewhat desperate one, the fact is partly ascribable to his
pioneering status in this and other respects. In a society that still
liked to live by fixed forms and characters, he was endeavouring
both to respect these forms and yet to live as a free spirit. His

favourite image of himself as a boat on the ocean, in need of a sheet-anchor,[40] overtly acknowledged the vulnerability of his position.

During his schooldays, however, and for some years afterwards, when he was, as Lamb put it, 'in the dayspring of his fancies', the dominant impression he gave was of power. Lamb's imagery is that of a Moses, setting forth to lead his people through the wilderness, touching a spring from the rock and bringing them to a land 'flowing with milk and honey', and it was in this rôle that Coleridge sometimes saw himself.[41] Even his own study-boy, whose reminiscences were by no means complimentary in all respects, remembered him finally as a figure of power:[42]

> a tall, dark handsome young man, with long black flowing hair; eyes, not merely dark, but black and keenly penetrating; a fine forehead, a deep-toned harmonious voice; a manner never to be forgotten, full of life, vivacity and kindness: dignified in his person, and, added to all these, exhibiting the elements of his future greatness.

According to De Quincey, a lady who knew him in Bristol in 1796 described him as the most beautiful young man she had ever seen, and likened him to Chaucer's squire.[43]

Coleridge's failure to fulfil his own promise was proverbial in his own lifetime and a source of frequent self-reproach. Yet it may also be argued that his attempts to bring the heart and imagination into unison and to explore nature both externally and in the processes of his own mind transposed his sensibility into a new key, which was, at the same time, attuned to the needs of late eighteenth-century England. It enabled him to evolve new syntheses and groupings among the ideas which were coming to the fore and to gain a purchase on concepts and impressions that were otherwise hard to seize or articulate. It encouraged him, for example, to take a fresh look at the human interests which were served by romance and to explore the possibilities of the form as an alternative mode of interpreting man's experience of the world. It also enabled him to come to terms with the new emphasis on process, a theme that would become increasingly important in nineteenth- and twentieth-century thought. Whatever one makes of the concept of the

Deity as a fountain, for example, one important feature is that it transforms the status of the Creator from that of a static law-giver into that of a Being which is itself in process. The concept of the Trinity which may be traced in Boehme and the Neoplatonists, similarly, is less a relationship between persons than an imaging of creative process – of a Being centred in the Father, of an energy going forth from that Being in the Son and of a returning, formative power in the Spirit.

At this moment in European intellectual history, when attention was being turned to the operation of active powers, moreover, such concepts provided speculative instruments with which to approach the processes of creation as they could be observed not only in the mind of the creative artist, but in the organic processes of nature itself. Cloistered as Coleridge's upbringing had been, strange as some of his speculations might seem, they had given him some unusually appropriate equipment with which to explore this new world.

3

Shoots and Eddies

At first sight, Coleridge's career between his discharge from the army in the spring of 1794 and the end of 1795 presents a clear and comprehensible shape. After the intervention of his brothers he returned to Cambridge for a term, determined to work hard for his degree. During a vacation walking tour that summer, however, he met Robert Southey, who impressed him both by his uprightness of character and his idealism; together they formed the plan of setting up a new community in America and courted the Fricker sisters as prospective fellow-participants. Coleridge then returned to Cambridge full of this 'pantisocratic' scheme but in November left for a trip to London, where he stayed for some time, becoming friendly with a number of leading radicals such as Frend (who had recently been expelled from the university), Gilbert Wakefield and George Dyer. Despite firm promises to return to Bristol he lingered so long in London that Southey was forced to go up personally and reclaim him for Pantisocracy and Sara Fricker. He now set up as a lecturer in Bristol, speaking on political topics of the day and also giving a course on theology. In the late summer he married Sara and settled with her in a cottage at Clevedon, but continued to lecture occasionally and wrote poems which were to be published the following year by Joseph Cottle. Meanwhile, the pantisocratic scheme was breaking up and by the end of the year Coleridge and Southey were estranged.

Presented so, it is a simple enough story of a young man whose idealism leads him into radical opinions and schemes which he is then forced to qualify and reconcile with the practical demands of his situation. At the same time, and remembering all that has been said about the activity of Coleridge's mind up to this time, we might be forgiven for asking whether such an account tells the whole story. Was Coleridge's inquiring spirit so closely channelled throughout these months, and was he so exclusively committed to public themes?

With this question in mind, it is instructive to turn to the documents that survive from the walking-tour of 1794, undertaken in the first flush of the pantisocratic idea. Hucks, Coleridge's walking-companion, left a journal of the tour and Coleridge wrote several letters describing it. From these it is clear that while the pantisocratic scheme occupied a good deal of their attention, particularly after they had left Oxford, they were also discussing many other things. And indeed pantisocracy itself was not just a political scheme; it reflected an entirely new spirit which was moving among young men at this time. Godwin then, in Hazlitt's words, 'blazed as a sun in the firmament of reputation',[1] and a new spirit of liberty and benevolence was felt to be abroad. It was in line with this enthusiasm that young men should set off on walking-tours. The tour of picturesque landscapes was in no way a novel phenomenon, of course: many eighteenth-century travellers spent their holidays in this way and reported their experiences. What was new was that such tours should be undertaken not by stagecoach or on horseback but entirely on foot. This stress on the equality of all men was accompanied by questionings concerning the relationship between man and nature. Was it the case that constant intercourse with nature had a beneficial effect on human beings? Hucks's reflections on the matter may owe something to his conversations with Coleridge, but they are also typical of his generation: 'There is an analogy in nature throughout', he writes, commenting on the exhilaration of their spirits, 'from the most torpid state of vegetable existence to the most refined subtlety of animal life', and he goes on to argue that if a man were to be shut out from nature, 'his would be a most comfortless state of existence, with a mind that could have no idea, if any at all, of the deity. . . .'[2] At the same time, Hucks is careful to guard against any straightforward assumption of cause and effect, introducing memory as the efficient cause of the response to nature:[3]

It is not therefore that there is any absolute impression made upon the mind, from the scene before us, whether it be bright with sunshine, or overcast with clouds, but it is memory which associates to it some event, or transaction of former years, which, though scarcely perceptible, is the cause of such an effect.

Man's relationship to nature was also in Coleridge's mind a good deal at this time. For whatever power in man it was that attuned itself to the outward world of nature, that might be the link around which a new universal brotherhood of man might be constructed. Pantisocracy itself involved a theory of nature as well as of man; it was not for nothing that the community was to be set up by a beautiful river, with husbandry in the midst of nature as its primary activity.

Coleridge's new acquaintance with the radicals and unitarians of the metropolis that autumn brought him closely into touch with the scientific thought of the time. At Christ's Hospital, as in other English schools at the time, there had been little or no formal science teaching. Nor was the position much better at Cambridge. Mathematics, of course, played a major part in the syllabus there, following the work of Newton, but there was little or no opportunity to learn about more recent discoveries. The work of Joseph Priestley, for example, was carried out by a man who was a unitarian divine; and it was in the Dissenting Academies of that sect that a student was most likely to find science on the syllabus.[4]

In France, on the other hand, scientific speculation had played a more central part in the intellectual life. As H. W. Piper has shown in his study,[5] the chemical and electrical discoveries of the time had stimulated much discussion concerning the active powers in the universe, some of which reached England.

It was, in fact, an unusually propitious time for such speculation. Scientific investigators, as yet unconfronted by the great nineteenth-century structures of investigation and discovery which would encourage the formulation of mechanistic patterns to explain any given phenomena (including those of the human mind), could theorise freely. Richard Saumarez, a surgeon whose ideas Coleridge later praised extravagantly, published in 1795 his short *Dissertation on the Universe*, in which he argued for the validity of Neoplatonist opinions and the immateriality of the human soul.[6] It was a time when men could look at the natural creation with new eyes and marvel at the mystery of the processes, organic and psychological, that were being disclosed. When he went to London towards the end of 1794, then, it is fair to assume that Coleridge's mind was occupied not only by political action (which would have led him back to Bristol sooner) but by other issues that were being discussed by informed people in the metropolis.

At this point it is useful to turn to a book not previously associated with his development: Richard Sulivan's *View of Nature*, published in six volumes that year. Although we have no direct record of Coleridge's having known the work, it is very difficult to believe that he did not read parts of it, at least, during the year after its publication. It is a work guaranteed to appeal to his kind of omnivorous curiosity, for Sulivan set out to bring together the whole state of contemporary knowledge concerning nature in a manner which should comprehend not only recent scientific work but the observations of classical authors, the common elements to be found in mythologies, and so on. An extraordinarily large number of topics discussed in its pages turn up in Coleridge's writings as important themes,[7a] and although the presence of any one or two might be coincidental, since Sulivan was drawing upon writers whom Coleridge might have read for himself, the very large number of instances involved makes it at once economical and reasonable to suppose that he came upon at least some of them in these volumes. The very manner of their juxtaposition in Sulivan constituted a positive invitation to the reader to pursue possible links between them.

Coleridge's apparent interest in the idea that there might be a correlation between the sun and the human heart, as correspondent fountains, has already been mentioned. In Sulivan's book, this idea is explicitly discussed at one point. He makes a series of connections between the operation of the sun (conceived in just these terms) and the process of circulation, as shown in the movements of the water in nature and blood in human beings. Circulation, he argues, seems to be the only principle by which the inexhaustibility of light can be accounted for; and this is analogous with other natural phenomena.

The blood, for instance, has a progressive motion in the bodies of all animals; water has a progressive motion in the earth and seas; wind has a progressive motion in the atmosphere; and all these are kept up by the grand principle of circulation. The blood returns into its own source; the water returns to the ocean whence it came; the air circulates with contrary currents in the atmosphere; the equatorial and polar parts always supply each other reciprocally, to restore the *equilibrium*: so that if the matter of the sun returns into itself, there is nothing singular in the case . . .   (Sulivan I 166–7)

Sulivan ends by putting together a quotation from Macrobius ('the sun is in the aether what the heart is in the animal') with Harvey's description of the heart of the animal as 'the sun of microcosm, from which flows all its strength and vigour'.[8]

Various writers cited by Sulivan were already available to Coleridge. Lucretius, for example, had himself put forward the fountain-theory quite explicitly, asserting that[9]

the Seeds of Fire from all Parts of the Universe meet in the Body of the Sun, and are there collected as into a Spring, from whence the Heat of the whole World is diffused abroad.

Nevertheless, this kind of eclectic discussion, encountered in the pages of a central and sober writer, would be likely to have encouraged Coleridge to think afresh about the possible validity of Boehme's speculation.

There is another reason for believing that Coleridge was reading Sulivan during the autumn of 1794 or so. In a striking passage, Sulivan attempts to locate the three fundamental principles of nature as follows:

(1) an universal power, energy, or spirit, which is the divine agent or efficient principle.
(2) an universal power of vegetation, by which all bodies in the earth increase in bulk, and grow from small to great.
(3) an universal plastic power, whereby every body in nature receives its peculiar and specific form.   (Sulivan II 92)

In its general shape this threefold principle is reminiscent of the Trinity of process which we have suggested Coleridge to have been formulating from his readings in Boehme and Platonic philosophy. There is an important difference, however. Where the 'Platonic' trinity consists of a central Being, the expressive Word that goes forth from that Being, and the Spirit of Love which returns to it, Sulivan's trinity is conceived in terms of a basic power, or energy, an expressive expansion (as seen in vegetation) and a plastic power, by which all things receive their form. It resembles the ancient scheme in its progression from ground to productive expression and from that expression to living form, but the ordering within that framework has changed significantly. The ground is identified here not with central Being but with a universal energy or genial warmth. The paradigm now figures itself, in fact, in organic terms, as a life-fostering power in the earth, a principle of growth in the vegetative body and an external shaping or fostering power. It may still be conceived against the biblical Creation imagery, however. In these terms, a restless chaotic energy is always in flux (as in the ocean at its stormiest), a shaping power can move over that chaos (or brood over it like a great winged bird). But it is not until the intervening Word ('Let there be Light') sets in motion the great creative process that this mass of restless energy can be transformed into an earthly paradise, character- ised by fecund earth, the expansion of vegetation and gentle temperate breezes blowing across it.

There is some reason to believe that Coleridge was attracted by this threefold formulation of Sulivan's, since on no less than three occasions in 1794 he used the biblical imagery of the spirit brooding on the face of the deep in a manner which suggested close attention to the paradigm involved. On 4 November he wrote to Southey of the effects on his spirits of his pinings after Mary Evans at this time, and of his belief that such 'mental Miseries' would 'vanish before an Effort (Whatever of mind we *will* to do, we *can* do!)'. He continued:

> What then palsies the Will? The Joy of Grief! A mysterious Pleasure broods with dusky Wing over the tumultuous Mind —'and the Spirit of God moveth on the darkness of the Waters'! She was VERY lovely, Southey! We formed each other's minds—our ideas were blended . . . (CL I 123)

The biblical imagery is not drawn upon lightly here. The leading idea is that in its unrealised state love is like Chaos before the Word of Creation. The creative elements, the darkness of the waters and the moving Spirit are present, but without the actualisation of love they can remain only a brooding presence

– even if it is still a darkly pleasurable one, enough to inhibit the will from positive action in other directions.

With this formulation we may compare another, two days later, in some lines from a poem sent in a letter to his brother:

> To me hath Heaven with liberal hand assign'd
> Energic Reason & a shaping Mind,
> The daring ken of Truth, the patriot's part,
> And Pity's Sigh, that breathes the gentle heart
> Sloth-jaundic'd all!   (CL I 128)

The last-named activities are those which Coleridge feels to be proper to his public career: the pursuit of truth, political activity, the cultivation of sympathy; but before naming them he speaks of his intellectual equipment: 'Energic Reason & a shaping Mind'. Again we glimpse the extremes of a threefold paradigm, yeasty energy on the one hand, shaping spirit on the other, existing without the central act, the *fiat* that would bring them into productive and dialectic activity. This time, however, Coleridge does not identify that lack with his lost love for Mary Evans; he simply refers, self-castigatingly, to 'Sloth'.

Finally, in December, he sent to Southey a sonnet addressed to Bowles, praising him because his poetry of sensibility had first awakened his heart to the needs of his fellow human beings and then had solaced him in his times of distress, taking the sting from 'vain Regret',

> While shadowy Pleasure with mysterious Wings
> Brooded the wavy and tumultuous Mind,
> Like that great Spirit, who with plastic Sweep
> Mov'd on the darkness of the formless Deep!
>   (CL I 136)

Sulivan's word 'plastic' now makes its appearance to reinforce the sense of a formless energic power and a shaping spirit which might, if brought into full activity, produce a paradisal state but which, in the absence of love, can remain only in a state of negative (even if semi-pleasurable) pain.

This paradigm of love and creativity may be traced elsewhere in Coleridge – it is as if he thought that the dawning of love in itself constituted the ultimate creative 'Let there be . . .'.[10a] But the growth of this pattern of thinking in his mind seems also to have led in another direction, encouraging him to think more about the nature of life itself, in the straightforward biological sense, and to ask whether the processes of growth in vegetable nature might not be a paradigm for other forms of creativity. Could it be that the expansion of the plant, rooted in the energies of the soil and assisted by the breeze that blew over it, really offered a miniature of the ideal creative process?

The evidence at this point is somewhat tenuous, but what there is suggests that Coleridge's speculations about the nature of life were particularly active during the winter of 1794. They would associate with the pattern of thinking just traced, as also with contemporary interest in the part played by electricity in all life; and the London intellectuals with whom Coleridge was associating at this time, such as Frend, Wakefield and Dyer, were particularly open to new ideas. Recalling the period later, Charles Lamb spoke of a smoky little room at the 'Salutation and Cat', 'with all its associated train of pipes, tobacco, Egghot, welch Rabbits, metaphysics and Poetry'.[11] Coleridge seems to have been indulging in ranging speculations of just the kind that books such as Sulivan's encouraged.

It may well be that he was also reading Lucretius with attention. This would have been natural, since his new friend Gilbert Wakefield was then working on his great edition. By 1796, certainly, Lucretius would provide a firm point of reference for Coleridge's own poetic ambitions. In *The Watchman* he wrote,

> If we except Lucretius and Statius, I know not of any Latin Poet, ancient or modern, who has equalled Casimir in boldness of conception, opulence of fancy, or beauty of versification.
>
> (Watchman 68 (9.3.96))

Writing to Thelwall a month later enclosing his poems, he wrote of the *Religious Musings* as a work which

> ... you will read with a POET'S Eye, with the same unprejudiceness, I wish, I could add, the *same* pleasure, with which the atheistic Poem of Lucretius.   (CL I 205)

If we wish to know in more detail what Coleridge gained from Lucretius, we are forced to go to statements made many years later. In 1830 he declared that Lucretius had 'preserved a complete view' of Epicurus' system;[12] in the *Philosophical Lectures* he had brushed aside the physiology of Epicurus by quoting Lucretius' account:

> First of all the mud was a milky substance with which the living things were nourished and . . . in the former state it was still better for it produced the living things themselves.
>
> (PL 217)

The exact terms used elsewhere to dismiss Epicurus are also worth attention; Coleridge speaks of his Summum Bonum as 'not worth the having, as in his overthrow of final causes & the intelligence he himself pourtrays'.[13]

This last sentiment is of particular interest in view of a reference in Sulivan to the belief that 'nature, producing and possessing intelligent beings, must be herself intelligent',[14] which comes in the midst of a long and highly relevant discussion of life, including references to the phenomenon of 'suspended animation' and to the extraordinary power of the 'vegetative spark' to remain in a seed for an astonishing length of time.[15] In the following summer Coleridge was reading *The Intellectual System of the Universe*, where the atheists' subordination of intelligence in the universe furnishes a main point for Cudworth's attack on their philosophy.[16]

We are still left asking where Coleridge saw that intelligence 'Pourtrayed' – and, indeed, what prompted him to speak in 1796 of Lucretius' 'boldness of conception'. He left one answer, perhaps, in the title he gave to a later notebook: 'Semina Rerum, Audita, Cogitata, Cogitanda of a Man of Letters. . .'.[17] The phrase 'semina rerum' occurs as a refrain in Lucretius' poem, expressing his central belief that matter is ultimately reducible not to atoms but to seeds. And this idea, at least, would find a ready echo in a mind which was learning from the avant-garde philosophy of the time that the universe might after all be not one of dead matter in motion, but, at its heart, an 'active universe'. Such a view might well change, not just one's abstract conception of the universe, but one's very mode of *perceiving* it. Whereas a universe contemplated in terms of atoms and their properties would in all important ways invite a quantitative analysis, set in a broad structure of space and time, a universe conceived as one of seeds automatically took on a dimension of infinity. To one who had learned from it to look everywhere in the universe for the 'seeds of things', each seed containing infinitely more, growing inside each for ever, Lucretius' system, for all its atheism and dismissal of intelligence, would indeed possess 'boldness of conception'.

There were other, more recent thinkers for Coleridge to be engaging with that winter. On 11 December he wrote of himself as a 'compleat Necessitarian': adding, 'but I go farther than Hartley and believe the corporeality of *thought*, namely, that it is motion...'.[18] I have argued elsewhere that the last, riddling assertion might represent a response to Godwin's query, in *Political Justice*, whether motion could exist where there was not thought and to his division of motion according to various functions associated respectively with 'gravitation, elasticity, electricity, magnetism and the motions of the vegetable and animal systems'.[19]

Lastly we may turn to Erasmus Darwin, arguably the most challenging and exciting intellectual figure of Coleridge's time. 'The Loves of the Plants', published while Coleridge was still at school, had been an attractive volume, beautifully illustrated, written in a light elegant verse that suited its subject. Those who were advanced enough in their views to discuss the idea of free love no doubt found something deeply engaging in Darwin's demonstration of the sexual vagaries of the vegetable world, where, he pointed out, many males and females lived together in the same flower; he compared this with the 'promiscuous marriage' of '100 males and 100 females' in Otaheite.[20] The next work, 'The Economy of Vegetation', which was less light-hearted in character, included discussion of turbulencies in nature such as the power of the Maelstrom, inundations of the Nile, and the behaviour of geysers in Iceland.[21] His culminating work of the time, *Zoönomia*, which was entirely serious, developed many ideas about human and animal physiology that had merely been touched on in notes to his previous volumes.

Certain changes may be traced in Coleridge's attitude to Darwin, corresponding to the work he had been most recently reading. A critical attitude towards the poetry remained constant, however. In 1796 he went so far as to say, 'I absolutely nauseate Darwin's poem';[22] in the *Biographia* he recalled how in a paper which he wrote with a friend for a literary society at Exeter during a Cambridge vacation he had compared *The*

Botanic Garden to 'the Russian palace of ice: cold, glittering and transitory'.[23a]

This last image deserves further scrutiny in view of its source. While eminently respectable, Cowper appealed to the young of the time as a liberal, who had expressed his hope for the fall of the Bastille several years before the event actually took place.[24] When Coleridge wished to avouch the moderateness of his political opinions to his brother in 1798, it was some verses from the same Book of *The Task* that he called to his aid.[25] And it is near the beginning of that book that Cowper describes the Russian palace of ice, in terms which are sensuously attractive:

> No forest fell
> When thou wouldst build; no quarry sent its stores
> T' enrich thy walls; but thou didst hew the floods,
> And make thy marble of the glassy wave...
>
> Silently as a dream the fabric rose.
> No sound of hammer or of saw was there.
> Ice upon ice, the well-adjusted parts
> Were soon conjoin'd, nor other cement ask'd
> Than water interfus'd to make them one.
> Lamps gracefully disposed and of all hues
> Illumined every side. A wat'ry light
> Gleamed through the clear transparency, that seemed
> Another moon new-risen, or meteor fall'n
> From heav'n to earth, of lambent flame serene...
>
> (V 131–4; 144–53)

The hint of Milton's Pandaemonium in these lines prepares us for the moral comment at the end, which is sharply drawn:

> 'Twas transient in its nature, as in show
> 'Twas durable. As worthless, as it seemed
> Intrinsically precious. To the foot
> Treach'rous and false, it smiled and it was cold.
>
> (V 173–7)

This then leads Cowper into a long analysis of tyranny and its origins, culminating with a rhapsodic praise of liberty and the affirmation that it can be found only in the enlightened individual:

> He is the freeman whom the truth makes free,
> And all are slaves beside.
>
> (V 733-4)

When Coleridge likened Darwin's poem to the Russian palace of ice, then, he was using a precise and familiar simile, which did not preclude a limited admiration. It was the versification of the poem (particularly 'The Economy of Vegetation') which drew his chief criticism. The poetry was, he said,

> ...a succession of Landscapes or Paintings—it arrests the attention too often, and so prevents the rapidity necessary to pathos.—it makes the great little.   (CN I 132)

The image of the Russian palace, on the other hand, suggests that Coleridge found much that was brilliant in Darwin's poem and saw its positive qualities as possible elements in a larger dialectic. Truly great poetry might combine this kind of brilliance with other, more permanent and profound qualities.

The existence of this admiration is attested to by Coleridge's borrowings from Darwin. Whatever he might think of his verses, he found the notes a rich quarry for images and ideas. In addition to the phenomena mentioned above, Darwin's eclectic mind had drawn together such items as the lyre in the Temple of Memnon, which emitted a musical sound at the touch of the rays of the rising sun, the luminosity of certain plants and inanimate objects and the luminous and electrical properties of creatures such as the glow-worm, the gymnotus and the torpedo.[26] When Coleridge praised Wordsworth's phrase 'green radiance' for the glow-worm,[27] he was perhaps implying an advance on Darwin, who had simply instructed the Nymphs of Fire to[28]

> Warm on her mossy couch the radiant Worm,
> Guard from cold dews her love-illumin'd form ...

To a young poet who had been pursuing the idea of correspondences in nature, Darwin's references to the mysterious properties of light and energy in living things could start a train of exciting possibilities in the mind. Coleridge's most direct borrowing is in fact to be found in a note on the 'flashing' of flowers affixed to his 'Lines Written at Shurton Bars', citing Haggern's observation that marigolds sometimes seemed to flash in the evening.[29] This note, which Coleridge used to justify his image of his love-charg'd heart flashing with ecstasy when rushing to greet Sara Fricker, was lifted bodily (and without acknowledgement) from Darwin. One feature which no doubt delighted him particularly was the image of the 'flash', which occurred also in Boehme. Scholars have noted other such borrowings from Darwin in his poetry.[30]

While it may seem reprehensible of Coleridge to have criticised Darwin's poetry with one hand while plundering his notes with the other, it should be pointed out in his defence that his main criticisms of Darwin were directed to the poetry. Some of his statements about the thought, by contrast, were positively adulatory. Just after meeting him (earlier in 1796) he had written,

> Dr Darwin possesses, perhaps, a greater range of knowledge than any other man in Europe, and is the most inventive of philosophical men. He thinks in a *new* train on all subjects except religion. (CL I 177)

'On the whole', he wrote a year later, 'I think he is the first *literary* character in Europe, and the most original-minded Man.'[31] Such criticism as he made in this area concerned his attitude to religion. He had gone to see him, we may imagine, hoping for sympathetic reception of his idea that the study of nature might be related to a reinterpretation of Christianity, only to find that on the latter subject the great scientist's mind was closed. Darwin, he complained afterwards, would not have rejected Hutton's *Theory of the Earth* without having studied it,

> but *all at once he makes up his mind* on such important subjects, as whether we be the outcasts of a blind idiot called Nature, or the children of an all-wise and infinitely good God... (CL I 177)

The disillusionment, which spread also to his intellectual methods,[32a] seems to have been all the more severe in view of the work which had begun to appear just before. A reference many years later which suggests that he had found Darwin's *Zoönomia* (the first volume of which came out in 1794) exciting and stimulating, deserves to be examined in detail:

So long back as the first appearance of Dr Darwin's Phyto-
nomia, the writer, then in earliest manhood, presumed to
hazard the opinion, that the physiological botanists were
hunting in a false direction; and sought for analogy where
they should have looked for antithesis. He saw, or thought
he saw, that the harmony between the vegetable and animal
world, was not a harmony of resemblance, but of contrast;
and their relation to each other that of corresponding
opposites. They seemed to him (whose mind had been
formed by observation, unaided, but at the same time
unenthralled, by partial experiment) as two streams from
the same fountain indeed, but flowing the one due west, and
the other direct east; and that consequently, the resemblance
would be as the proximity, greatest in the first and rudimental
products of vegetable and animal organisation. Whereas,
according to the received notion, the highest and most perfect
vegetable, and the lowest and rudest animal forms, ought to
have seemed the links of the two systems, which is contrary to
fact. Since that time, the same idea has dawned in the
minds of philosophers capable of demonstrating its objective
truth by induction of facts in an unbroken series of correspondences in nature. From these men, or from minds enkindled
by their labours, we hope hereafter to receive it, or rather
the yet higher idea to which it refers us, matured into *laws*
of organic nature; and thence to have one other splendid
proof, that with the knowledge of LAW alone dwell Power
and Prophecy, decisive Experiment, and, lastly, a scientific
method, that dissipating with its earliest rays the gnomes of
hypothesis and the mists of theory may, within a single
generation, open out on the philosophic Seer discoveries that
had baffled the gigantic, but blind and guideless industry of
ages.   (Friend I 469–70)

Although Coleridge scrambles the title of Darwin's *Zoönomia*
(1794–6) with that of his *Phytologia* (1800), we may agree with
the editor of *The Friend* that he meant the former: he would
hardly have referred to 1800 as 'earliest manhood' and it is the
Zoönomia that fits his argument.

To this day, particularly if read with some exercise of
historical imagination, *Zoönomia* is an attractive work. By com-

parison with the staidness of most contemporary studies, its discussions of psychology, including the psychology of perception, give the sense of an engaged and informed intelligence at work; we are reminded once more of the unusually open state of scientific thinking at the time.

If we go on to ask what part of the volume might have prompted the speculation described by Coleridge we find ourselves drawn to the section entitled 'Of Vegetable Animation', which discusses the various ways in which vegetables resemble animals. Darwin begins with an account of the mimosa, or sensitive plant, 'whose leaves contract on the slightest injury', proceeds to list various anatomical resemblances to animals (the roots of vegetables are said to resemble the lacteal system, for example) and answers the question whether vegetables have ideas of external things by asserting that they have the senses of heat and cold; of moisture and dryness; and of light and darkness. He also suspects the agency of a 'voluntary power' in the circular movement of the tendrils of vines, and believes that the anthers and stigmata are themselves really 'animals' – attached to the parent tree, but capable of spontaneous motion.[33]

The doctrine of evolution which seems implicit in all this is furthered by the idea (voiced also in *The Botanic Garden*) that the anthers and stigmata might mark the point at which the insect creation begins.[34a] Coleridge, on the other hand, was, according to the account just quoted, drawn to argue that the difference between plant and anther marked, not a point of continuity, but a chasm which had existed from the beginning of creation, a polarity between opposing forces always at work in the world of life. If the previous account of his developing ideas is accepted, moreover, it will readily be seen how these concepts could enmesh themselves into a view of nature in which the phenomena of life were seen as a threefold process of evolving form, free-playing energy and shaping spirit. In the vegetable creation, it is the form that predominates: from the seed upwards, the activity of energy is mainly devoted to the elaboration of that form. In the animal creation, by contrast, a new feature is introduced by the existence of a fund of energy more freely at the organism's disposal. The shaping spirit is here more vividly displayed in patterns of movement created by the animal itself, whether singly, as with the sinuous gliding of the snake, or communally, as in the interweaving dance of small flies.

This passage of Coleridge's deserves close attention, therefore. If taken seriously, it helps to explain his later assertions that he had developed certain theories about the nature of the organic before he went to Germany. It also helps to explain certain of the ideas at work in his poetry, where the relationship between vegetable forms and animal energies is important.

For the moment, we need only draw attention to one particular theme which featured in his later thinking, and which would seem to have focused itself there in connection with the theory just discussed; though some elements may date from still further back. This was the distinction between movement in a direct line and the various circling or cycling movements which often characterise animal energies when exercising themselves in a state of free play or idleness.

In the vegetable creation, it could be argued, there was little free movement of this kind. The vegetable grew by expansion and seemed to possess only limited sensibility. But at one of the rare points at which any kind of 'voluntary power' might be detected – in the movement of vine-tendrils – the movement assumed a spiral form, as Darwin had noted.

In the animal world, on the other hand, there was a constant tendency to circular movement, particularly in flying creatures. A similar phenomenon might be observed in snakes, which were forced to employ curving motions, even when proceeding in a direct line, and which found it natural to wreathe themselves spirally around an upright stem or pillar.

The various patterns involved seem to have fascinated Coleridge. They could be found in other instances of energy in free motion, as in the movement of water. A stream, while flowing steadily onward to the sea, would be caught in constant eddies: moving both through and around them. The larger motions of water involved constant further circulation of various kinds, by which, whether through evaporation and condensation in the air, or through underground streams, it was restored to its ultimate springs. In such a process the coiling movement of the serpent turned into ultimate harmony – the snake with its tail in its mouth[35a]. But it was also true that in its fiercer manifestation the free energy of water could circle more destructively, towering up in the spiralling pillar of the sandstorm or the waterspout, or opening into the vortical destruction of the whirlpool.[36]

All these phenomena may be related back to the distinction which Coleridge made in *The Friend*. In vegetable growth, form expands from a central spring of life; except in rare cases, energy is no more than a circulation within that form. In the animal, on the other hand, the form of the organism's growth is only one part of the phenomenon: it also has power to produce active forms either through exercise of its own limbs or through association with fellows of its species. Such forms are created essentially as movements in time and have a tendency towards the circular.

An account of Coleridge's ideas on these lines can be dated only tentatively. Various of the speculations involved might have taken place either in London at the end of 1794 or in Bristol during the summer of 1795. There is however a unified quality about them which suggests that they were more likely to have first been developed together in the forcing-house atmosphere of London, encouraged by the congenial company of Lamb and other sympathetic friends.

When he was brought back by Southey from London early in 1795, Coleridge determined once more to devote himself to practical activities. Already he had made a vow of the kind in his last letter to Mary Evans on Christmas Eve;[37] the political situation, meanwhile, was deteriorating and firm action on the part of the liberal-minded was called for if free speech were not soon to be totally suppressed. Coleridge lectured boldly on the theme. His chief offering to his audiences at Bristol, however, was a longer series on 'Revealed Religion, its Corruptions and Political Views'.[38]

This series may well have been devised with larger plans in mind. Throughout his career, Coleridge was fond of devising lecture-courses and teaching-schemes with the idea of learning along with his audiences or pupils.[39a] If he needed to know about particular aspects of theology or philosophy, one way of purchasing the necessary time (and of ensuring his own application) was to offer several lectures or arrange a study-class on the subject in question. In the 1795 course, certainly, Coleridge draws heavily on the work of Priestley, Cudworth and other defenders of Christianity who had taken up the challenge offered by study of philosophy and the natural world.

So far as our present purposes are concerned, only one or two features of the lectures need be discussed. The first is that the lectures are evidently conceived in terms of Coleridge's 'public' philosophy at this time; at one point, indeed, he speaks sardonically about the Platonic version of the Trinity, though his description of Plato as 'the wild-minded Disciple of Socrates who hid Truth in a dazzle of fantastic Allegory, and is dark with excess of Brightness'[40] betrays a different subterranean direction in his thought. Elsewhere, he makes a point that may partly derive from Sulivan. Discussing instinct, Sulivan had declared,

> It is not owing to learning, or to experience, that infants apply themselves to their mother's breasts, that they put things to their mouths; or that they extend their hands to such objects as please them . . .   (Sulivan III 162)

In his first lecture Coleridge argued that the instinct towards motion in infants from the very earliest age must presuppose the existence of a Deity.

> A considerable Length of Time is necessary to teach the use of Motion: but before he could have learnt this, he must have perished from want of Food. Or suppose what is impossible that without innate Ideas he should be produced with a knowledge of the use of motion, or rather that as he lay helpless on the bosom of his unconscious Mother his Food luckily grew up around him. Who was present to teach him that the Pains which he felt proceeded from the want of Food or that opening his Mouth & chewing were the means of rendering useful what by accidental(ly) stretching out his hand he had acquired   There being no innate Ideas, I am unable to conceive how these Phaenomena are explicable without Deity—   (Lectures (1795) 103)

The general argument here owes something to Hartley (as the editor points out), but the specific conjunction of sucking and stretching is more reminiscent of Sulivan.

The delivery of the lectures gave Coleridge an opportunity to consider basic metaphysical questions concerning the existence of God and His attributes. And although he drew heavily on Priestley's writings, he evidently became aware that he disagreed with some aspects of them. In his *Disquisitions on Matter and Spirit*, Priestley had tried to maintain that man was totally matter and that the concept of separate spirit should be abolished. When man died, he argued, he did not live on in any sort of spiritual existence but simply awaited the recreation of his body in physical form at the resurrection of the dead.[41]

The factor in Priestley's thinking which allowed it to include this idea and retain coherence was no doubt provided by the new facts and properties which his scientific investigations had revealed. His own work on oxygen, along with other scientific work of the time, had given a new and exciting dimension to matter. Priestley's divine creator (though he tries to guard against such a conclusion) gives the sense of an energic God, moving like a yeast in matter.

Although Priestley defended himself against charges of pantheism by asserting that God was both immanent in his creation and transcended it, the logic of his arguments was by no means clear, as Coleridge came to see. 'How is it that Dr Priestley is not an atheist?' he asked in March 1796, '– He asserts in three different places that God not only *does*, but *is*, every thing. – But if God *be* every Thing, every Thing is God – : which is all, the Atheists assert – . An eating, drinking, lustful God – with no *unity* of *Consciousness* – these appear to me the unavoidable Inferences from his philosophy . . .'[42] Coleridge's interest in such questions did not end with the lectures. They may be seen at work in his chief poetic work during the summer of 1795, the lines which he contributed to Southey's *Joan of Arc* and later published separately as part of 'The Destiny of Nations'.[43] Here, his aim was to link the ideal of political freedom (as championed by Joan) with the sense that true freedom could be discovered only within an awareness of God's nature as Father. As he develops the theme in his drafts he uses his trinitarian paradigm of God in two forms, first conceiving the Logos as literally a 'Word' and so making the Spirit a kind of sound and echo:

Mind! Co-eternal Word! forth-breathing Sound!

then following this by a formula which stresses the element of cycling process:

Birth and Procession; Ever re-incircling Act!   (PW II 1026)

During that summer he was also reading an associated work, Andrew Baxter's *Enquiry into the Nature of the Human Soul*. Baxter was a straightforward thinker, not particularly subtle but able to spot the flaw in an argument. His work (by contrast with Priestley's) was designed to argue firmly for the immateriality of the soul and to oppose any theories which would turn the universe into a total machine. In particular he took issue with Newton, who towards the end of his life had supposed the existence of a subtle and elastic fluid diffused through all bodies and open spaces, providing the medium within which gravitation could operate and associated with attractions, repulsions and influences throughout the physical and animal creation. The idea had been taken up by Hartley, who, in his *Observations on Man*, used the conception of aether as a model for the kind of medium within which he believed association of ideas to take place.[44] Baxter's discussion of the question, in which he argued cogently against the possibility of such a fluid's existing physically on the terms that Newton had postulated was taken up by Coleridge, and inserted (with insufficient acknowledgement) as a long note[45] to his lines about those who 'cheat themselves'

> With noisy emptiness of learnéd phrase,
> Their subtle fluids, impacts, essences,
> Self-working tools, uncaused effects, and all
> Those blind Omniscients, those Almighty Slaves,
> Untenanting creation of its God.   (PW I 132)

Speaking later about his contributions to *Joan of Arc*, Coleridge spoke of the 'vast exertion of all his intellect' involved and claimed that the comparative industry as between himself and Southey ought to be judged 'by the quantum of mental exertion, not the particular mode of it.'[46] The following passage, which contains the most concentrated expression in the work, witnesses to the pressure of his thought at this time:

> But Properties are God: the naked mass
> (If mass there be, fantastic guess or ghost)

Acts only by its inactivity.
Here we pause humbly. Others boldlier think
That as one body seems the aggregate
Of atoms numberless, each organized;
So by a strange and dim similitude
Infinite myriads of self-conscious minds
Are one all-conscious Spirit, which informs
With absolute ubiquity of thought
(His one eternal self-affirming act!)
All his involved Monads, that yet seem
With various province and apt agency
Each to pursue its own self-centering end.
Some nurse the infant diamond in the mine;
Some roll the genial juices through the oak;
Some drive the mutinous clouds to clash in air,
And rushing on the storm with whirlwind speed,
Yoke the red lightnings to their volleying car.
Thus these pursue their never-varying course,
No eddy in their stream. Others, more wild,
With complex interests weaving human fates,
Duteous or proud, alike obedient all,
Evolve the process of eternal good.   (PW I 133)

Although lines such as these are sometimes dismissed as philosophical poeticising, they can be thought of with more justice as
a very successful attempt to express in verse the processes of
thought. The thinking involved does not derive from any single,
readily identifiable source; if, for example, we ask how Coleridge
came by the idea that the naked mass 'acts only by its own
activity' the answer is that he found it in Andrew Baxter's book:
the first chapter is devoted to a discussion of the matter, in
which this very phrase occurs. The 'bolder' account of God's
activity, on the other hand, might owe something to Sulivan,
who answered the problem of matter and its activity by his
supposition of a 'universal energy' which could be regarded as
being everywhere at work:

Matter . . . is in itself absolutely inert, or inactive, and is put
in motion; therefore, motion must be communicated from
some external agent. But we find warmth and heat in all parts
of the earth, more or less. This proves, that all parts are more

or less in motion, and consequently, that there is an universal agent, or spirit, or divine power.   (Sulivan II 92–3)

In his subsequent discussion, Sulivan speaks of matters still closer to Coleridge's 'infant diamond' and the 'genial juices' in his oak. Growth, he says, can be found in all substances:

... we see that all kinds of spar grow and increase in bulk, by peculiar juices and surrounding fluids. We see crystals, efflorescences, even metals, talks and asbestos, growing from stony substances, or an earthy root.   (Sulivan II 93)

Coleridge's attempt to define the 'divine power' more precisely as a system of monads likewise seems to have no single source. He may have derived the plural form from Leibnitz,[47a] but the idea of a monad as an active force in matter is hardly Leibnitzian. That element seems rather to come from Pythagoras, who according to Enfield's *History of Philosophy* (the first volume of which Coleridge borrowed from the Bristol Library in March 1795) taught[48] that God

is the Universal Mind; diffused through all things; the source of all animal life; the proper and intrinsic cause of all motion, in substance similar to light; in nature like truth . . .

He also said:[49]

The Monad, or unity, is that quantity, which being deprived of all number, remains fixed . . . It is the fountain of all number.

Coleridge's picture indirectly involves a similar fountain image, in that his 'Monads' are regarded as powers which act each with a purpose of its own – some directly as natural forces, 'no eddy in their stream', others in more complex fashion, as those which weave the fates of human beings. (In an earlier draft he had tried a different metaphor, which also employs an imagery of directness and eddying: 'Absolute Infinite, whose dazzling robe/Flows in rich folds, and darts in shooting Hues/ Of infinite Finiteness!'.)[50]

One problem which remains unsolved here is that of the freedom of the human will. Coleridge trifled with it for a moment in his drafts and then dismissed it from present consideration. Instead, he closed his contribution with some lines in which he affirmed the nature of God to be at once omnipresent and (his favourite word that year[51]) 'omnific' – revealing himself, that is, in direct vision to the receptive eye of the prophet, but also working obliquely through the energies of fanaticism, however misguided they might seem:

> 'Glory to Thee, Father of Earth and Heaven!
> All-conscious Presence of the Universe!
> Nature's vast ever-acting Energy!
> In will, in deed, Impulse of All to All!
> Whether thy Love with unrefracted ray
> Beam on the Prophet's purgéd eye, or if
> Diseasing realms the Enthusiast, wild of thought,
> Scatter new frenzies on the infected throng,
> Thou both inspiring and predooming both,
> Fit instruments and best, of perfect end:
> Glory to Thee, Father of Earth and Heaven!'
>
> (PW I 146–8)

Coleridge's contributions to *Joan of Arc* display his wider purposes at this time and give some hint of his growing desire to investigate the larger principles involved in all political and social issues. The poetic and intellectual labour involved, however, also led him towards one of the best poems he ever wrote.

Among the drafts for *Joan of Arc*, there is a passage, not afterwards used, which points away from the general rhetorical course of the poem. In good heroic vein, Coleridge demands an adequate instrument for his hymn and locates it in a harp, which 'hanging high between the Shields/Of Brutus and Leonidas, gives oft/A fateful Music, when with breeze-like Touch/Pure spirits thrill its strings.'[52] But the theme of the Aeolian harp, once broached, leads momentarily in another direction, as he dwells more luxuriously on its music:[53]

> The zephyr-travell'd Harp, that flashes forth
> Fits and coy wooings of wild Melody
> That sally forth & seek the meeting Ear,
> Then start away, half-wanton, half-afraid
> Like the Red-breast forced by wintry snows,
> In the first visits by the genial Hearth,
> From the fair Hand, that tempts it to—

Or like a cone of flame, from the deep sigh
Of the idly-musing Lover dreaming of his Love
With thoughts & hopes & fears, sinking, snatching,
                                        as warily, upward
Bending, recoiling, fluttering as itself . . .

In these lines, Coleridge turns away from his current preoccupation with public prophecy to contemplate the effects of the wind-harp when listened to in a mood of indolence. His meditations become more subtle as he considers how it attracts without satisfying the ear of the listener. The play of energy involved is then imaged in the behaviour of the robin, the light winged creature which is at once attracted to and cautious of the 'genial' warmth of the fire. (Once again, Coleridge is drawing on his paradigm to indicate the relationship between winged life and a life-sustaining, yet also potentially destructive source of energy.) The 'fair hand that tempts it', following on the use of 'half-wanton' for the bird, hints at the erotic, with its similarly ambiguous pleasures.

The sequel to this divergent meditation is found not in *Joan of Arc* but in the more relaxed poem which Coleridge wrote later that summer, *The Eolian Harp*.[54] Here, instead of being invited to contemplate the universe at large, we are in a local and recognisable landscape. Yet in describing that scene he deftly picks up elements of his larger vision. On this evening the warmth of the nearby earth, the beanplants that grow into flower from it and the breeze that blows over those flowers provide a beautifully apt illustration for the trinity of genial energy, growing vegetation and shaping spirit that we found also in Sulivan. There is more to the scene than that, however. The warm sensibility of the two lovers; the jasmine and myrtle on the walls of the cottage, the sight of the evening star, the sound of the sea, the fragrance from the beanflowers, all help to suggest the presence of a general spirit, playing over and interfusing itself with every component of the scene.

If the scents ('exquisite' . . . 'Snatch'd from yon bean-field') speak most directly of that spirit, the breeze of evening is its most comprehensive agent: it not only bears the fragrance given off by the innate energy of the beanflower but also carries the sound of the sea, which in turn enforces the sense of peacefulness ('tells us of silence'). As it stirs the strings of the Aeolian harp also, it wakens the music of nature. And that music itself suggests the play of erotic energies in a basically chaste situation:

> . . . by the desultory breeze caress'd,
> Like some coy Maid half yielding to her Lover
> It pours such sweet upbraiding, as must needs
> Tempt to repeat the wrong!

These lines no doubt owe something to Pope's

> As some coy Nymph her Lover's warm Address
> Nor quite indulges, nor can quite repress.
>
> (*Windsor Forest* 19–20)

and to James Ridley's description (in *Tales of the Genii*) of carvings which showed 'coyly willing virgins; who seemed, even in the ivory in which they were carved, to show a soft reluctance'.[55] But the more pervasive debt is to Milton's unfallen Adam and Eve in *Paradise Lost*, resting in a bower of flowers that include myrtle and jasmine and indulging to the full their innocent sensuousness.

The sounds awakened by the breeze in the harp again suggest Milton's lovers, who 'Lulled by nightingales embracing slept'.[56] But the paradisal note is also becoming more generalised, with images of honey culled from flowers by the 'birds of Paradise':

> Such a soft floating witchery of sound
> As twilight Elfins make, when they at eve
> Voyage on gentle gales from Faery Land,
> Where *Melodies* round honey-dropping flowers,
> Footless and wild, like birds of Paradise,
> Nor pause, nor perch, hovering on untam'd wing. . . .
>
> (*Poems* (Ev) 52)

At this point, recalling Erasmus Darwin, we may trace a complex undertheme. For Darwin, it will be remembered, the crucial juncture in nature is that at which the insect approaches the vegetable, being drawn towards it by its quest for honey. The image of the snatches of melody that drift 'half-wanton, half-afraid', like the red-breast approaching the hearth (whose flames rise and fall in response to the sighs of the lover himself) have now given place to still subtler sensations. Now it is the scents floating from the beanfield, the ambiguous response from the maiden, 'coy' yet 'half-yielding', and the birds of paradise, hovering around 'honey-dropping flowers', that work together to suggest an imagery of forms and potent energies. The concept, with its carefully qualified sexuality, is then applied to the whole of animated nature. The breeze which passes over the beanfield, releasing its scents, now becomes an image of fantasies passing over the brain, and then of the 'intellectual breeze' which passes over all animated things (including human beings) in a manner which at once unifies them all in its energising action yet assists the individual identity of each.

In the midst of creating an atmosphere of magic and romance, that is, Coleridge has launched an important speculation. Can it be that the mood of heightened sensibility in which he finds himself this evening is in fact a central key to the significance of nature herself? That the correspondence now sensed between all the components of this scene, linked as it is by the caressing breeze, is in fact present at a more subtle level throughout nature, as a link between all living things, including human beings?

> And what if all of animated nature
> Be but organic Harps diversly fram'd,
> That tremble into thought, as o'er them sweeps
> Plastic and vast, one intellectual Breeze,
> At once the Soul of each, and God of all?
>
> (Poems (Ev) 53)

His speculations are immediately checked. From Sara, at his side, he senses a reproof (real or imagined) at such 'thoughts/ Dim and unhallow'd'. The mood changes abruptly as he turns, with a gesture of due obeisance, towards the 'INCOMPREHEN-SIBLE', acknowledging his own guilt and praising him for the gift of 'PEACE, and this COT, and THEE, Heart-honor'd Maid!'

The pietism of the closing lines has been censured by many critics, who catch a whiff of insincerity. And the change of mood is hardly rendered more convincing by the nature of the speculations just set in train, which seem harmless enough. The conception of a plastic spirit, 'at once the Soul of each, and God of all' is not necessarily unattractive even to orthodox Christians, who might easily find ways of subsuming it to their own beliefs. As William Empson has pointed out, also, Coleridge in later revisions 'twice added further heretical or profane thoughts for his bride to have reproved'.[57]

When we consult the terms of the poem's previous development, however, we may suspect that Coleridge was already conscious of proceeding towards a point which he could hardly have wished to reach. In a marginal comment written some years later, he returns to the image of the Aeolian harp:[58]

> The mind does not resemble an Aeolian harp, nor even a barrel-organ turned by a stream of water, conceive as many tunes mechanized in it as you like, but rather as far as objects are concerned a violin or other instrument of few strings yet vast compass, played on by a musician of Genius.

If a meditation on genius was also working in Coleridge's mind when he wrote his poem, the need for a check to his thoughts is more explicable. For the natural sequel of the speculation there would have been not to continue the pleasant speculation concerning the forms of nature, but to assert boldly the nature of genius in the individual, and in the poet himself. In other words, Coleridge would have found himself asserting that the 'universal Soul' to be discerned in nature at large was also active in every human being, working as his genius, and that it was the poet's special privilege to possess this genius in larger measure. But he could no sooner envisage such a conclusion before the other side of his experience rushed in to check and admonish him not only against the idea itself but against its possible sensual implications, encouraging as it might a spontaneity of behaviour like that which he had indulged in, disastrously, at Cambridge.

The logical connection is not simply pietistic, therefore. And one or two positions are still reserved by the imagery. Philosophy may be an 'aye-babbling spring' but it is still a spring – which leaves an outlet open to Coleridge's visionary universe. And the pietistic tone yields slightly at a second look:

> For never guiltless may I speak of Him,
> Th' INCOMPREHENSIBLE! save when with awe
> I praise him, and with Faith that inly *feels!*
>
> (Poems (Ev) 53)

The point about feeling is reinforced by a footnote quoting Citoyenne Roland on the 'sense' that she finds lacking from atheism. Coleridge, it seems, *can* feel free of guilt on those occasions when he approaches God either with a sense of sublimity ('praising him with awe') or with a feeling heart. His conception of religion remains distinctly less rigorous than that which a more conventional orthodoxy would demand.

If there is a flaw in Coleridge's attitudes, then, it may be seen as the enlargement of a flaw to be traced also in Milton: the flaw, that is, of a religious thinker who tries to enlarge the boundaries of puritanism without fully considering the bases on which puritanism ultimately rests.

We return to the core of the poem: the vision of animated nature as breathed upon and physically informed by a single shaping spirit. For Coleridge himself, the train of imaginative speculation encouraged by this concept had important and permanent effects. It made him more directly responsive to the world of living things in general. Studying the world of animals and insects, he came to delight particularly in winged creatures, ranging from the butterfly (the ancient emblem for the human 'psyche'[59]) to the nightingale and the eagle – each of which in some sense expressed its energies in response to light.

In the case of birds, some moral reference was often close at hand; Coleridge's feeling for flowers, and particularly scented flowers, was more direct. It was not only the beanflower, with its extraordinarily powerful effect of fulfilling sweetness, that attracted him. It is rather as if he believed all flowers to retain some paradisal quality that was less easily retained in the freer energies of the animal creation. He was particularly attracted to the rose and myrtle – flowers which he associated particularly with human love. In designing a seal for himself in 1808, he asked for a rose or myrtle in blossom as its centre;[60] and when Mrs Gillman actually gave him a myrtle-tree for his room twenty years later he seized the occasion to write a panegyric on flowers such as the rose, eglantine, honey-suckle, jasmine and geranium, concluding:

none of these are the MYRTLE! . . . O precious in its sweetness
is the *rich* innocence of its snow-white Blossoms!

(CL VI 678)

The association of myrtle with innocent love provides a key to the total shape of *The Eolian Harp*, a thin line of continuity which enables Coleridge to round his poem with an acceptance of the blessings of home and security and so relate himself back to the note of peace at the beginning of the poem. For the modern reader, on the other hand, the poem reads better as one of interrupted process: it is the speculation in the middle of the poem that works most actively in the mind.

This was equally true, it might be argued, of Coleridge's own imagination. Whenever caught by the idea that, as Lavater had put it,[61] 'The world that surrounds us, is the magic glass of the world within us', he would, despite his intervening willingness to check his own speculations, find himself returning again to the nexus of ideas involved, wondering at the mysterious and unfolding growth of flowers, delighting in the circling and spiralling energies of creatures at play and still more attentive to those points of intercourse between the animal and vegetable creations that had been focused for him by Darwin's image of an insect taking nectar from a flower.

4

Primary Consciousness

Our investigation so far has dealt mainly with Coleridge's view of the external world and of the possibility of detecting some significance in certain of its elements in their most benevolent form; whether the light and energies of nature, for example, might in their inner form yield knowledge of the divine creative principle that worked behind or within those phenomena.

Beneath these preoccupations, however, there lurks another, again related to the eighteenth-century world-picture. We mentioned earlier the sense of alienation induced by awareness that the mechanical system of the heavens, for all its magnificence, bore very little intimate correlation with human concerns. It was also the case that the atomism of contemporary physics left unsolved the basic question how communication between living things ever took place at all. The logical deduction from a universe in which things move according to preordained laws would seem to be that all living beings act either in accordance with similar laws or from the urges of self-preservation and self-aggrandisement. Was it indeed possible to account for their behaviour on any other terms?

From an early stage, Coleridge seems to have seized on one crucial point: the mystery that is involved in all recognition. How did it come about that living beings could not only signal meaningfully to one another but *recognise* one another's signals? The question, which is relevant to all animal behaviour, is particularly so to the growth of human language, since only a little reflection is required to see the logical difficulty of explaining how, if each individual is a self-contained and self-serving organism, the process of communication by signs is ever initiated in the first place.

The first difficulty, that of cosmic alienation, had been recognised by Newton himself, who, as mentioned earlier, proposed in a late work the existence of a subtle 'aether', through which the workings of gravitation might be operating.[1] This supplementary theory was applied by Hartley to human beings in trying to explain the medium within which association of ideas might be supposed to take place. In a similar spirit, Berkeley produced *Siris*, his treatise on tar-water, claiming that the healing powers which he believed to lie in that substance were due to its concentrating a subtle essence, diffused throughout the universe and forming a chain between all living beings and the divine.[2] For the same reason, thinkers were constantly attracted to any theories which dealt in influences, attractions, repulsions and other kinds of movement which were not readily explicable.

In the search for signs of subtle linkage, the phenomenon of magnetism aroused particular interest, as providing a suggestive paradigm for the study of similar attractions between living beings and more particularly of the belief in human free-will. William Law, for example, had argued that if a needle touched by a lodestone could reason it would no doubt be able to account for itself in a very satisfactory way without ever fully comprehending the part played by magnetism in its behaviour. The human soul, he thought, could be regarded in much the same way. He continued:[3]

And let me tell you, my dear friend ... that there is much more in this *instance* than you imagine. For all is *magnetism*, all is *sentiment, instinct*, and *attraction*, and the *freedom* of the will has the government of it. There is nothing in the universe but magnetism, and the impediments of it. For as all things come from God, and all things have *something* of God and goodness in them, so all things have *magnetical* effects and *instincts* both towards God and one another. This is the *life*, the *force*, the *power*, the *nature* of everything, and hence every thing has all that is really good or evil in it; reason stands only as a busybody, as an idle spectator of all this, and has only an imaginary power over it.

Those who were coming to distrust the hegemony of reason, on the other hand, might turn to Law for support in their belief in certain other powers of the human psyche.

The disadvantage of Law's belief, from a rationalist point of view, was that whereas the Newtonian laws, if regarded as central, left reason a full part to play in the ordering of human conduct, a view of the world which placed so much stress on magnetism defended divine wisdom at the risk of enfeebling human reason. If, like Law's magnetised needle, it could never apprehend directly those processes of the universe that involved human instincts and affections, reason's authority was seriously disabled. For Law, this was not a serious problem. In his hands the doctrine of cosmic magnetism was no more than a way of buttressing the existing moral system: it was basically the occasion of an argument by analogy, designed to convince the doubter that God's moral laws worked upon him through direct attraction and instinct. Towards the end of the century, on the other hand, what had begun as analogy began to assume more directly the guise of physical correspondence, with the advent of Anton Mesmer, who demonstrated hypnotic techniques and announced the existence of a superfine fluid, interpenetrating all bodies, which, if tamed and harnessed by certain techniques, could be brought into the service of human healing. Mesmer had an extraordinary fashionable success; his methods were practised widely and his disciples recorded many hundreds of cases in which they claimed that cures had been wrought with its aid. And since the forces in question were held to exist throughout the universe, providing, among other things, the necessary medium through which gravitational attraction could take place, the doctrine revived possibilities previously raised by Newton's 'aether'.[4]

As Robert Darnton points out in his book *Mesmerism and the End of the Enlightenment in France*, the contemporary intellectual atmosphere in France provided a propitious setting for such theories. The recent invention of ballooning had brought into common use a mode of transport hitherto thought impossible: Parisians could see the refutation of previous scepticism on the subject being physically enacted above their heads. (Faced with this *renversement*, many took seriously the claim of a watchmaker that he would walk across the Seine with the aid of a pair of elastic shoes.)[5] The discovery of electricity, similarly, followed by that of oxygen, drew attention to the existence of strange forces in nature, and made it easier to believe that

Mesmer and his disciples might be drawing upon a force hitherto unacknowledged by orthodox science.

Although mesmerism had an immediate success when the first 'animal magnetisers' began practising in London (it was said that three thousand besieged the house of one leading hypnotist, seeking admission[6a]) the practice seems not to have had the full or lasting impact which it had in certain continental countries. The first great wave of enthusiasm took place during Coleridge's schooldays at Christ's Hospital, however, sweeping London at a time when his sensibility was unusually receptive to vivid new ideas. In due course he no doubt came to dismiss Mesmer's 'superfine fluid' along with Newton's 'aether', but the apparent facts disclosed by mesmerism in practice were harder to dispose of.

At this time, as is well known, psychological thinking was dominated by Hartley's ideas, the appeal of which was twofold. On the one hand, they offered an explanation of the nature of mental processes which seemed to fit neatly with the universe proposed by Augustan rationalism. All sense-experience was conducted in the body through a series of vibrations in the nerves. These gradually established paths for themselves through the nervous system and also touched with other common vibrations so as to form common patterns of association. Thus the mind, which began life like a rased wax tablet (in Locke's terminology), gradually took upon itself more and more the patterns established by repeated association. More and more complex ideas were gradually built up through these processes.[7]

A further advantage of Hartley's theory was the fact that it made the human mind less like a mirror for reflecting incoming sense-perceptions than it was made to seem in some contemporary psychological theories. The core of his system lay in the theory that such perceptions set up vibrations, and that these vibrations were carried into their centre in the medullary substance of the brain, where they continued to vibrate and to set up 'vibratiuncles', which could be reawakened when necessary by the processes of recognition and memory. Thus the medullary substance became, as Hartley put it, 'the seat of the sensitive soul, or the sensorium, in man.'[8]

Just as the Newtonian theory accounted for the movements of the heavens Hartley's view seemed to explicate the human nervous system. Hartley's belief in the 'sensitive soul' also encouraged cultivation of 'sensibility': by becoming 'tremblingly alive'[9] to the feelings and sufferings of others, human beings could enlarge their sympathies and hope to act with compassion in their society. There was also the possibility of a more radical interpretation. For if the processes of association were as straightforward as Hartley maintained, and if some way could be found to improve the ideas which were being impressed upon men – if, for example, children could be brought up to associate the beautiful, the true and the good with their earliest impressions, the whole human condition might be improved. And if the processes once set in motion proved irresistible and mutually propulsive, the movement towards human perfection might actually accelerate.

Such an optimism was further reinforced if the human being was regarded as subject to other forces working below the level of conscious attention. If there were indeed subtle attractions and instincts in the universe, and if human beings could be acted on by forces such as those of the hypnotist's art, might it not be possible to attune the processes of association to these underlying powers?

At this point we may turn back to Darwin's *Zoönomia*. Like Godwin, Darwin maintained that there were different forms of motion in the universe and argued that the 'primary motions' of matter could be divided into three classes, of which the first (and only the first, one assumes) belonged to Newton and Newton's laws:[10]

> 1st The gravitating motions include the annual and diurnal rotations of the earth and planets, the flux and reflux of the ocean, the descent of heavy bodies, and other phaenomena of gravitation.

To these he added, secondly, the 'chemical motions', distinguished by being generally attended with an evident decomposition or new combination of the active materials, and then one other class:

> The third class includes all the motions of the animal and vegetable world; as well those of the vessels, which circulate their juices, and of the muscles, which perform their locomo-

tion, as those of the organs of sense, which constitute their ideas.

It is to this last class that Darwin proposed to devote himself particularly in his book; his account of the various workings of the body brings home to the reader the miraculous range of activities involved. We have already mentioned his discussions of animation in vegetables; in addition much of the volume is given up to the discussion of human psychological phenomena. He draws attention to ways in which sense-experience may be said to begin not from external impressions but from various activities inside the body. A chapter on phenomena such as ocular spectra and after-images (contributed by his son)[11] demonstrates that in important respects human 'perception' is actually projected from within. Darwin also discusses the importance of touch and how children learn new figures not simply by sight but by putting objects to their mouths (which presupposes an organising force within them that is capable of putting together the two types of experience). He further points out (importantly for our later argument) that the sensations of heat and touch seem to depend on different nerves.[12]

Another important section of the volume is devoted to sleep and dreams, and particularly to certain curious features of the sleeping state.[13] Volition, Darwin points out, is then suspended – particularly in nightmare. In both sleep and reverie, likewise, the sense of time is lost. We are untroubled by inconsistencies, moreover; the sense of surprise is totally lacking. Yet in other respects our life is going on as usual: our growth, for example, is unaffected.

In these and many other comments in Darwin's volume, one discovers materials for a view of the human psyche by which the normal division between the waking and sleeping states could be extended into the projection of two distinguishable 'consciousnesses': a waking consciousness, in which the human organism uses all its powers to achieve a knowing relationship with the world of objects, and a sleeping consciousness, in which the mind, devoid of will or surprise, follows its own instincts more freely.

Although Darwin does not proceed to any firm conclusions, he throws out further ideas which point in the same direction. He distinguishes between two senses of the word 'volition': one in which we act immediately according to our own desire or aversion and another in which, between the feeling of desire or aversion and the initiation of action, there is time for reflection and delay. 'It is probable', he remarks, 'that this twofold use of the word volition in all languages has confounded the metaphysicians, who have disputed about free will and necessity.'[14] To Coleridge such an idea would surely be provocative; nor would his attention be likely to flag when, in pursuit of his discussion of 'diseases of volition', Darwin went on to distinguish as follows between madness and delirium:[15]

> Madness is distinguishable from delirium, as in the latter the patient knows not the place where he resides, nor the persons of friends or attendants, nor is conscious of any external objects, except when spoken to with a louder voice, or stimulated with unusual force, and even then he soon relapses into a state of inattention to every thing about him. Whilst in the former he is perfectly sensible to every thing external, but has the voluntary powers of his mind intensely exerted on some particular object of his desire or aversion ...

Coleridge, who used several of Darwin's ideas, later made a distinction between mania and delirium in terms very similar to these.[16] I believe that his interest was deeply involved, in fact: that he was urged on by all these separate distinctions in Darwin (between sleep-consciousness and waking-consciousness; between two sorts of volition; between delirium and madness) to probe the possibility that there existed, within human consciousness, a radical division, valid at all these levels. On the one hand, it might be argued, there was the world of outward phenomena, as organised by the theories of Newton and Locke, to which the mind attached itself through its waking experience and the working of the Hartleyan association of ideas; on the other the world of inward life, not directly available to consciousness, but indirectly accessible by way of the work of dreams, showing its nature most vividly perhaps, in states of delirium.

It was not only in dreams and delirium that this power might be traced, however; it might be assumed to be co-present, at a hidden and secret level, in all processes of perception – and more particularly in imaginative creation. Here again Darwin had some pregnant hints to offer. Having early on discussed the 'spirit of animation' and its power to assume whatever physical form it chooses, he gives, towards the end of his volume, some examples of the operation of transforming powers in animals and human beings. Some animals, for example, change the pigmentation of their coats according to the season: the final cause, he remarks, is understandable, but the efficient cause is almost beyond conjecture.[17] And having noted that vegetable buds and bulbs which are produced without a mother are always exact resemblances of their parent, he goes on to suggest that the real power of imagination in generation may belong to the male, so that the art of begetting beautiful children might perhaps be taught by affecting the imagination of the male parent.[18] Again, the work of some mysterious shaping power within the organism is presupposed.

The exact point in 1794–5 when Coleridge read Darwin is, as I have said, not easy to determine. Since he tended to read such books hot from the press, the most likely assumption is that it had already passed under his eye by the end of 1794, when he was in London (the idea that he had already begun formulating theories under its guidance by then receives some support from the fact that when Lamb was writing to him later about his period of madness he mentioned that he had imagined himself to be young Norval (from Home's *Douglas*) during his illness:[19] a fact which might suggest that the question of retaining identity in disordered states of the mind had earlier been discussed between them when Coleridge was in London) and that the psychological observations made by Darwin continued to reverberate in his mind during the following months.

One of the most distinctive features of *Zoönomia* is that Darwin makes no hard and fast distinction between the phenomena of the vegetable and animal worlds, on the one hand, and those of the human world on the other. He moves rapidly between discussions of animal instinct and theories about human illness, for example. And his use of psychological terminology contains one example of this cross-hatching which is of crucial importance for our discussion. On the one hand he discusses the behaviour of insects as embodying a form of 'volition'; on the other he discusses certain human ailments under the heading 'diseases of volition', explaining that he is using volition in a slightly different sense from the normal, to denote the behaviour of the human being in relation to the objective world.[20]

When we consider these ramifications we can glimpse further possible implications for Coleridge's thinking at this time. For it becomes possible to suppose that he not only began to think in terms of two levels of consciousness, but grafted that idea on to the distinction between the organic and the vital in nature which, as he later reported, he had been prompted to make when he first read the book. His separation of the two principles, in other words, according to which the vegetable creation was the chief exponent of the organic and the insect creation the exponent of the vital, made it possible also not only to correlate the insect creation with external human 'volition' but to correlate the vegetable creation with the deeper human will. It became possible to argue, that is, that while human beings were made in the condition of animals who could behave with the instinctive communality of insects, their energies at the mercy either of some inward instinct to preservation or of external threats to their survival, according to the dominant circumstances of the movement, their central aspiration was towards the condition of the vegetable creation, where energies were primarily governed by the inner form of the growing vegetative organism. *There* was the great exemplar of the human will – as opposed to volition; under that condition the human being was no longer at the mercy of the energies of the moment but under the dominance of an indwelling *idea*.

This is not to say that in such a view the function of the human being was to forsake the play of energy for the pure development of inward form (which would have been to suggest that the ideal existence was a calm vegetable one), but that the human being, in the full exercise of his animal energies, was called on to take still as his ideal the paradigm of the vegetable creation and submit them to such an inner form; just as, many years later, the ultimate aspiration and achievement of Yeats's dancer is to realise in dynamic form that which the 'great-rooted blossomer' shows forth in steady and static manifestation.[21]

Such a step as we suppose him to have taken is so crucial in understanding Coleridge's development that we ought to linger over the reconstruction and discuss some of its further implications. It seems to help explain his idea of the organic, his theory of will and his doctrine of the imagination. To interpose his emblems of the organic and the vital is in each case enlightening. The ideal of the organic might be envisaged as a paradise tree with a serpent entwined about it, that of the vital as a body of insects working together to create some communal form. One ideal emblem of the relationship between these two modes would be, say, a beanfield visited by numerous bees, not unlike that in *The Eolian Harp*.

In any attempt to relate the waking state to the vital and the sleeping state to the organic phenomenon of dreaming must have an important place. Andrew Baxter, whose work has already been mentioned, devoted a good deal of space to it, and we know from an account written many years later that Coleridge read him attentively on the subject that summer. Pausing during a discussion of dreams in a later notebook, he wrote, of Baxter,

> ... by the bye, I must get the Book—which I have never seen since in my 24th year I walked with Southey on a desperate hot Summerday from Bath to Bristol with a Goose, 2 vol. of Baxter on the Immortality of the Soul, and the Giblets, in my hand—I should not wonder if I found that Andrew had thought more on the subject of Dreams than any other of our Psychologists, Scotch or English— (NB 35.36)

What was Coleridge recalling in delivering this eulogy? Baxter's discussion, which comes in the second volume, still makes fascinating reading. He dwells particularly on the creative genius shown by the dreamer. This could not, he claims, be caused by the 'soul', since that is asleep; yet it is also a curious feature of the dream that although the whole thing is being created by oneself, the distinction between self and other selves is just as clearcut as in everyday life. He therefore proposes that the dream may afford an occasion on which other life-principles are enabled to operate through one's own sensory apparatus.[22]

The idea seems to have attracted both Coleridge and Southey. It would seem that their joint revision of Southey's *Joan of Arc* that summer may have been associated with a desire to give some firmer status to her story by interpreting the significance of her visions. If, after all, human dreams were simply the fantasies of an overheated imagination, the value of her career and teachings was correspondingly limited; but if 'vision' could sometimes be regarded as springing authentically from a reality which was glimpsed directly by the subconscious as it could not be by the conscious mind, her teachings and activities on behalf of liberty might be seen as grounded in an apprehension of truth.

Several passages in *Joan of Arc* are given over to the discussion of prophetic vision, the strong implication being that Joan was directly in touch with 'Nature's ... Energy', which was 'vast' and 'ever-acting', though whether the effects of that Energy were good or ill depended on the state of the vessel:

> Whether thy Love with unrefracted ray
> Beam on the Prophet's purgéd eye, or if
> Diseasing realms the Enthusiast, wild of thought,
> Scatter new frenzies on the infected throng ...
>
> (PW I 147)

Baxter's main concern, though not altogether unconnected, was slightly different: it was to protect the rationality of the waking soul by arguing that the irrationality of many dream appearances was due to their being fostered by spirits, which as daemonic forces could be either good or bad. (Something of the same sort was subsequently asserted by Swedenborg, as Coleridge later pointed out.)[23]

An important feature of Baxter's work lay in the wealth of material adduced, and the attention which it invited to the mysterious nature of the forces which operated in the subconscious during sleep. One or two specific points in Baxter might be expected to arouse particular attention, such as his discussion of Hume's theory that dreams and visions of fear were produced by cold,[24] or his suggestion that the work of dreams was essentially protective, guarding the sleeping human being from total incursion of terror. He cites an opinion, ascribed to Tillotson, that

> if our imaginations were let loose upon us, we should be always under the most dreadful terrors, and frighted to distraction with the appearances of our own fancy ...

and that an overruling power therefore restrains these effects.[25]

Darwin had focused attention upon the difference between sleeping and waking states; Baxter, previously, had tried to solve the problems which this difference posed for the rationality of the conscious mind by suggesting that in its unconscious state it was open to external daemonic forces, and so revived certain theories of the ancients. Another author should finally be mentioned who (as I believe) prompted Coleridge, during the summer when he was reading Baxter, to make one further leap of the speculative mind, which, like the others, gave an important impetus to his subsequent thinking. One reason for positing such a leap is that it throws light on some curious and riddling elements in Coleridge's later speculations – including his use of the terms 'single touch' and 'double touch', which has never been satisfactorily explained.

Although Coleridge never set out fully the theory involved, he sometimes made statements which give some indication of the themes involved: as, for example, in a note which he made at the end of a book on animal magnetism.[26] Here he argues that faith, understood as a sort of unifying energy, is most likely to exist in weak and credulous, but sincere, sensitive and warm-hearted men; he thinks this to be the case with those who believe in animal magnetism. And he goes on:

> I think it probable, that Animal Magnetism will be found connected with a Warmth-Sense: & will confirm my long long ago theory of Volition as a mode of *double Touch*.

Tantalisingly sibylline as this is, it throws one or two distinct rays of light on the matter. The phenomenon of animal magnetism, we gather, is to be associated with a warmth-sense; and this will then be seen to throw light on his theory that volition is a mode of 'double Touch'.

We may go further. 'Long long ago' suggests something more than ten or fifteen years; this type of nostalgic language is normally reserved by Coleridge for his youth. And there is good reason for supposing that the theorising in question belongs to that period of his life. Animal magnetism, as has already been stated, had been a new craze in the London of his schooldays, and he could not have escaped hearing about its remarkable effects. There were also constant references to such phenomena in the periodicals of the time. The *Conjuror's Magazine* for 1792 contained an account of a somnambulist at Vevey in Switzerland who in his sleep-walking would remember things that had happened during previous fits. Magnets, it was reported, had been held to him, with interesting effects.[27]

The invocation of the 'warmth-sense' also suggests speculations dating from Coleridge's youth. In addition to its relevance to the human heart (Descartes, it should be noted, devoted a long section of his *Discourse on Method* to a description of the physical workings of the heart, including the regulation of the warmth sense in the human body[28]), we have noted Baxter's mention of Hume's theory that dreams and visions of fear were produced by cold and Darwin's statement that the sensations of heat and of touch were dependent on different nerves. Coleridge's use of the term 'volition' also points to Darwin, who, as we have seen, distinguished two senses of the word. But what of the specific term 'double touch'?

The attempt to solve this particular riddle involves some intricate detective work concerning Coleridge's early reading. We may begin with a remark that occurs in *The Friend*. Coleridge is arguing for the primacy of acts of mind, as shown particularly in the work of mathematicians. He goes on

> The celebrated EULER, treating on some point respecting arches, makes this curious remark, 'All experience is in contradiction to this; sed potius fidendum est analysi: *i.e.* but this is no reason for doubting the analysis'.   (Friend I 476)

A similar comment on Euler appears in *Aids to Reflection*, where Coleridge is urging on much the same basis more frequent usage of the terms 'subjective' and 'objective'.[29] The editor of *The Friend* searched diligently through Euler's works for a source, but without success; we may assume that, in that precise form at least, it is not there. Since the formal opening to Coleridge's statement, coupled with the repetition of it in *Aids*, leaves one with the sense of an unexplained residue, however, it is worth pointing out that there is a passage in Euler which mentions the arch (though not in a mathematical context) and which involves a comment not unlike the one quoted in *The Friend*. In his *Letters to a German Princess* Euler describes a number of scientific phenomena, mostly of a familiar kind, and goes on to discuss the mode in which we look at the sky.[30] Everyone, he points out,

'considers the azure expanse of heaven as a flattened arch'; he
continues:

> Though this vault, however, has no real existence, it pos-
> sesses an undoubted reality in our imagination; and all man-
> kind, the philosopher as well as the clown, are subject to the
> same illusion. On the surface of this arch we imagine the
> sun, the moon, and all the stars to be disposed, like so many
> brilliant studs affixed to it; and though we have a perfect
> conviction of the contrary, we cannot help giving in to the
> illusion.

Although this is not exactly the same point as that in the
remark that appears in *The Friend*, the resemblance is strong
enough to make one ask whether Coleridge is not, twenty years
later, trying to throw a context of Latin grandeur and mathematical prestige around a point which, discovered long before,
and in a different context, had further precipitated his interest
in the power of subjective forces in the human psyche.

There are various factors to support the idea that Coleridge
read the *Letters to a German Princess* in 1795. It was first published in English in that year, at a time when we know
Coleridge's interest in scientific theory to have been strong, and
some things in it fall naturally into the genre of speculative
science that we have been considering. Euler discusses at length
the question of Monads and draws attention both to the mystery
involved in gravitation ('the question is, What is the cause of
this attraction?') and to the difficulty involved in believing that
rays of light emanated from the sun simply as water from a
fountain which was running to waste, since if so, he argued, it
would soon be exhausted; he also mentions, dismissively, the idea
that matter might be endowed with the faculty of thought.[31]
Just as Baxter (to whom he refers) argues that our dreams act
as a benevolent curb against the incursive power of total imagination, so Euler makes a similar point about the universe at
large: the slight opacity of the air which renders it blue is a
merciful circumstance, for if the air were completely transparent, the sun would shine directly from a black vault.[32]

There is enough circumstantial evidence here to suggest that
Coleridge would have been attracted to Euler's book in 1795
and found in it yet another stimulus to trains of thought

concerning the mysteries of nature and the human mind. The impact of Euler's passage concerning the arch of heaven would be likely to be increased by the fact that a similar illusion had been noted by Lucretius;

> And thus all the Stars seem fixed in the vaulted Sky, when they are all in continual motion.
> The Sun and Moon, by the same Rule appear fixed, when Experience tells us that they move.   (IV 392–3; 396–7)

Lucretius, also, discusses some common instances of illusion: giddy boys imagine that the walls are turned about and that the pillars run round; the appearance of objects under water is misleading; if one presses a finger under one's eyes every object will appear double.[33] There are also further references to the appearance of the sky:

> The Sun, to Mariners, seems to rise out of the Sea, and there again to set and hide his Light; for they see nothing but the Water and the Sky . . .
> So when the Winds drive the light Clouds along the Sky in the Night, the Moon and Stars seem to fly against the Clouds and to be driven above them in a Course quite opposite to that in which they naturally move.   (IV 434–7; 445–8)

When we recall how the Ancient Mariner later asserts of the sun's rising 'Out of the sea came he', or how he sees the heavenly bodies sometimes as fixed and sometimes as moving, we may legitimately suspect that Coleridge reflected on the nature of illusion and the degree to which it was capable of enslaving human perception. If so, Euler and Lucretius stand out as affording the most readily available stimuli for such speculation.

We have not yet touched upon the most important section of *Letters to a German Princess*, however, so far as the sense that Coleridge was 'conjuring over' Euler's text at this time is concerned. A later chapter in the work is actually entitled 'On the Double Touch': and this is the only place outside Coleridge's own work, so far as I have been able to discover, where the term is found.

At first sight, it must be acknowledged, there is no obvious link between Coleridge's theories and Euler's chapter. Most of

Coleridge's later theorisings on the subject are concerned with analyses of physical touch and sensation, including the ways that children learn by touch and the phenomenon of 'seeing double'. Euler's chapter, by contrast, is on the properties of the magnet and the problem of inducing magnetism in metals so that it will be retained.

Before we dismiss the idea of a possible connection, however, it is worthwhile to turn back to that marginal note which Coleridge wrote long afterwards in Wolfart's *Mesmerismus*. In this Coleridge pointed out that it is no sound objection to the facts of animal magnetism to say that its most successful Professors had been men of weak judgement, since these were precisely the sort of men ('weak & credulous, but sincere, sensitive and warm-hearted Men') who were most likely to be successful magnetisers. He continued by mentioning Tieck's direct evidence to him of Wolfart's power of fixing the needle in the Mariner's Compass by pointing his finger on it, and concluded with his tantalisingly brief reference to Animal Magnetism as connected with a Warmth-Sense and his 'long long ago' theory of Volition as a mode of double Touch. Why, we ask, should double Touch be related to Volition – or either of them to animal magnetism and a warmth-sense? Yet there is a strong suggestion that at some point in the past these terms had all had a living relationship in his mind.

It becomes possible to suggest an answer to the problem if we remember that in the late eighteenth century the phenomena of animal magnetism and those of ordinary physical magnetism were not rigidly separated from one another. Sometimes, as in William Law's passage, the principle of magnetism was regarded as central to an understanding of human attractions and instincts. And in the case of sleep-walking, which as a mysterious working of the subconscious fell into the same class as hypnotism, we have seen that an experiment had actually been carried out in which metal magnets had been held to the body of a man while sleep-walking. Coleridge himself later mentions an investigation by physicians appointed by Louis XVI to look into the matter of magnetic healing. While sceptical on the subject of 'animal' magnetism, they had concluded that Mesmer's claims to have carried out cures with a mineral magnet were grounded in fact.[34]

Euler's section on 'double touch' was concerned with the difficulties inherent in magnetising metals. He spoke of two methods: with one, 'simple touch', where a pole of the lodestone was applied to the metal, limited success was achieved. The other, far more successful, was known as 'double touch'. Both poles of the lodestone were applied to the metal and this (by supposedly creating a 'vortex') resulted in more lasting magnetisation.[35]

The theory now to be advanced is that Coleridge, his mind already full of speculations about phenomena of consciousness, came across this passage in Euler and saw in its terms a possible mode of accounting for certain of the 'facts of mind' in which he had been interesting himself. Darwin's assertion that the sense of warmth and the sense of touch are mediated by separate nerves was available to suggest the vehicle of separate organisation for the two modes of consciousness involved. Supposing that developed human consciousness had not one pole (that by which we make contact with the outside world, of which touch is the final arbiter) but two: an outer sense of touch and an inner sense which was in direct communication with the inner life-forces of the universe? The first could be said to govern waking life, in which the external world was perceived, and finally tested, by touch; the second would be more operative in states of dream or hypnotism or somnambulism or trance. It could further be argued that it was with the maturation of the human being, as it was with Euler's magnetism: the natural state of the newborn infant was one of single touch: its relationship to the mother was straightforward and direct. Through a set of delicate alignments throughout his life, he was then required to magnetise himself to particular people and places where the warmth of affection could still combine with accumulated experiences of knowledge by touch to make him feel 'at home'. If the adult were suddenly to be plunged back into a pure state of 'single touch', on the other hand, the abrupt withdrawal of his or her magnetisation to the known and familiar landscape might well induce a state of utter terror. In dreams, particularly nightmares, or in hypnotic states where the sense of magnetic attachment to particular times and places was suddenly withdrawn, the dreamer's magnetic energy would be left searching for a focus of security. In the specific case of 'single touch' known as hypnotism, this could be found by direct alignment with the hypnotist's will.

A similar interpretation could be extended to nightmare. In this case one could be said to be experiencing the phenomenon of 'single touch' in its pure form. When the body was asleep and made numb by some cause (cramp or indigestion, for example), the operation of 'double touch' which gave it its comfortable sense of being at home in the world of objects was suspended, so that external sensation was experienced in the pure form of single touch. As a result the inward power of imagination, forced to find a form with which to meet the sensation, would reach back to an equivalent state in the past, which would be most likely to have been experienced in a moment of pure terror. The result would be the pure horror felt in connection with some imaginary dream-event, which is experienced in nightmare. And the whole process is in fact described in just this way in a later note of Coleridge's:

> Nightmair is . . . a state not of Sleep, but of Stupor of the outward organs of Sense . . . while the volitions of *Reason* . . . are awake, tho' disturbed . . . and when ever this derangement occasions an interruption in the circulation, aided perhaps by pressure . . . the part deadened—as the hand, or his arm, or the foot & leg, on this side, transmits double Touch as single Touch: to which the Imagination therefore, the true inward Creatrix, instantly out of the Chaos of the Elements or shattered fragments of Memory puts together some form to fit it.
>
> (CN III 4046)

When we look at these later developments, we may see that their apparent origin in a speculation about certain psychological processes helps to explain other aspects of his later thought and terminology. It seems to have given him, for example, a fine speculative instrument with which to probe the appeal of romance. The strange power which such fictions exerted, particularly on children, could be associated with their ability to penetrate to the primary level of consciousness by the exercise of certain powers of charm (including sometimes literal incantations). Once the human being had been thus seduced into suspending the operations of his normal checks on objective reality, the romance was free to exert its power – which would be all the greater for the directness of their access to the primal regions of consciousness.

The effects of the theory may, I think, be discovered in Coleridge's celebrated formula concerning that 'willing suspension of disbelief for the moment which constitutes poetic faith';[36] we may also trace its workings in a strange little anecdote included in an early notebook:

> A country fellow in a village Inn, winter night—tells a long story—all attentive &c, except one fellow who is toying with the Maid—/The Country Man introduces some circumstance absolutely incompatible with a prior one—/The *Amoroso* detects it/—/&c The Philosophy of this.—Yes! I don't tell it for a true story—you would not have found it out—if you had smooring with Mall—   (CN I 232)

Why there should be a 'philosophy' involved in the story is not at first clear; once the anecdote is read off against the theory of primary consciousness, however, it becomes more readily comprehensible. What the countryman is in effect saying, translated into psychological terms, is: I was simply telling you a romance; and if it had not happened that your primary level of consciousness was already very satisfactorily and exclusively engaged by the warmth of your flirtation with the maid, you too would have very willingly suspended your disbelief and not been seeking to find fault with my story.

The action of the anecdote, it will also be noted, takes place in an inn on a winter's night, which seems important in terms of the theory just outlined. Warmth, according to that, could be said to assist the co-operation of primary and secondary consciousness, helping to magnetise a human being to the world and to his fellows. Hence the observable and familiar phenomena of conviviality and love in a warm atmosphere. Cold, on the other hand, tended to separate the operation of the two levels of consciousness, leaving the human being more exposed to the 'primary' emotion of fear. In a cold atmosphere one was more likely to have a sense of the supernatural and even (by release of that same primary 'shaping spirit') to see ghosts. Hume's assertion that dreams are the result of cold[37] could now be set in a larger context of meaning, for cold would be seen as the likely *occasion* of projected illusion rather than its cause.

This line of argument may be related to certain of Coleridge's later statements: such as his joke that he did not believe in ghosts since he had seen so many himself, or his mention of Hume and stress on the extreme cold described in the first scene of *Hamlet*, just before the appearance of the ghost.[38] (In view of his interest in Descartes in the earlier period, also, we may note how neatly the famous story of the philosopher being closeted in a warm room with a stove for some time before his great maxim revealed itself would have fitted this line of thought.)[39]

The point is relevant to Coleridge's own poetry of the supernatural, where experiences of extreme cold or extreme heat alike may be seen to disturb the 'secondary consciousness' and its purchase upon the external world of sense. In the one case, cold is related to the sense of death and the experience of fear; in the other heat connects to the sense of life and the experience of love. But it is also germane to Coleridge's sense of the matter that these two spheres of primary consciousness should be seen as closely connected, so that an experience of fear may, as if by natural reaction, pass into one of love, and *vice versa*. Examples of such connections will occur to every reader of *The Ancient Mariner* or of *Christabel* – where, for instance, the fact that the night is 'chilly but not dark' is mentioned just before the discovery of Geraldine behind the oak-tree.

At the same time, the presupposition of such a connection is one of Coleridge's more controversial theories, and it is possible that he would not have adopted it so readily had it not reflected the idea (to be encountered in Boehme's *Aurora*) that there was a subtle link between the wrath of God and the love of God. At this point it is relevant to quote a series of phrases from Boehme which Coleridge transcribed (about 1796) either from memory or directly from the seventeenth-century translation:

> throned angels—upboyling anguish
> Leader of a Kingdom of Angels.
> Love-fires—a gentle bitterness—
> Well-spring—*total God*
>
> Sick, Lame, & Wounded—Blind, and Deaf and Dumb—
> Why sleep ye, O ye Watchmen—
> Wake from the sleep of whoredom, trim your Lamp—
> Sound, sound the Trumpets—for the Bridegroom comes—

O man, thou half-dead Angel—
a dusky light—a purple *flash*
crystalline splendor—light blue—
    Green lightnings.—   (CN I 272–3 var.)

These quotations from Boehme are in sequence with a previous run of phrases culled from Jeremy Taylor and seem to have been devised for use in some piece of rhetorical verse or prose. The first two lines look like an attempt to sketch the process of rebellion against God, the second two the process of reconciliation. There follows a series of rhetorical invocations culminating in the characterisation of man as 'half-dead Angel'; this is followed by a highly characteristic movement to Boehme's imagery of light and colour, which may have been seen by Coleridge as offering material for describing the drama of alienation from, and reconciliation with, the fountain of lights.[40]

By now, we may begin to recognise, at least dimly, the universe of *The Ancient Mariner*, where rediscovery by the Mariner of a 'spring of love' in his heart enables him to regain a sense of relationship with the life of the world about him. Boehme's imagery also ministers to the life of the later poem in a more intimate and detailed way, however, for the drama of the Mariner's desolation and reconciliation takes place against a similar imagery of colours and flashing lights.

Coleridge later claimed to have formulated a theory of colours of his own which he would have reduced to form and published had Southey not diverted his attention from such studies to poetry.[41] The reference to Southey suggests that the investigation he had in mind might have taken place in 1794–5, at the height of their co-operation; and this would fit the evidence that he was then deeply interested in Darwin's work, for that contained some work on colour-perception. Opposite an early page of the first volume, in fact, there appears a red circle on an otherwise blank background; the reader is invited to conduct a now familiar experiment on his own perception by looking at it steadily for a minute and then gently closing his eye – when a green circle of the same dimension should appear.[42] To anyone familiar with later experimental psychology the phenomenon is familiar enough. But to a reader examining the phenomenon with other interests in mind, the phenomenon is important as providing a clear example of the organism's power to *create* a colour from within its own resources. As such it might well arrest the attention of anyone who was investigating the creative resources of the human organism.

At the end of his volume Darwin reprints a paper on ocular spectra by his son, R. W. Darwin of Shrewsbury, in which the question is investigated more fully, and with many examples.[43] That Coleridge was interested in ocular spectra during the period of his association with Southey is also suggested by a reference to the phenomenon in a letter of 1803, in which he is recalling those days. He is afraid, he says, to give his opinion on a literary project of Southey's for fear that he should infect him with fears rather than furnish him with new arguments and 'prick you with *spurs*, that had been dipt in the vaccine matter of my own cowardliness'. He goes on:

> While I wrote that last sentence, I had a vivid recollection— indeed an ocular Spectrum—of our room in College Street—/ a curious instance of association/you remember how incessantly in that room I used to be compounding these half-verbal, half-visual metaphors. (CL II 961)

There is plenty of evidence from the notebooks and writings of this period of this last-mentioned habit; and it is easy to see how in addressing himself to Southey he might not only fall back into precisely the style of writing that they had delighted in years before, but find himself projecting involuntarily the re-membered scene of their collaboration. And if we suppose that this projection were itelf an example of a phenomena discussed during those months, the circle draws itself still more tightly.

How would such a phenomenon fit the framework of the theory outlined earlier? Clearly it would have considerable interest as an example, from the world of concrete perception, of the kind of projection from the inward organism that also takes place during the operation of the dream. More importantly, it could be argued to connect with the kind of physical 'irradiation' in human beings which always fascinated Coleridge. If the organism were capable of creating colours without any direct stimulus from the external world, it was more possible to believe in the existence of some central luminary power, acting below the level of waking consciousness. (Darwin pointed out that long attention to the phenomenon would alternately destroy and revive the operation of the spectrum.)[44]

This power of originating light could in turn be related to the phenomenon of animal magnetism (helping to explain the power of the eye in hypnotic fascination) and to the whole realm of so-called apparitions. Such phenomena, if associated also with the warmth sense, might be held to operate in similar, yet contrasting fashions, according to whether the organism happened to be suffering from extreme cold or extreme warmth at the time. If the organism were unusually warm, then the images which might be projected from within would be essentially images of figures who were intimately loved.

The idea that Coleridge entertained this idea might gather some support from examples such as his discussion in *Frost at Midnight* of the power of his fire not only to originate images of loved ones and familiar country scenes during his schooldays, but to enforce his faith in the superstition that the 'stranger' fluttering on the grate really portended the arrival next day of a friend from home; or the later accounts of images associated with Sara Hutchinson.

This particular aspect of the ocular spectrum, its ability to appear, as if magically, out of the past when the circumstances of the recipient were particularly propitious, was to give Coleridge the material for some of his most interesting psychological observations, connected with the extraordinary powers of memory. It was the working of these powers, in fact, which suggested a limitation to Hartley's theories – that the mechanical processes studied by Hartley were subject at a deeper level to the operations of certain active forces, such as the recurrence of particular states of the emotions.

A developed form of the same theory could also offer a solution for certain artistic problems of the age. The conflict between the 'rational' art of the eighteenth century and contemporary cultivation of 'genius and sensibility' might turn out to be no true conflict at all if the two areas concerned were seen to correspond to different levels of consciousness. While the rational artist reached his greatest achievements through masterful representation of the external world (a work in which secondary consciousness was brought centrally into play), the genius, it might be argued, worked largely from primary consciousness, putting himself in touch with its forces and so under the power of the imagination, 'the true inward Creatrix'. At his most inspired, possessed and intoxicated by an irradiating power of creativity, he might hope to illuminate the whole of external nature by his vision.

If one went on to believe, finally, that the creative level of the mind actually *corresponded* to the workings of life in nature, that there was a relationship between the interplay of form and energy in the plant and the interplay of image and energy in the creative mind, then one could say that a genius of this kind was initiated into a knowledge of nature that transcended (while also subsuming) the cold organising vision of the rationalist. While the latter was mathematically plotting the movements of nature, the enhanced sensibility of the genius enabled him to 'see into the life of things'.

Viewed from certain angles, such claims might appear wildly arrogant; and this may explain why Coleridge was comparatively reticent in making them. From another point of view, however, he could think of himself as simply drawing attention to powers which he believed to exist in every human mind; indeed several of his artistic experiments during subsequent years look like attempts to discover whether poems drawing upon them might not provoke an equivalent response in the popular mind.

Awareness of these speculations should alert the reader to certain unusual word-usages in Coleridge's writings; and particularly to his use of the word 'genial'. As used by him it often carries the connotations of warmth and kindliness which it still has today; but when we look to the apparent association between warmth and the operation of primary consciousness discussed above, we see that the other possible sense of the word, as meaning 'of genius', or 'to do with genius' shades naturally into it. When Coleridge uses the word 'genial' in fact, semantic play of this kind is often present, suggesting a link between fostering warmth and genius. (Both usages were current in Coleridge's day, though the use of 'genial' as meaning 'to do with genius' is more common in German, where 'genialische' often carries this sense.)

The most crucial question of all takes us deeper still. If the primary consciousness could be said to be exposed to the infinite, could it know anything more about that infinite than the intensity of its own horror when exposed to it? If not, then the utmost that the fear and trembling of nightmare could do was to make human beings seek out metaphysical truths which were elsewhere revealed authoritatively. But supposing that the genial power of the human being could in some sense *know* the truth directly? Supposing that the complementary moments of vision which often seemed to follow immediately upon some blood-chilling experience of fear corresponded to some important truth about the metaphysical significance of human love? The possibility never ceased to haunt Coleridge: for, if true, it offered a key to 'the riddle of the world'. If, on the other hand, such moments of vision were simply delusory, then one was left, with the sense of reality which they nevertheless communicated, confronting that riddle still more bewilderingly.

The moral implications of Coleridge's ideas were not necessarily acceptable in his time. They could give rise to strictures such as Carlyle's, that his doctrines did not involve sufficient manliness: that they were an attempt to '*steal* into Heaven'.[45] Yet it is possible to acknowledge the potency of such criticisms and still insist that the pursuit of this particular path enabled Coleridge, by entering psychological territories which were resolutely ignored by his contemporaries, to make observations which, by their insistence on the active and creative powers of the mind, were more than a century ahead of their time.

It could also give a distinctive colouring to his whole way of thinking, which it would never lose. Even when he produced his rather sober *Aids to Reflection* thirty years later, one long section would still begin with the firm affirmation, 'In Wonder all Philosophy began'.[46]

5

Riddling Energies

Although it helps to explain the erratic course of Coleridge's public career if we come to believe that his social and political interests were accompanied by an undercurrent of compulsive esoteric speculation and research into the more mysterious elements of human nature, we may still be led to ask why references in the surviving records should be comparatively rare.

One answer has already been mentioned in connection with the closing lines of *The Eolian Harp*. When tempted to read a universal philosophy from the pleasures of nature, Coleridge recognised warning signals from memories of his career in 1793. Delight in the processes of 'animated life' had once before licensed impulsive behaviour and led him close to a total disaster. The demands of marriage and family called for a more conventional faith.

His early married life with Sara Fricker had turned out, in fact, to be unexpectedly happy. The beanfield with its paradisal scents and harmonised energies had been a not altogether empty augury. When he looked back on the period in 'Reflections on having left a Place of Retirement' the myrtles, jasmines and roses were still vivid in his memory; his picture of the 'son of Commerce' from Bristol who sauntered by one Sunday and was made to 'muse with wiser feelings', recalls Milton's image of Satan 'forth issuing on a summer's morn' like a city-dweller and finding himself, at the sight of Paradise and its innocent pleasures, 'stupidly good'.[1]

The decision to leave Clevedon had been due partly to the need to keep his wife and help their dependents, but still more to current events. As John Cornwell has pointed out,[2] the state of popular feeling in the late autumn of 1795 led to legislation which seemed to endanger the right of free speech. Coleridge re-entered the fray with a new lecture, later published as *The Plot Discovered,*[3] and planned a magazine, *The Watchman,* bearing the 'seditious' motto, 'That All may know the TRUTH, and that the TRUTH may make us FREE!'[4]

The Watchman ran for no more than ten issues. Contemporary agitation was losing momentum through changes in the political climate during its run; Coleridge meanwhile was beset by domestic troubles and private disillusionments. Southey, having talked him into marriage with Sara, had defected from the Pantisocratic scheme and even talked now of becoming an Anglican clergyman.[5] Darwin, visited during the *Watchman* tour of 1796, turned out to be less impressive than he had hoped.[6]

Other troubles struck deeper. Lamb, who had been an enthusiastic auditor of Coleridge's speculative discourses, suffered a period of temporary madness in 1795, and his resumption of correspondence with Coleridge was followed by an appalling incident in September, when his sister, in a fit of insanity, took up a carving-knife and murdered her mother. Lamb destroyed Coleridge's previous correspondence and urged him to write 'as religious a letter as possible'.[7] When Coleridge did so, Lamb still rebuked him for offering the assurance that he would be 'an eternal partaker of the Divine Nature'.[8] Later, he urged him to cultivate simplicity in his poetry:

> for simplicity springs spontaneous from the heart, and carries into daylight its own modest buds and genuine, sweet, and clear flowers of expression. I allow no hotbeds in the gardens of Parnassus.
>
> (LL I 55–6 (Marrs I 60–1))

Lamb's tragedy, with its inevitably sobering effect, was followed by the strange case of William Gilbert. In 1796 Gilbert, a barrister from the West Indies who had spent some time in London, was a prominent personality in Bristol. Coleridge, who may have met him through the movement against the slave-trade, published an essay of his in *The Watchman* in April and included a part of his poem *The Hurricane* in May.[9] By December, however, when he sent a copy of the complete poem to Thelwall, he was disturbed at Gilbert's mental condition, referring to him as an Astrologer here, who *was* a man of fine Genius, which, at intervals, he still discovers.—But, ah me! Madness smote with her hand, and stamped with her feet and swore that he should be her's—& her's he is.—He is a man of fluent Eloquence & general knowlege, gentle in his manners, warm in his affections; but unfortunately he has received a few rays of supernatural Light thro' a crack in his upper story. I *express* myself unfeelingly; but indeed my heart always achs when I think of him. (CL I 286)

Behind these sentences lies a bizarre story. According to Cottle, Gilbert, who had been in an asylum near Bristol for about a year in 1787, was gifted with unusual eloquence (his brain 'seemed to be in a state of boiling effervescence'[10]); despite some evidences of derangement he exerted a strong impression on many who heard him. Finding himself in London shortly after publishing his poem, he placarded the walls there with the largest bills that had ever been seen, announcing 'The Law of Fire' (the title of his forthcoming book on physics). In 1798, however, he departed unexpectedly and suddenly from Bristol. Thinking that he might be making his way to Africa (where he had expressed interest in the tribe of 'Gibberti' as possible kindred) his friends alerted William Roscoe to try and intercept him at Liverpool, but without success; it was assumed that he had come to an unfortunate end. Not until many years later did it transpire that he had in fact travelled to Charleston in America, where he lived peaceably to a good age.[11]

Something more than simple madness or eccentricity is involved. Wordsworth later quoted a long extract from the notes to *The Hurricane* in a note of his own to *The Excursion*; he also mentioned in a note to 'The Brothers' that his account of Leonard's obsessions at sea was indebted to a description by Gilbert of a calenture (a description which has not, apparently, survived).[12] In both cases, it would seem, he had been impressed by Gilbert's insight into the nature of 'genial power'.

Gilbert was, in fact, an enthusiastic exponent of the idea of Genius. His mention of Swedenborg and the sub-title of his poem, 'A Theosophical and Western Eclogue', are evidence that he had been influenced both by the theosophical movement which had grown up in England following the introduction of Swedenborg's ideas and by contemporary admiration for America. The hurricane itself is seen (in a kind of Sweden-borgian correspondence) as symbolising the movement for free-dom in America, whose 'SPIRIT, or GENIUS or PRINCIPLE' is seen now to be infusing itself into Europeans.[13] Gilbert's idea that every country has such a principle is expressed as follows:[14]

> ... all Countries have a specific *Mind*, or determinable *prin-ciple*. This character may be traced with as much satisfaction in the vegetable as in the animal productions. Thus, *Strength* with its attributes, viz. *Asperity*, &c. is the character or mind of England. Her leading productions are the Oak, Peppermint, Sloes, Crabs, sour Cherries. All elegance, all polish, is super-induced; and primarily from France, of which *they* are Natives.

The resemblance to some of Coleridge's ideas which may be detected here becomes more distinct when we turn to Gilbert's account of the statue of Memnon, followed by his comment on the 'Celestial Philosophy of the IDEA':[15]

> LIGHT and SOUND are CORELATES. Creation proceeded in *darkness*, while it proceeded in *silence*. At length GOD SPAKE —*Let there be* LIGHT! *And there was* LIGHT—*ipso facto* ...
>   MEMNON is a solitary instance of this in human productions or works of art; but the Crowing of Cocks, and Singing of Birds, are among instances of it, where moral powers predomi-nate rather than physical—that is in the works of the FATHER of LIGHTS ...
>   With the Greeks, *Phoebus* and *Apollo* were the *same* person; or LIGHT and SOUND were twin streams from one *spring* ...

The notes continue with a reference to Fire as '*visibly* the Pri-mary, or rather the ESSE of BEING; because FIRE alone has MOTION in itself, or can impart motion, that is, *inherent* motion to any body ...'; to magnetic attraction; and to a contrast between two kinds of fountain: 'EUROPE is the *fountain* of *Slavery*; AMERICA the FIELD of FREEDOM: The *Fountain* of it is GOD in *Man*, and FIRE in NATURE.'[16] Gilbert also moves by way of the tradition that the Abyssinians never leave their country ('I strenuously maintain that a *total aversion* from *travelling* can only consist with being at the *ultimate* of *Enjoyment* and the Primary of Being'), to the assertion that by Eleusis he means 'the PHILOSOPHY of the Springs of Nature'.[17] Later he writes,[18]

> While the MYSTERIES of ELEUSIS were sacred to CERES, it is evident, they must have contemplated SEEDS and EARTH; or the Springs and Fountains of PLANTS. But that they did not turn '*their backs to bright reality*' . . .

A footnote by Gilbert at this point reminds us that the final quotation is in fact taken directly from Coleridge.

In the 'Advertisement' to his poem, Gilbert refers to discussions with 'a friend' – clearly Coleridge – about metre.[19] The fact that he could quote a line from Southey's *Joan of Arc*, identifying it correctly as Coleridge's, shows him to have been intimately acquainted with his poetry. His discussions of genius, of Light and Sound as 'corelates' and as springing from a single sunlike fountain, of God's 'Let there be Light', of expansion and magnetic attraction, and of seeds in the earth as the 'springs and fountains of Plants' strongly suggests, moreover, that he was reproducing, in however garbled a form, images and ideas that he had first heard on the lips of Coleridge himself. It may be that alarm at Gilbert's fate was another reason for Coleridge's lapse into comparative silence on these subjects, at least in public.

Even so, however, it should be noted that various references in the latter part of that year betray a revival of former interests. There are evidences of Coleridge's having read widely in mythology, in books of travel and in ancient histories – looking, perhaps, for the 'mythological' elements which they had in common.[20] With the further evidence of his psychological concerns now before us, it may also be suggested that he was looking for confirmation of his suspicion that the imagination of man might have veiled access to a realm of knowledge not directly revealed in nature and that this knowledge might in turn support his own, liberalised version of Christianity, whereby Jesus had come to reveal that all men were (at least potentially) 'sons of God'.[21]

The status given to moon and sun in ancient mythology might suggest the existence of two corresponding forces in the subconscious, the one passive, vegetative and silently expansive, the other active, animal and freely energetic. The one corresponded to a light-receiving principle, like that of the moon, the other to an energy like that of the sun, which was always liable to become destructive. The Swedenborgian concept of a 'true' sun, reconciling light and heat, might thus be one possible analogue for the unfallen state of the human mind. (A memorandum in a notebook of the time runs, 'To reduce to a regular form the Swedenborgian's Reveries—'[22].) The paradigm could be further expressed in terms of liquids and their behaviour. At the one extreme, passive ice, accumulating from without according to an inner principle, at the other the distorted fountain, or the Typhoon; behind both, the possibility of an original spring illuminated by light, a fountain of the sun.

A letter to Thelwall in November contains the most open references to such subjects among writings of that year. Of his current interests he writes:

> Metaphysics, & Poetry, & 'Facts of mind'—(i.e. Accounts of all the strange phantasms that ever possessed your philosophy-dreamers from Tauth [Thoth] the Egyptian to Taylor, the English Pagan,) are my darling Studies.   (CL I 260)

He goes on from this to say that he is about to read a new work by Dupuis (a book in which Dupuis argued that all religions are descended from sun-worship[23]) and then quotes a poem written in September on his way home to see his baby son, who had been born while he was away:

> Oft of some *Unknown Past* such fancies roll
> Swift o'er my brain, as make the Present seem,
> For a brief moment, like a most strange Dream
> When, not unconscious that she dreamt, the Soul
> Questions herself in sleep: and Some have said
> We liv'd ere yet this *fleshly* robe we wore . . .
>   (CL I 260–1 (cf. 246))

In discussing the latter lines later, Coleridge refers both to Plato and to Fénelon's followers, 'almost all' of whom believed that men were 'degraded Intelligences who had all once existed together in a paradisiacal or perhaps heavenly state'.[24] The lines in question are remarkable not only for their confluence of ancient and modern philosophy but also for the running together of two separate psychological phenomena: the well-known experience now known as that of 'déjà vu', in which it seems to the person involved that all the circumstances of a particular moment and situation have taken place on some other occasion, and the experience in which the mind becomes conscious that it has been dreaming, yet still does not wake up. The associating of all these ideas suggests that Coleridge had been giving thought to unusual states of mind, to the problems which they presented under a 'common-sense' view of human experience and to the possibility that metaphysical implications might be present.

By the end of 1796, Coleridge had turned aside from schemes to influence society by direct actions of his own, such as those involved in lecturing and journalism. He now wished to retire to a small cottage where he could be largely self-sufficient, earn a small sum by writing and reviewing and devote the rest of his time to study. The plan may have been partly due to increasing hostility to criticism on the part of the Government. As father of a newborn child Coleridge could not afford to risk imprisonment. At the same time, it would seem that as a non-violent radical he was deeply disturbed, both by the increasing violence of the government in France and by the general apathy of Englishmen when confronted by reasoned arguments. It may be significant that the most forceful of his writing at this time is to be found in his letters to Thelwall, who under these new policies of the administration was one of the last major radicals left at liberty.

In letters to other correspondents, Coleridge had found himself adopting a pietistic tone of voice. Writing a letter of consolation to Benjamin Flower, he had drawn upon phrases also to be found in his notebook[25a] to describe his own chastenings:

—I have known affliction, yea, my friend! I have been myself sorely afflicted, and have rolled my dreary eye from earth to Heaven, and found no comfort, till it pleased the Unimaginable High & Lofty One to make my Heart more tender in regard of religious feelings. My philosophical refinements, & metaphysical Theories lay by me in the hour of anguish, as toys by the bedside of a Child deadly-sick. May God continue his visitations to my soul, bowing it down, till the pride & Laodicean self-confidence of human Reason be utterly done

away; and I cry with deeper & yet deeper feelings, O my
Soul! thou art wretched, and miserable, & poor, and blind,
and naked!—   (CL I 267)

After describing Charles Lamb's affliction, he had returned to
the religious theme;

> The Terrors of the Almighty are the whirlwind, the earth-
> quake, and the Fire that precede the still small voice of his
> Love. The pestilence of our lusts must be scattered, the strong-
> layed Foundations of our Pride blown up, & the stubble &
> chaff of our Vanities burnt, ere we can give ear to the
> inspeaking Voice of Mercy, 'Why *will* ye die?'—   (Ibid)

Although such sentiments were familiar enough within the
English religious tradition of the time, we may note that they do
not readily square with the view of God and his workings that
Coleridge had been evolving in, say, *The Destiny of Nations*.

They also raised further possibile questions. Was there really
an identifiable relationship between the terrible energies of
nature and the still small voice of God's love? As a sceptic, also,
Thelwall forced him to inspect the shaky foundations of his
religious position more closely than did Lamb or Flower. Since
Thelwall was a man in touch with many intellectual and
cultural movements, including poetry, Coleridge set out for him
the present state of his own development and poetic ideals:

> I feel strongly, and I think strongly; but I seldom feel
> without thinking, or think without feeling. Hence tho' my
> poetry has in general a *hue* of tenderness, or Passion over it,
> yet it seldom exhibits unmixed & simple tenderness or
> Passion. My philosophical opinions are blended with, or
> deduced from, my feelings: & this, I think, peculiarizes my
> style of Writing.   (CL I 279)

When he turned from poetry to religion, he defended the
Christian position forcefully, defining its basic tenets as follows:

> . . . the Religion, which Christ taught, is simply 1 that there is
> an Omnipresent Father of infinite power, wisdom, & Goodness.
> in whom we all of us move, & have our being & 2. That when
> we appear to men to die, we do not utterly perish; but after this
> Life shall continue to enjoy or suffer the consequences & natural

effects of the Habits, we have formed here, whether good or evil.   (CL I 280)

There is an admirable vigour in the letters to Thelwall. Statements such as those just quoted make it clear that Coleridge was still trying to pursue simple and forceful ends, seeking a new kind of radicalism which should be grounded not in the atheism favoured in France but in a Christianity reduced to certain basic elements.

His various readings in mythology and ancient philosophy were no doubt associated with this purpose. The study of ancient religions suggested that two doctrines in particular characterised the beliefs of all men at all times and in all ages: a belief in the immortality of the soul and a belief in the unity of God. Coleridge sets out to demonstrate that one God to be of 'infinite power, wisdom & Goodness' (one notes the survival of the Platonic trinitarian paradigm mentioned earlier) and to infuse the belief in immortality with a moral content by supposing that the quality of the afterlife will be conditioned by habits that have been set up during an individual's lifetime.

In his own letter, Thelwall made some shrewd criticisms of the Christian religion. Despite the vigour of his subsequent defence, Coleridge must have recognised that the position which he was endeavouring to establish involved him in difficulties of a kind which we shall encounter again in these pages. On the one hand he could not join hands wholeheartedly with those radicals who were seeking for a sweeping change in the political organisation of the country. Recent events in France suggested that such changes would be merely deleterious unless accompanied by the adoption of intellectual and moral values which nourished the growth of wisdom and goodness. His own definition of the Christian religion, on the other hand, was open to the objection that in this form it carried no clear historical authority. Its claim to universality consisted in his welding of certain distinctive Platonic and Christian tenets to a generally acceptable belief in a single God and in the immortality of the soul. No clear argument for such a version could be drawn from Christian history or from the phenomena of religion at large.

The strength of the position, on the other hand, was that it reconciled various elements and needs in Coleridge's society. Had he remained in and developed it, he would no doubt have had many followers and admirers. He needed a wider acceptance for his ideas, however. If so intelligent a man as Thelwall remained unmoved by his arguments and rhetoric, what hope was there of drawing society at large to such a rallying point?

The debate with Thelwall continued, culminating in the latter's visit to Alfoxden the following summer. It may well be, as D. M. Robbins has argued,[26] that Coleridge hoped, from his position of retirement, to feed the active Thelwall with ideas for him to develop in his radical speeches and writings. He came near to expressing such an aspiration openly, in fact, in a letter to Thelwall:

> I am not *fit* for *public* Life; yet the Light shall stream to a far distance from the taper in my cottage window. Meantime, do *you* uplift the *torch* dreadlessly, and shew to mankind the face of that Idol, which they have worshipped in Darkness!
>
> (CL I 277)

What did he mean, however, by saying that he was not fit for public life? Hardly that he was not equipped to write for the newspapers or lecture on public platforms: he had shown a marked aptitude for both activities. What he seems to have meant was that, finding the free exercise of his mind incompatible with full allegiance to a particular party, he wanted now to devote himself to study and thought, in the hope of throwing light on certain fundamental issues which must underlie all social and political discussion.

The stakes were high. If Coleridge could draw together the various threads of his thought and beliefs in a single work, his achievement might match that of Milton in the late seventeenth century. The chief hope of attaining such a height of achievement, however, lay in bringing together the two worlds of intellectual life: his continuing allegiance to certain basic moral tenets of Christianity and his imaginative attraction to more esoteric ideas. Could it be that there was, after all, a discoverable link between the life of God ('in whom we all of us move, & have our being'[27]) and the imaginative life of man as it operated in the depths of the subconscious? If this could be demonstrated, the way would be open for new departures in religious and political thought.

From this point of view, the most important passage in his correspondence with Thelwall is in a letter which he wrote a fortnight later, on 31 December. In this, he moved from brief discussion of the possibility of immortality to a more extended passage on the nature of life.

The passage in your letter respecting your Mother affected me greatly.—Well, true or false, Heaven is a less gloomy idea than Annihilation!—Dr Beddoes, & Dr Darwin think that *Life* is utterly inexplicable, writing as Materialists—You, I understand, have adopted the idea that it is the result of organized matter acted on by external Stimuli.—As likely as any other system; but you *assume* the thing to be proved—the '*capability* of being stimulated into sensation' *as a property* of organized matter—now 'the Capab.' &c is *my* definition of *animal Life*—Monro believes in a plastic immaterial Nature—all-pervading—

> And what if all of animated Nature
> Be but organic harps diversely fram'd
> That tremble into *thought* as o'er them sweeps
> Plastic & vast &c—

(by the bye—that is my favourite of *my* poems—do *you* like it?) Hunter that the *Blood* is the Life—which is saying nothing at all—for if the blood were *Life*, it could never be otherwise than Life—and to say, it is *alive*, is saying nothing —& Ferriar believes in a *Soul*, like an orthodox Churchman— So much for Physicians & Surgeons—Now as to the Meta-physicians, Plato says, it is *Harmony*—he might as well have said, a fiddle stick's end—but I love Plato—his dear *gorgeous* Nonsense! And *I, tho' last not least*, I do not know what to think about it—on the whole, I have rather made up my mind that I am a mere *apparition*—a naked Spirit!—And that Life is I myself I! which is a mighty clear account of it. Now I have written all this not to expose my ignorance (that is an acci-dental effect, not the final cause) but to shew you, that I want to see your Essay on Animal Vitality— of which Bowles, the Surgeon, spoke in high Terms—Yet *he* believes in a *body* & a *soul*. (CL I 294–5)

Some of the information here, though by no means all, is

derived from an article in the *Manchester Memoirs*.[28] In general, the passage shows not only that Coleridge had thought intensely about the nature of life, but that he was once again juxtaposing modern scientific observation and theory with the beliefs of the ancients. Thelwall himself had written an essay on Animal Vitality (containing, presumably, the view mentioned by Coleridge) which he was anxious to see.[29a] Coleridge's own view on the subject, presented here, unfortunately, in riddling terms, suggests that at this time he was trying to associate the nature of life with the nature of his own central identity, and that he was inclined to locate this in the subconscious.

It is at this point that his own dilemma becomes manifest, however, for while he wishes to demonstrate the existence of a correspondence between the divine power and human nature, this particular correspondence, if established in simple terms, would negate the moral responsibility of the individual human being. If Life is to be equated with 'I myself I', where does the possibility of moral transgression enter?

Coleridge duly established himself in Nether Stowey at the end of 1796, but there found that, although his desire to have more time for further study and thought was now satisfied, the isolation of his position, with only his wife and Thomas Poole to talk with, was deeply unsettling. According to his statement in *Biographia Literaria*, in fact, he found himself overwhelmed by doubts concerning his true beliefs:

> I retired to a cottage in Somersetshire at the foot of Quantock, and devoted my thoughts and studies to the foundations of religion and morals. Here I found myself all afloat. Doubts rushed in; broke upon me '*from the fountains of the great deep*' and fell '*from the windows of heaven.*' The fontal truths of natural religion and the books of Revelation alike contributed to the flood; and it was long ere my ark touched on an Ararat, and rested.   (BL I 132–3)

Even while Coleridge is describing his state of doubt, however, it will be noted that his *imagery* is drawn from the paradigm discussed earlier. His turmoil, described in terms of the Flood, takes up the two biblical phrases that describe the event;[30] these in turn suggest an allegorical reading of the Flood story as on the one hand a transformation of the fountainous energies of the deep into destructive forces and on the other the obscuring of light from the windows of heaven. Twenty years later, Coleridge is still displaying his symbolic leanings – even in the midst of a record of his intellectual doubts.

Coleridge now goes on to explain the dilemma in which he found himself:

> The *idea* of the Supreme Being appeared to me to be as necessarily implied in all particular modes of being as the idea of infinite space in all the geometrical figures by which space is limited. I was pleased with the Cartesian opinion, that the idea of God is distinguished from all other ideas by involving its *reality*; but I was not wholly satisfied. I began then to ask myself, what proof I had of the outward *existence* of anything? (BL I 133)

The intervening and subsequent arguments of this later account are largely Kantian, and include a long quotation from one of his works. The main core of his dilemma, however, follows quite logically from the development we have been tracing; as Coleridge sums it up a little later in his discussion,

> For a very long time, indeed, I could not reconcile personality with infinity; and my head was with Spinoza, though my whole heart remained with Paul and John ... (BL I 134)

He goes on to relate his growing conviction that 'religion', as both the corner-stone and the key-stone of morality, must have 'a *moral* origin'. The argument, once unravelled, is that while his study of nature led him towards the sense of an infinite deity as its fountainous centre, his experience of human personality led him to demand a religion founded on a moral basis. Yet we are conscious of a certain wisdom after the event. Was his 'heart' so fully committed then to the moral view as he suggests?

Shortly after his characterisation of life as 'I myself I' (and probably in the second half of January) Coleridge sent to Lamb a poem which Lamb referred to as 'your dream' and which was later published as *The Raven*.[31] It is in many ways a slight poem, easily overlooked, and might not be worth noticing at all were it not for the fact that within the year its author was to write another poem, *The Ancient Mariner*, in which another bird figures prominently. In direct contrast to the albatross, the sociable bird who 'loved the man who shot him with his bow', however, the raven is black, solitary and associated with melancholy. The poem tells how he came across a group of pigs who had been eating beneath an oak and who had left a single acorn uneaten; how he picked up the acorn and buried it; how he returned to find it grown into an oak tree where he was able to nest and rear his young; how a woodman came and chopped down the tree; how the ship which was built from its wood was destroyed by a storm at sea on its maiden voyage; and how the raven circled above the wreck, cawing joyfully as he heard the cries of the drowning, for 'They had taken his all, and *Revenge was sweet!*'

While the cynical quality of the poem provides an interesting contrast to the more benevolent implications of the later poem, it may also be noted that the bare narrative contains an elaboration of the vegetation/animation theme. The raven rescues the one surviving seed; the tree which grows from it eventually shelters his family; when the woodman's action deprives him of that rooted home he is cut off from his fostering shelter. His subsequent action in the storm is that of an energy expressing itself in pure, circular motions: 'The old raven flew round and round, and cawed to the blast'.

Further evidence that the paradigm of vital energy was in his mind is provided by a note which Coleridge appended to the lines in which he described the raven's adventures during the years while the tree was growing: he described how an artist had once proposed illustrating the poem and that for the lines in which the raven went away and travelled 'Many Autumns, many Springs ... Many Summers, many Winters' Coleridge had suggested the device of 'A *Round-about* with four seats, and the four seasons, as Children, with Time for the shew-man.'[32] The fact that Coleridge's imagination again figured a circling movement is perhaps significant. Yet if the larger pattern was indeed in his mind, he also found the fact embarrassing – both, perhaps, on account of the slightness of the narrative, and of the cynicism involved. When he reprinted his poem in *Sibylline Leaves* he gave it the elaborate subtitle 'A Christmas Tale, told by a schoolboy to his little brothers and sisters' and added a couplet at the end, pointing a pious little moral:

We must not think so; but forget and forgive,
And what Heaven gives life to, we'll still let it live.

(PW I 171n)

But then in one copy of the volume containing these new lines,
he had further thoughts again, and added a manuscript note:

Added thro' cowardly fear of the Goody! What a Hollow,
where the Heart of Faith ought to be, does it not betray? this
alarm concerning Christian morality, that will not permit
even a Raven to be a Raven, nor a Fox a Fox, but demands
conventicular justice to be inflicted on their unchristian conduct, or at least an antidote to be annexed.   (PW I 171n)

These twists and turns of attitude suggest that Coleridge was
fully aware of amoral implications in his poem. No doubt a work
of this kind came more easily to his mind early in 1797, when
he had just given up politics and public life, and when he was
particularly conscious of his own isolation and of the destructive
tendencies of mankind in general. He must often have been
visited by a sardonic and satiric sense of human folly and a
despairing feeling that the power of his own imaginative life
actually cut him off from the rest of mankind.

It may also be pointed out that Coleridge's use of the raven
did not cease with that poem. In his *Osorio*, written later that
year, the various hints at a beneficence in natural process are
overshadowed by the sardonic isolation of the Moorish woman
Alhadra who, seeking revenge, finds even that desire thwarted
by her contempt for all things, and cries,

... would to Alla
The raven and the sea-mew were appointed
To bring me food, or rather that my soul
Could drink in life from the universal air!

(PW II 584)

It would hardly have escaped Coleridge's symbol-seeking mind
that in *Macbeth* the raven helps to symbolise the isolate life of
the castle ('The raven himself is hoarse/That croaks the fatal
entrance of Duncan/Under my battlements'), while Macbeth
is later to look wistfully at the homeward flight of the more
gregarious crow:

> Light thickens, and the crow
> Makes wing to the rooky wood . . .　　　　(III. ii)

Indeed (as Reginald Watters has noticed) there would seem to be an echo of a meditation on these lines in 'This Lime Tree Bower . . .', written the following summer, where Coleridge, watching the flight of a rook, derives a welcome sense of linking life even from the strange creaking of its wingbeat.[33ᵃ] (In Coleridge's own case, however, the use of the image of the raven bringing food suggests that such a meditation, once welded to the well-known tradition that Elijah was fed by ravens,[34] could also produce a reassuring sense of his own status as an isolated but justified prophet.)

Osorio contains an attempt to explore the nature of evil actions in something of the manner to be found in Shakespeare's play, with its hints at a benevolent order in nature, the resources of which are available to the forces of good. In Coleridge's play, however, both the great forces which contend for Spain at the time of the play are portrayed as equally mistaken. Roman Catholicism is represented by the Inquisitor Francesco, while the Moors who struggle to resist the imposition of established Christianity find their spokesman in Alhadra, who declares that the proof of the divine authority of Mahomet's Law is that it fits the soul of man. She characterises that fittingness as follows:

> Ambition, glory, thirst of enterprize,
> The deep and stubborn purpose of revenge,
> With all the boiling revelries of pleasure—
> These grow in the heart, yea, intertwine their roots
> With its minutest fibres!　　　　(PW II 586)

After the long clash of Moorish and Catholic forces in the play, she also delivers the final speech, announcing that if she had a band of suitable men she would destroy all the strongholds of the cruel,

> Till desolation seem'd a beautiful thing,
> And all that were and had the spirit of life
> Sang a new song to him who had gone forth
> Conquering and still to conquer!

Such an ending explicitly affirms the 'spirit of life' only to assert that before the spirit can assert itself properly in such a place,

bloodshed must be endured. The logic of drama, with its need
for a strong ending, has enforced a final dominant note that is
sardonic and even borders on the cynical.

In a later note on *Osorio*, Coleridge indicated his recognition
of certain imperfections, including the omission of some information necessary for a full understanding of the plot. He regretted
that he had not explained the full development of Osorio's
character, in spite of having 'most clear and psychologically
accurate ideas of the whole of it'. Osorio, he said, was

> A man who, from constitutional calmness of appetites, is
> seduced into pride and the love of power, by these into
> misanthropism, or rather a contempt of mankind; and from
> thence, by the co-operation of envy, and a curiously modified
> love for a beautiful female ... into a most atrocious guilt. A
> man who is in truth a weak man, yet always duping himself
> into the belief that he has a soul of iron.　　(Carlyon I 144)

He also claimed that from the writing he had learned a 'most
important lesson, namely, that to have conceived strongly, does
not always imply the power of successful execution'.[35]

Between the conception and the execution the pressure of
strictly dramatic factors had thwarted the giving of full weight
to more benevolent themes. During the action, however, the
opposing attitudes of Catholics and Moors are in fact both
implicitly criticised by those of the hero and heroine, Albert
and Maria, who have grown up together as devotees of nature.
Albert spends a good deal of time studying plants; when at one
point he is presented as a sorcerer, his semi-fictitious guise
includes an intimate knowledge of the workings of the energies
of nature – which turn out to behave like the Monads of the
Joan of Arc passage, and are all presented as circling and
spiralling in a 'living wheel' – whether in the desert sandstorm,
the ocean typhoon or the Lapland whirlpool:

> O ye numberless
> And rapid travellers! what ear unstun'd
> What sense unmadden'd, might bear up against
> The rushing of your congregated wings?
> Even now your living wheel turns o'er my head!
> Ye, as ye pass, toss high the desart sands,

That roar and whiten, like a burst of waters,
A sweet appearance, but a dread illusion,
To the parch'd caravan that roams by night.
And ye build up on the becalmed waves
That whirling pillar, which from earth to heaven
Stands vast, and moves in blackness. Ye too split
The ice-mount, and with fragments many and huge,
Tempest the new-thaw'd sea, whose sudden gulphs
Suck in, perchance, some Lapland wizard's skiff.
Then round and round the whirlpool's marge ye dance,
Till from the blue-swoln corse the soul toils out,
And joins your mighty army.   (PW II 551)

This powerful description is then followed by the singing of a
charm which invokes all the elements of a peaceful moonlight
scene by the sea-shore:

Hear, sweet spirit! hear the spell
Lest a blacker charm compel!
So shall the midnight breezes swell
With thy deep long-lingering knell.
And at evening evermore
In a chapel on the shore
Shall the chanters sad and saintly,
Yellow tapers burning faintly,
Doleful masses chant for thee,
Miserere, Domine!

Hark! the cadence dies away
On the quiet moonlight sea,
The boatmen rest their oars, and say,
Miserere, Domine!   (PW II 552)

Once again Coleridge has demonstrated his facility in the field
of magic and his sense of possible hidden powers which may
prove dangerous unless charmed into peaceful harmonic activity.
The passages quoted are two of the best in the play. Yet he has
also been careful to avoid any commitment to belief in magical
powers: the ceremony just described is presented as a sham,
setting up a suitably supernatural ambience for other events
which are being enacted. Although it is clearly part of Cole-

ridge's belief that the passions described by Alhadra as intertwining their roots with the minutest fibres of the heart are alien to its true nature, he finds it difficult to demonstrate the point, a subtle one, convincingly in a drama where military powers are manifested vividly and physically in front of the audience, but where the forces of nature must work silently.

A similar difficulty beset the projected 'Wanderings of Cain', which was planned later that autumn. This, according to Hazlitt's account, was to have been a prose-tale set partly or wholly in the Valley of Rocks, and to have been 'in the manner of, but far superior to, *The Death of Abel*.'[36] Salomon Gessner's *Death of Abel* was one of the most popular works available in the late eighteenth century, sold by packmen in its thousands.[37] It would seem that the two poets, having completed their dramas, were looking for another means of reaching a public beyond the leisured classes. In the event the tale was not completed and Coleridge was later to recall with amusement the sight of Wordsworth, his 'taste so austerely pure and simple', trying to imitate the *Death of Abel*. '*The Ancient Mariner* was written instead', he concluded.[38]

In that comment, there may be some indication of a thematic link between the two tales, since if popular success had been the sole motive, Coleridge would surely have written that the 'Lyrical Ballads' were written instead. And as critics have pointed out, from Lowes[39] onwards, the theme of a man who has killed and is forced to wander for ever in remorse (which also survives in the figure of the Wandering Jew) links immediately with that of *The Ancient Mariner*.

The chief point that separates the surviving fragments of the 'Wanderings' from the orthodox histories of Cain lies, as R. H. Wells has pointed out,[40] in the treatment of Abel, who appears to Cain in suffering form as a 'Shape':

They were all three under the rock, and within the shadow. The Shape that was like Abel raised himself up, and spake to the child: 'I know where the cold waters are, but I may not drink, wherefore didst thou then take away my pitcher?' But Cain said, 'Didst thou not find favour in the sight of the Lord thy God?' The Shape answered, 'The Lord is God of

the living only, the dead have another God.' Then the child
Enos lifted up his eyes and prayed; but Cain rejoiced secretly
in his heart. 'Wretched shall they be all the days of their
mortal life,' exclaimed the Shape, 'who sacrifice worthy and
acceptable sacrifices to the God of the dead; but after death
their toil ceaseth. Woe is me, for I was well beloved by the
God of the living, and cruel wert thou, O my brother, who
didst snatch me away from his power and dominion.' Having
uttered these words, he rose suddenly, and fled over the
sands: and Cain said in his heart, 'The curse of the Lord is
on me; but who is the God of the dead?'   (PW I 291)

This 'Shape that was like Abel' appears not only in the part
which Coleridge published but in two other manuscript fragments. In one, appearing as an orb of fire, he impresses upon
Cain the enormity of his guilt 'and that he must make some
expiation to the true deity, who is a severe God, & persuades
him to burn out his eyes'. In another he 'persuades Cain to
offer sacrifice for himself & his son Enoch by cutting his child's
arm & letting the blood fall from it'.[41*]
   The manuscript fragments also make it clear, however, that
this apparition is not the true Abel, who appears at the end of
the second fragment to dissuade Cain from sacrificing his child
and takes him under his protection, while the evil spirit, throwing off the countenance of Abel and assuming his own shape,
flies off pursuing a flying battle with Michael.
   The conclusion bears a resemblance to that of the Apocryphal
Book of Tobit, which had earlier been an object of interest to
Southey and Coleridge.[42] But the most significant feature of the
passage quoted is to be found in the references to the 'god of
the living' and the 'god of the dead'. In one fragment, Cain
replies to the false Abel's demand for physical sacrifice by saying
that 'God himself who had inflicted this punishment upon him,
had done it because he neglected to make a proper use of his
senses, &c.' The implication of the passages seems to be that the
Shape that is like Abel is an apparition conjured up by Cain's
own faulty consciousness – perhaps as a further result of his
failure to make 'a proper use of his senses.' For those who do
make a proper use, it would follow, 'God is a God of the living';
but those who do not become so obsessed by death that they

begin to image their very God as a God of the dead; in conse-
quence, they are likely to be ravaged by their own destructive
energy.

That this poem should have been planned on a trip to the
Valley of Rocks is fitting enough, for that desolate setting might
well be thought of as the kind of scene that would be sought out
by a man under the sway of a death-consciousness ('You might
wander on and look round and round, and peep into the crevices
of the rocks and discover nothing that acknowledged the influence of the seasons.'[43])

It is also possible that this same expedition was marked by the
composition of *Kubla Khan*,[44] in which Coleridge's current
concern with the status of energy finds a new point of focus. I
suggested earlier that it was essential to his scheme of things to
associate the workings of creative genius with those of the
primary and secondary consciousness; in that sphere the exercise
of animal energy is a resource more immediately at hand than
the welling up of direct inspiration. Coleridge's ideas on the
subject may be assimilated to those expressed in his later distinction between 'commanding genius' and 'absolute genius'. In
the decline of human beings, it could be argued that what is
primarily lost is the primary level, the area of passive enlightenment and active realisation of vegetative form. Once that is no
longer available, the man of genius, forced to live by the animal
energies of his personality, directs them outwards to objects in
the external world, imposing his creative powers upon them and
bending them to his will. Such men

> must impress their preconceptions on the world without, in
> order to present them back to their own view with the
> satisfying degree of clearness, distinctness, and individuality.
> These in tranquil times are formed to exhibit a perfect poem
> in palace, or temple, or landscape-garden; or a tale of romance
> in canals that join sea with sea, or in walls of rock, which,
> shouldering back the billows, imitate the power, and supply
> the benevolence of nature to sheltered navies; or in aqueducts
> that, arching the wide vale from mountain to mountain, give
> a Palmyra to the desert.   (BL I 20–1)

But since they have no sure and steady life in their primary
being, their energies are at the mercy of whatever forces may

be at work around them: if there is some violent working among
the other inhabitants of their civilisation, their energies will
automatically be drawn to express it, and they will therefore
emerge as leading agents of destruction:

> But alas! in times of tumult they are the men destined to
> come forth as the shaping spirit of Ruin, to destroy the
> wisdom of ages in order to substitute the fancies of a day, and
> to change kings and kingdoms, as the wind shifts and shapes
> the clouds.   (BL I 21)

The man of 'absolute genius', on the other hand, retains
contact with his primary consciousness and is therefore able
to organise his energies by its light. Whatever he creates is
recognised as bearing the stamp of a numinous authenticity,
so that while he himself remains calm and happy, caring
little for the world and its demands, those who see his work
may be at once attracted and fearful, recognising a mystery
which communicates with them at the very roots of their
being.

This, it will be seen, is also the basic argument to be traced
within the stanzas of *Kubla Khan*. Much of the imagery of the
poem derives from Coleridge's reading in mythology and
comparative religion, as viewed in the light of contemporary
beliefs that the descendants of Cain built places sacred to the
sun because they were trying to recreate the paradise-garden
which had been lost by the first man, and to set up a firm
defence against the awareness of death which had consequently
come to obsess them.[45] Kubla Khan's earthly paradise, a circular
enclosure by the sacred river with perfumed trees and sparkling
streams, can be matched by many descriptions of places sacred
to the sun in accounts that were available to Coleridge.[46] The
imagery of the second stanza, equally, is full of images of per-
verted energy.

At the end of the second stanza there is a very marked
rhythmical break and in the published versions the following
six lines form a separate unit.[47a] The change of movement
suggests a new departure in the sense, an attempt to present an
ideal beyond that at which Kubla was aiming in the first
stanza. Forced to acknowledge that the reconstructed earthly
paradise is necessarily precarious, the man of commanding

genius still dreams of a construction which would not be vulnerable, and in which all extremes, such as those of movement and
stasis, of heat and cold, would be reconciled.

The most important transition in the poem, however, comes
between the end of these lines and the final stanza – the movement from 'He did ... but ...' to 'I would ... if ...' is another
version of the transition between the world of 'it is' and the
world of 'I am' which plays a crucial part in Coleridge's
philosophy. In this and other respects the structure of the poem
expresses the complex nature of Coleridge's own problems as
thinker and artist at this time. The opening lines of the last
stanza introduce the conclusion triumphantly; yet they also
constitute what is essentially a conjuror's stroke.[48a] The scene is
changed instantaneously from that surrounding the troubled
Kubla Khan and his vulnerable aspirations to that of the inspired
poet of absolute genius, creating effortlessly through his 'sym-
phony and song'. We have moved from the world of nature,
with all her ambiguities, to that of the 'absolute' genius which
triumphantly resolves them.

It is nevertheless a conditional resolution, unavailable to the
poet except under special conditions. The mediating figure
projected as necessary to its attainment is 'a damsel with a
dulcimer' who is also an 'Abyssinian maid'; and she has been
seen before only in a vision. The evidence in sources available
to Coleridge would suggest that her specific attributes mark
her, in her mythological significance, as a votary of Isis and
perhaps one of the cave-dwellers in Abyssinia who were thought
to preserve there the reliques of ancient wisdom. The troglo-
dytes of that country played a small lyre, known as the
sambuca, or dulcimer, which was elsewhere said to be the soft
feminine complement to the louder lyre of Apollo. Such music,
considered in the light of our earlier discussion, becomes an apt
emblem of the stimulating of inspiration as it might work
passively in the primary consciousness, to call forth the strong
active music of creative power.[49]

In these respects there can be traced through the poem the
same sense of the ambivalence of natural energies that was to
be found in Coleridge's dealings with *The Raven*. Once raised
into a human context, however, those energies are 'genial
powers', their contradictions potentially resolvable through the

abilities of the creative genius to charm them into visionary harmony.

The poem is not to be summed up by that pattern, of course, for the interacting rôles of dream and reality, playing in and out of its structure, are themselves riddling – all the more so when one reflects that Kubla's enterprise can itself be seen as an analogue of the poetic act. In such terms, *Kubla Khan* is a poem about poetry – in some respects even a poem about itself.

There are many such ramifications involved, some of which I have pursued elsewhere.[50] In its totality, however, the poem does not present itself for final 'interpretation'. It offers itself to the reader rather as a simulacrum of Coleridge's own poetic intelligence, which at one and the same time accepts the final incomprehensibility of the universe and yet proceeds resolutely to efforts of harmonising interpretation. And if we accept Coleridge's own account that the poem was composed somewhere between the waking and sleeping state, the facts surrounding its composition act as a comment upon the very powers which he was investigating: in his own career, it seems, the incomprehensible could be harmonised only by invoking the depths of that creative unconscious which was itself incomprehensible. It is a riddle that can be read many ways, but which in every direction turns out to honour the kind of intelligence that Coleridge was cultivating at this time.

For *Kubla Khan*, the poem, does exist; and it has value.

6

The Characters of Life

On one point, Coleridge's *Biographia* account of his intellectual struggles in 1797 is strangely silent. The spring of that year marked the time of his first full intimacy with William and Dorothy Wordsworth; during that summer and autumn whole days were spent in walking and conversing; poems were read, written and discussed, intellectual issues debated, collaborations planned. Yet the only mention of this that reaches Coleridge's pages is a brief discussion, several chapters later, of the principles on which the *Lyrical Ballads* were planned.

The omission is all the more surprising when we consider the contemporary evidences of his deepening admiration. In the spring he reported that Wordsworth's conversation had roused his feelings a little from the state of 'calm hopelessness' into which they had fallen.[1] Recording Wordsworth's complaint that Southey wrote 'too much at his ease', he went on to describe, by contrast, 'the march of Milton' – 'his severe application, his laborious polish, his deep metaphysical researches, his prayers to God before he began his great poem, all that could lift and swell his intellect, became his daily food' – and outlined the studies which he would regard as necessary before he himself could embark on an epic poem.[2] Poole, he said, had formed the opinion that Wordsworth was the 'greatest Man he ever knew'; he himself concurred. 'I feel a *little man by his* side'.[3] In July, he wrote: 'Wordsworth is a very great man – the only man, to whom *at all times* & *in all modes of excellence* I feel myself inferior.'[4] The following spring he wrote:

> The Giant Wordsworth—God love him!—even when I speak
> in the terms of admiration due to his intellect, I fear lest those

terms should keep out of sight the amiableness of his manners . . .   (CL I 391)

The clear import of these and other references is that Coleridge
valued Wordsworth's company not simply for his abilities as a
poet but for his intellect. If so, their conversations must have
been playing an important part in his own intellectual development at this time.

Wordsworth's reported remark about Southey provides one
reason for Coleridge's enthusiasm. In place of Southey's intellectual cautiousness, which must always have damped his own
play of mind, he found himself in the company of a man who
found it natural to think strenuously and even to court disturbance of received ideas.

Wordsworth's breadth of vision (Coleridge's consciousness of
which surely helped shape his picture of 'the march of Milton')
was matched by the focused delicacy of Dorothy's perceptions.
There is little sign that she was attracted to Coleridge's more
metaphysical speculations (except when they resolved themselves
into vivid imagery) but she had the capacity for a quivering,
half-attracted, half-fearful response to the minutest manifestations of life in nature which was directly relevant to his central
ideas and even seemed to set her for him above normal moral
categories. Describing her to Cottle as 'exquisite', he emphasised
that he was referring specifically to her mind and heart and then
quoted some lines from *Joan of Arc*:

. . . her manners are simple, ardent, impressive—.

> In every motion her most innocent soul
> Outbeams so brightly, that who saw would say,
> Guilt was a thing impossible in her.

Her information various—her eye watchful in minutest
observation of nature—and her taste a perfect electrometer—it
bends, protrudes, and draws in, at subtlest beauties & most
recondite faults.   (CL I 330)

In such company, Coleridge found his mental activity focused
increasingly upon observations of the actual life of nature: his
descriptions look back directly to his accomplishment in *The
Eolian Harp*. In 'This Lime-Tree Bower My Prison' his description

of the scene about him on a summer evening is faithful both to the details of the scene and to the quality of his registering sensibility:

> I watch'd
> The sunshine of each broad transparent Leaf
> Broke by the shadows of the Leaf or Stem,
> Which hung above it: and that Wall-nut Tree
> Was richly ting'd: and a deep radiance lay
> Full on the ancient ivy which usurps
> Those fronting elms, and now with blackest mass
> Makes their dark foliage gleam a lighter hue
> Thro' the last twilight.   (CL I 335–6)

Even in this passage Coleridge's concerns extend beyond a simple rendering of the minute details of nature. There is a binding emphasis throughout on the work of translucence, the 'accidents of light and shade'. One reason for this emerges sharply when he comes to describe the splendour of the sunset which he imagines his friends watching near the Bristol Channel:

> Ah slowly sink
> Behind the western ridge; thou glorious Sun!
> Shine in the slant beams of the sinking orb,
> Ye purple Heath-flowers! Richlier burn, ye Clouds!
> Live in the yellow Light, ye distant Groves!
> And kindle, thou blue Ocean!

As this larger description proceeds, Coleridge suggests the possibility of a more mystical effect, by which this extreme in nature may be wedding itself to powers in the depth of human consciousness. Contemplating such a scene, he says, his friend

> May gaze till all doth seem
> Less gross than bodily, a living Thing
> That acts upon the mind, and with such hues
> As cloathe the Almighty Spirit, when he makes
> Spirits perceive His presence!   (CL I 335)

Although the phrase 'a living Thing/That acts upon the mind' was dropped from the published version, it is important to the poem at the time of writing, helping to explain Coleridge's footnote on that occasion, 'You remember, I am a *Berkleian*'.

He is involving himself with the possibility that the work of a
sunset upon the perceiver is, like the connections described in
Berkeley's *Siris*, an actual physical work, a correspondence which
runs deeper, therefore, than simple delight. The idea not only
prefigures Wordsworth's

> sense sublime
> Of something far more deeply interfused,
> Whose dwelling is the light of setting suns . . .
>
> (WP II 262)

but temporarily moves beyond it to indicate an apprehension
mediated through some even more intimate 'interfusion' (perhaps through some direct magnetism between the sun and
human organic sensibility).

Further effects of Coleridge's conversation on Wordsworth are
detectable in some of the entries in the Alfoxden notebook.
There, for example, Wordsworth writes some lines describing a
man who would

> . . . gaze upon the moon until its light
> Fell like a strain of music on his soul
> And seem'd to sink into his very heart. (WP v 340)

– which might suggest an influence from Coleridge's 'light/
sound' correlation. Another fragment ends, 'In all forms of
things/There is a mind', another refers to

> . . . unknown modes of being which on earth,
> Or in the heavens, or in the heavens and earth
> Exist by mighty combinations, bound
> Together by a link, and with a soul
> Which makes all one.   (WP v 340–1)

There is nothing quite like this in Wordsworth's earlier poetry.

The mention of the heart as the place where the harmonising
light of the moon finds its final location reminds us of other
speculations which have been discussed above, particularly those
which derived from Coleridge's reading of Boehme. It seems
likely that Boehme's hint of a set of 'spring-correspondences' in
the world, extending across the ebullience of water-springs, the
vitality of animal and vegetable organisms and the operations of
the human heart was a fruitful theme between the two poets at
this time.

To such a topic, Wordsworth was able to bring his salutary grasp of the actual. By contrast with Coleridge's early incarceration in the town, he had grown up in a countryside where the presence of springs and streams was a prominent element, providing, particularly in winter, a refreshing contrast to bleaker aspects of the landscape. In the same way, his early surroundings had made him unusually sensitive to the seasonal work of spring in transfiguring the permanent forms of nature. Someone who had lived through Lakeland winters, the scene dominated by the still forms of mountains and lakes, with large areas bare or covered by snow, could not but respond to the change when the fixed forms of trees broke simultaneously into bud and leaf, when the song of birds was heard again, and when wild flowers suddenly showed themselves in unlikely corners. At this level, the idea of a fountainous life-force in the universe made contact with the straightforward facts of Wordsworth's childhood existence. Dorothy's immediacy of response to all manifestations of life, similarly, was the personal enactment of a sense of a subterranean link between the activities of all living beings.

There was another, related respect in which Boehme's allusive imagery seems to have provided a stimulus for the thought of the two poets at this time. We may approach it by way of the terms which Coleridge uses in the *Biographia* to describe the benefits he received in youth from Boehme and other mystic writers:

> They contributed to keep alive the *heart* in the *head*; gave me an indistinct, yet stirring and working presentiment, that all the products of the mere *reflective* faculty partook of DEATH, and were as the rattling twigs and sprays in winter, into which a sap was yet to be propelled from some root to which I had not penetrated, if they were to afford my soul either food or shelter.   (BL I 98)

Here, as elsewhere, Coleridge's imagery repays examination. When we turn to *Aurora* we discover that this relationship between life and death in nature is something that Boehme himself dwells on. Writing of the activity of heat and cold in air and water, and of the importance of air and water to the life of all living things, he continues,

Now in these two qualities two other Species or kinds are to be observ'd, *viz. a living* and a *dead* operation. The Ayr is a living quality, if it be temperate or moderate in a thing, and the Holy Ghost reigneth in the Calmnesse or *Meeknesse* of the Ayr, and all the creatures rejoyce therein.

But there is a *fierceness* or wrath also in it, so that it killeth & destroyeth by its terrible disturbance . . .

The Water also contains a fierce *deadly* Spring, for it killeth and consumeth. . .   (i 24–6)

Here the opposition between life and death, the sense that air and water have both a living and a dead operation, directs the reader to the natural world in a manner which reminds him vividly of the strange and merciful correspondences which relate her workings to human needs.

At such a moment in Boehme we seem close to the imagery of benevolent streams and 'living air' that occurs in both *The Ancient Mariner* and *Tintern Abbey*. The following passage from *Aurora* is still more suggestive:

Behold and consider a *Tree*, on the outside it hath a hard, grosse *Rind* or *Bark* which is Dead benumm'd, and without Vegetation, yet it is not *quite* Dead, but in a faintnesse or imbecility, and there is a great difference between it and the Body, which groweth next under the Rind or Bark. But the Body hath its Living Power, and breaketh forth through the *withered* Rind, and generateth many faire *young* Bodys or Twigs, all which stand in the *old Body*.

But the *Rind* is as it were dead, and cannot comprehend the *Life* of the Tree, but only hangs to it, and is a *Cover* to the Tree in which worms doe Harbour, which in the End destroy the Tree.

And thus also is the whole House of this world: the *outward* Darknesse is the House of God's Wrath, wherein the Devils dwell, and it is rightly the House of Death, for the Holy Light of God hath *dyed* therein . . .

Now the Love alwaies breaketh *through* the House of Death, and generateth *holy* heavenly Twigs in the great Tree; which Twiggs stand in the Light: For they spring up through the shell or *skin* of Darknesse as the Twiggs do through the shell or Bark of the Tree, and are *One Life* with God. (*Aurora* xxiv 7–9, 11)

For Boehme, the tree provides dramatic evidence of the relationship between a form which is dead, and an energy within which is essentially alive: the mysterious process by which the tree is roused each spring to put forth new shoots, only to retire each winter leaving a still more elaborate body of death, is thrown into relief by his account. Boehme's assumption that the body of death is the 'House of God's Wrath' (which he can fully sustain only by the introduction of destructive worms into the trunk) is less striking than his exposition of the life/death process. And it is the same process, we find, that is attracting the attention of the two poets to nature at this time.

The chief signs of such a preoccupation occur during the first autumn and winter at Alfoxden. In the late summer of 1797 Coleridge completes *Osorio*, with its long passage describing the atmosphere created by change of leaf; he also writes of the scritch-owl,

Its note comes dreariest in the fall of the year

In his most precise account of the circumstances under which *Kubla Khan* was composed, he specifically includes the information that it was produced in 'the fall of the year'.[5]

In Wordsworth's case, the sense of contrast between the forms of death and the animating energies of nature is particularly strong during the following spring. In March he shelters in a holly grove during a hailstorm and finds himself contemplating the strange paradox created by the contrast between the stillness of the living holly grove and the convincing sense of life which is created there by the dance of the dead balls of ice:

The leaves in myriads jump and spring,
As if with pipes and music rare
Some Robin Good-fellow were there,
And all those leaves, in festive glee,
Were dancing to the minstrelsy. (WP II 127–8)

He is also arrested by the sight of a thorn on the Quantocks which is almost completely dead but which is yet able to harbour new life:

> Of leaves it has repaired its loss
> With heavy tufts of dark green moss
>   (WP II 240 app. cr.)

It is this thorn, seen on a stormy day, when the dramatic atmospheric conditions bring it vividly to his attention, that is to prove the precipitating stimulus for his poem 'The Thorn'.[6]

The most striking feature of the passage from Boehme, however, is its use of a phrase that is to reverberate in Coleridge's own writings – the phrase in the final sentence concerning the love that springs up as the twigs do 'and are *One Life* with God.' In 'The Pedlar' Wordsworth's description of his visionary boyhood experiences (written probably after June 1797) includes the lines[7]

>   Wonder not
> If such his transports were; for in all things
> He saw one life, and felt that it was joy.
> One song they sang, and it was audible,
> Most audible then when the fleshly ear,
> O'ercome by grosser prelude of that strain
> Forgot its functions, and slept undisturbed.

By 1802 the phrase was to have become formalised in Coleridge's mind. In a letter to William Sotheby he wrote,

> Nature has her proper interest; and he will know what it is,
> who believes & feels, that every Thing has a Life of its own,
> & that we are all *one Life*.   (CL II 864)

This formulation (which, it will be noticed, repeats Boehme's stress) is associated with an adumbration of the Fancy/Imagination distinction. The most extended exposition of it comes in a passage which Coleridge adds many years later to *The Eolian Harp* to give further point to the scene he is describing there:

> O! the one Life within us and abroad,
> Which meets all motion and becomes its soul,
> A light in sound, a sound-like power in light,
> Rhythm in all thought, and joyance every where—
> Methinks, it should have been impossible
> Not to love all things in a world so filled ...   (PW I 101)

Ideally the process of the 'one Life' might be seen as manifested outwardly in the joint play of sun and breeze in nature; but it also takes subtler forms. In 'This Lime-Tree Bower my Prison', for example, the contrast between the distinct forms created by the vegetative process and the informing and unitive energy that plays throughout nature is a central theme, culminating in the address to the friend to whom

> No sound is dissonant which tells of Life.

In this poem the basic processes of life are examined closely (if also subtly and unobtrusively) in the description of the 'rifted dell' which his friend will visit

> where many an Ash
> Twists it's wild limbs beside the ferny rock,
> Whose plumy ferns for ever nod and drip
> Spray'd by the waterfall.   (CL I 335)

Between this draft and first publication (assisted perhaps, as J. D. Gutteridge has noted,[8] by Dorothy's observations at the same spot) Coleridge expanded these lines into a longer description. Now he pictured his friends actually winding down to

> . . . that still roaring dell, of which I told;
> The roaring dell, o'erwooded, narrow, deep,
> And only speckled by the mid-day sun;
> Where its slim trunk the ash from rock to rock
> Flings arching like a bridge;—that branchless ash
> Unsunn'd and damp, whose few poor yellow leaves
> Ne'er tremble in the gale, yet tremble still,
> Fann'd by the water-fall! and there my friends
> Behold the dark green file of long lank weeds,
> That all at once (a most fantastic sight!)
> Still nod and drip beneath the dripping edge
> Of the blue clay-stone.   (PW I 179)

The scene enables Coleridge to examine the elements of life as they subsist at their lowest ebb and minimal manifestation. In the darkened dell a possible correspondence between the lowest workings of nature and the inmost functions of the human body is discernible. Such life as subsists there receives little benefit from sunlight or freshly blowing breeze. Yet movement still continues, as in the human body during sleep. Some vital force persists, manifesting itself in the few poor yellow leaves of the branchless ash which are fanned only by the movement of the waterfall. It is seen in a still more 'fantastic' form in the nodding and dripping of the long lank weeds which are kept in motion, but only by the dripping from the blue clay-stone.

This theme of a buried life so untouched by light and warmth that it might seem positively sinister is also taken up in *Osorio*. One of the key-scenes in the drama takes place in a cavern, where the guilty character Frederick, whose torch has just been put out by the falling water in the cave, finds himself oppressed by the incessant dripping noise. He is then afraid of something moving. Osorio goes to look and reports that

> A jutting clay-stone
> Drips on the long lank weed that grows beneath;
> And the weed nods and drips.   (PW II 563–4)

The implication seems to be that phenomena which may be sinister and fearful to a mind that has been disturbed by guilt are simply attractive to the eye of innocence.

In 'This Lime-tree Bower', on the other hand, the innocent eye is sovereign. It is Coleridge's major moral theme in the poem that

> . . . nature ne'er deserts the wise & pure,
> No scene so narrow, but may well employ
> Each faculty of sense, and keep the heart
> Awake to Love & Beauty.   (CL I 336)

The existence of possible sympathetic links between the life of nature and the life (including the moral life) of man continued to work in the minds of Coleridge and Wordsworth during the winter and spring. Wordsworth was even willing to entertain, at least for a time, the idea that the forces of spring might act not only physically, but morally for the good of those human beings who were willing to expose themselves to them. When he wrote,

> One impulse from a vernal wood
> May teach you more of man,
> Of moral evil and of good,
> Than all the sages can.   (WP IV 57)

there is no reason to believe that he did not want his words to be considered seriously. How, indeed, did communication and sympathy between human beings come into existence if there were not some such concealed force at work in the world? And if so, why should it not manifest itself most clearly when life was springing up freshly all around? Coleridge's theory of the two levels of consciousness, the one representing an active use of energy through the organs of perception, the other expressing a deeper, subconscious vegetative process which was essentially passive, can be seen to fit not only this idea of the 'one impulse' but the equally well-known lines:

> The eye—it cannot choose but see;
> We cannot bid the ear be still;
> Our bodies feel, where'er they be,
> Against or with our will.

> Nor less I deem that there are Powers
> Which of themselves our minds impress;
> That we can feed this mind of ours
> In a wise passiveness.   (WP IV 56)

The sense that Wordsworth is here giving actuality and definition to ideas that had been originally adumbrated by Coleridge is further reinforced when we turn from a line of Coleridge's published in 1796,

> New life and joy th'expanding flow'ret feels (PW I 96)

to Wordsworth's more direct and personal asseveration of 1798:

> And 'tis my faith that every flower
> Enjoys the air it breathes.   (WP IV 58)

Any attempt by the two poets to generalise further from such instances would of course have met with certain objections – and they were fully aware of them, as we shall see. In one area of human experience, however, the case could be put at its most positive. In childhood, it could be argued, particularly if the child were frequently exposed to nature, the primary consciousness and its links with the 'one life' were to be seen in a pure form. A child who had not been forced by prolonged exposure to the world of sense and reason to organise its perceptions around cut and dried quantitative categories could manifest its sense of the unity of existence with unusual vividness.

This is the perception which lies at the heart of Wordsworth's 'We are Seven'.[9] The little girl whom he had met in the ruins of Goodrich Castle many years before,[10] and who refused to accept that the number of people in her family was diminished by the death of two of them was displaying the activity of a life-consciousness that had not yet been modified by formal education and heavier experiences of personal loss.

Yet for all Wordsworth's delight in this reinforcement of the idea from an actual remembered experience of his own, there remained a residuum of uneasiness, betrayed for example by the fact that he found it most natural to compose the stanzas of 'We are Seven' in reverse order, beginning with the last. Despite his speed of composition he was still, according to his own account,[11] without an opening stanza to give the theme of the whole when he came in for tea, and it was in fact Coleridge who furnished him with it:

> A simple child, dear brother Jim
> That lightly draws its breath,
> And feels its life in every limb,
> What should it know of death?   (WP I 236n)

His welcoming acceptance of Coleridge's intervention suggests a point of limitation in Wordsworth's ability to enter the world of the 'one life'. He could respond to the idea of a universal life-force of some kind, for this corresponded to his own emotional experiences in nature as remembered from boyhood; he could readily believe, on the same grounds, that the child, being naturally attuned to that power, was exhibiting the nature of its deeper sensibility when it gave way to unconfined joy. But the Coleridgean location of that recognition in the nerves and veins of the child, so that its very lightness of breath and ability to 'feel its life in every limb' became open manifestations of the same life-power: this was a more difficult belief for Wordsworth.

Coleridge was evidently willing to pursue the possible physical links between the forces of nature and the as yet unviolated primary consciousness of childhood and early youth as far as he could. In the spring of 1798 he wrote *The Nightingale*, a poem which goes further than Wordsworth in asserting the power of nature, at least in certain moods, to fill the receptive observer with shared joy. Against those who have heard about the nightingale only in a context of civilisation, where its song has come to be thought of as melancholy, Coleridge affirms the essential 'merriness' of the nightingale:

> That crowds, and hurries, and precipitates
> With fast thick warble his delicious notes,
> As he were fearful that an April night
> Would be too short for him to utter forth
> His love-chant, and disburthen his full soul
> Of all its music! (PW I 265)

The succeeding lines, which contain some of the best and most sensuous nature-poetry that Coleridge ever wrote, look forward directly to Keats. When he writes of the birds as

> Stirring the air with such an harmony,
> That should you close your eyes, you might almost
> Forget it was not day!

we immediately recognise the world of the *Ode to a Nightingale*. Entry into such a world, however, raises for Coleridge (as it was to do for Keats) further questions about the reality of the world created by the human imagination. He introduces into the scene a girl who belongs both to the 1790s, with its surviving mansions and absentee landlords, and to the world of Gothic romance, but who differs from the conventions of both by making her devotions not in a church or private chapel but in a nearby wood:

> A most gentle Maid,
> Who dwelleth in her hospitable home
> Hard by the castle, and at latest eve
> (Even like a Lady vowed and dedicate
> To something more than Nature in the grove)
> Glides through the pathways. . . (PW I 266)

As the description proceeds, we are made aware that Coleridge is exploring another link in nature's possible chain of subliminal powers:

> she knows all their notes,
> That gentle Maid! and oft, a moment's space,
> What time the moon was lost behind a cloud,

> Hath heard a pause of silence; till the moon
> Emerging, hath awakened earth and sky
> With one sensation, and those wakeful birds
> Have all burst forth in choral minstrelsy,
> As if some sudden gale had swept at once
> A hundred airy harps!

The 'As if' here stands guard over a speculation which has taken Coleridge far into a world that was partially projected in *The Eolian Harp*. Could it be that, as some of the French magnetists had suggested, the moon exercised a positive magnetic influence on living organisms? After all, the influence of the moon not only over the tides but over the disturbed human mind had long been well known (Coleridge himself, in a schoolboy poem, had addressed her as 'Mother of wildly-working visions!'[12]). Was it possible that this apparently sinister process was an unusually overt manifestation of a magnetism which was always, and normally more benevolently, at work in human beings?

The workings of such a speculation may be detected in Wordsworth's description of the delight felt for the moon by the idiot in his *Idiot Boy*, which was written in the groves near Alfoxden in 1798; and also, perhaps, in his hopes for Dorothy in *Tintern Abbey* ('Therefore let the moon/ Shine on thee in thy solitary walk').[13] In the last section of *The Nightingale* it emerges – again in guarded form – in Coleridge's anecdote of his baby Hartley, telling how when his baby son woke up crying one evening he hurried him into their little orchard:

> And he beheld the moon, and hushed at once,
> Suspends his sobs, and laughs most silently,
> While his fair eyes, that swam with undropped tears,
> Did glitter in the yellow moon-beam!   (PW I 266–7)

'Well—' continues Coleridge (bracing himself against the reader's anticipated cynicism), 'It is a father's tale'. He concludes, therefore, with an acceptable public moral: he will, he proposes, make Hartley 'Nature's playmate' and ensure that he grows up familiar with the nightingale's song, so that he may associate the night with joy.

The Nightingale is a key poem in the evolution of what might be termed the 'child of nature' motif in Coleridge's writing.

That motif appears first in a section of *Osorio* which he published
separately as 'The Foster-Mother's Tale', describing

> A pretty boy, but most unteachable—
> And never learnt a prayer, nor told a bead,
> But knew the names of birds, and mock'd their notes,
> And whistled, as he were a bird himself:
> And all the autumn 'twas his only play
> To get the seeds of wild flowers, and to plant them
> With earth and water, on the stumps of trees.   (PW I 183)

The last thing related of this boy is that he

> seiz'd a boat,
> And all alone, set sail by silent moonlight
> Up a great river, great as any sea,
> And ne'er was heard of more: but 'tis suppos'd
> He liv'd and died among the savage men.

Despite the deliberate ambiguity of the conclusion, the import of
the tale as a whole is that the boy had kept alive a realm, or level,
of consciousness which education or strict religious observance
would gradually have deadened, and which finds an ultimate
fulfilment (however unsatisfactory) when he sails up the river in
silent moonlight to join others whose primitive consciousness
has been unviolated by processes of civilisation.

The theme of the child of nature under moonlight is taken up
again in 'The Wanderings of Cain'. It is perhaps significant that
the only part of the tale which rendered itself naturally into
poetry in Coleridge's mind was that which concerned Cain's son
Enos, who remains at his side, a child still dominated by consciousness of life, delighted by the play of squirrels and puzzled
that they should run away from him:

> Encinctured with a twine of leaves,
> That leafy twine his only dress!
> A lovely Boy was plucking fruits,
> By moonlight, in a wilderness.
> The moon was bright, the air was free,
> And fruits and flowers together grew
> On many a shrub and many a tree:
> And all put on a gentle hue,

Hanging in the shadowy air
Like a picture rich and rare.
It was a climate where, they say,
The night is more belov'd than day.
But who that beauteous Boy beguil'd,
That beauteous Boy to linger here?
Alone, by night, a little child,
In place so silent and so wild—
Has he no friend, no loving mother near? (PW I 287)

As in *The Nightingale*, there is a strong suggestion that nature
includes a primary process of benevolence which attracts to her,
and works directly in, those who still preserve innocency of
mind and behaviour. The theme receives its most sophisticated
treatment, however, in the opening of *Christabel*,[14] in which a
maiden, similar in innocence to the heroine of *The Nightingale*,
goes out at night into a wood, where the forces of nature are
more equivocally disposed. The moon which illuminates the
scene is diminished by intervening clouds to smallness and dull-
ness; the birds which respond to it are no longer joyful nightingales but gloomy owls, the life-force in the trees has not yet
made its presence felt, for 'the spring comes slowly up this way',
so that the only motion is that of the single leaf left over from
last season. The forces of life are not acting negatively, however:
they are simply at their lowest ebb in this they correspond to
the nature of the daemonic force that is embodied in Geraldine.

The encounter of Christabel with Geraldine and Coleridge's
own difficulty in completing his poem are part of a larger problem mentioned earlier: that of knowing how much weight to
give to 'life-consciousness' within the facts of the world as we
know them. Among other things, as we have seen, that problem
associated itself with the large body of unproven theorisings
surrounding animal magnetism. Some of the straightforward
psychological phenomena associated with his current ideas, on
the other hand, were convincing enough to allow of less guarded
use in the *Lyrical Ballads*. That he and the Wordsworths felt joy
rather than melancholy when listening to nightingales was a
fact; that country people often derived positive pleasure from
looking after idiot children was a fact;[15] that an old and infirm
man, hardly able to talk at all, might still set out on an epic

journey to see his son who was dying in a distant hospital was a fact.[16] In some sense, then, and whatever the truth or otherwise of their physical theories, the belief on the part of the magnetists that an invisible link connected all men to one another – a link more powerful apparently among those who had been brought up in the midst of nature – corresponded to observable human experience. Hazlitt records Coleridge's pleasure at this time in the account of a fisherman who was trying to explain how he and his friends had undertaken a dangerous rescue:

> . . . he did not know how it was that they ventured, but, Sir, we have a *nature* towards one another. (HW XVII 121)

Further perspicuous observation of nature drew attention not only to the relationship between life-processes and death-processes in all organic life, animated or vegetating, but to the strange capacity of the 'life-consciousness' of the human observer to impose itself upon the natural scene about it, deriving a strong sense of life from objects which are yet known to be, in themselves, devoid of it. Such reflections sharpened perception of the phenomena involved: on 1 March Dorothy Wordsworth wrote in her journal:

> The shapes of the mist, slowly moving along, exquisitely beautiful; passing over the sheep they almost seemed to have more of life than those quiet creatures. The unseen birds singing in the mist. (DWJ I 11)

On 1 February she had sheltered in a holly grove during a storm and observed the effects of the wind: 'The trees almost *roared*, and the ground seemed in motion with the multitudes of dancing leaves, which made a rustling sound, distinct from that of the trees.' The very first entry of her journal in January had described the effects of a fresh winter's day:

> The green paths down the hill-sides are channels for streams. The young wheat is streaked by silver lines of water running between the ridges, the sheep are gathered together on the slopes. After the wet dark days, the country seems more populous. It peoples itself in the sunbeams . . .

The last two sentences take the conception of 'animation' in nature a stage further; in certain weathers the scene seems to be

actually 'populous'. Wordsworth described a similar effect in a
contemporary verse fragment:

> these populous slopes
> With all their groves and with their murmurous woods,
> Giving a curious feeling to the mind
> Of peopled solitude.   (WP V 341)

In his chief conversation poem of this spring, written a month
after Dorothy's first entry, Coleridge inverted the effect. In the
opening to *Frost at Midnight* he described how the stillness of
night-time made it almost impossible to believe in the life that
he knew to be going on all round his cottage:

> Sea, hill, and wood,
> This populous village! Sea, and hill, and wood,
> With all the numberless goings-on of life,
> Inaudible as dreams!   (PW I 240)

For Coleridge, the mystery of life's continuance in the night's
stillness is akin to the mystery of watching a sleeping person
who gives no outward sign that his or her mind is at that
moment vividly peopled by a dream. In this poem, moreover, the
strangeness of the sense is sharpened by the fact that the only
human being present with him is his baby son, Hartley, the
workings of whose consciousness would be partly hidden even if
he were awake, so that they are now, as it were, doubly inaccessible.

It is altogether beneficial to this poem that Hartley is at its
centre, replacing the fictitious heroes and heroines of previous
poems. The behaviour and capabilities of a real child give new
definition to the 'child of nature' theme, which had also been
pursued by Coleridge in his notebook observations. An entry
headed 'Infancy and Infants' included several vignettes which
may have been intended for poetry and which show not only a
feeling for the charm of childhood but a concern with issues of
nature and environment:

  1. The first smile—what kind of *reason* it displays—the first
     smile after sickness.—
  2. Asleep with the polyanthus held fast in its hand, its bells
     drooping over the rosy face.

3. Stretching after the stars.—
4. Seen asleep by the light of glowworms.
5. Sports of infants—their incessant activity, the *means* being the end.—Nature how lovely a school-mistress—A blank-verse moral poem—(Children at houses of Industry.—) . . .

(CN I 330)

The indignation at child-labour which is suggested in the last parenthesis later found expression in writings directed specifically against it; at this time, however, the question of nature's influence is more important and finds expression in a 'blank-verse moral poem', *Frost at Midnight*, which is subtler than these notebook foreshadowings might lead one to expect. The entry at the foot of the previous page

> The reed-roof'd Village, still bepatch'd with snow
> Smok'd in the sun-thaw   (CN I 329)

becomes part of the climax to a poem where, instead of describing 'Children at houses of Industry', Coleridge evokes, through vivid recreation of his own childhood, the faults of an education rooted in a mechanist world. At the same time, sitting in his cottage at a dead time of year and night, he evokes (often by negatives) the sense of a living world about him. The natural sounds described in recent poems: birdsong, the sound of streams, the blowing of the breeze – all of them signifying present life-forces – are absent. The freezing process receives no assistance from wind; the only animal noise is the sinister-sounding owlet's cry; the child sleeps peacefully. Even the thin blue flame on the fire is motionless. The only convincing sign of life comes, para-doxically, from the film of dead soot fluttering on the grate, which affords a sense of its companionship with his own idling imagination:

> Methinks, its motion in this hush of nature
> Gives it dim sympathies with me who live,
> Making it a companionable form,
> Whose puny flaps and freaks the idling Spirit
> By its own moods interprets, every where
> Echo or mirror seeking of itself,
> And makes a toy of Thought.   (PW I 240–1)

More than one critic has drawn out the reminiscences of Cowper's *Task* in these lines and the following.[17] Like his predecessor, Coleridge draws on the country superstition that the film in the grate betokens the arrival of a stranger. He recalls how at school the sight of such a film on his study grate sometimes supervened on a waking dream in which he had already been projecting (presumably into the flames of the fire itself) pictures of his own birthplace. As a result, the power of the dream would continue into the next day, so that if the door of his school-room opened he would find his heart leaping up in the expectation that some 'stranger' from his home town was about to appear:

> Townsman, or aunt, or sister more beloved
> My play-mate when we both were clothed alike!

In this section Coleridge has moved beyond Cowper, to an evocation of the part in which the phenomena of 'primary consciousness' are strongly suggested. The warmth of the fire has already linked in his imagination with the heat of a hot fair-day and the sound of bells ringing 'from morn to evening'; this induces a more personal link which, when furthered by the play of the soot-film (with its own suggestions of a fluttering heart) induces first the image of some townsman, who would have been welcome as a straightforward physical link with Ottery, then the aunt, who would have had the more intimate bond of family affection and finally the sister, most welcome of all, since his play with her in childhood had been the nearest he had known to a total human sympathy.

At this point in *Frost at Midnight* Coleridge breaks off to address Hartley, the baby whose peaceful sleep at his side is another, if less active, manifestation of life in the present stillness. He now transfers the link of sympathy with his long-dead sister into the father–child relationship, expressing the hope that Hartley, as 'Nature's play-mate', will achieve a more intimate relationship with her than the circumstances of his own life have allowed.

At this point there may also be a buried link between the reminiscence of his day-dreams by the fire at school and the bitter reminiscence of the same school-days which he introduces as a contrast with the education proposed for Hartley:

> For I was reared
> In the great city, pent 'mid cloisters dim,
> And saw nought lovely but the sky and stars.

Coleridge's reading of Boehme at Christ's Hospital, with all its possible implications for his philosophy of the human heart, has been discussed earlier; it may be that even in those days his gazing into the fire behind the barred grate created an emblem of life imprisoned by death. The image of bars occurs again in a later reminiscence of Christ's Hospital: this time of his glimpse of the beauties of the heavens.[18a]

> At eve, sky-gazing in 'ecstatic fit'
> (Alas! for cloister'd in a city School
> The Sky was all, I knew, of Beautiful)
> At the barr'd window often did I sit,
> And oft upon the leaded School-roof lay . . .

When these two glimpses of beauty seen through bars are put together, they seem like natural forerunners of the imprisoned sun in *The Ancient Mariner*, which peers 'as if through a dungeon grate'. It is not impossible that that image of contrast between the vital energy and the imprisoning bars of mortality first came to him at school as he looked into the grate of his fire, or through barred windows at the sky.

Certainly the imagery in question, coupled with the central image of frost in the present poem, prompts one to look again at the imagery of ice, as it had developed over the years. In 1791, when he wrote a poem on the death of his sister, he used a rather conventional image: 'On me thy icy dart, stern Death, be prov'd . . .'[19] Traditionally, the association of ice with death strikes fear. Ice is the opposite of life, the natural enemy of the warm beating heart.[20a] Boehme's use of the symbol, however, might encourage a modification of that response. Viewed dispassionately, the principle of concretion which manifests itself in ice is as beautiful as the work of the sun. It stands at the opposite extreme, perhaps, but not as positive antagonist. Seen within the spectrum of life, indeed, it defines a necessary extreme, corresponding to one of the two forces which Coleridge traced in all organic phenomena: the principle of expansion and the principle which strives for unity within that expansion.[21] In vegetables, on this view, the principle of unity is paramount, in animals the principle of energy. And just as the sun might be seen as the animal principle taken to a logical conclusion, with energy and expansion predominant over a principle of unity that yet holds it tenaciously in the form of a sphere, so ice may be seen as the principle which takes the vegetative to its logical end. Unity here takes full precedence; any energy involved is devoted to the single end of realising its unified form.

If we follow this line of thought further it will be seen that in *Frost at Midnight* Coleridge is celebrating his own deliverance from the hectic and overwrought musings of his schooldays, where contemplation of the relationship between the human heart and the forces of death and restraint too often led to inordinate actions, and his entry into a more benevolent world, where the relationship between ice and death is less horrifying, since even the self-binding work of frost is seen to contain an active and creative principle.

This subterranean process plays a part in the transition from the first part of the poem to the second. For Coleridge at this time is coming to believe that the excesses of his youth were partly produced by a system of education which barred him from the consolatory influence of nature's processes. (His self-critique was perhaps assisted by Wordsworth, who in *The Prelude* was to discuss the defects of Coleridge's upbringing while also drawing attention to the advantages of his own education in the midst of nature.[22]) It therefore becomes natural for him to propose for Hartley an education which will bring him closer to those same forms and so leave his spirit free to be moulded by the greater 'Spirit' who expresses himself through them.

First, however, he addresses the sleeping child as one who in his own right exhibits the spirit of life,

> Whose gentle breathings, heard in this deep calm,
> Fill up the interspersèd vacancies
> And momentary pauses of the thought!

The relief which his own gentle breathing gives to the silence will for this child be repeated by his presence in nature as a whole. He will not only be given freedom but will find a similar freedom working in the very breezes of nature; he may then go on to discover both in the beauty of the permanences of nature

('By lakes and sandy shores, beneath the crags/Of ancient mountain . . .) and in the impermanencies which mirror those permanencies ('the clouds,/Which image in their bulk both lakes and shores/And mountain crags') the forms of the language

> which thy God
> Utters, who from eternity doth teach
> Himself in all, and all things in himself.

The slight eccentricity of the words 'thy God' should be noted, particularly when read in conjunction with the description of him as 'Himself in all, and all things in himself'. This God is not necessarily identifiable with the orthodox Christian God; there is a sense in which the description not only mirrors Coleridge's favourite formula for life ('Each thing has a life of its own, and we are all one Life'[23]) but echoes the interpenetrative quality of the earlier imagery. The child of nature wanders like a breeze; he sees the lakes and shores and mountain crags, which are in themselves permanent; but he also sees the clouds that can imitate all these – and which are in turn shaped and moved by nature's breezes. And this shifting pattern, to which the poet refuses to give permanent focus, becomes the mirror of a divine creative process which can likewise be seen in various aspects, between the free energy of the breeze and the fixities of permanent matter, and which can never, as a whole, be firmly contained in the finite human mind.

Although the mind may be thwarted in its attempts to hold this pattern in one, the achievement of the human mind in contemplating the pattern is self-liberating. No longer are the seasons set into the contrast of life-affirming summer against death-betraying winter; all seasons become sweet, for all tell of life. That central life displays its processes not only in the mysterious unitive work of fertility which clothes the general earth with greenness, but in the separative and dramatic winter scene where the singing of the robin contrasts with its dead surroundings of snow and bare branch – these in turn being offset by the fact that the apple-tree is mossy and that, as the energy of the sun causes the frost which might otherwise become a deadly permanence to expand into vapour, the nearby thatch 'smokes in the sun-thaw'.

As the paragraph comes to a close, the contrasts are still more dramatic. We move between the wild energy of the storm-blast and the intervening silences which, rendered trance-like by what has come between, make the listener attentive to the noise of the eave-drops – a very simple work of nature, continuing regardless of the riot beyond. And finally we return to the work of frost:

> Or if the secret ministry of frost
> Shall hang them up in silent icicles,
> Quietly shining to the quiet Moon.

In the original published version there was a comma after 'Moon', and the poem concluded,

> Like those, my babe! which ere tomorrow's warmth
> Have capp'd their sharp keen points with pendulous drops,
> Will catch thine eye, and with their novelty
> Suspend thy little soul; then make thee shout,
> And stretch and flutter from thy mother's arms
> As thou wouldst fly for very eagerness.   (PW 1 243n)

Humphry House said that the decision (taken for an edition ten years later) to end *Frost at Midnight* with the 'quiet Moon' was one of the best, artistically, that Coleridge ever made.[24] At one level the judgement can hardly be questioned. This new exposition of the 'secret ministry of frost' reinterprets the opening line, sealing the whole poem into the mode of trance. Everything in the poem now echoes and counterpoints within a larger sense of containing peace. House went on to say, however, that 'once the vista of domestic detail was opened there was no reason why it should not be indefinitely followed, with increasing shapelessness.' This is less convincing. The domestic detail, it will be observed, opens into a new sense of joy and eagerness, of expansion after the contracting sense induced by the icicles. We end, in other words, with a vision of Hartley's primary consciousness responding so directly to the sight of sun on ice that it seems to be taking wing. One of Coleridge's reasons for cancelling the lines was perhaps a waning confidence in the power of primary consciousness, which made it natural for him to seek a more publicly available conclusion. His more immediate explanation, however, was that they destroyed 'the rondo, and return upon itself of the Poem'.[25] Whatever the reasons, conscious or unconscious, for its adoption, however, the new, self-sealing conclusion confides the process of the poem to the meditative mind and in so doing stresses further the theme of natural harmony. In its original form the poem concludes with a sense of growth, of a process of contraction and expansion which is as active in the pure emotional life of the child as it is in the silent life of the organism. It is an ending full of potentialities.

With or without the original ending the dominant note of *Frost at Midnight* is still in some sense one of reconciliation. This is not the only way of seeing the processes of life however: the ambiguities involved in natural energy, which we discussed earlier, stretch into the whole realm covered by this poem also. Looking back to his first meeting with Coleridge in January 1798, Hazlitt was to remember how Coleridge complained of Godwin's presumption 'in attempting to establish the future immortality of man, "without" (as he said) "Knowing what Death was or what Life was" – and the tone in which he pronounced these two words seemed to convey a complete image of both'[26] – which gives the impression of a language more portentous than anything in *Frost at Midnight*.

The full force of Coleridge's remark emerges when we turn to *The Ancient Mariner*. In that poem, death appears at times in all its terror: never more so than in the incident of the spectre-ship. As the Mariner looks out to sea, he sees something which he can at first characterise only as a 'speck', a 'mist' or a 'shape'. It behaves, however, with all the appearance of life:

> And, an it dodg'd a water-sprite,
> It plung'd and tack'd and veer'd   (PW II 1034)

Hardly has he seen it as a boat and found strength to hail it, before its movement changes into total steadiness, as it drives between them and the sun to create against the horizon a sudden image of imprisonment:

> And straight the Sun was flecked with bars
> (Heaven's Mother send us grace!)
> As if through a dungeon-grate he peered
> With broad and burning face.   (1800 vn, PW I 193)

The sense of energy burning through the bars of a limiting

mortality is increased by the terms in which the Mariner questions the boat as it draws nearer:

> Are those *her* ribs through which the Sun
> Did peer, as through a grate?   (Ibid.)

It is with the sight of the crew, finally, that the pattern involved is forged into seizable images. The 'ribs' of the boat are now made actual in the skeletal form of the 'fleshless Pheere':

> *His* bones were black, with many a crack,
>   All black and bare, I ween;
> Jet-black and bare, save where with rust
> Of mouldy damps and charnel crust
>   They're patch'd with purple and green.

(PW II 1035)

The present tense into which Coleridge shifts as he describes this figure dominates the ensuing description of his companion – a strangely ambiguous figure who seems at first to possess the pleasantest qualities of life:

> *Her* lips are red, *her* looks are free,
>   *Her* locks are yellow as gold:
> Her skin is as white as leprosy,
> And she is far liker Death than he;
>   Her flesh makes the still air cold.   (PW II 1035)

The cumulative effect is one of beauty until the moment when the word 'leprosy' strikes a chill into the reader – which is promptly reinforced by the suggestion that she is actually communicating cold to the air about her. It seems that we are exploring the idea of a life subsisting without the means of warmth and communication which is provided by mortal existence, with the further implication that such a conception is more terrifying than that of death itself.

It is this woman who wins the Mariner: nearly twenty years later Coleridge gives her a name – that of 'the Nightmare Life-in-Death', who 'thicks man's blood with cold'. Perhaps the most important clue to the appropriateness of her victory, however, is given in the original phrase, 'her looks are free'. The Mariner too was totally free when he shot the albatross. But if he imagined that freedom was simply identifiable with life, he has

now to learn the truth: total freedom could belong only to a life
outside the mortal body. The welcome communicative warmth
of human existence brings with it the necessity of limiting one's
own freedom in order to maintain and further that communication.

When the Mariner finally returns to his native land it is one
of the mercies of his restoration that he finds himself once again
surrounded by the forms of rooted, vegetative existence, where
if life feeds upon life the process is less savage than in the ocean.
The man from whom he immediately seeks absolution is the
Hermit, who values such mercies:

> He kneels at morn and noon and eve—
> He hath a cushion plump:
> It is the moss, that wholly hides
> The rotted old Oak-stump.

This new version of 'death in life' and 'life in death' (closely
analogous to the thorn and moss that attract the narrator's
attention in 'The Thorn'), couples the rootedness of a death-
form with the work of self-renewing life. The Hermit, at least,
'knows what death is, and what life is'. He is by no means blind
to the more sinister elements involved, however. When he
originally sees the Mariner's vessel which, with its deathly
silence, warped planks and thin sails, has now turned into the
form originally bodied forth in the spectre-ship, the first image
which comes to his mind is a more sombre version of death in
life (winter branches above a forest-brook), followed by a vision
of life at its most sinister, with the hooting owl and the eating of
the off-spring of the devouring wolf:

> The skeletons of leaves that lag
> My forest-brook along;
> When the Ivy-tod is heavy with snow,
> And the Owlet whoops to the wolf below
> That eats the she-wolf's young.

The Pilot, who lacks the Hermit's larger organic awareness, falls
back on superstition: 'Dear Lord! it hath a fiendish look!'

Despite the general atmosphere of vitality and benevolence in
the poem as a whole, features such as this forbid one to read
The Ancient Mariner simply as a poem about 'the sacramental

vision, or . . . the "One Life" '.[27a] Life-in-Death is a figure of
nightmare: she and the various experiences of terror in the poem
remind us continually that in all life, with its necessary processes
of destruction, there is an element of inevitable fear. A similar
fear haunts the second stanza of *Kubla Khan* (the composition
of which poem, I have suggested elsewhere, might have been
prompted partly by the preceding experience of walking through
the woods near Porlock in late autumn) and the opening of
Christabel – though the heroine, walking out of castle which is a
world of death into woods which show hardly a single sign of life,
seems immune to it.

It is in *The Ancient Mariner* that this nightmare sense is most
fully rendered, nevertheless; we need to turn to that poem once
again, therefore – looking at it this time in terms of Coleridge's
view of human consciousness and its potentialities.

7

An Exploring Fiction

Of all Coleridge's poems, *The Ancient Mariner* has raised the most problems of interpretation. For many readers, to be sure, the problems are lessened by their willingness to read the poem without taking too seriously the full implications of all the detailed incidents. John Livingston Lowes, for instance, found it possible to write a brilliant study of Coleridge's artistry in the poem on the assumption that his delight in speculative thought had been an unfortunate trait, which hindered his ability as a poet and which could safely be disregarded. Coleridge's true poetic calling, he thought, had been to create marvellous imagery.[1]

One can readily sympathise with such an approach; there can be no doubt that a chief value of the poem is its rare power to start a vivid work in the reader's imagination. The more one looks into Coleridge's early intellectual career, however, the more difficult it becomes to believe that he wrote the poem during a holiday from thought. If, as De Quincey asserted, 'Logic the most severe was as inalienable from his modes of thinking as grammar from his language',[2] it is hard to imagine how this man, who was at the time preaching in Unitarian pulpits, could have left a long ballad which seemed to have a straightforward moral content yet which contained so many knotty moral points for critical readers to puzzle over, without knowing something of what he was doing.

So far as the 'moral' itself is concerned, the kind of puzzle which arises was long ago summed up in Sir Leslie Stephen's acerbic comment:[3]

> The moral, which would apparently be that people who sympathise with a man who shoots an albatross will die in prolonged torture of thirst, is open to obvious objections.

More recently, William Empson has remarked that if one is looking for the kind of practical moral action prescribed by the poem it is hard to get beyond the familiar Victorian 'Don't pull poor pussy's tail, because God loves all his creatures.'[4]

In addition to this central problem, however, there are incidental puzzles in the narrative. The game of dice between the crew of the spectre-ship might seem to negate any validity of free will in the poem, for instance; and despite the suggestions of avenging justice working through nature, the elements often seem to act with pure wantonness rather than according to an intelligible pattern of moral retribution or reclamation. It is not easy to know how much of the Mariner's narrative is to be trusted, moreover. Can we be sure that *any* of the events after the onset of his thirst-agony have an 'objective' existence ('supernatural' or otherwise)? Possibly not – yet in some sense we are expected to believe that the boat was actually brought, crewless, from the South Seas to the northern sea-port from which it originally set out.

Faced with the endless labyrinths set up by such questionings, some recent critics have argued that, despite the Mariner's final assertions and injunctions, the poem is really 'about' the unintelligibility of the universe. One, while acknowledging an inherent improbability in the supposition, has concluded that Coleridge 'deliberately embodied a view of nature contrary to the one he was stating in more discursive poetry written at the time' – using the ballad form as a convenient cover for his heresy.[5*]

The poem certainly draws some of its subterranean power from the intellectual struggles and doubts through which Coleridge had been passing, and if one attends exclusively to such aspects it can be interpreted quite legitimately as presenting an oblique exposition of nature's essential amorality. But it is hard to believe that in 1797 he would have allowed himself to work so deviously in writing a serious poem as to present an exoteric moral which he meant to be totally subvertible once critical attention was given to the poem's contents.

In the long run much must depend on the elements to which the reader chooses to attend. Penn Warren and others have sought moral coherence in the poem by investigating its symbolic structure. I myself have pointed out that, from the part played by certain of the natural elements, notably the sun and moon, and their continuity with elements in Coleridge's reading and with his uses of similar symbolism in previous poems, it is possible to trace a large coherent symbolic structure, in which the ambivalence both of the sun (glorious and destructive by turns) and of the moon (presiding over both beneficence and cursing) can be resolved by seeing them against Coleridge's master conception of the divine as an ideal sun, 'that shall unite heat and light', which is in turn imaged directly in the dawn-vision.[6] E. E. Bostetter, on the other hand, argued that overattention to the poem's symbolic structure may do violence to another fact about it: that reading it is not necessarily a pleasant experience. The Mariner's alternating experiences of terror and relief may, in the mind of a susceptible reader, induce a state not far from that of nightmare.[7]

With these considerations in mind, we should look again at the larger processes of the poem's creation, so far as they can be inferred from contemporary evidences.

The nature of the current political and social atmosphere, to begin with, would support the supposition that Coleridge intended to make a strong affirmative point. The general pressure of his shared enterprise with Wordsworth was – at least in general terms – towards the reinterpretation of nature: a new version of 'justifying the ways of God to man'. But there was also a contemporary sense of urgency. R. H. Wells has cogently aligned their aims with those of Godwin, who was later to recall how, when he was writing *Caleb Williams* (published in 1794), one thought was constantly uppermost in his mind:[8]

> I will write a tale, that shall constitute an epoch in the mind of the reader, that no one, after he has read it, shall ever be exactly the same man that he was before!

The parallel with the closing lines of *The Ancient Mariner* is, as he points out, striking.

Although it would be unwise, and probably wrong, to draw too hasty an analogy between the composition of *Caleb Williams* and that of *The Ancient Mariner*, the existence of this parallel may be seen to reflect an urgency which was natural enough in the aftermath of the French Revolution. For a time the revolution had seemed to promise a profound change in the habits and institutions of mankind; the Reign of Terror, on the other hand, had seemed to demonstrate the dangers of interfering with the established order. In 1797 the debate was still continuing. Was this a world in which it was possible for human beings to be changed and where the French hopes would eventually be realised in a new order? Or were there certain forces which would always exert too powerful a counterweight in favour of 'things as they are' (the alternative title of Godwin's novel)?

Some of the work we have considered already can be viewed as marking an endeavour on the part of Wordsworth and Coleridge to achieve a breakthrough of the kind that Godwin had aimed at. There are signs that the dramas of both men were aimed at galvanising their audiences into a sense of the injustices which the revolutionaries had sought to remedy. One of the most striking instances is to be found in the speech in *Osorio* where Albert (the character most in touch with nature) looks round the dungeon in which he is confined and complains at the corruption of human energy that must be set up in a prisoner by such restriction:

> Is this the only cure? Merciful God!
> Each pore and natural outlet shrivell'd up
> By ignorance and parching poverty,
> His energies roll back upon his heart,
> And stagnate and corrupt till changed to poison,
> They break out on him like a loathsome plague-spot!
> Then we call in our pamper'd mountebanks—
> And this is their best cure!

He cites, in contrast, the restorative processes of Nature:

> Thou pourest on him thy soft influences,
> Thy sunny hues, fair forms, and breathing sweets,
> Thy melodies of woods, and winds, and waters,
> Till he relent, and can no more endure
> To be a jarring and a dissonant thing
> Amid this general dance and minstrelsy;
> But bursting into tears wins back his way,
> His angry spirit heal'd and harmoniz'd
> By the benignant touch of love and beauty. (PW II 586–7)

The passage, which marks a high point in affirmation of nature and her powers, was later extracted as 'The Dungeon', and included in the first edition of *Lyrical Ballads* along with Wordsworth's poem 'The Convict', which concludes with an address to the prisoner:

... My care, if the arm of the mighty were mine,
Would plant thee where yet thou might'st blossom again.

(WP I 314)

At another point in *Osorio*, where Coleridge relates the sudden chilling of a character to his subterranean sense of guilt, he seems to be exploiting the hypnotic possibilities of presentation in the warm and darkened theatre directly. The scene in which Albert performs as sorcerer is introduced by a strain of music 'from an instrument of glass or steel – the harmonica or Celestina stop, or Claggett's metallic organ'.[9] The glass harmonica was used by mesmerists in Paris to produce an appropriate atmosphere during their hypnotic sessions.[10]

As we have seen, however, the logic of dramatic creation and Coleridge's unwillingness to allow actuality to the magic powers invoked by Albert produced events which dwarfed both Albert's urgent moral declamations and his evocation of supernatural atmosphere, persuasive as each might have been at the moment of delivery. The plan for a successor to *The Death of Abel*, another attempt to affect a large popular audience, had also proved abortive.[11]

At the same time, such setbacks did not invalidate the body of existing evidence that the behaviour of a human being could, on occasion, be changed – sometimes dramatically; and there are indications that Coleridge, in particular, had been interesting himself in accounts of such 'conversions', religious or otherwise. We may mention John Wesley's famous experience of 'heart-warming' and the phenomena, familiar in Coleridge's Bristol and elsewhere, of large-scale conversions, sometimes violent, during the excitement of Methodist gatherings.[12] Coleridge's own characterisation of Methodism as 'a stove', which reflects his awareness of all this, may in turn be connected with the well-known story of Descartes' report, mentioned above,[13] that his major enlightenment took place after he had been closeted for a long time in a room with a hot stove. In another popular book of

the time (which, as Bernard Martin has pointed out,[14] Wordsworth knew, and probably read in the winter of 1797–8), John
Newton, the well-known Evangelical and friend of Cowper,
described a spiritual crisis which he had passed through in his
unregenerate days while undergoing dangers and privations at
sea; this had later been confirmed into a 'fully Christian' conversion during a fever at Sierra Leone, when he was almost
delirious.[15]

In addition to the literature of religion, we know that Wordsworth had received from William Gilbert a description of the
'calenture', a raging fever which was liable to attack sailors who
had been at sea for a long time. In a hallucination characteristic
of this condition the sufferer would imagine that the sea was
really a plain of grass – and sometimes leap overboard to try and
reach it.[16] In view of this, it is worth paying particular attention
to De Quincey's story that Coleridge, shortly before writing
The Ancient Mariner, had been thinking of writing 'a poem on
delirium, confounding its own dream-scenery with external
things, and connected with the imagery of high latitudes'.[17]

Phenomena of this kind associate themselves readily with a
theory of 'primary consciousness' such as that outlined earlier.
Under certain extreme pressures, it could be argued, the mind
sinks into its primary being and relaxes its normal tenacious
grasp of the external world. The conditions are then propitious
for a reorientation at the heart of sense-experience, leading, when
the sufferer recovers, to a new organisation of its dealings with
the external world.

In later years, Coleridge was fond of expounding a theory of
delirium and mania related to the distinction already quoted
from Erasmus Darwin. 'The excess of fancy is delirium, of
imagination mania', he said in 1810, according to Crabb Robinson;[18] and only a month before his death he was still making a
similar point:

> You may conceive the difference in kind between the Fancy
> and the Imagination in this way, that if the check of the
> senses and the reason were withdrawn, the first would become
> delirium, and the last mania.   (TT 23 June 1834)

If we now proceed to associate mania with primary consciousness
and delirium with secondary consciousness, we may begin to see

the possibility of a theory to explain how conversion could work (as, apparently, in the case of John Newton) during processes of delirium. As the consciousness loses its hold on the external world, there is a disordering of the processes of association, which causes them to work randomly. In such a state, the mind might be thought to be more open to the impact of forces subsisting in the primary consciousness.

In *The Ancient Mariner*, there are two specific references to such states of disordered consciousness, or 'swound'. The first, reflecting De Quincey's point, comes in relation to images of Antarctic cold; the ice makes noises like those 'in a swound'. Much later, the Mariner finds the blood flung into his head by an extreme motion of the boat and actually falls to the deck 'in a swound': while in this condition he hears Two Voices talking (and referring to his state as a 'trance').[19] An interpretation of the psychological work of the poem's action suggests itself under which the journey through the polar regions acts as an equivalent to delirium in disordering the senses. The Mariner is then exposed to the full impact of nature's primary forces, and exposed to them in a state which swiftly reduces his own sensations to those of single touch (heat and thirst); while his actual swoon, coming as an intermission during his later experiences, affords him an unusual access to the primary forces at work behind life, heard in actual dialogue, before his 'living life return'd'.

A reading of Coleridge's poem, on these terms would give particular weight to the breaking down of the Mariner's sense-organisation during his period of exposure to the forces first of ice and then of heat (a kind of externalised swoon-experience) and to his subsequent glimpse of other possible hidden modes of organisation in the world during the later stages of that exposure and during his actual swoon.

If we turn from Coleridge the esoteric psychologist to Coleridge the Unitarian preacher, we discover that he had for some time been contemplating the nature of religious experience as a path which could bring one through desolations and then, by way of ardent prayer, to final self-annihilation and identity with God. The path, hinted at first in 'Religious Musings', is shown in more detail in a notebook entry indicating the successive stages of prayer:

First Stage—the pressure of immediate calamities without
earthly aidance makes us cry out to the Invisible—
Second Stage—the dreariness of visible things to a mind
beginning to be contemplative—horrible Solitude.
Third Stage—Repentance & Regret—& self-inquietude.
4th stage—The celestial delectation that follows ardent
prayer—
5th stage—self-annihilation—the Soul enters the Holy of
Holies.—   (CN I 257)

This scheme (which may have been intended for a sermon) is
cast in the mould of traditional piety: it demonstrates the way by
which a human being, living within the ordinary terms of civilisation, might, through misfortunes, be assisted to the discovery
of a mode of true prayer.

The Mariner's experiences are not quite like this, however.
The sufferings to which he is exposed are more extreme than
those that normally afflict civilised man, and his 'conversion', if
that is what it is to be called, is not to a new religious position
but to a more generalised version of the Catholicism in which
he started out.

The phrases of Boehme quoted earlier from Coleridge's notebook offer another possible shape for the significance of the
events that overtake him:

> throned angels—upboyling anguish
> Leader of a Kingdom of Angels
> Love-fires—a gentle bitterness—
> Well-spring—*total God*   (CN I 272)

The first entries here can be closely connected to the idea that
in his primary consciousness man becomes aware of the nature
of infinity. On these terms, the presence of upboiling anguish
(like the 'mighty fountain' in *Kubla Khan*) is a direct visitation
from a disordered subliminal self. Once its nature is accepted,
however, the way is open for the recognition that, since wrath-
fires burn from the same elements as love-fires, all such experiences of anguish point back to an ultimate power which is, in
itself, less a fountain than a well-spring, displaying in its depths
the true form of infinity, and thus demonstrating the nature of
'total God'.

The entries overleaf in the notebook, which do not seem to derive from Boehme, are even more interesting:

in that eternal & delirious misery
  wrathfires—
              inward desolations—
an horror of great darkness
  great things that on the ocean
      counterfeit infinity—   (CN I 273)

The first line, referring specifically to delirium, invites attention in terms of the distinction between mania and delirium outlined above. In mania, we have argued, the primary consciousness is itself disorientated, so that one may even lose the sense of one's own personal identity; connection with the external world, while remaining apparently normal in the area of secondary consciousness, is continuously disturbed by disorientations from the primary level. In delirium, on the other hand, connection with the objective world of time and space being cut off, the primary consciousness is exposed to the play of its own forces, which, if unable to relate themselves directly to their infinite source, will 'counterfeit' it by producing an imagery of wrathfires, coupled with a sense of great horror and oceanic vastnesses.

The phrase 'counterfeit infinity' is, as W. Schrickx has pointed out,[20] from Cudworth's *Intellectual System*, which Coleridge borrowed in both 1795 and 1796. Cudworth asserted that infinity of duration, or eternity, was, in fact, 'nothing else but *Perfection*':[21]

> ... and because Infinity is Perfection, therefore can nothing, which includeth any thing of Imperfection, in the very idea and essence of it, be ever truly and properly infinite, as number, corporeal magnitude, and successive duration. All which can only, *mentiri infinitatem, counterfeit* and *imitate infinity*, in their having more and more added to them infinitely, whereby notwithstanding they never reach it or overtake it. There is nothing truly infinite, neither in knowledge, nor in power, nor in duration, but only one absolutely perfect Being or the holy Trinity.

Coleridge is taking the point a little further, by introducing an element of fear and desolation into the forms that 'counterfeit infinity'. The import of his phrases links closely with that of the well-known lines in Wordsworth's contemporary play, *The Borderers*:

> Suffering is permanent, obscure and dark
> And shares the nature of infinity.   (ll.1543-4)

Coleridge is apparently working his way towards some work which might embody these ideas in a setting of remorse and guilt. Lamb, meanwhile, in February 1797, reminded him of a former project for a long poem on the Origin of Evil, suggesting as further alternatives a dream poem describing a Utopia in one of the planets (the moon for instance) or a five days dream which should 'illustrate in sensible imagery Hartley's 5 motives to conduct.'[22ª] Coleridge was already moving beyond Hartley, however, to consider experiences, such as splendid sunsets, where (to quote the later formulation) 'we associate ideas in a state of excitement'.[23]

There now supervenes the walk, in November, during which *The Ancient Mariner* was planned. For details of the plan's development we are indebted to two accounts by Wordsworth, who later said that the spectre-ship was the first element to be introduced:[24]

> 'The Ancient Mariner' was founded on a strange dream, which a friend of Coleridge had, who fancied he saw a skeleton ship, with figures in it . . .

Wordsworth also suggested the committing of some crime that should bring about a spectral persecution:

> I had been reading in Shelvocke's Voyages, a day or two before that while doubling Cape Horn they frequently saw Albatrosses in that latitude, the largest sort of sea-fowl, some extending their wings twelve or thirteen feet. 'Suppose,' said I, 'you represent him as having killed one of these birds on entering the South Sea, and that the tutelary Spirits of those regions take upon them to avenge the crime.' The incident was thought fit for the purpose and adopted accordingly.
> (WP I 361)

Wordsworth's idea is in line with his assertion, in the 'Lines left upon a Seat in a Yew-tree' that

> he who feels contempt
> For any living thing, hath faculties
> Which he hath never used . . . (WPI 94, ll.52–4)

His own initial plan for the poem may have been for the crime
to have been punished through a spectral persecution by deathly
forms such as those in the skeleton ship, until the seaman who
committed the crime was brought to a larger sense of the nature
of life. According to his account, he also suggested the navigation
of the ship by the dead men.

Such conceptions brought into focus many of the issues of
mysterious energy and of the relationship between life and death,
that the poets had been exploring together. (Wordsworth's
further contribution, the lines

> And thou art long, and lank, and brown,
> As is the ribb'd Sea-sand

suggests that an obsessional concern with images of life and
death was dogging the poets even as they walked along the sea-
shore.) But it also brought into play Coleridge's conception of
the modes by which a consciousness might be changed and
sleeping faculties awakened. This element in the shaping of the
poem was inevitably his, taking him, as he tried to hammer out
ways in which those faculties might be aroused, into areas of
dream and trance where he was peculiarly at home.

The conception of the Mariner himself took its place naturally
among the poets' current efforts to interpret general human
experiences on a universal scale. For the account of his conversion
to be valid it was important that the central events should happen to a man who was an ordinary human being, rather than a
man of unusual educational advantages such as the hero of
Wordsworth's 'Lines left in a Yew-tree'. (Wordsworth himself,
in connection with that poem, recorded his boyhood pleasure
when he took an untutored lad, the companion of an itinerant
conjuror, to see the same view and found him delighted by the
scene.[25]) Yet by the same token it became difficult to project a
hero who would have the mental equipment to comprehend in
any exact terms what had happened to him. In reading *The
Ancient Mariner*, certainly, it is hard to believe that the Mariner
fully understands what happened to him on the ocean, or ever
will. Our impression is rather of a man who is now strangely at

the mercy of energies in his primary consciousness. He has become, by reason of those daemonic energies, a natural hypnotist
('For that which comes out of thine eye, doth make/My body
and soul to be still' says the Wedding-guest[26]); he is continually
driven to seek out a receptive listener; but the power to comprehend the full significance of the experiences which he relates is
lacking: it is his fate, as a figure of 'life in death', simply to suffer
a persistently renewed 'burning' of the heart, which must be
expiated – and only for a limited time – by telling his story again.

A larger understanding of his experiences, along with those
of his shipmates, is not to be sought from his own account, therefore, for that is contained within the limits of a mind that is
bounded by superstition. We need rather to consider the rôle
played by superstition itself in any theory of primary and
secondary consciousness.

Coleridge had a long-standing interest in the phenomenon, as
we may see even from his early 'Songs of the Pixies'.[27] Hazlitt
records that in 1798, at Stowey, 'He lamented that Wordsworth
was not prone enough to believe the superstitions of the place'.[28]
He seems to have regarded the workings of superstition as not
altogether unlike those of delirium, acting as an intermediary
between the world of firmly organised sense-experience and
buried awareness of – or capability of awakening to – further,
more profound forces.

A Christianised version of this theory may be traced in the
passages contributed to *Joan of Arc* in 1795, where he recounted
several of the 'legends terrible, with which/The polar ancient
thrills his uncouth throng' and continued,

> Wild phantasies! yet wise,
> On the victorious goodness of high God
> Teaching reliance, and medicinal hope,
> Till from Bethabra northward, heavenly Truth
> With gradual steps, winning her difficult way,
> Transfer their rude Faith perfected and pure.
>
> (PW I 135–6)

The theory involved is set out as follows:

> For Fancy is the power
> That first unsensualises the dark mind,
> Giving it new delights; and bids it swell

With wild activity; and peopling air,
By obscure fears of Beings invisible,
Emancipates it from the grosser thrall
Of the present impulse, teaching Self-control,
Till Superstition with unconscious hand
Seat Reason on her throne.   (PW I 134)

Coleridge may have regarded it as significant that superstitions and superstitious attitudes were particularly well-preserved among country folk, who were close to the processes of vegetative and animal life, and among sailors, whose well-known credulity might be linked to their constant exposure to the energies of nature in their extremest forms. It was possible that their superstition concerning the killing of birds was due to their isolation from the normal processes of life, which impressed upon them the mysterious powers inherent in the life-process – mysteries no longer properly acknowledged, however, but surviving as dim awarenesses in the depths of human consciousness. Such seamen no longer had any equipment to handle such ideas directly, but their superstition marked a wariness, a sense of something needing to be respected and propitiated. In the same way, their religious worship of the saints and the Virgin belonged with a sensed need for help from beyond their own limited individualities.

In the case of seamen, however, it could also be argued that the energies to which they were constantly exposed brought them within range of an awareness of the actual nature of the forces involved. Wordsworth's account of his narrator in 'The Thorn' (who, it will be remembered, becomes fascinated by the obsessive grief of a single human being, sitting by a single organism of vegetable life) is apposite here. He had envisaged, he says, someone like a captain of a small trading vessel, living in retirement in a village:

Such men, having little to do, become credulous and talkative from indolence; and from the same cause, and other predisposing causes by which it is probable that such men may have been affected, they are prone . . . to exhibit some of the general laws by which superstition acts upon the mind. Superstitious men are almost always men of slow faculties and deep feelings; their minds are not loose, but adhesive; they have a reasonable share of imagination, by which word I mean the faculty which produces impressive effects out of simple elements ... but they are utterly destitute of fancy, the power by which pleasure and surprise are excited by sudden varieties of situation and an accumulated imagery. (WP II 512)

Wordsworth's terms here, particularly his brief hint at the 'predisposing causes' by which such a man might have been affected – presumably his periods of exposure at sea – could be applied to Coleridge's Mariner, who might also, without too much exaggeration, be described as a man of 'slow faculties and deep feelings' with a mind 'not loose, but adhesive'. Like the narrator of Wordsworth's poem, moreover, his very inability to understand the nature of the phenomena that fascinate him draws him back to them again and again.

When we look at the Mariner's final state, then, we see that it is not, as in the conventional story of conversion, that of a man who has moved from one state of consciousness to a happier one, in which he now feels himself more at home. On the contrary, he has become a perpetual wanderer. If he has reached any firmness of mind it is in the single, over-riding conviction that has over-taken him as a result of his experiences. Through experiencing the ultimates of suffering and mental alienation, he has come to believe that the supreme human accomplishment is to be found in the exercise of love.

Despite such divergences, however, there is much in the annals of religious conversion, particularly as related by simple men, that links with the Mariner's central experiences. When the albatross falls from the Mariner's neck, the moment of relief is cognate with that in *The Pilgrim's Progress* when Christian, after many initial trials, comes to the cross and feels his burden, loosed from his shoulders, tumble away into the mouth of the nearby sepulchre. Even the imagery is not dissimilar. 'He looked there-fore, and looked again, even till the springs that were in his head sent the waters down his cheeks'.[29] And in real life John Wool-man, whose spiritual autobiography Coleridge mentioned ap-provingly in a letter of February 1797,[30a] describes how his first religious stirrings came through remorse at killing a mother-robin on her nest; later he speaks of 'feeling the spring of Divine love opened': and still later, of the 'well of living-waters; or the spring-ing up of living-waters' as the sign of a good Quaker meeting.[31]

By such usages, the biblical imagery of springs and waters had been drawn effortlessly into the language of personal religious experience.

Even the simplicity of the Mariner's final words to the Wedding-Guest has its model in religious tradition. It was said of the aged St John that when he grew too old to walk into assemblies of the faithful he would still be carried there, and that on such occasions he would give a single injunction, repeated over and over again: 'Little children, love one another.'[32] So, it might be argued, the experiences of the wisest of the saints and those of a simple man exposed to the extremes of nature might in the end foster the same single condensation of wisdom.

So far, then, the Mariner is to be regarded as a representative human being. But when we look more closely at some of his detailed experiences – and more particularly at the language and imagery with which they are described – we begin to see that the implications of his 'conversion' range much further. Within that fairly simple awakening there is being indicated the work of a more subtle and intricate transformation of the psyche, particularly relevant to the circumstances of the time when the poem was written. We recognise certain points of contact, in other words, between the Mariner's experiences and those of the young men who had come to a sense of hopeless isolation as a result of the political events of their time, including the aftermath of the French Revolution and the declaration of war on France by England.

Coleridge and Wordsworth, as we have seen, were particularly troubled by this phenomenon. Wordsworth has left an account in *The Prelude* of his own cynicism, which was so powerful at one stage that he 'yielded up moral questions in despair';[33] Coleridge in an early poem described how his sense of isolation had sometimes made him fancifully wish to actualise it more fully by becoming a lighthouse-keeper:

> Even there—beneath that light-house tower—
> In the tumultuous evil hour
>   Ere Peace with Sara came,
> Time was, I should have thought it sweet
> To count the echoings of my feet,
>   And watch the storm-vexed flame.

And there in black soul-jaundic'd fit
A sad gloom-pamper'd Man to sit,
And listen to the roar . . .

Then by the lightning's blaze to mark
Some toiling tempest-shatter'd bark;
Her vain distress-guns hear;
And when a second sheet of light
Flash'd o'er the blackness of the night—
To see *no* Vessel there!   (PW I 98)

He goes on to describe how his love for Sara had restored him to
a sense of humanity, replacing his gloomy desire for stimulation
from violent flashes like those just described by the pleasurable,
milder 'flash' of physical affection.

The progress of Coleridge's marriage had not altogether fulfilled the promise of these hopes, however, and at the beginning
of 1797 he was, as we have seen, being drawn towards sardonic
self-isolation. The composition of *The Raven* suggests a mind
which still finds it easy to fall into such attitudes.

Further light is cast on this aspect of his development by a
letter written to John Thelwall in October 1797, just before he
embarked on his major poems. Thelwall, we are to assume, had
been describing the sublime beauties of nature; Coleridge commented:

—I can *at times* feel strongly the beauties, you describe, in
—themselves, & for themselves—but more frequently *all
things* appear little—all the knowledge, that can be acquired,
child's play—the universe itself—what but an immense heap
of *little* things?—I can contemplate nothing but parts, & parts
are all *little*—!—My mind feels as if it ached to behold &
know something *great*—something *one* & *indivisible*—and it
is only in the faith of this that rocks or waterfalls, mountains
or caverns give me the sense of sublimity or majesty!—But
in this faith *all things* counterfeit infinity!— 'Struck with the
deepest calm of Joy' I stand . . .

and he goes on to quote the lines from 'This Lime-Tree Bower'
concerning his occasional sense of ecstatic unity with nature.

The introduction of the quotation into this particular context helps to correct any impression that Coleridge was by now so deeply under the influence of the Wordsworths as fully to share their immediacy of response to nature. What he is saying amounts in fact to a confession of his limited success in that direction. He would like to know a state where all things in nature are seen as beautiful, but this happens only rarely. Direct response to the beauties of nature comes to him normally as a subsidiary benefit, dependent upon his own efforts to apprehend the unity of all existence. The effort required (and the rarity of the experience itself) are commented on directly just afterwards:[34]

> It is but seldom that I raise & spiritualize my intellect to this height—& at other times I adopt the Brahman Creed, & say —It is better to sit than to stand, it is better to lie than to sit, it is better to sleep than to wake—but Death is the best of all! —I should much wish, like the Indian Vishna, [Vishnu] to float about along an infinite ocean cradled in the flower of the Lotos, & wake once in a million years for a few minutes—just to know that I was going to sleep a million years more.

This passage contains a swift transition from the directly confessional to a more complicated mode, combining self-deprecatory humorous comment on his own indolence with references to Eastern mythology which are detailed enough to suggest a more serious undertow. For although critics are fond of rehearsing the evidences concerning Coleridge's lack of determinate identity, it is also true that he had, at some deep level, an extraordinarily firm ontological personeity, which his own efforts to identify his own being with the being of God helped to fortify. And this kind of being, which could never be brought into communication with the world – which sometimes, indeed, led, through failure of grasp of the actual, to reverses in the world of sense – could respond to the beauties of nature in a very different way. For a moment the sardonic attitude which underlay *The Raven* peers out again as he reports to Thelwall that the feeling he has just described had actually been put into the mouth of Alhadra, the Moorish woman who seeks revenge in the last act of *Osorio*, when a moorish priest has just mentioned the owl:

> 'It's note comes dreariest in the *fall of the year*'—/this dwells on her mind—& she bursts into this soliloquy—

The hanging Woods, that touch'd by Autumn seem'd
As they were blossoming hues of fire & gold,
The hanging Woods, most lovely in decay,
The many clouds, the Sea, the Rock, the Sands,
Lay in the silent moonshine—and the Owl,
(Strange, very strange!) the Scritch-owl only wak'd,
Sole Voice, sole Eye of all that world of Beauty!—
Why, such a thing am I?—Where are these men?
I need the sympathy of human faces
To beat away this deep contempt for all things
Which quenches my revenge!—O would to Alla,
The Raven & the Seamew were appointed
To bring me food—or rather that my Soul
Could drink in life from the universal air!
It were a lot divine in some small skiff
Along some Ocean's boundless solitude
To float for ever with a careless course,
And think myself the only Being alive!   (CL I 359)

Coleridge breaks off his train of ideas immediately, leaving no
further clues as to his precise meaning. He has said enough,
however, to give pause to any critic who would make him at this
time too ready a believer in the power of nature to induce auto-
matic moral benefits in man. Instead, he is insisting on the
necessary ambiguity of his response to a nature which can either
produce such a sense of isolation in him as to make human
society welcome simply as a guardianship against the incrusta-
tions of total contempt – or occasionally, as in the experience
described in 'This Lime-Tree Bower', where all things in his
range of vision temporarily 'counterfeit infinity' in a more
enjoyable manner than that described in his notebook, enable
him to perceive in the glory illuminating a natural landscape the
lineaments of an infinity that exists, springlike, in the heart of
every human being.

In recording such ambiguities of attitude, he was by no means
out of touch with Wordsworth, who had also in the past been
drawn into a stance of sardonic isolation. The fact that he had
not finally succumbed, which he attributed partly to Dorothy's
influence, had led him to the conclusion (quoted in part above)
that pride

Howe'er disguised in its own majesty
Is littleness; that he, who feels contempt
For any living thing, hath faculties
Which he has never used: that thought with him
Is in its infancy.   (WP I 94, ll 51–5)

J. D. Gutteridge has pointed out that shortly after Wordsworth
read these lines at Stowey, Coleridge was writing to Southey, 'I
am . . . less *contemptuous,* than I used to be, when I argue how
unwise it is to feel contempt for any thing—';[35] in the drafts for
'The Wanderings of Cain', as we have seen, Cain asserted that
he had been punished because he 'neglected to make a proper
use of his senses'; even now, however, Coleridge is still uncom-
fortably aware that in many moods the universe appears to him
as 'a heap of *little* things'.[36]

The means of escaping such a state would seem to have been
an important topic in his dialogue with Wordsworth, who
among the first of his drafts for *The Excursion* wrote of the
benefits afforded by the Pedlar's early reverence for nature:[37]

There littleness was not, the least of things
Seemed infinite, and there his spirit shaped
Her prospects, nor did he *believe*—he saw.

The alternate state of mind, which insists primarily on an analytic approach, is attacked in some lines of early 1798, describing
how we by

still dividing and dividing still,
Break down all grandeur, still unsatisfied
With our unnatural toil, while littleness
May yet become more little; waging thus
An impious warfare with the very life
Of our own souls!   (WP v 402 (cf. 139))

The passage which relates most closely of all to Coleridge's ideas
is a cancelled passage for *The Prelude* (in a manuscript with
'Peter Bell') which follows some lines about the harmonies
created by nature, as perceived in youth:[38]

By such communion I was early taught
That what we see of forms and images
Which float along our minds and what we feel

Of active, or of recognizable thought
Prospectiveness, or intellect or will
Not only is not worthy to be deemed
Our being, to be prized as what we are
But is the very littleness of life
Such consciousness I deem but accidents
Relapses from the one interior life
That lives in all things, sacred from the touch
Of that false secondary power by which
In weakness we create distinctions, then
Believe that *all* our puny boundaries are things
Which we perceive and not which we have made
—In which all beings live with god, themselves
Are god, existing in one mighty whole.

When the last lines actually found their way into *The Prelude*, it was as part of a tribute to Coleridge himself, as one who, while knowing the importance of silence, was no slave to 'that false secondary power':

To thee, unblinded by these outward shows
The unity of all has been revealed . . . (1805 II 225–6)

In these lines, with Wordsworth actually using the term 'secondary power' in relation to the analytic side of the mind and subordinating it to 'the one interior life/That lives in all things' we have strong presumptive evidence of his fascination with the idea of a primary level of consciousness, inaccessible to immediate scrutiny, at which the human psyche maintained an immediate correspondence with all other living things through workings of the 'one Life'.

In Wordsworth's writings this idea bears heavily upon another. Human perception operates between similar poles. In the one extreme, all forms freeze into fixity; in the other, nothing has form; the very consciousness feels itself caught into a vortex of tearing energies.

These nightmare extremes correspond to possible modes under which the universe offers itself to perception. Seen under one aspect it is basically a universe of dead forms, with living movements a mere accidental excrescence on the surface of some, perhaps only one, of them. Alternatively, it may be seen as a mighty ocean of warring lifeless energies moving on one another in restless destruction, with the world as a small pocket of fragile stability in its midst. Yet normal human perception refuses to be taken over by either mode: through its almost miraculous power to blend forms and energies in unified acts of perception it preserves itself from the dreary extreme of the one vision and the terrible extreme of the other, mapping out for itself a path which makes possible the pleasures and sensitivities of everyday life.

If there is a bias involved, on the other hand, it is (in Western civilisation at least) towards fixity. The need for order and a stable life attracts the mind into channels of precision, raising an ever-present danger that the consciousness will itself harden in its own habitual stances, so that everyday life will come to be seen as mere mechanism.

Read in the light of these ideas, The Ancient Mariner may be seen as a subtle psychodrama, exposing the inner forces of human mental organisation. We are to picture the crew of the ship on its setting forth as composed of ordinary human beings whose perceptions have in the course of time settled into channels prescribed by superstition and by a religion which yet preserves within its apparently superstitious observances a recognition of the harsher extremes just mentioned. At first, their psychic equipment is adequate to the needs of their voyage. When they pass into the polar regions the cold of the area serves merely to stimulate their senses. The language suggests an atmosphere of striking beauty and of great dreamlike energies abroad: it is 'wondrous' cold; the ice is 'green as Emerald'; the sounds are reminiscent of noises projected from within oneself during a swoon.

Yet these touches also remind us that the voyagers have moved into a region which is dangerously near one polarity of their own conscious experience. If ice and snow are a stimulus to the animal energies of any living thing that finds itself among them, they also loom above and over them, rearing themselves into great indeterminate forms which, by 'counterfeiting infinity' quantitatively, may strike a chill desolation into the perceiving sensibility. The action of the Mariner, therefore, may be seen as a counterblow to such desolation. By drawing his cross-bow and shooting the albatross he cuts across the oppressiveness of the scene with a distinct action, transfixing the albatross into definite form.

The Mariner's shipmates know only the superstition involved; they do not understand the subterranean recognition of interdependency of life on which that superstition is based. While at first condemning the Mariner, therefore, they are equally ready, once the mist and snow have disappeared, to exchange their condemnation for approval. The effect of that disappearance, however, is the removal of all screening between the ship and the sun: it is left totally exposed to heat. The new situation aptly fits the original offence. The Mariner allowed himself to be governed by an urge towards fixity and definiteness; he now finds himself immobilised in a still ocean. The breeze has stopped, the sun is registered in the mind as a shrunken burning circle above the mast. The saltness of the water thwarts the desperate urge to drink. The only visible movements are horrifying, disgusting or maddening.

The torture continues. 'Withered', the word used to describe the state of their tongues, provides an imagery of vegetable death which is exacerbated in the image 'chok'd with soot'. And when the dead albatross is hung round the Mariner's neck 'instead of a cross' we are reminded both of the act which he performed with his cross-bow and of the fact that the crucifixion is, in itself, an emblem of fixity and definiteness, of all the destructive modes by which human beings try to reduce the complexities of human life to manageable form.

Despite an initial suggestion of freedom and release, the subsequent arrival of the spectre-ship only compounds the predicament. It introduces two figures who are fixed in the modes of life and death respectively, and who play a game which seals destinies with equal definiteness. In the case of the crew those fates are realised almost immediately.

> With heavy thump, a lifeless lump
> They dropp'd down one by one.

The sight and sound of their deaths is, meanwhile, part of the Mariner's own fate, confirming his fixity of isolation into a state of 'life in death'. He remains trapped like an ever-living insect in some ever-torturing substance. His ability to perceive motion continues as a mechanism, but the only movements, apart from the 'million million slimy things' – which again counterfeit infinity quantitatively, and so instil despair – are inside himself: the 'wicked whisper' which desiccates his very heart, or the beating of his eyeballs 'like pulses' – *suffering* a movement which in normal human life operates more unobtrusively and benevolently. Above all, his eyes are caught and held by the fixed curse that glitters in the eyes of the dead.

But in spite of the apparent hopelessness of the situation, which might seem to preclude the very possibility of release, a new process is eventually set in motion. The Mariner looks up at the sky and sees that not everything there is fixed: the moon, moving up the sky, is a reminder that peaceful movements are an irrefragable feature of the universe at large. This recognition opens his consciousness to the subsequent, more penetrating perception of the water-snakes, moving in free energy and impressing their beauty on several senses at once. Simultaneously, all counterfeitings of infinity give way to the true infinity in the depths of his being, experienced as a gushing spring of love.

This crucial event does not mark an end to the Mariner's sufferings, but it sets his experiences in a new mode. His continuing remorse is interspersed with visionary experiences which pierce the mechanisms of the universe to display its heart as fountainous. The most vivid of these comes when the dead seamen, enacting their fate by continuing to work the ropes of the ship ('They rais'd their limbs like lifeless tools—/We were a ghastly crew') break off at dawn to hymn the fountain of light and sound:

> The day-light dawn'd—they dropp'd their arms,
>   And cluster'd round the mast:
> Sweet sounds rose slowly thro' their mouths
>   And from their bodies pass'd.
>
> Around, around, flew each sweet sound,
>   Then darted to the sun:
> Slowly the sounds came back again
>   Now mix'd, now one by one.   (PW II 1039)

Such visions set the rôles of fixity and motion in a new context, which suggests that what are perceived as sterile opposites may on a larger view be seen as the inter-related poles of a dynamic process. In the events immediately following, it is true, they are vividly dramatised as physical phenomena. After the boat has stood still at noon, 'fix'd' to the ocean by the sun, it suddenly

stirs and makes a bound, which throws the Mariner into a swoon.
While in that state, however, he hears a dialogue between two
voices, the one questioning and reproaching, the other speaking
mercifully.

> 'Is it he?' quoth one, 'Is this the man?
> By him who died on cross,
> With his cruel bow he lay'd full low
> The harmless Albatross.
>
> The spirit who bideth by himself
> In the land of mist and snow,
> He lov'd the bird that lov'd the man
> Who shot him with his bow.'
>
> The other was a softer voice,
> As soft as honey-dew:
> Quoth he, 'The man hath penance done,
> And penance more will do.'

The dialogue between these two demonstrates the larger process
in action. Fixity and motion are now seen not as threatening
extremes but as twin polarities in the process of life. The first
voice, it will be noticed, is aware primarily of the land of mist
and snow. He immediately relates the Mariner's act of transfixing the albatross with his bow to the act of devotees of the
Law in nailing Christ to the cross. The focusing point of his
questionings is not totally fixed, however, for he knows that in
the world of life, at least, there proceeds out of solidity and coldness a sense of yearning, personified in the spirit from the world
of ice who loves the bird who loves the man who shoots him; he
cannot, however, extend his vision further. The second voice, by
contrast, expresses a vision which springs from the other pole of
life – expressing the warm, expansive and unpredictable power
which (in nature, for example) causes trees to secrete honey-dew.
His voice is closer to the depths of absolute genius, speaking
quietly and effortlessly out of primary consciousness.

The transposition of values inherent in these speeches, replacing nightmare fixities and motions by a vision of free-playing
life-energies and expansive forms, moving dialectically within a
larger life-process, assigns new prominence to the primary con-

sciousness, the active rôle of which is also suggested by the assertion that the movement of the ship is dependent upon the Mariner's remaining within its domain:

> . . . slow and slow that ship will go
> When the Marinere's trance is abated.

While his trance continues, on the other hand, the strange duality of extreme motion and extreme fixity is reiterated. As before, the First Voice, knowing primarily of fixity, responds wonderingly to the action and energy involved:

> What makes that ship drive on so fast?
> What is the Ocean doing?

while the Second Voice speaks again out of a vision of communicative benevolence and expansiveness

> Still as a Slave before his Lord,
> The Ocean hath no blast:
> His great bright eye most silently
> Up to the moon is cast—
> If he may know which way to go,
> For she guides him smooth or grim.
> See, brother, see! how graciously
> She looketh down on him.

The contrast between the stillness of ocean and moon and the driving motion of the boat also suggests the double process inherent in hypnotism, where the link between magnetiser and magnetised seems static, yet the controlled actions of the magnetised patient are undertaken within an illusion on his part of freedom.

When the Mariner wakes from his trance, the processes of alternation are resumed, but never again with the same overwhelming power. First he is aware of the eyes of his shipmates, still gazing at him:

> All fix'd on me their stony eyes
> That in the moon did glitter.

Then that spell in 'snapt', so that he is released – but released into the steady, panic-ridden motions of a man dominated by fear:

> Like one, that on a lonely road
>   Doth walk in fear and dread,
> And having once turn'd round, walks on,
>   And turns no more his head:
> Because he knows, a frightful fiend
>   Doth close behind him tread.

Fear, however, as often in Coleridge, is prelude to a more beneficial sense. He is aware of a breath of wind which yields no sign
of physical existence by sound or movement but which is yet felt
on the cheek, restoring to him a fostering sense of contained identity. This is followed by sight of his native country in a moment
of total calm and steady vision:

> The harbour-bay was clear as glass,
>   So smoothly it was strewn!
> And on the bay the moon light lay
>   And the shadow of the moon.

Yet this glimpse of the ordinary world transfigured with
beauty is to be the setting for still another revelation of the
extremes between which he is living – seen now, perhaps, in
their ultimate form. First he sees his shipmates in an enhanced
and more sinister version of their fixity. Aware of a redness
reflected on to his own flesh, he turns to see the cause:

> I turn'd my head in fear and dread,
>   And by the holy rood,
> The bodies had advanc'd, and now
>   Before the mast they stood.

> They lifted up their stiff right arms,
>   They held them strait and tight;
> And each right-arm burnt like a torch,
>   A torch that's borne upright.
> Their stony eye-balls glitter'd on
>   In the red and smoky light.

The new vision, more fearful than any that preceded it, since the
stiff arms are actually seen to be burning, is immediately followed
by another – expansive where the other was static. And this time
the Mariner's invocation of the cross is tempered by the oath 'O

Christ!' which focuses attention rather on the human being associated with that emblem of fixity. Just as sweet sounds had earlier
come out of the shipmates' mouths, so now each corpse is seen to
be surmounted by 'a man all light, a seraph-man':

> This seraph-band, each wav'd his hand,
>   It was a heavenly sight:
> They stood as signals to the land,
>   Each one a lovely light . . .

This, the last experience of the Mariner's before he suffers the
impulse and vortex that destroy his boat and restore him to the
human world, briefly replaces the endless alternations of fixity
and motion by a satisfying pattern of moving lights, offering a
more hopeful vision of human potentialities.

The Mariner's awareness has now undergone a change – expressed in the very stanza by which he relates himself back to
the scene where he and the Wedding-Guest are actually standing:

> What loud uproar bursts from that door!
>   The Wedding-guests are there;
> But in the Garden-bower the Bride
>   And Bride-maids singing are:
> And hark the little Vesper-bell
>   Which biddeth me to prayer.

If the noise of the wedding-feast sounds less harmonious now
than at the beginning of his tale it is described without any
marked moral judgement. But as he passes to the singing in the
garden-bower the Mariner conveys something of the new apprehension that he gained during his solitary experiences. This brief
paradisal glimpse modulates quickly and naturally (by way of the
'little Vesper-bell', with its suggested sweetness of note) into the
main resource which he now feels to be actually available to him:
that of attending the vesper service and praying in a spirit of love.

Read in its narrative position, the diction of the stanza is not
obtrusive; yet when compared with that with which he began his
tale it is seen to betray the extraordinary transformation which
has gradually overtaken him. More and more, we realise, we have
been listening not to the archaic phrases of a Renaissance
mariner, but to the accents of a man of early romantic sensibility.
When he tells of his dawn vision:

> Sometimes a dropping from the sky
> I heard the Lavrock sing;
> Sometimes all little birds that are
> How they seem'd to fill the sea and air
> With their sweet jargoning.
>
> And now 'twas like all instruments,
> Now like a lonely flute;
> And now it is an angel's song,
> That makes the heavens be mute . . .

We are (despite the archaism of 'Lavrock') less aware of the mariner-narrator than of Coleridge himself walking on the Quantocks (where 'high o'er head the sky-lark shrills') or of Dorothy listening to the sounds of unseen birds in a mist or of the youthful Wordsworth hearing a flute played in a lonely place by a schoolfriend. When he speaks of the sails making a 'noise like of a hidden brook/In the leafy month of June' or says of the breeze,

> It raise'd my hair, it fann'd my cheek,
> Like a meadow-gale of spring . . .

we pick up echoes of the North Somerset scenery in which Coleridge was living, giving a new actuality to Boehme's imagery of clear-running streams and soft breezes. And when the Mariner goes on to say of the final seraph-band that they imparted no voice –

> No voice; but O! the silence sank,
> Like music on my heart.

we need only recall Wordsworth's fragment about the man who would

> . . . gaze upon the moon until its light
> Fell like a strain of music on his soul
> And seem'd to sink into his very heart.
>
> (WP v 340)

to see how far the Mariner has become for the time being a surrogate for the shared sensibility of the two poets.

In this respect, the development of the Mariner's discourse is one of Coleridge's most spectacular feats. The mode by which, without the reader's being aware of inconsistency, he gradually infuses the superstitious, sometimes crabbed speech of the earlier part of the poem with a lyrical utterance attuned to the workings of his own sensibility is a marvellous piece of poetic conjuring.

The full process is also necessary to the poem's larger effect. Just as Wordsworth found it necessary to set at the heart of *The Excursion* a narrator who had none of his own educational advantages yet could plausibly be represented as having reached the same truths through reading some crucial books while living among the great forms of nature, so Coleridge wishes to suggest the universal availability of processes by which he and Wordsworth have been rescued from the despondency set up by the later events of the French Revolution. Conversely, the final words of the Mariner extend beyond the terms of Christian piety in which they are expressed, to cover the experiences of every human being who after being exposed to great privations has returned to find the 'littleness' of his or her native surroundings less dreary or boring than they seemed earlier.

It was primarily for this reason, we may suggest, that *The Ancient Mariner* was originally placed as the opening poem to *Lyrical Ballads*. Insofar as the Mariner's experiences corresponded to those of Wordsworth and Coleridge during the years after the French Revolution his final state could be said to give a tone to the collection as whole. Some of the stories there might seem ridiculous, some of the language unworthy of serious attention (so the argument would run) but to a reader who had experienced in any form such extremes of physical and mental hardship they would no longer be so: they would emerge instead under the illumination of an envisioned relief.

So far the argument holds good, and is true to the experience of many later readers as well. Generations of critics, however, have also expressed a dissatisfaction with the last stanzas of Coleridge's poem, a feeling that they do scant justice to the fullness of the poem's effect; and this judgement, also, deserves serious consideration. A part of the difficulty may be traced to the fact that by not allowing the Mariner fully to understand what has happened to him, Coleridge has forfeited some of the benefit gained by his initial status as a universal figure. But it is true that the reader, also, is not given firm clues to the nature of the significance which the Mariner has half-seen, half-missed.

Even if he turns to the last lines concerning the Wedding-Guest, which involve more direct narration, he finds no immediate assistance. The Mariner has told him that he will wake up a sadder and wiser man the following morning and so he does; but why? Why, for that matter, does he finally 'turn from the Bridegroom's door'? Is not the wedding-feast an open and immediate occasion for the expression of the love that the Mariner has just enjoined upon him? If there is at the heart of the universe a joyful harmony such as the Mariner described, would it not be well for him to begin cultivating it? Boehme, after all, following the Gospels, had envisioned heaven itself in the form of a wedding dance:

> The Musician has wound up his Pegs and tuned his Strings; the Bridegroom cometh, take *heed* thou dost not get the *hellish Gout* in thy feet, when the Round beginneth, lest thou be found uncapable or *unfit* for the Angelical Dance, and so be thrust out from the *Wedding*, seeing thou hast no *Angelical Garment* on.   (*Aurora* V 33)

Read from a different point of view, however, Boehme's passage offers a possible answer to our questions. Perhaps the Wedding-Guest has seen too clearly the possibility of such a ceremonial dance at the heart of nature to find satisfaction – at least for the moment – in its earthly counterpart. The counterfeit at hand, with its 'uproar', can offer no substitute for sights and sounds such as those that have just been evoked.

This does not altogether solve the problem, however. It may account for his now being a 'wiser' man; but why should he also be 'sadder'? Should not the awareness of such a possibility rather induce joy?

One reason for his sadness lies in the fact that the Wedding-Guest, like the Mariner himself, has been granted no direct means of access to the joy described. It has been presented to him as a tantalising and even compelling possibility, but not as an available resource. Another, more powerful, is that as a possibility it is not merely attractive but potentially transforming – sufficient, if taken seriously, to change human beings generally and their relationships with each other. To this extent, therefore, the Wedding-Guest is in a position akin to that of Wordsworth, who, in lines written while Coleridge's poem was being completed, turned aside from the joy that he felt breathing through the whole of nature on a spring morning to ask,

> If I these thoughts may not prevent,
> If such be of my creed the plan
> Have I not reason to lament
> What man has made of man?

(WP IV 58 app. cr.)

Such a reading of *The Ancient Mariner* presupposes that the Wedding-Guest's interpretation of the Mariner's tale is focused on moments of vision rather than upon the moments of fear: a reading which may understandably be questioned by readers who experience more directly the moments of nightmare, or who approach the poem with a scepticism which questions the Mariner's own view of the things that happened to him. That it was Coleridge's original purpose to suggest this, however, may be supported by all that has been said concerning his view of the intimate relationship between fear and vision. On such a view, it is the 'ministry of fear' to open the consciousness to a full acceptance of moments of revelation when they occur. This, in fact, is the manner in which we 'associate ideas in a state of excitement'. Once the primary consciousness has been opened by excitement of any kind, but particularly by fear, it is common for objects of nature to be seen in a sharper light immediately afterwards, it is being suggested, and this perception may be closer to the heart of nature herself.

The Wedding-Guest's behaviour in the poem fits this pattern closely. He is seized upon by the Mariner when he himself is in a state of aroused excitement, just about to enter a scene of anticipated enjoyment; he is held back by a man whose very appearance and behaviour instil fear; and he is told a tale in which fearful experiences and visions of great beauty regularly alternate. He is unusually fitted, therefore, to be as impressed by the events as was the Mariner, and to share his repeated sense of beauty and wonder at the revelatory scenes.

If Coleridge supposed that the same process would then extend itself to every reader of the poem, on the other hand, he was to be disappointed. The poem had a somewhat blank reception at its first appearance, some even professing incomprehension. These included Southey, who stated in an anonymous review:[39]

We do not sufficiently understand the story to analyze it. It is a Dutch attempt at German sublimity. Genius has here been employed in producing a poem of little merit.

Southey's dismissal is worth close inspection, however. If his reference to 'Genius' suggests a certain pique at the new alliance between Wordsworth and Coleridge, his gibe in the previous sentence betrays some awareness of the new modes that were being employed. His use of the term 'Dutch' might possibly include a covert reference to the Behmenist overtones in the poem:[40] certainly his reference to German sublimity, coupled with his assertion earlier that the poem, in spite of the author's claims, was not in the style of the 'early English poets', suggests a recognition that the ballad-form of this poem was not that of the old English ballad of the kind collected by Thomas Percy, but that of the 'long ballad' recently reintroduced into Germany by Gottfried Bürger,[41] and this debt turns out to be relevant to questions discussed above.

Bürger's ballads, particularly in the English translation by Walter Scott, are more polished and rounded than their historical predecessors. Internal rhymes are more frequently used and rhythms strongly regular. For present purposes, however, the most important feature of Bürger's verse is his powerful enactments, through rhythmic control, of movement followed by stasis. When at the climax of *The Chase*, for example, the Earl insists, against entreaty, on entering a sanctuary, it is to find that the chapel suddenly disappears, leaving him alone in a desolate landscape:[42]

> Still dark and darker round it spreads,
> Dark as the darkness of the grave;
> And not a sound the still invades,
> Save what a distant torrent gave.

In *The Ancient Mariner* there are several instances of similar shifting effects, which reproduce by variation of rhythmic movements the interplay of movement and stasis, of excitement and calm and thus provide a narrative counterpart to the dialectic between motion and fixity that is, on our reading, crucial to the poem's meaning.

Study of these rhythmic effects helps to emphasise one of the most striking qualities of the poem: the sheer verve of the writing. Indeed, insofar as the poem can be seen to reflect questions that perpetually moved in Coleridge's mind and the desolations to which they sometimes led, the Mariner's response to the bright movements of the water-snakes can be seen to mirror the poet's delight at the play of energies of his own mind. So long as it can sustain such a pitch of activity, such a mind can continue to wrestle with the enigmatic processes of nature, the incessant problems surrounding 'the riddle of the world', without ultimately allowing itself to be overwhelmed by them. And the very act of doing so keeps it true to its own moral destiny – at least on one reading of human experience. Complaining in 1796 that Priestley had asserted in three different places that 'God not only *does,* but *is* every thing' it will be remembered,[43] Coleridge had asked,

> Has not Dr Priestly forgotten that *Incomprehensibility* is as necessary an attribute of the First Cause, as Love, or Power, or Intelligence?— (CL I 192–3)

The existence of this statement casts new light on a little epigram, addressed 'To Mr Pye on his Carmen Seculare', which Coleridge contributed to the *Morning Post* in 1800:

> Your Poem must *eternal* be,
> *Eternal!* it can't fail,
> For 'tis *incomprehensible,*
> And without head or tail! (PW II 959)

As sometimes happens with Coleridge's jokes, a serious point is inextricably intertwined with the humorous one, which rests upon a concept of the eternal combining a sense of the incomprehensible with the image of the serpent with the tail in its mouth. 'The common end of all *narrative,* nay of *all* Poems', Coleridge wrote again, many years later, 'is ... to make those events, which in real or imagined History move on in a *strait* Line, assume to our Understandings a *circular* motion—the snake with it's Tail in its Mouth'.[44] Elsewhere he declared that ideally a short poem should end with a return upon itself – 'the snake coiled with its tail round its head'.[45] When, therefore, in the *Biographia,* he comes to claim (incorrectly) that the published epigram had been addressed, not to Mr Pye but to himself, as author of *The Ancient Mariner*,[46] new depths of irony open. If he had indeed produced in his ballad a poem which kept alive all the variant energies that contributed to the incomprehensibility of the world, yet which also contrived, through invoking the processes of the primary consciousness, to make those energies finally dance the circle which brought the Mariner back to a home country which, through transformation of his central perceptions, he could now see in a new light; then, however, absurdly 'incomprehensible' the resulting work might be to a casual reader, a discerning one might see that it did, in an important sense, mirror the relationship of humanity to 'the eternal'.

At another and less controversial level, the poem might be said to mirror that relationship in its very structure. The relationship between the energies of the inquiring mind that an intelligent reader brings to the poem and the poem's refusal to yield a single comprehensive interpretation enacts vividly the everlasting intercourse between the human mind, with its instinct to organise and harmonise, and the baffling powers of the universe about it. In this sense, the poem may be read as an experimental fiction of a very 'modern' kind.

Coleridge himself, however, was playing for higher stakes, as may be seen from a letter which he sent to his clergyman brother the same spring, describing his current attempts to create 'such works as encroach not on the antisocial passions':

> —in poetry, to elevate the imagination & set the affections in right tune by the beauty of the inanimate impregnated, as with a living soul, by the presence of Life—in prose, to the seeking with patience & a slow, very slow mind 'Quid sumus, et quidnam victuri gignimur[']—What our faculties are & what they are capable of becoming.   (CL 1 397)

There, if anywhere, we may see the 'moral purpose' of *The Ancient Mariner* set out. The quest to discover 'what our faculties are & what they are capable of becoming' is accompanied by the attempt to impregnate the inanimate, 'as with a living soul, by the presence of Life' – and that brings into play the devotion to moments of harmony and revelation in nature that he had been cultivating with the Wordsworths. Coleridge is concerned not only to present 'the riddle of the world' but to offer a possible

key to its solution. *The Ancient Mariner*, with its bafflements
and inductions of harmony, is thus a brief, limited experimental
model for much more extensive and ambitious works which
might, without violating the essential intractability of human
experience, cause it to be glimpsed in a single unified movement.

For the purposes of this more limited experiment, on the other
hand, Coleridge had enabled himself to circumvent the 'slow,
very slow' nature of the wider investigation by invocation of a
different poetic resource. In places he was drawing less on the
ballad (whether traditional or Bürgeresque) than on the nursery
tale:

> The wedding-guest sate on a stone,
> He cannot chuse but hear:
> And thus spake on that ancyent man,
> The bright-eyed Marinere.

In other details, such as that of the wedding-guest listening 'like
a three years' child', or the 'little vesper-bell', or the effect of
repetition within stanzas such as

> He prayeth best who loveth best,
> All things both great and small:
> For the dear God, who loveth us,
> He made and loveth all.

· there is a foreshortening, a rounding of the work of imaginative
energy into recreation of perceptions retained from childhood,
which inhibits the reader from questioning the details of the story
too persistently.

In thus allowing the poem to fall back on familiar rhythms and
long-retained images Coleridge had for this occasion, at least,
resolved some of his artistic and intellectual problems in a
manner which is consonant with one of his later assertions concerning genius:

> To carry on the feelings of Childhood into the powers of
> Manhood, to combine the Child's sense of wonder and novelty
> with the Appearances which every day for perhaps forty years
> had rendered familiar,
>
> With Sun and Moon and Stars throughout the year,
> And Man and Woman—

this is the character and privilege of Genius, and one of the marks which distinguish Genius from Talents.   (Friend II 73)

In this respect, the effect of the poem as a whole may be seen to reflect his larger claims in the same passage:

> to find no contradiction in the union of old and new, to con-
> template the ANCIENT OF DAYS with feelings as fresh as if they
> then sprang forth at his own fiat, this characterizes the minds
> that feel the Riddle of the World, and may help to unravel it!

Between the childlike rounding of imagery and syntax in some places, and the bounding, eager movement of the narrative in others, however, there falls the suspicion of a shadow, which was to darken over Coleridge's later work. Successful as the occasional nursery-rhyme diction is within the scope of *The Ancient Mariner*, one recognises it as another (albeit more successful) attempt to deal with the check that he had elsewhere felt obliged to impose (as in *The Eolian Harp*) upon his more adventurous speculations. Once again, the need for further intellectual questioning and exploration is foreclosed by giving a level to the story which involves assigning its narration to a sensibility more simple than his own.

In effect, moreover, the limitations of the device also made the poem unsatisfactory in certain respects as an introduction to *Lyrical Ballads*, since it lent a certain naiveté of tone to the whole. collection which, though partially balanced by 'The Nightingale', was not fully countered before the concluding 'Lines written above Tintern Abbey'. The fact that other poems in the collection were being written from a sophisticated point of view was, as a result, partially obscured.

It was perhaps considerations of this kind that led Wordsworth to conclude that the inclusion of the poem had been an injury to the volume and to place it later in the second edition, together with a series of criticisms: the principal person had no distinct character; he did not act but was continually acted upon; the events having no necessary connection did not produce each other; and the imagery was somewhat laboriously accumulated.[47] All these may be seen as registering a sense on Wordsworth's part that the serious intent of his contributions had somehow been compromised by the presence of Coleridge's poem, and an uneasiness about the blurring of other intellectual issues. Yet as criticism directed to the poem itself it was clearly unfair, as Charles Lamb was not slow to point out:

> ... I was never so affected with any human Tale. After first reading it, I was totally possessed with it for many days.—I dislike all the miraculous part of it, but the feelings of the man under the operation of such scenery dragged me along like Tom Piper's magic Whistle. I totally differ from your idea that the Marinere should have had a character and profession.— This is a Beauty in Gulliver's Travels, where the mind is kept in a placid state of little wonderments; but the Ancient Marinere undergoes such Trials, as overwhelm and bury all individuality or memory of what he was.—Like the state of a man in a Bad dream, one terrible peculiarity of which is, that all consciousness of personality is gone.
>
> (LL I 240 (Marrs I 266))

Lamb could tread the poem's mazes with such assurance, we may suggest, because he not only recognised its romantic power and psychological subtlety, but picked up more distant echoes, dating from the time when Coleridge was making his first attempts at a language that should bind heart and imagination. 'I never so deeply felt the pathetic', he wrote in another letter, directed this time to Southey's criticisms, 'as in that part, "A spring of love gush'd from my heart,/And I bless'd them unaware—" '.[48]

Such a comment directs us back to the central impact of the poem. Coleridge had come closer than he was ever to come again in devising a language for the heart's imagination. In so doing he had rediscovered a note which had been sounded by Shakespeare and some of his contemporaries and successors, but which had long been absent from English poetry. He had also enabled himself to speak on occasion with the accents of simple, heartfelt passion:

> We drifted o'er the Harbour-bar,
> And I with sobs did pray—
> 'O let me be awake, my God!
> Or let me sleep alway!'

At such moments, Coleridge achieves that 'true voice of feeling' which Keats and many of his successors were to make a criterion of poetic success.

If as he claimed, his poem is strictly inimitable,[49] the reason is not to be sought in passages such as this, however, for the true voice of feeling cannot easily be appropriated by a single poet. It is rather the general matrix of alternations between nightmare and vision, movement and fixity in which such actions are set that give the poem its special character. Even to readers who have not fully analysed the working of such modes, they are still apprehended as an essential part of the experience of reading the poem; and it is through them, perhaps, pre-eminently that the poem has gained its power to induce in generations of readers a uniquely powerful imaginative experience – reminding them vividly, among other things, that, as human beings, they are both fearfully and wonderfully made.

8

Animated Nature

Shortly after writing *The Ancient Mariner*, Coleridge went to sea for the first time, boarding a packet-boat bound for Hamburg. While William and Dorothy Wordsworth lay below, racked with sea-sickness, he joined a riotous group of Danes – one of whom, in the ebullience of intoxication, declared him to be 'a god' – and entered on a Bacchanalian progress which culminated in a 'sort of wild dance on the deck'.[1]

His appearance, however, was far from Dionysian, as his companions had already noticed:

> dressed as I was all in black with large shoes and black worsted stockings, they very naturally supposed me to be a Priest. (CL I 421)

There were also opportunities for observations of a different kind;

> About 4 o'clock I saw a wild duck swimming on the waves— a single solitary wild duck—You cannot conceive how interesting a thing it looked in that round objectless desart of waters. (CL I 426)

Through these various differing facets we catch something of the complexity of Coleridge's personality at this time: the vital spirits, the sobriety of his social self-presentation, the eye for isolated pathos.

During the preceding months these factors had all contrived to exist together, the poet and visionary keeping house with the Unitarian preacher and political commentator through the common purpose of evoking human sympathy. An extended example of his success in reconciling these various sides of his personality may be found in the poem 'Recantation' (later retitled 'France: an Ode'), his response to the suppression of the Swiss cantons by the French in 1798 and to all that that implied of abrogation from the brave principles of the original Revolution.[2a] In declaring his final disillusionment with the French Republic, he turned from such falsities of action to the true spirit of liberty, which he believed could be traced to the very energies of nature. The clouds, the ocean-waves, the forests (whether they were listening passively to the sounds of nightbirds or more actively making solemn music of their own under the impact of the wind), the rising sun, the 'blue rejoicing sky': all are seen as manifestations of liberty in nature herself. In a final ecstatic moment, standing on a sea-cliff where the murmur of the pines is heard in concert with that of the distant surging waves, Coleridge affirms his belief in the power of liberty:

> Yes, while I stood and gazed, my temples bare,
> And shot my being through earth, sea and air,
>   Possessing all things with intensest love,
>   O Liberty! my spirit felt thee there.

The theory of a link of energies in nature here culminates in a voicing of the belief that man, through sufficient intensity of outgoing sympathy, can at times feel its activity.

The closing lines make a good ending for a poem with a rhetoric which is primarily one of protest, but if taken seriously revive questions that have arisen before. Is there indeed some subtle connection running through the energies of nature? If so, how certain can we be that its energies are on the side of liberty and goodness? And in any case, if it is only in the pitch of generous self-projection on a high cliff that these links are sensed, what is their relevance to the fate of mankind generally?

These questions are faced in a much more local and particular manner in *Christabel*, a poem which, as has already been noted, represents Coleridge's last major exploration of the 'child of nature' theme, undertaken now against a setting where the powers of nature are presented working at so low an ebb as to appear ambiguous in their moral valency.

According to Coleridge's later account, the poem was first conceived in the context of his other contributions to *Lyrical Ballads*:

it was agreed, that my endeavours should be directed to persons and characters supernatural, or at least romantic; yet so as to transfer from our inward nature a human interest and a semblance of truth sufficient to procure for these shadows of imagination that willing suspension of disbelief for the moment, which constitutes poetic faith. (BL ɪɪ 6)

It was in the spirit of this plan, he goes on, that he wrote *The Ancient Mariner* and was preparing, among other poems, *The Dark Ladie* and *Christabel*, 'in which I should have more nearly realized my ideal than I had done in my first attempt'.

In the light of our discussion so far we are justified in giving some attention to the nature of the 'human interest' and 'semblance of truth' that were to be transferred from 'our inward nature' for the purposes of this poem. There are many obvious links between the Mariner's experience and Christabel's, for example; the main difference being that while he enters on his voyage as one who has allowed his feelings for life to atrophy, she as clearly retains them. One 'truth' that is presumably intended to emerge is that a consciousness which retains such links will not easily be seduced into evil behaviour.

There is another way in which the story seems to express humanity's 'inward nature', as Coleridge understands it. Where *The Ancient Mariner* shows us a man brought face to face with the powers of life and death in their extreme versions, *Christabel* presents those same powers in a different guise. The poem opens with a young girl entrusting herself to the world of vegetation by entering a forest at night and proceeds by the introduction there of a figure who expresses the energies of life in free play. The world of the nearby castle, meanwhile, is not unlike that of the enclosure decreed by Kubla Khan: a fortified structure ostensibly organised to preserve life but also masking a fear and desolation on the part of those who enclose themselves in it.

In the midst of this deathly home, Christabel alone retains a strong relationship with the sense of life – which is passed on most immediately, according to Coleridge's theory, through the link between mother and child. Christabel's mother died when she was born, but a strong link of sympathy remains. Christabel has not yet, however, learned to deal adequately with the energies of the world about her. They are the province rather of her father, a figure of 'commanding genius' who has lost his basic sense of relationship with life since the death of his wife, but who is still powerful in the exercise of command. When Christabel wishes to pray for her distant lover, therefore, she finds it natural to leave the castle secretly and go into the nearby woods, where she seeks out the strongest organic form she can discover, a great oak, for her devotions. Yet nature is not at this time informed with vital energy. The strong link of joy which was suggested in earlier poems by the relationship between moonlight and nightingales' song is here replaced by the more sombre suggestions of owls hooting under a veiled moon. If the link is still there, it is heavily muted, to a point where it might seem sinister rather than joyful. The spirit of life is represented solely by the one last leaf on the tree – a dead leaf which retains only the semblance of life to be derived from the wind that sometimes blows it into motion.

It is in this setting that Christabel has her first encounter with Geraldine, who embodies a complementary life-principle. Where Christabel's affinities are with the organic, Geraldine's are with the vital powers of nature, not here controlled by organic form, but subsisting in free activity, to be taken into the services of whatever higher powers are dominant at any particular time. So she is at once beautiful and secretly ravaged by hideous wastings; in touch with both the higher and the lower powers; attractive and fearful. She has distinct affinities with the figure of Life-in-Death in _The Ancient Mariner_, but without her immediate nightmare quality. Her most striking characteristic is that while Christabel is a creature of flesh and blood (there are various references in the poem to the movements of her blood), Geraldine is a white figure, 'with blue-veined feet': there is little or no suggestion that red blood flows in her veins.

The relationship between Christabel and Geraldine, then, is between two great powers of life, working in separation from one another. Christabel and her dead mother are linked by the power of the organic that subsists deep in the primary consciousness, expressing itself most readily in outgoing love. It is characteristic of Christabel's mother that she should have left behind her a distillation of vegetative powers, the 'cordial wine' made from wild flowers which Christabel gives to Geraldine, and which restores her briefly to her true stature, the vital in her working in harmony with the organic:

> She was most beautiful to see
> Like a lady of a far countrée.

The words associated with Geraldine all have connotations of energy: 'wild', 'glittering', 'bright'. The exact nature of her deformity, by contrast, is never made clear. (Coleridge's one explicit description, of her skin as like the 'Sea-wolf's hide', was made only in one copy and never published.[3]) What are being suggested primarily are the workings and ravages of free energy when separated from their living principle. Such a conception may be applied to many occult monsters, such as the werewolf or the vampire, creatures of outlawed energy which prey upon the warmth of human life. A similar yearning for human warmth exists in Geraldine, along with a potential destructiveness which makes the most fitting expressive symbol for her that of the snake, with its free destructive energy.

Because of her links with the energies of the primary consciousness, it is fitting that Geraldine should also possess hypnotic powers. The fascination which she exercises over Christabel – the 'spell' which becomes 'lord of her utterance' – is recognisably that of animal magnetism:

> But vainly thou warrest,
>> For this is alone in
> Thy power to declare,
>> That in the dim forest
> Thou heard'st a low moaning,
> And found'st a bright lady, surpassingly fair;
> And didst bring her home with thee in love and in charity,
> To shield her and shelter her from the damp air.

It is in the conclusion to Part One, however, describing the state of Christabel during and after the 'trance' imposed upon her by Geraldine, that Coleridge's esoteric theories are most fully in evidence. Precisely what is happening to her during this time is again not clear; but the central implication is that in some way deep psychic energies are being roused and worked upon. The effects of these workings are presented in the same ambiguous form as much else in the poem, but with a final accent always upon reassurance. If she weeps when she wakes, the tears leave her lashes bright:

> And oft the while she seems to smile
> As infants at a sudden light!

We are reminded of Hartley being taken out to see the moon, and of the implied beneficial effects from the light and impulse of that exposure. Christabel is like Enos, the child of nature, who preserves his central innocent vision; more specifically, she is

> Like a youthful hermitess
> Beauteous in a wilderness . . .

There is an implication, however, that during her trance she has been removed from all the reassuring experiences of 'double touch', to a point where the movements of her blood have almost ceased. Now, we are told,

> . . . if she move unquietly,
> Perchance, 'tis but the blood so free
> Comes back and tingles in her feet.

The further conjecture that the 'vision sweet' which she subsequently enjoys is of her mother, suggests that the primal organic link is reasserting itself in the depths of her consciousness, unviolated by the previous incursions of free energy: the section ends with the lines:

> But this she knows, in joys and woes,
> That saints will aid if men will call:
> For the blue sky bends over all!

The last line brings us back sharply to theories discussed earlier. The fact that human beings naturally see the blue sky as bending over them, despite the fact that it actually does nothing of the sort, was for Coleridge, we earlier suggested, a supreme example of the benevolent operation of the human imagination when double touch is powerless to magnetise it to tangible objects of the external world.[4] Such faith, therefore, is at one with the primal innocence which links and harmonises the energies of experience embodied in Geraldine.

Despite the neatness of their assurance, however, these closing lines pose in a more striking form questions which are raised by the poem as a whole. In what sense is it true that 'saints will aid if men will call'? Only, we must believe, in a very esoteric one. An outcry from the primary being will find an answer in the life-echoing universe: that seems to be the psychological point involved for Coleridge, who, beyond certain limited sympathies, had little of the Roman Catholic in him by nature. The further implication is that for Christabel and others like her the invocation of saints is a valuable and convenient fiction, through which the true work of the inner spirit finds expression.

The validity of such ideas is associated therefore with that of Coleridge's larger theories, which have in this poem focused themselves on the primal link between mother and child. Normally, on such theories, the link could be expected to extend itself into the long work of education through sense and double touch which is initiated at the mother's breast. But in Christabel's case her mother died in the hour that she was born. How then could she have come to know anything of the link between the fountainous impulsive self-giving of the mother and the light of love from her eyes? Coleridge's answer, to be found in a later note about the poem, would seem to be that such knowledge is, in fact, instinctive:

> Christabel—My first cries mingled with my Mother's Death-groan/—and she beheld the vision of Glory ere I the earthly Sun—when I first looked up to Heaven, consciously, it was to look up after or for my Mother—&c &c   (CN III 3720)

The full theory involved seems to be that any child born into the world will find a re-establishment of the link of life that it had known in the womb; if it is fortunate enough to have a truly loving mother, its subsequent course in the world will be set by its earliest education between its tactile adventures at the mother's breast and its constant assurances of love from its mother's eyes. But because Christabel's mother was already dead, she was forced instead to look up directly to the sky; and this is the explanation for the unusual bond with nature that she has formed over the years.

When the ingenuity of the theory has been acknowledged, we are still left asking about the extent of its validity. Is the link between mother and child really so centrally significant? That vital issues are in question few will doubt who have studied psycho-analytic work on the relationship involved and the importance that it can play in establishing or undermining the ontological security of the child. When the theory is drawn out into the semi-religious suggestion that the light and impulse of the mother's devotion are really living analogues of the divine love, on the other hand, many readers will draw back in scepticism.

Nor is it clear that Coleridge himself would have given whole-minded allegiance to the theories which lie buried in his poem. It may be truer to the facts to say that for him they had the status of an 'And what if . . .?' statement, and that his presentation of them in suasive fictional form rather than as dogmatic assertions was deliberate, enabling him to see how they looked, both to himself and his readers, when examined in such a guise. That he took the ideas involved seriously is to be seen from their reappearance in later writings; but they were never to be stated unambiguously in his published works. They provided apparently, an area for further exploration rather than doctrines for unambiguous proclamation.

The kind of perplexity which Coleridge felt about these and other ideas is suggested in some lines which he inserted in his translation of *Wallenstein*:

> He walked amidst us of a silent spirit,
> Communing with himself: yet I have known him
> Transported on a sudden into utterance
> Of strange conceptions; kindling into splendour
> His soul revealed itself, and he spake so
> That we looked round perplexed upon each other,
> Not knowing whether it were craziness,
> Or whether it were a god that spoke in him.
>
> (PW II 767)

Such lines may well reflect the experience of drawing out his theories in the company of men such as Wordsworth: a flow of ebullient ideas, produced in the heat of enthusiasm, might later, examined with a cooler eye, come to seem less plausible, yet still leave a fascination at the phenomena that had been temporarily drawn together, and the links between man and nature that had been thereby adumbrated.

Perplexities concerning the exact status of such ideas may well have played a strong part in the decision to spend the winter of 1798 in Germany. *The Ancient Mariner* could be published without difficulty as a poem of the supernatural and as an experiment, but *Christabel* was less tractable. If the ideas there transferred from 'our inward nature' did in some way indicate the point of correspondence between nature and humanity, it was important that further investigation should take place; Coleridge may, indeed, have been reluctant to continue the poem in the absence of further knowledge.

Various other reasons for the trip can be brought forward, ranging from the practical fact that the non-renewal of the Wordsworths' lease at Alfoxden had made it necessary for a move of some kind to take place, to possible issues of political expediency (E. P. Thompson has pointed out that the poets' known sympathies with Thelwall, coupled with the impending pressure on local gentlemen to join the militia made their immediate situation in England precarious.[5])

For Coleridge, however, an important reason for joining the Wordsworths was undoubtedly provided by the intellectual attractions of contemporary Germany. He had earlier spoken of a plan to take his wife and child to Jena for a time.[6a] During the previous few years, translations of works such as Schiller's dramas and Bürger's long ballads had drawn attention to a flourishing and adventurous literary scene.[7] The political and cultural state of Germany was also a source of interest. Undamaged by the revolutionary movements that had swept across France, less philistine than England, the German city-states, with their flourishing universities and strong cultural traditions presented a face of progress, enlightenment and benevolence.

It should also be noted, however, that the most important reason which Coleridge offered for his visit, both before and afterwards, was his interest in science and philosophy. He had an interest in theology, it is true: when he reached Göttingen he had Eichhorn's lectures on biblical criticism reported to him.[8] It was Blumenbach's lectures on physiology, however, that he actually attended.[9] He made some preliminary encounters with writings of Kant, similarly, but the philosopher who seems most to have occupied his attention was Spinoza. A year or two later, Henry Crabb Robinson, who had not at this time met him, reported hearing that he had become a Spinozist during his visit to Germany.[10]

The idea that Coleridge's decline as a poet was due to the fact that he 'forsook poetry for metaphysics', one of the most familiar in literary criticism, has a long history. Wordsworth is partly responsible: after Coleridge's death, he expressed his regret that 'German metaphysics had so much captivated the taste of Coleridge, for he was frequently not intelligible on the subject';[11] ten years later he was saying much the same:[12]

> in his opinion Coleridge had been spoilt as a poet by going to Germany. The bent of his mind, which was at all times very much to metaphysical theology, had there been fixed in that direction.

Wordsworth's exact terms should be noted, however. The emphasis is on *Germany*, and upon his being *fixed* in the direction of metaphysical theology. Wordsworth can hardly have found Coleridge's metaphysics in general damaging; for he himself drew heavily on those ideas. When he elsewhere described Coleridge's later state as 'hyper-metaphysical'[13] he was perhaps expressing more truly what he meant. Our examination of Coleridge's early thinking before he went to Germany, moreover, supports the view that what he meant by metaphysics differed in important ways from what he was to encounter in Kant and others. Carlyon, chief witness of his conversations in Germany, is a somewhat uncomprehending reporter; the context in which he introduces his discussion is, however, noteworthy. First he talks of the nightingales which could be heard from the walls of Göttingen, and of how Coleridge used to maintain, as he had done elsewhere, that they were the reverse of melancholy. Having quoted from the relevant poem, he then continues

> He had a great wish to make us metaphysicians, and the perseverance with which he would occasionally re-word the same train of thought, for the edification of his pupils, was quite extraordinary. It was in fact far from an easy matter for any unpractised person to keep pace with him in threading his metaphysical labyrinths. The impressions made upon the minds of his hearers often gave an abundant consciousness of new light: but they were too like the impressions of a seal

upon wax, when the seal adheres; there the impressions were, but where was the capacity of communicating them to others?

(Carlyon I 91)

On a later excursion, Carlyon recalls,

...He frequently recited his own poetry, and not unfrequently led us rather farther into the labyrinth of his metaphysical elucidations, either of particular passages, or of the original conception of any of his productions, than we were able to follow him. (Carlyon I 138)

Carlyon then quotes the first lines of *Christabel,* particularly those describing the hootings of owls, as a humorous example of a passage on which Coleridge commented at full length. He also makes it clear that commentary of this kind was devoted particularly to that poem and *The Ancient Mariner,* commenting that *Religious Musings,* which might have been expected to be a subject for exposition, was not included.[14] The implication throughout is that what Coleridge meant by metaphysics at this time was intimately related to his two major poems of the previous year.

Coleridge continued to explore related ideas as opportunity arose – and particularly when in congenial company. In late 1798, for example, when he had been suffering from a temporary blindness – the result, he said, of hearing that his child Berkeley was dangerously ill – he sent a letter to William and Dorothy Wordsworth, commenting on the fact that the eye seemed to have a life of its own:

O! what a life is the eye! what a fine and inscrutable essence!
Him that is utterly blind, nor glimpses the fire that warms
him;
Him that never beheld the swelling breast of his mother;
Him that ne'er smiled at the bosom as babe that smiles in its
slumber;
Even to him it exists, it stirs and moves in its prison;
Lives with a separate life, and 'Is it the spirit?' he murmurs:
Sure, it has thoughts of its own, and to see is only its language.

(CL I 452)

Still more striking are the letters which Coleridge wrote the following April, after hearing that Berkeley had in fact died some weeks earlier. To his wife he commented on the difficulty of realising the event when Berkeley had been, since he left England, necessarily a creature of his imagination; he went on to extend the idea:

> . . . Dear little Being!—he had existed to me for so many months only in dreams and reveries, but in them existed and still exists so livelily, so like a real Thing, that although I know of his Death, yet when I am alone and have been long silent, it seems to me as if I did not understand it.—Methinks, there is something awful in the thought, what an unknown Being one's own Infant is to one!—a fit of sound—a flash of light—a summer gust, that is as it were *created* in the bosom of the calm Air, that rises up we know not how, and goes we know not whither!—But we say well; it goes! it is gone!—and only in states of Society in which the revealing voice of our most inward and abiding nature is no longer listened to, (when we sport and juggle with abstract phrases, instead of representing our feelings and ideas) only then we say it *ceases*! I will not believe that it ceases—in this moving stirring and harmonious Universe I *cannot* believe it!—Can cold and darkness come from the Sun? where the Sun is not—there is cold and darkness!—But the living God is every where, & works every where—and where is there room for Death?—To look back on the life of my Baby, how short it seems!—but consider it referently to non-existence, and what a manifold and majestic Thing does it not become?—What a multitude of admirable actions, what a multitude of *habits* of actions it learnt even before it saw the light? and who shall count or conceive the infinity of its thoughts and feelings, it's hopes and fears, & joys, and pains, & desires, & presentiments, from the moment of it's birth to the moment when the Glass, through which we saw him darkly, was broken—and he became suddenly invisible to us? (CL I 481–2)

A few days earlier, writing to Poole, he had commented on the range of possibilities in greater detail (prompted partly, it seems, by Priestley's belief that newborn infants could not achieve immortality, since they were not yet conscious):

> I find it wise and human to believe, even on slight evidence, opinions, the contrary of which cannot be proved, & which

promote our happiness without hampering our Intellect.—My Baby has not lived in vain—this life has been to him what it is to all of us, education & developement! Fling yourself forward into your immortality only a few thousand years, & how small will not the difference between one year old & sixty years appear!—Consciousness—! it is no otherwise necessary to our conceptions of future Continuance than as connecting the *present link* of our Being with the one *immediately* preceding it; & *that* degree of Consciousness, *that* small portion of *memory*, it would not only be arrogant, but in the highest degree absurd, to deny even to a much younger Infant.—'Tis a strange assertion, that the Essence of Identity lies in *recollective* Consciousness—'twere scarcely less ridiculous to affirm, that the 8 miles from Stowey to Bridgewater consist in the 8 mile stones. Death in a doting old age falls upon my feelings ever as a more hopeless Phaenomenon than Death in Infancy/; but *nothing* is hopeless.—What if the vital force which I sent from my arm into the stone, as I flung it in the air & skimm'd it upon the water—what if even that did not perish!—It was *life*—! it was a particle of *Being*—! it was *Power!*—& how could it perish—? *Life, Power, Being!*—organization may & probably *is*, their *effect*; their *cause* it *cannot* be!—I have indulged very curious fancies concerning that force, that *swarm* of motive Powers which I sent out of my body into that Stone; & which, one by one, left the untractable or already possessed Mass, and—but the German Ocean lies between us.—It is all too far to send you such fancies as these!—'Grief' indeed,

> Doth love to dally with fantastic thoughts,
> And smiling, like a sickly Moralist,
> Finds some resemblance to her own Concerns
> In the Straws of Chance, & Things Inanimate!

(CL I 479)

He continued by commenting on the strange lack of direct grief which he now felt, and then quoted Wordsworth's 'A slumber did my spirit seal . . . ', which had been sent to him some months previously – and which seems to have been conceived very much within the same sphere of speculation.[15]

Perhaps the most striking word in the account is 'swarm',

applied to his 'motive Powers'. It suggests a Coleridge actively pursuing his idea that the operations of the mind should be conceived in terms of a vegetative power stimulated by energies of animation which cluster and shape themselves like flying insects or birds.

Coleridge's interests while he was in Germany ranged very widely: he explored various aspects of German history and literature and went on one or two walking tours. He also seems to have begun collecting data concerning psychology from the magazines which were beginning to circulate there.[16] Walking through Germany he compared the scenery with that of the West Country, particularly that near Holford and Porlock – perhaps recalling the stimuli that had surrounded the composition of *Kubla Khan*.[17a] There are also, however, signs of intermittency in his intellectual ebullience, the most ominous being a statement in March 1799:

> I have, at times, experienced such an extinction of *Light* in my mind, I have been so forsaken by all the *forms* and *colourings* of Existence, as if the *organs* of Life had been dried up; as if only simple BEING remained, blind and stagnant.   (CL I 470)

As in the passage about his temporary blindness, the link between light and organic life is heavily stressed.

On his return to Stowey, his interests and plans again showed considerable diversity, ranging from a rapt reading of Spinoza to projects for poetic colaboration with Southey. In spite of various trials, he was basically happy; and it has sometimes been suggested that if he had been content to subside at this point into the society which he had left before his departure for Germany he might have had a happier life.[18] Bringing up his family in the benign company of Thomas Poole, contributing to the life of the little Somerset community yet still in touch with a larger culture through books and visits to Bristol, he would have been in a position to produce a series of fine works in peace.

It is in some ways an attractive thesis. Yet it is also difficult to see how Coleridge's intellectual appetites could long have been satisfied by such a society. With his growing sense of all that was happening in intellectual life in London and on the continent of Europe, he needed to be working in a larger centre, and with men whose concerns were more like his own.

Such considerations may help to explain one of the more extraordinary episodes of his career, which followed just afterwards in 1799. Coleridge wrote to Southey on 15 October that he was off to Bristol and might be going to London.[19] Once in Bristol, however, he set off with Cottle to Sockburn in County Durham, where Wordsworth was visiting the Hutchinsons. During several weeks he seems not to have been in touch with his wife, for at the beginning of December he was forced to write to Cottle from London in order to discover her whereabouts.[20]

In simple human terms, Coleridge's behaviour to Sara at this time is hard to understand or justify. It cannot but have contributed to the coldness which was overtaking the marriage. At another level, however, the attractions of the Wordsworths' society are obvious. With Southey and his other friends he could enjoy pleasant discussions of literature and culture without being called to any particular effort. In the company of the Wordsworths, by contrast, his faculties were always on the stretch. A letter to Dorothy characterising John Wordsworth, whom he had recently met for the first time, illustrates the point neatly:

> Your Brother John is one of you; a man who hath solitary usings of his own Intellect, deep in feeling, with a subtle Tact, a swift instinct of Truth & Beauty. He interests me much.
>
> (CL I 543)

Each quality in turn adds a new dimension, suggesting the diversity of ways in which Coleridge felt his own sensibility being exercised by the company of his friends.

Even so, however, Coleridge might not have been so heavily attracted to them at this time had it not been for another important encounter. Biographers have noted that his visit to Bristol was the occasion of his first meeting with Humphry Davy, which was to be followed by strong mutual admiration during the subsequent years. The significance of this particular meeting does not, however, become fully apparent until it is set in the full context of Coleridge's intellectual interests during the preceding years. Davy, working with Beddoes at the Pneumatic Institute in Bristol, was a young man with ambitions rather like Coleridge's own, both in range and intensity. Growing up in a nearby part of England, he too had been fired by the late

eighteenth-century vision of the 'man of genius' and his potentialities. He had written a poem entitled 'The Sons of Genius'[21]
and set out to become both poet and man of science. In 1799,
when he met Coleridge, he was still moved by strong enthusiasms
and was in fact then in an unusually excited state, having
recently begun investigations into the properties of nitrous oxide
and its power of inducing euphoria. His experiments were the
talk of Bristol: even the staid Southey was overcome with enthusiasm, writing to his brother Tom of the initial effects,[22]

> Oh Tom! I have had some; it made me laugh and tingle in
> every toe and finger-tip. Davy has actually invented a new
> pleasure, for which language has no name. Oh Tom! I am
> going for more this evening! It makes one so strong, and so
> happy! So gloriously happy!

Coleridge also took part in the experiments, reporting his reactions in a brief paper. At a first inhalation he experienced

> a highly pleasurable sensation of warmth over my whole
> frame, resembling that which I remember once to have ex-
> perienced after returning from a walk in the snow into a warm
> room.

On the third occasion, he says,

> I could not avoid, nor indeed felt any wish to avoid, beating
> the ground with my feet; and after the mouthpiece was re-
> moved, I remained for a few seconds motionless, in great
> extasy.   (DW III 306–7)

On the last he experienced 'more unmingled pleasure than I had
ever before experienced'.

These reactions (which were echoed by many other partici-
pants) were shared by Davy himself. After many experiments
throughout the year, he set out on Boxing Day 1799 to intoxi-
cate himself with nitrous oxide, first habituating himself to it
and then inhaling twenty quarts.

> By degrees, as the pleasurable sensations increased, I lost all
> connection with external things; trains of vivid visible images
> rapidly passed through my mind, and were connected with
> words in such a manner, as to produce perceptions perfectly

novel. I existed in a world of newly connected and newly modified ideas. I theorised—I imagined that I made discoveries.

(DW III 289)

On coming round from this state, his emotions were 'enthusiastic and sublime', but the ideas were feeble and indistinct.

... One collection of terms, however, presented itself: and with the most intense belief and prophetic manner, I exclaimed to Dr Kinglake, 'Nothing exists but thoughts!—the universe is composed of impressions, ideas, pleasures and pains!'

(DW III 290)

Since by this time Davy had already conversed with Coleridge it is possible that his language reflects his ideas. Certainly, however, Davy's experiments must have been of immense interest to him, being relevant not only to his general interest in 'facts of mind' but more specifically to the theories discussed earlier. For here was evidence of a 'vital force' physically at work in nature, producing in those who inhaled it just such an expansive warmth as might have been predicted from the theory of 'single touch'. For a time it must have seemed to Coleridge as if his theories were being triumphantly supported (if not indeed demonstrated) by the objective methods of chemistry.

The existence of such implications helps to explain why Coleridge made so many enthusiastic and even extravagant claims for Davy in the years following. And it may be that it was the wave of excitement associated with nitrous oxide that encouraged him to stay so long with the Wordsworths – for it was Wordsworth who was in the best position to understand what Davy's experiments meant to Coleridge.

The general stimulus of the Wordsworths' company was further supplemented by experience of the warm family life of the Hutchinsons at Sockburn in County Durham and first stirrings of love for Sara, later to be Wordsworth's sister-in-law. The Lake District itself, now discovered for the first time, also proved highly attractive: and after various periods in London and the Lakes, Coleridge decided to settle his family in the North. By May 1800, he had found a house which he described to Godwin (echoing the terms of Davy's rapture over nitrous oxide) as being 'of such a prospect, that if, according to you & Hume, impressions & ideas *constitute* our being, I shall have a tendency to become a God – so sublime & beautiful will be the series of my visual existence.'[23] His more serious scheme of things was slightly different. Ideas and impressions might not *constitute* the being, but they were an important part of its active and passive life. It was important for its health, therefore, that there should be constant influx of fine impressions and efflux of good ideas. One could not become a god, but one might in this way maintain one's state as a 'son of god', in Coleridge's own sense of the term.

Such, at least, are the implications in a letter to Davy describing a picnic on the island in Grasmere Lake as they finally moved up to take possession of their new home:

> We drank tea the night before I left Grasmere on the Island in that lovely lake, our kettle swung over the fire hanging from the branch of a Fir Tree, and I lay & saw the woods, & mountains, & lake all trembling, & as it were *idealized* thro' the subtle smoke which rose up from the clear red embers of the fir-apples which we had collected. Afterwards, we made a glorious Bonfire on the Margin, by some alder bushes, whose twigs heaved & sobbed in the uprushing column of smoke—& the Image of the Bonfire, & of us that danced round it—ruddy laughing faces in the twilight—the Image of this in a Lake smooth as that sea, to whose waves the Son of God had said PEACE! May God & all his Sons love you as I do—   (CL I 612)

The acount involves an interesting alternation between vision and energy: first the peaceful impression of the view seen through the smoke of their small fire, and so 'idealized'; then the bonfire and the dance round the bonfire, reminiscent of the expressive obeisance to absolute energy in *Kubla Khan* – and finally the whole reflected back into the supreme stillness of the lake. The progression from idealising form to dancing energy, the whole then being contained in an embracing context of peace, which is typically Coleridgean, may also be traced in some of Wordsworth's nature poetry at this time.

It was a good beginning, to be complemented by pleasurable effects on Hartley's health. Coleridge told Davy triumphantly that Hartley was 'a spirit that dances on an aspen leaf' and that the air was 'a perpetual Nitrous Oxide' to him. His spirit of joy, indeed, was at present powerful enough to engulf experiences of pain:

> Never was more joyous creature born—Pain with him is so wholly trans-substantiated by the Joys that had rolled on before, & rushed in after, that oftentimes 5 minutes after his Mother has whipt him, he has gone up & asked her to whip him again. (CL I 612)

The activities of his children provided opportunities for more detailed observation of natural joy. Sometimes that joy seemed to be closely linked with the corresponding forces in nature, as when he saw them playing and giving themselves up to the energies of nature until they themselves were whirling and eddying:

> Hartley & little Derwent running in the Green, where the Gusts blow most madly—both with their Hair floating & tossing, a miniature of the agitated Trees below which they were playing/ inebriate both with the pleasure—Hartley whirling round for joy—Derwent eddying half willingly, half by the force of the Gust—driven backward, struggling forward, & shouting his little hymn of Joy. (CL II 872)

Such was Hartley's pleasure in these scenes that Coleridge was reluctant to have him christened:

> I look at my doted-on Hartley—he moves, he lives, he finds impulses from within and from without—he is the darling of the Sun and of the Breeze! Nature seems to bless him as a thing of her own! He looks at the clouds, the mountains, the living Beings of the Earth, & vaults & jubilates! Solemn Looks & solemn Words have been hitherto connected in his mind with great & magnificent objects only—with lightning, with thunder, with the waterfall blazing in the Sunset—/—then I say, Shall I suffer the Toad of Priesthood to spurt out his foul juice in this Babe's face? (CL I 625)

The strange and complicated workings of instinct in the animal and insect worlds, meanwhile, prompted a closer look at these manifestations of the 'one life'—and he was gratified that Hartley showed so great a pleasure in them:

Ants having dim notions of the architecture of the whole System of the world, & imitating it, according to their notion in their ant-heaps—& even these little Ant-heaps no uncomely parts of that great architecture—Hartley's intense wish to have Ant-heaps near our house/his *Brahman* love & awe of life/N.B. to commence his Education with natural History—

(CN I 959)

In his own cultivation of the sense of life during this time, Coleridge himself appears at his most attractive. Wordsworth's description of him in his 'Castle of Indolence' Stanzas fills out the picture. Despite his 'low-hung lip . . . Deprest by weight of musing Phantasy . . . ',

> Noisy he was, and gamesome as a boy;
> His limbs would toss about him with delight,
> Like branches when strong winds the trees annoy.
> Nor lacked his calmer hours device or toy
> To banish listlessness and irksome care;
> He would have taught you how you might employ
> Yourself; and many did to him repair,—
> And certes not in vain; he had inventions rare.
>
> Expedients, too, of simplest sort he tried:
> Long blades of grass, plucked round him as he lay,
> Made, to his ear attentively applied,
> A pipe on which the wind would deftly play;
> Glasses he had, that little things display,
> The beetle panoplied in gems and gold,
> A mailéd angel on a battle-day;
> The mysteries that cups of flowers enfold,
> And all the gorgeous sights which fairies do behold.

(WP II 26–7)

From Dorothy Wordsworth's *Journals* we catch supporting glimpses of Coleridge planning to sow laburnum in the nearby woods, or making a small lake by damning a stream.[24] In October 1800 he decribes to Davy a walk in which he was forced to shelter from a storm and sat, 'worshipping the power & "eternal Link" of Energy'.[25]

At the same time, his setting was slowly darkening. The

dialectic between vital forces and organic form had derived some
of its validity from the fact that he felt it as a continuously
operative fact of his own mind. At its best, the creative process
seemed to consist of harmonised energies, in the midst of which
forms of creation effortlessly arose, like the temple or city built
to music by the inspired poet of classical mythology. But he also
recognised that such periods of energy alternated with times of
sloth. In December 1800, for instance, he wrote to Davy of the
phenomenon by which we are

> one while cheerful, stirring, feeling in resistance nothing but a
> joy & a stimulus; another while drowsy, self-distrusting, prone
> to rest, loathing our own Self-promises, withering our own
> Hopes, our Hopes, the vitality & cohesion of our Being!—
>
> (CL I 649)

In the second set of formulations there lurks an image of hope as
a force which ought to move supportively around the organic
core of a person, but which may also atrophy, to the detriment of
that central being. Two years later, that same force was waning
fast as he faced his inability to resolve his domestic discordancies.
In the 'Letter to Sara Hutchinson' he commented on the change,
concluding with a rueful glance towards the elm/vine relationship – an ideal which for him was now to be placed in the past:

> There *was* a time when tho' my path was rough,
> The Joy within me dallied with Distress;
> And all Misfortunes were but as the Stuff
> Whence Fancy made me Dreams of Happiness:
> For Hope grew round me, like the climbing Vine,
> And Leaves & Fruitage, not my own, seem'd mine!
>
> (CL II 796)

The operation of the spiralling energies of vitality in himself is
not, he now recognises, to be induced simply by intent observation of the energies of nature in the external world: particularly
when the inward mind is oppressed by the precise negative of
that process, that sense of his own duties and responsibilities
which 'plucks out the wing-feathers' of his own mind. The final
version of the poem, in fact, by a precise reversal of the imagery,
produces serpents which coil harshly round a living form and
crush it:

> Hence, viper thoughts, that coil around my mind,
>   Reality's dark dream!   (PW I 367)

– 'Reality's dark dream' because they image, negatively, that
play of energies around the organic mind (like the serpent around
the staff of the healing god) that had characterised his being in
happier times. Now, he can project that state as possible only for
Sara, entering on her new life as a part of the Wordsworth
household. In the past she and Coleridge have sometimes stood
attentive to the sounds of life in nature:

> O Sara! in the weather-fended Wood,
> Thy lov'd haunt! where the Stock-doves coo at Noon,
>   I guess, that thou hast stood
> And watch'd yon Crescent, & it's ghost-like Moon . . .
>   (CL II 792)

Although the promise of those sounds is unlikely ever to be
fulfilled in their own relationship, she can still hope to enjoy a
pleasure like that of her favourite stock-doves, by sharing the
domestic happiness of her sister and friends:

> . . . feeling in thy Soul, Heart, Lips, & Arms
> Even what the conjugal & mother Dove,
> That borrows genial Warmth from those, she warms,
> Feels in her thrill'd wings, blessedly outspread . . .
>   (CL II 798)

The crucial phrase is 'genial Warmth'. Coleridge is drawing on
his theory of vitality and the power of genius to suggest that
Sara, in her vicariously maternal rôle, will still be open to warm-
ings of her animal spirits which will guarantee the continuance
of primal joy, keeping alive in her mind that combination of
secure love and spiralling energy which will maintain her as an
inhabitant of the universe of life by producing a correspondent
eddying vitality of perception:

> To thee would all Things live from Pole to Pole,
> Their life the Eddying of thy living Soul . . .
>   (CL II 798)

And that process will in turn be an echo of the similar process at
the heart of the universe which communicates itself by a combination of illumination and energy:

O dear, as Light & Impulse from above,
Thus may'st thou ever, evermore rejoice!

In the 'Letter' Coleridge does not speak of his poetic powers as being finally dead (which would be absurd in view of the quality of his writing) but of his 'shaping spirit of Imagination' as being 'suspended'. He still hoped that the suspended animation would end, and in a letter gave a witty account of what he hoped to find restored, drawing on his observation of the kinds of energies exhibited by various birds in flight:[26a]

> ...I wished to force myself out of metaphysical trains of Thought—which, when I trusted myself to my own Ideas, came upon me uncalled—& when I wished to write a poem, beat up Game of far other kind—instead of a Covey of poetic Partridge's with whirring wings of music, or wild Ducks *shaping* their rapid flight in forms always regular (a still better image of Verse) up came a metaphysical Bustard, urging it's slow, heavy laborious, earth-skimming Flight, over dreary & level Wastes. To have done with poetical Prose (which is a very vile Olio) Sickness & some other & worse afflictions, first forced me into *downright metaphysics*/for I believe that by nature I have more of the Poet in me. (CL II 814)

Even if the poetic power was not restored, he still found the inherent paradigm of life working in his mind, with a sense that the life power was itself infinite, and that it was only his own weaknesses and afflictions that were preventing him from producing it into creativity.

At the beginning of the following year he reiterated his belief in the universal link of life:

> ...I never find myself alone within the embracement of rocks & hills, a traveller up an alpine road, but my spirit courses, drives, and eddies, like a Leaf in Autumn: a wild activity, of thoughts, imaginations, feelings, and impulses of motion, rises up from within me...The farther I ascend from animated Nature, from men, and cattle, & the common birds of the woods, & fields, the greater becomes in me the Intensity of the feeling of Life; Life seems to me then a universal spirit, that neither has, nor can have, an opposite. God is every where, I have exclaimed, & works everywhere; & where is there *room*

for Death? In these moments it has been my creed, that Death exists only because Ideas exist/that Life is limitless Sensation; that Death is a child of the organic senses, chiefly of the Sight; that Feelings die by flowing into the mould of the Intellect, & becoming Ideas; & that Ideas passing forth into action re-instate themselves again in the world of Life. And I do believe, that Truth lies inveloped in these loose generalizations.—I do not think it possible, that any bodily pains could eat out the love & joy, that is so substantially part of me, towards hills, & rocks, & steep waters! And I have had some Trial.   (CL II 916)

In this passage Coleridge comes closest, perhaps, to expressing the philosophy of life that he had recently been exploring. The consciousness is seen engaged primarily with life – and therefore with the 'ideas' of life that eddy and circulate continuously within the world of sense. Death becomes an idea externally impressed from without, its dominance in the mind a result of perpetual analytic inspection of the forms of the world of sense and the phenomena of nature. For this reason, paradoxically, proper awareness of the nature of things cannot be gained so long as the mind is in too close a proximity to animated nature; it grows as the climbing traveller rises to contemplate hills, rocks, steep waters – forms that counterfeit infinity, being too great and powerful to be stamped into finality by the processes of the mind, and cannot therefore minister to the sense of death.

In spite of what Coleridge was saying, however, the sapping of the sense of joy that he had spoken of in the 'Letter to Sara Hutchinson' continued, so that by October he was forced to confess again that, in spite of constant exposure to beautiful stimuli, he was not truly happy. In order to explain his predicament he devised another variation on his imagery of the organic and the vital, speaking of

A sense of weakness—a haunting sense, that I was an herba-ceous Plant, as large as a large Tree, with a Trunk of the same Girth, and Branches as Large and shadowing—but with *pith within* the Trunk, not heart of Wood/—that I had *power* not *strength*—an involuntary Imposter—that I had no real Genius, no real Depth/—/This on my honor is as fair a state-ment of my habitual Haunting, as I could give before the Tribunal of Heaven.   (CL II 959)

The simile is not quite as self-deprecatory as it might appear
to a casual reader, since it involves both terms of Coleridge's life-
principle. One requisite of genius, under this, is a strength of the
absolute self, the central organic form around which the vital
powers play. Coleridge is arguing that while he has the vital
powers of genius, they are rendered impotent for want of that
central strength of being.

Not long afterwards he produced an account of certain diseases, drawing on the same distinction to suggest that in certain
'great and innocent' minds, the overbalance of the vital feelings,
by comparison with the 'organic perceptions', resulted in an
explosive reaction from the consuming faculties, such as stomach,
lungs and bowels, at the expense of the five senses used in active
perception.

Images in sickly profusion by & in which I talk in certain
diseased states of my Stomach/Great & innocent minds
devalesce, as Plants & Trees, into beautiful Diseases/Genius
itself, many of the most brilliant sorts of English Beauty, &
even extraordinary Dispositions to Virtue, Restlessness in good
—are they not themselves, as I have often said, but beautiful
Diseases—species of the Genera, Hypochondriasis, Scrofula, &
Consumption! This was at first a Joke; but is now no longer
so/for under the 3 Genera Hypochond., Scrofula, & Consumption (under Hypochondriasis implying certain sorts of Epilep-
tic winds & breezes, gusts from the bowels of the Volcano
upward to the Crater of the Brain, rushings & brain-horrors,
seeming for their immediate proximate Cause to have the
pressure of Gasses on the stomach, acting possibly by their
specified noxious chemical & [...] Properties as well as by
their general property of mechanical Pressure) under these
names I include (no matter how rightly) all those Diseases
which proceed from or produce, in one word, which *imply* an
overbalance of the vital Feelings to the Organic Perceptions,
of those Parts which assimilate or transform the external into
the personal, or combine them thus assimilated (stomach,
lungs, Liver, Bowels, & many others, no doubt, the use of
which is not yet known) over the Eyes, Ears, Olfactories,
Gustatories, & the organ of the Skin.   (CN I 1822)

It was his recognition of these intractable weaknesses that

prompted him to think of spending a year in some warmer
climate and finally drove him to Malta.

Despite his growing inability to rejoice in the beauties of the
external world, Coleridge continued to hope that this was due to
weakness in himself and that the joy he had known in earlier
years could be expressed and made manifest by others such as
Wordsworth, who retained an absolute strength at the centre of
their being. He also continued to hope that Davy's investigations
of the powers of nature might result in an objective demonstration of the validity of his theories. 'Humphry Davy in his
Laboratory,' he wrote, 'is probably doing more for the Science of
Mind than all the Metaphysicians have done from Aristotle to
Hartley, inclusive.'[27]

As Richard Haven has pointed out, Davy's own scientific
thinking during these early years was much more speculative
than it later became. In the very year that he met Coleridge he
published an essay suggesting that 'the laws of gravitation, as
well as the chemical laws (would) be considered as subservient to
one grand end, *Perception*.'[28] The essay was criticised for its
scientific shortcomings, and there are signs that Davy became, as
a result, more cautious. For many years he seems to have concentrated on limited scientific work within the acceptable framework of experimental method, while privately considering the
possibility that he might be on the brink of more extraordinary
and far-reaching discoveries. A letter of Coleridge's in 1807
suggests how far his private ideas continued to outrun those in
his published writings:

> Davy supposes that there is only one power in the world of the
> senses; which in particles acts as chemical attractions, in
> specific masses as electricity, & on matter in general, as planet-
> ary Gravitation. Jupiter est, quodcunque vides [Jupiter is
> whatever you see]; when this has been proved, it will then
> only remain to resolve this into some Law of vital Intellect—
> and all human Knowlege will be Science and Metaphysics the
> only Science.   (CL III 38)

A year or so later, he was wishing that he could give his life,
if that could give Davy enough health to discover 'the Element of
the metals, of Sulphur and of Carbon'.[29] The ultimate aim was to
discover 'the *synthetic* Idea of the Antithets, Attraction and

Repulsion'. If one could discover a concept that would reconcile *those*, then, surely, one would indeed be at the unity of things.

Coleridge also used imagery drawn directly and wittingly from the organic/vital paradigm to describe his friend. 'Every subject in Davy's mind has the principle of vitality,' he wrote, 'Living thoughts spring up like turf under his feet'[30] – cleverly combining the sense of an energetic man striding over grass with a corresponding sense that grass itself embodies the vital power of organic nature, not only rearing itself into its own form, but also springing back into it as necessary. The image of a common elasticity in man and in vegetating nature is thus made to support the very ideas which Davy is producing. For the same reason, he was not unduly disturbed by reports of Davy's success in the fashionable London world; instead he invoked his old image of the serpent entwining itself around the staff (encountered long before in the emblems of Mercury and Aesculapius in Tooke's *Pantheon*[31a]) to describe his faith that Davy's genius would turn all to good:

> ... may that Serpent, the World, climb around the Club, which supports him, & be the symbol of Healing—even as if in Tooke's Pantheon you may see the thing *done* to your eyes in the Picture of Esculapius.   (CL II 1042 (cf. 745))

While Coleridge continued to hope that Davy's experiments would support his own beliefs, Davy, in turn, describing Coleridge's genius as designed to create 'the new world of intellectual form', was drawn to use Coleridgean imagery:[32]

> Brilliant images of greatness float upon his mind: like the images of the morning clouds upon the waters, their forms are changed by the motion of the waves, they are agitated by every breeze and modified by every sunbeam.

The imagery conveys both the quality of Coleridge's mind and something of his favourite subject-matter as well – even if it may also suggest a certain sensed intellectual fragility. Before his friend left for Malta, Davy sent a farewell letter which was still more extravagant in admiration. Coleridge's creative energy was now uppermost in his mind:

> In whatever part of the World you are, you will often live with me, not as a fleeting idea but as a *recollection* possessed

of creative energy, as an *Imagination* winged with fire in-
spiriting and rejoicing.—

You must not live much longer without giving to *all men*
the *proof of power*, which those who know you feel in admiration. Perhaps at the distance from the applauding and
censuring murmurs of the world, you will be best able to
execute those great works which are justly expected from you;
you are to be the historian of the Philosophy of feeling—Do
not in any way dissipate your noble nature/Do not give up
your birth-right——

May you soon recover perfect health; the health of strength
and happiness! May you soon return to us confirmed in all the
powers essential to the exertion of *genius*——You were born
for your Country and your native land must be the scene of
your activity. I shall expect the time when *your spirit* bursting
through the clouds of ill health will appear to *all men* not as
an uncertain and brilliant *flame* but as a fair and permanent
light, fixed though constantly in motion, as a sun which gives
its fire not only to its attendant *Planets*; but which sends
beams from all its *parts* into all worlds . . .   (CL II 1103n)

In writing this, Davy is bearing witness to the existence of
elements in Coleridge's thought that have not so far been fully
given to the world. Like him, he is equating the rôle of genius
among men with that of the sun in the universe; he is also
picturing Coleridge himself as a man of creative energy and
'winged' imagination.

Coleridge, in reply, was less optimistic. Such hopes were now
rare with him, he said, repeating his image of the insubstantial
tree to describe his failing organic powers:

There *is* a something, an essential something wanting in me. I
feel it, I *know* it—tho' what it is, I can but guess. I have read
somewhere that in the tropical climates there are Annuals [as
lofty] and of as ample girth as forest trees. So by a very dim
likeness, I seem to myself to distinguish power from strength
& to have only the power. But of this I will speak again: for if
it be no reality, if it be no more than a disease of my mind, it is
yet deeply rooted & of long standing & requires help from one
who loves me in the Light of knowledge.   (CL II 1102)

In subsequent years his self-disillusionment deepened until he could actually turn his imagery of the organic back upon itself, rejecting some of his early enthusiastic notes concerning Boehme as products of a time when he had been[33]

> intoxicated with the vernal fragrance & effluvia from the flowers and first-fruits of Pantheism, unaware of its bitter root.

It is possible that the comment contains a covert reference to opium – itself a distillation from a beautiful flower: Coleridge may have felt that over-trust in the innocence of the vegetative had helped betray him into his dependency. Whether or not this is so, however, he inverted his favourite imagery of vital power to describe the condition by which he had been led to the drug, claiming that he had had recourse to it

> only as the means of escaping from pains that coiled round my mental powers, as a serpent around the body & wings of an Eagle! (CN II 2368)

Such imagery devolved readily into a still darker image: the engulfing vortex which, by comparison with the serpent which simply coils and crushes, seizes the victim and whirls it helplessly in coils of energy. Coleridge had described the whirlpool in one of his school exercises and in his *Joan of Arc* lines used a vortical image of a different kind:

> the Profound
> That leads with downward windings to the Cave
> Of Darkness palpable, Desert of Death . . .
> (PW I 140, ll 292–4)

At the nadir of his emotional fortunes, during the quarrel with Wordsworth in 1810, he wrote in his notebook, simply and starkly:

> Whirled about without a center—as in a nightmair—no gravity—a vortex without a center. (CN III 3999)

He also used the image of the Maelstrom (which he may first have come across in Darwin's notes to *The Botanic Garden*[34]) to provide a more sophisticated description of the insidious mode by which a bad habit could take hold of a human agent who had begun in a state of freedom:

This, I long ago observed, is the dire Curse of all habitual Immorality, that the impulses wax as the motives wane—like animals caught in the current of a Sea-vortex, (such as the Norwegian Maelstrohm) at first they rejoice in the pleasurable ease with which they are carried onward, with their consent yet without any effort of their will—as they swim, the servant gradually becomes the Tyrant, and finally they are sucked onward against their will ...   (CL IV 553)

The opposite vision, that of a peaceful circling energy around a strong organic centre, hardly recurs in his writings. There is, however, at least one notable exception. 'This Lime-Tree Bower', it will be remembered, contained a memorable vignette of circling energy and harmonising peace:

> And tho' the rapid bat
> Wheels silent by and not a swallow twitters,
> Yet still the solitary humble-bee
> Sings in the bean flower.   (CL I 336)

While at Göttingen he had experienced a similar scene one beautiful May evening, with a pleasant undertone of humming that surged occasionally into shriller clarity:

> The nightingales in a cluster or little wood of blossomed Trees singing—and a bat wheeling incessantly round & round.— The noise of the Frogs not unpleasant—resemble the humming of spinning wheels in a large manufactory, now & then a distinct sound, sometimes like a Duck, & sometimes like the shrill note of Sea-fowls.—   (CN I 421)

Coleridge later drew on this remembered experience for a passage in *The Friend*, interpolating it into a narrative which is otherwise largely literal translation from a German original to describe the voice of the heroines and its effect upon a receptive listener:

> If you had listened to it in one of those brief Sabbaths of the soul, when the activity and discursiveness of the Thoughts are suspended, and the mind quietly *eddies* round, instead of flowing onward (as at late evening in the Spring I have seen a Bat wheel in silent circles round and round a fruit-tree in full blossom, in the midst of which, as within a close Tent of the purest White, an unseen Nightingale was piping its sweetest

notes) in such a mood you might have half-fancied, half-felt, that her Voice had a separate Being of its own . . .

(Friend II 173)

Interestingly enough, Southey picked on precisely this passage for criticism:[35]

. . . the description of Maria's voice and countenance is too beautiful for its place; it is too much like poetry. We should beware of mingling fancy with the narration of what we believe to be the truth . . . an air of fiction is thrown over them.

Coleridge replied that the passage had been inserted 'in order to *unrealize* it even at the risk of *dis*naturalizing it', acknowledging however that he had 'not only thought the Voice part & Philomel out of place, but in *bad* taste per se'.[36]

Such an explanation provokes as many questions as it answers. Why should Coleridge have wished to 'unrealize' the passage? And what is the difference between unrealising and 'disnaturalizing'? Surely any writer would wish to make such a story more, not less real?

There is, I believe, an answer, which has to do with Coleridge's statement, many years later, in connection with his tendency to allegorisation, that he had been accustomed from childhood 'to *abstract* and as it were unrealize whatever of more than common interest my eyes dwelt on; and then by a sort of transfusion and transmission of my consciousness to identify myself with the Object.'[37] The process described involves a strenuous attempt to seize the essence of a scene of object, and at the same time, by creating a similar and corresponding state of mind in himself, interfuse his consciousness with it, so creating a stable centre to the perceived world. Like the dawn-vision in *The Ancient Mariner*, the images of fruit tree and bat, with the voice singing from within, gives a possible visionary centre to the story being related, inviting the reader to organise his perceptions around it. It 'unrealizes' the object only in order to create a steady central harmony between an eddying in the consciousness and an eddying in the scene, and so suggest a different possible ordering of 'reality'.

As the years went by, Coleridge's belief that he could demonstrate his view of nature on a large scale lost momentum. He

remained ready to seize on any phenomena that seemed in any
way to fit the paradigm, however. Reading *Antony and
Cleopatra*, for example, he comes across Antony's reference to
the hair that, soaked in swamp-water, will acquire a serpent's
poison, and comments:

> This, however, so far true that a horse-hair thus treated will
> become the supporter of apparently one worm, tho' probably
> of an immense number of small slimy water-lice. The hair will
> twirl round a finger and sensibly compress it. It is a common
> experiment with the schoolboys in Cumberland and Westmor-
> land.   (Sh C 1 87)

The idea of a horse-hair spiralling round the human finger
through the combined energies of the water-lice inhabiting it,
had presumably been picked up when he was living in the Lake
District. Similarly he notes an observation that fruit-stains will
easily wash out from a fabric so long as the fruit remains in
season, but become indelible if allowed to remain longer[38] – if
true an interesting illustration of the 'link of life'. His most
sustained attempt to give large expression to his theory, contained in the manuscript 'Hints towards the Formation of a
more Comprehensive Theory of Life' (written, apparently, soon
after he joined the Gillman household in 1816) makes considerable use of contemporary German scientific work while still
imposing an original organisation on the data. After this, discussion of the question is rare and largely allusive.

For Coleridge himself, the main continuing value of the
theory now lay in its potentialities as a tool for thinking about
animated nature, and more particularly about phenomena of
mind – sometimes wittily, as when he wrote to Sotheby in 1808,

> ... my thoughts are like Surinam toads—as they crawl on,
> little Toads vegetate out from back & side, grow quickly, &
> draw off the attention from the Mother Toad ... (CL III 94–5)

(the use of the word 'vegetate' is particularly telling).

In certain cases, the imagery could be used to give a new
incisive edge to a familiar word. The term 'revolution', for
instance, could be reinterpreted, by way of a literal reading, as a
process which could be either vortical and destructive or progres-

sive and creative. Speaking of his initial reaction to the French Revolution, he writes 'I was a sharer in the general vortex, though my little World described the path of its Revolution in an orbit of its own.'[39] When he describes *The Prelude* as Wordsworth's 'Poem on the growth and revolutions of an individual mind',[40] in the same way, his linking of the organic to the vital is not accidental but provides a precisely worded characterisation of the dynamic workings of genius as he sees them. The underlying formula emerges again many years later when he describes Swedenborg as 'a man of Philosophic Genius, radicative and evolvent'.[41]

This in turn bears on his use of related terms, such as 'evolution'. Thus he looks at the moon, 'dim-glimmering through the window-pane' and sees his response as the awaking of a hidden truth of his inner nature: 'it is Logos! the Creator! and the Evolver!'[42] Of nature he observes in 1817 that 'the whole Process is cyclical tho' progressive'.[43] Sensibility is described as 'a power that in every instant *goes out* of itself and in the same instant retracts and falls back on itself' – illustrated for him by the Pythagorean and Platonic Geometricians in 'the production, or self-evolution, of the point into the circle'.[44]

The pattern could readily be applied to human and social processes. In 1826 he could express a wish (if by now without much hope) that his son Hartley 'could but promise himself to be a *Self* and to construct a circle by the circumvolving line'.[45] It provided a ready shorthand for criticising those who failed to exploit their energies in an outgoing manner, as when he criticised Wordsworth's 'self-vorticity',[46] or lamented the 'all-sucking, all-whirling Money-Eddy' which he believed to be at the centre of England's troubles.[47] In one of his most despairing self-examinations he declared that there had always been a 'cold hollow spot' in his heart,[48]

as if a snake had wreathed around my heart, and at this one spot its Mouth touched at & inbreathed a weak incapability of willing it away.

To examine the fate of the paradigm more fully would take us into a long examination of Coleridge's later thought. Within our present scope, however, it is enough to remark that however persistently it might survive there, it ceased after 1803 to possess his psyche with its full former power. In the nature descriptions of the previous years there is an edge of running illumination which itself helps fulfil Coleridge's own paradigm: the stream of sensibility runs glittering as if in sunshine or moonlight. Despite the extraordinary sensitivity of later descriptions, that particular vivid vitality is lost in the later period, the paradigm itself remaining rather as a set of tantalising possibilities.

There is, however, one important footnote to be added. A few years before Coleridge's death, two German botanists, Schimper and Braun, who were studying phyllotaxis, the arrangement of leaves on the stems of growing plants, noted that this followed a spiral form and investigated further. What they discovered was surprising. One might readily imagine that the exact nature of such spirals would be dependent upon a variety of circumstances: the shape of the supporting stem, the strength and vitality of the plant itself, the incidence of rainfall, the accidents of light and shade. In point of fact, however, one would be wrong. The fact which emerged from these studies was that the spirals of vegetation always obeyed a mathematical law: that there was, indeed, a so-called 'magic formula' involved in these arrangements, corresponding to the Fibonacci series in mathematics.[49]

Excited by news of the current work, Goethe wrote an appendage to his earlier *Metamorphosis of Plants* entitled 'On the Spiral Tendency of Vegetation';[50] other scientists investigated the phenomenon further. The more general tendency of life-forms to move and formulate themselves in curves of various kinds was studied considerably in the following century; the most extensive survey appearing in Theodore Cook's *The Curves of Life*, published in 1914. Spiral patterns have since been found to be repeated in the most minute phenomena of the life-process, as when Crick and Watson identified the form of the DNA molecule as that of a double helix.[51]

Fascinating as such phenomena are in the light of Coleridge's speculations, however, the exact nature of their significance remains as unknown as in his day. Their mathematical form may be discoverable, but this simply means that the ratiocinative investigator who is also looking for meaning and purpose will finally be left in something of the plight which Coleridge himself (with his usual eye for an apt organic image) confessed to after a similar investigation:

I found myself unaware at the Root of Pure Mathematics—
and up that tall smooth Tree, whose few poor Branches are all
at it's very summit, am I climbing by pure adhesive strength
of arms and thighs—still slipping down, still renewing my
ascent. (CL II 714)

For some scientists, nevertheless, it is precisely phenomena such
as these that have remained most challenging, most indicative of
mysteries that cannot be penetrated by traditional experimental
methods.

During the years of his most adventurous speculations, the
chief value of Coleridge's interest in the wide relationship between forms and energies in nature as it affected his actual
writings was that it gave him a rare equipment for observing
and describing certain aspects of the natural world. As we have
also seen, however, all these activities were overshadowed by his
central interest in discovering whether or not it was possible to
establish the existence of valid correspondences between patterns
of growth and activity in nature and similar patterns in the
human psyche. In addition to the many observations of nature
just examined, the rôle of the psychological element in the potential correspondences had come to preoccupy him increasingly –
and even crucially – during the period we have been considering;
it is to that therefore that we ought now to turn.

9
Light and Impulse

Among the concerns that drew Coleridge to Germany, it is natural to include his interest in animal magnetism. In addition to the discreet hints of natural magnetism in *The Nightingale* and the overt presentation of hypnotic powers in the original *Ancient Mariner* and Part One of *Christabel*, he had been working with Wordsworth on a joint poem, *The Three Graves*, which involved cognate phenomena.

The latter poem, several parts of which survive,[1] is set in a village and devolves around the effects of a curse. In certain respects it is a natural successor to Wordsworth's 'Goody Blake and Harry Gill'; Wordsworth's collaboration may indeed have been offered in response to Coleridge's regret (expressed to Hazlitt at Nether Stowey) that he was 'not prone enough to believe in the traditional superstitions of the place'.[2] The belief in the power of cursing which is deep-rooted in most peasant societies had recently received some support from a case-history reported by Erasmus Darwin; from Coleridge's theory of primary consciousness it could be argued that in its effective form that power worked by summarily breaking the magnetic connections that link human beings to one another, causing certain subtle faculties that otherwise minister to life and health to wither at their roots.

It would follow from this that the most effective malediction, severing the most powerful unconscious link of all, would be that of a mother cursing her child; and this is precisely the kind that is involved in *The Three Graves*. The story concerns a young man, Edward, who, while preparing to marry the girl he loves, finds himself being pursued by her mother. His scornful rejection of her falsehoods and advances leads her in turn to curse both her daughters; the title of the poem suggests that in the completed poem all three women would eventually have died.

Just before the existing fragment ends, Edward has a moment of remorse for his treatment of the mother in which he cries, 'O God, forgive me! ... / I have torn out her heart'.³ His recognition suggests a key to the poem's action. His scorn, however strong the provocation, penetrated to the very heart by which she lived and so set inexorably in motion the destructive impulse towards her daughters.

The terms in which she curses the daughter in the room above carry the image a stage further:

> Thou daughter now above my head,
>   Whom in my womb I bore,
> May every drop of thy heart's blood
>   Be curst for ever more. (PW I 273)

There is an implication, not simply that the mother's curse is directed to the heart and heart's blood which are the central agency of life but that, by its very nature, it is peculiarly able to penetrate that normally spontaneous centre. The further ramification of Coleridge's theory that would associate primary consciousness with the warmth-sense in human beings is suggested by association of the cursing with changes in the weather and by a subsequent 'shivering' in the daughter, Mary – reminiscent of Harry Gill's teeth-chattering after Goody Blake's similar curse.

There is a problem of credibility at this point, obviously, since we are no longer dealing with speculations so firmly guarded as those in *The Nightingale* and the supernatural fictions. This story, by presenting itself in a guise of sober fact, directs attention to its own machinery. In such a setting, moreover, the cursing and its effects tend to intrude with a melodramatic force that borders upon the absurd. It may be that the difficulty of using such material effectively in a naturalistic context was recognised by Coleridge at the time of writing, lending urgency to his hopes that further light on the subject might be forthcoming in Germany.

If so, however, he was due for a sharp disappointment. Blumenbach, whose lectures he attended and who was one of the leading physiologists in Europe, was at the time a total sceptic on this subject. Not only was he unwilling to explore the field; he did not even believe in the phenomenon of hypnosis in the first place.[4]

It is likely that Blumenbach's extreme scepticism had a decisive effect on Coleridge's attitude, at least for the time being. Certainly it is hard to find an alternative explanation for the abruptness with which he dropped the subject immediately afterwards. *The Three Graves* remained uncompleted in manuscript and the revision of *The Ancient Mariner* for the edition of 1800 included the removal of his open reference to the Mariner's hypnotic powers. His only other mention of the subject during the next fifteen years was a disparaging side-glance in *The Friend*.[5]

In a mind so wide-ranging and inquisitive as Coleridge's, it might seem that the loss of a single speculative instrument of this kind would be of comparatively little importance: there would be many other interests to take its place. Yet there is reason to believe that the validity of this particular phenomenon was unusually important to him as poet. It had provided him with a key-link by which he could hold together a series of psychological speculations and apparently supernatural phenomena. 'The sudden charm, which accidents of light and shade, which moon-light or sun-set diffused over a known and familiar landscape',[6a] for example, was attractive on any count; but if one could suppose that there was a subtle physical force involved – that there existed, literally, a ground of Being –

> something far more deeply interfused,
> Whose dwelling is the light of setting suns . . .
>
> (WP II 262)

a mode of speculation was invoked that could be extended to certain mysterious aspects of human behaviour which were well fitted to poetic treatment. Such a belief, by its own subtle operation, could also encourage the evocation of charmed atmospheres by the poet himself, and, assist his rhythmic expression – even, perhaps, the very 'chaunt' which Hazlitt found characteristic of Wordsworth and Coleridge's recitation of poetry at this time.[7] After the German visit, certainly, the atmosphere which one associates with some of Coleridge's previous poetry does not recur with its old power. The effect is not totally disastrous, but there is an absence of the former 'entrancement' which does not seem to have been directly willed by the poet himself.

It also follows from our reconstruction of Coleridge's early thinking that a sapping of his faith in the phenomenon of hypnotism would carry implications for his psychological ideas as a whole, since in its original form the theory of single and double touch rested, we argued, partly on a foundation involving magnetism. Although removal of the 'magnetic' element from the theory deprived it of some of its suggestive power, on the other hand, it was not a fatal undermining. For whether or not magnetism was involved, Coleridge could continue to argue that his theory had, in its more general terms, provided an illuminating account of certain aspects of human behaviour. It remained the case that confidence in the reality of sense-perception seemed disproportionately affected by the availability of confirmation through varying sense-modes (notably sight and touch); discrimination between levels and qualities of consciousness, equally, had provided useful modes for examining the processes of sensation and thought. The functional value of such ideas was independent of any 'magnetic' dimension involved.

The attempt to link the main levels of consciousness with the distinction between the organic and the vital was also unaffected – indeed it may have been encouraged, as an alternative mode of explanation. The primary level of consciousness, it could be argued, found its true focus in the basic organic life of the individual, while his vital spirits, working through the activity of the senses, could either swarm around that inward centre or attach themselves to the forms of the outer world. To the primary level belonged the operations of memory, of image-making and of a central, unific identity; to the active energy of the senses the gathering and arrangement of impressions furnished by the outside world. The vital spirits, playing between these two spheres, would ideally keep the self in relationship to the outside world while preserving the integrity of its inner life, so 'constructing a self by the circumvolving line'. In less happy circumstances, however, they might either attach themselves too exclusively to the organic centre, producing for example, the 'self-vorticity' which, as mentioned above,[8] he thought to be a negative element in Wordsworth's genial power, or (more commonly) fix themselves so firmly and exclusively to the world of external forms that they became lifeless instruments of analysis, simply devoted to manipulating a world of objects. In the latter case there might be, in the strict sense, no true self at all. 'Poor Lloyd', wrote Coleridge in 1800,

> . . . every Hour new creates him—he is his own Posterity in a perpetually flowing Series—& his Body unfortunately retaining an external Identity, THEIR mutual contradictions & disagreeings are united under one name, & of course are called Lies, Treachery, & Rascality!　　　　　(CL I 563)

'The same circumstances', he continued, 'that have wrenched his Morals, prevent in him any salutary Exercise of Genius . . .': in other words, his loss of connection with his own organic centre had also deprived him of the formative power which might otherwise have allowed his genial powers to flourish. At times, Coleridge was still tempted into more extravagant speculation, as when he heard that Godwin's tragedy was about to be produced in London and wrote offering his good wishes. As before, however, the speculation which he allowed himself concerning the possibility of mysterious influences between living beings was immediately checked:

> Indeed, indeed, Godwin! such a stream of hope & fear rushed in on me, when I read the sentence, as you would not permit yourself to feel. If there be any thing yet undreamt of in our philosophy; if it be, or if it be possible, that thought can impel thought out of the visual limit of a man's own scull & heart; if the clusters of ideas, which constitute our identity, do ever connect & unite into a greater Whole; if feelings could ever propagate themselves without the servile ministrations of undulating air or reflected light; I seem to feel within myself a strength & a power of desire, that might dart a modifying, commanding impulse on a whole Theatre. What does all this mean? Alas! that sober sense should know no other way to construe all this except by the tame phrase—I wish you success.—　　　　　(CL I 624)

Despite such doubts concerning the exact status of his own theories, their activity in his mind provided Coleridge with speculative instruments of considerable scope. Upon their foundation may be seen to rest the idiosyncratic qualities of certain larger features in his later thinking, such as the distinctions between imagination and fancy, between genius and talent and between reason and understanding. In each case the distinction receives its true Coleridgean impress only when set in the context of psychological theories which locate the basic source of imagination, genius and reason at the level of organic being that is known chiefly to the primary consciousness; fancy, talent and understanding being seen, by the same token, as the prerogative of those who have lost contact with that primary level and must therefore focus upon the 'fixities and definites'[9] offered by the external world of forms.

The indications are, in fact, that Coleridge's disillusionment concerning animal magnetism did little to check his interest in these aspects of his theory; if anything it incited him rather to look for psychological data (including case-histories) which would provide solid evidence against which to test them. Describing his conversation in May 1799 Carlyon recalls how when they were standing on one of the Hartz mountains and contemplating the nearby peaks, a member of the party commented on the fact that only man seemed to respond to such scenery with any pleasure. Whilst agreeing, Coleridge dwelt on the paradox that man did so in spite of being short-lived:

> Eighty-four years is almost his farthest limit, whilst the rocks and mountains are, many of them, undoubtedly pre-Adamitical. Hence he drew an argument for the immortality of the soul; since, that being admitted, the means will be no more than adequate to the end. (Carlyon I 138)

Such a comment would hardly have sprung to Coleridge's lips had he not already devoted some thought to the nature of pleasurable experience and its association with the sense of immortality. In cold blood, he seems to be saying, there is little reason for a mortal to contemplate the existence of mountains with pleasure; we would simply expect him to be irritated by their permanence in comparison with his own transitoriness; the fact of his warm-blooded delight in their existence becomes, therefore, an argument in favour of his having a subconscious knowledge of his own immortality.

The obvious objections to which the argument is open were evidently obviated for Coleridge by his belief in the existence of many other such intimations. For a modern sceptic, the sense of immortality which haunts human beings may be no more than an obstinate delusion; for Coleridge it was seriously to be considered as a possible pointer to primary truth. 'All intense passions,' he wrote some years later, 'have faith in their own eternity, & thence in the eternity of their objects.'[10]

There were other ways in which passion could be thought of as bringing into the open aspects of primary consciousness which were not normally exposed. In a letter from Germany Coleridge wrote of some verses written by a girl suicide just before she died with her lover, commenting on the strangeness of the fact that at such a moment she should have felt herself impelled to write in rhyme and going on to suggest that she might actually have been led by the 'wild nature of the verse' to the thoughts which she expressed in them.[11] The implication, again, is that passionate grief actually brings the creative faculties into play – an idea elsewhere illustrated for him in the speech of Constance in *King John* which began 'Grief fills the room up of my absent child/—'.[12] In such cases the excited working of primary consciousness could be seen to involve a compulsive projection of form which was in turn dominated by an obsessive energy of repetition.

After Coleridge's return from Germany, the lack which had been left in his thinking by doubts concerning animal magnetism was partially replenished by his learning of Davy's discoveries. Here, at least, there was no doubting the evidence: everyone who participated in the experiments acknowledged the extraordinary mental and physical effects experienced. Coleridge's reference to the 'sensation of warmth' that spread over his frame on inhaling the gas suggests that the relationship between primary consciousness and the warmth-sense may have been in his mind as he participated, particularly since we find him observing shortly afterwards (on using a warm footbath) that 'the first Plunge into very warm Water produces precisely the same sensation, as a Plunge into exceedingly cold Water would' and then, in a letter to Davy several weeks later, asking him for an explanation of the same phenomenon 'in a philosophical Language divested of corpuscular Theories.'[13]

The kind of significance which he attached to Davy's experiments is shown still more clearly by a letter of July 1800, where

he wrote of a case which he had come across in a German magazine (*Moritz's Magazine for Experimental Psychology*). This
recorded a case of fever in an adolescent which lasted for four
weeks and was then exacerbated by convulsions and a strong
delirium:

> The subject of Death, & his old occupations as a merchant's
> clerk formed the subjects of his Discourse—in which he dis-
> covered a power of mind, a regularity, a logic, an eloquence,
> wholly unknown in him in his state of health.   (CL I 605)

During one of the paroxysms, a vein was opened, and the blood
proved to be almost black: it burst from the vein and foamed
violently. When the paroxysms were over, so far from appearing
exhausted he was then in extremely high spirits. Asked how he
felt during the onset of an attack, he spoke of a sensation of heat
from the stomach spreading upwards until it reached the head,
after which he felt more and more dizzy and drunken until he
lost all consciousness. When the attacks finally ceased, he was
restored to good health, but retained no consciousness of anything that had happened while they lasted. Both at the beginning
and end of his account, Coleridge drew a parallel with the effects
of nitrous oxide; the account evidently offered further potential
material to his consideration of the extraordinary ability of
'genial' power to manifest itself at times when the conscious
powers were suspended.

The euphoria created by participating in Davy's experiments
also helps to explain an intellectual excitement to be traced in
certain notebook entries made during his subsequent tour of the
North. These are concerned partly with the relationship between
his psychological enquiries and his metaphysical interests. He is
considering the paradox of the relationship between unity and
diversity, including the strange power of the mind to see things
disparately yet at the same time hold them in unity – a phenomenon which would be explained more easily if two levels of consciousness could be shown to co-exist in all waking experience.

Just before, Coleridge had projected the distinction into
religious terms, planning to co-operate with Southey in a poem
on Mahomet in which there would have been two chief religious
protagonists: Mahomet himself, as representative of impersonal
Theism, with all its associated traditional machinery, and a fetish

worshipper (an 'Okenist + Zoo-magnetist with the Night-side of Nature') who 'adored the sensible only, and held no religion common to all men, or to any number of men other than as they chanced at the same moment to be acted upon by the same influence.'[14] Now as he passed through the North he reflected in successive notes on the nature of Plato's genius and then on the perception of natural imagery:

> The sunny mist, the luminous gloom of Plato—
> Mist as from volcano—
> Waterfall rolled after long looking at like a segment of
> a Wheel—the rock gleaming thro' it—
> Amid the roar a noise as of innumerable grasshoppers or
> of spinning wheels.   (CN I 528–9)

The internal and external are again closely related here: first the sense of illumination through mist, then the sense of oneness in diversity as perception insists on turning the diverse movement of the waterfall into the single movement of a wheel – coupled with a complementary sense of diversity within oneness as its single roar gives the impression of being made by innumerable sounding insects or small wheels.

The relationship between the diversity of phenomena and the extraordinary unifying power of perception was much in his mind during the tour: after looking at a landscape and noting how a road against a hill looked exactly like the opening to a womb, he wrote in another notebook entry:

> If I begin a poem of Spinoza thus it should begin/I would
> make a pilgrimage to the burning sands of Arabia, or &c &c
> to find the Man who could explain to me there can be *oneness*,
> there being infinite Perceptions—yet there must be a *oneness*,
> not an intense Union but an Absolute Unity . . .   (CN I 556)

In the same way he meditated upon the 'spot-sprigged' print of the Blackwall Ox of Darlington, (possibly an object in the Hutchinsons' house at Sockburn). Both, perhaps, on account of its ability to survive, as an image, the decay of the paper on which it was printed, and its ability to reflect his own vicissitudes of mood, it caused him to revert to the tantalising intimations of immortality created by the phenomena of ideas and memory:

> . . . viewed in all moods unconsciously, distinctly, semi-

consciously, with vacant, with swimming eyes—a thing of
nature thro' the perpetual action of the Feelings!—O God!
when I now think how perishable Things, how imperishable
Ideas—what a proof of My Immortality—What is Forgetful-
ness?— (CN I 576)

This meditation on the imperishability of ideas took place on
the afternoon after an event which was to have far-reaching
effects on Coleridge's life, and which he recorded tersely in a
later notebook:

> Nov. 24th—the Sunday—Conundrums & Puns & Stories &
> Laughter—with Jack Hutchinson—Stood up round the Fire,
> et Sarae manum a tergo longum in tempus prensabam/ and
> tunc temporis, tunc primum, amor me levi spiculo venenato,
> eheu! et insanabili, &c [I took hold of Sara's hand for a long
> time behind her back/and at that time, then first, love (pricked)
> me with its light arrow, poisoned, alas! and incurable]
> (CN I 1575)

It is no accident, perhaps, that Coleridge stresses the warmth
of the scene: both literally in the fireside, and more meta-
phorically in the conviviality of the company. As the relationship developed there are further signs that Sara's chief virtue in
his eyes was a temperate warmth of nature which he found
lacking in his wife. Not only did Sara Coleridge, with her
capacity for 'freezing looks', lack 'Habits of heart-nursing
Sympathy',[15] but he found her devoid of physical warmth – at
least of a tender and communicative kind: she was, he said,
'warm in anger, cold in sympathy'.[16] When warmth did come
from her, it came violently and explosively: 'like a geyser in
Iceland' he once complained late in life.[17a] In the Hutchinson
household, by contrast, he seems to have sensed an atmosphere
in which his 'genial powers' might expand and flourish.

In the autumn of 1799 this was a new and inviting prospect,
which did not portend unhappiness, or even danger for his
marriage: awareness of the happiness of the Wordsworths in the
company of the Hutchinsons was rather opening a new dimension in possible personal relationships. The only other record of
the visit in the contemporary notebook which bears upon the
emotions is a two-line fragment: 'The lingering Bliss,/ The long
entrancement of a True-love's kiss.'[18]

As his coach rolled towards London after the trip, Coleridge's spirits were high. Pulling out his notebook he recorded a strange phenomenon: just after sunrise the coach passed in front of a hill, so that shortly afterwards the sunrise took place all over again. This repetition of a fountainous and transforming movement was followed by an extraordinary display of animated energy in action as hosts of starlings were seen in the air:

> Starlings in vast flights drove along like smoke, mist, or any thing misty (without) volition—now a circular area inclined (in an) arc—now a globe—(now from a complete orb into an) elipse & oblong—(now) a balloon with the (car suspended), now a concaved (semi) circle & (still) it expands & condenses, some (moments) glimmering and shivering, dim & shadowy, now thickening, deepening, blackening!—
>
> (CN I 582 (cf. 1589))

Such forms, created by the working of the shaping power of instinct in a community of flying birds, afforded a fine image for the workings of genial power in nature generally, with its unpredictability and wantonness of shaping, yet its over-riding ability to create momentary and shifting images. On a longer view, however, the most interesting feature of the description is the phrase 'any thing misty (without) volition' (later altered to 'a body unindued with voluntary Power'[19]), for this introduces Coleridge's conception that the model for the perfect operation of will is to be found not in animated behaviour but in central vegetative form. The starlings, by contrast, simply emblematise the constant play of energies towards form when no single controlling and shaping power from within is available.

During the tour, Coleridge had been having fruitful conversations with Wordsworth. It is conceivable that a plan of their future actions, whereby Wordsworth would concentrate on his great poem (and in particular that part of it which was to become *The Prelude*) while Coleridge would focus his attention, for the time being at least, upon his psychological investigations, was first sketched out by the two poets during this tour.[20a] Certainly it is possible to trace, particularly in the early books of *The Prelude*, statements by Wordsworth which suggest the impact of Coleridge's ideas: we need only recall the passage

describing the baby as being in direct harmony with the controlling principle of the universe:

> . . . blest the Babe,
> Nursed in his Mother's arms, the Babe who sleeps
> Upon his Mother's breast; who, when his soul
> Claims manifest kindred with an earthly soul,
> Doth gather passion from his Mother's eye!
>
> (W Prel (1805) II 239–43)

These feelings, Wordsworth continues, pass into his torpid life
'like an awakening breeze', so that the child, encouraged to see
things as unities, becomes gradually convinced that

> there exists
> A virtue which irradiates and exalts
> All objects through all intercourse of sense.
> No outcast he, bewildered and depressed:
> Along his infant veins are interfused
> The gravitation and the filial bond
> Of Nature that connect him with the world.
>
> (Ibid. 258–64)

Such a child is preserved, at least for the time being, 'an inmate
of this *active* universe': he or she is at one with the dynamic
principle that controls the whole of nature.

Though much of his time in 1800 was taken up by the move
to the Lakes described earlier, Coleridge continued to pursue
lines of thought related to his psychological theories. He seems
to have been interested in the processes by which 'genial power'
was brought into activity – particularly the possibility that
strong irritation of the nervous system might serve to set in
train an awakening and eradiation in the central organic powers.
A casual remark in a letter to Godwin in September illustrates
the theme:

> The scenes of Wicklow may be superior, but it is certain, that
> you were in a finer irritability of Spirit to enjoy them.
>
> (CL I 620)

The powers that thus responded, passively, to beautiful scenes
might also be brought into direct creative activity by irritable
stimulation. Trying to return to *Christabel* he attempted the

experiment of exposing himself to the impact of very powerful natural forces. In the end, however, it was a stimulus of a different kind that released his sleeping powers:

> I tried & tried, & nothing would come of it. I desisted with a deeper dejection than I am willing to remember. The wind from Skiddaw & Borrodale was often as loud as wind need be —& many a walk in the clouds on the mountains did I take; but all would not do—till one day I dined out at the house of a neighbouring clergyman, & some how or other drank so much wine, that I found some effort & dexterity requisite to balance myself on the hither Edge of Sobriety. The next day, my verse making faculties returned to me, and I proceeded successfully—till my poem grew so long & in Wordsworth's opinion so impressive, that he rejected it from his volume as disproportionate both in size & merit, & as discordant in it's character.— (CL I 643)

It is altogether appropriate that so physiologically analysable a process should have preceded the production of Part Two of *Christabel*, which, as already noted, reflects in its contents the changing concerns of Coleridge since he left England for Germany. In place of the enchantment that was interwoven into the very texture of the earlier narrative, a bleaker, more analytic quality prevails.

In part, of course, this reflects the changed scene against which the action is now taking place: H. N. Coleridge's memorable point that we are now witnessing 'witchery by daylight'[21] has its validity. The change of atmosphere is also relatable to the recent shift in Coleridge's ideas, however. The atmosphere in Part One was associated with a sense of possible magnetic links between all living organisms, as typified in the owls that hooted only when the moon was shining and the hypnotic power exercised over Christabel by Geraldine. That emphasis now gives place to suggestions concerning the actual means by which influence of a subconscious kind may be exerted over one human being by another.

The idea that a stimulus which penetrates deeply enough into the psyche could initiate an important working in the primary consciousness had apparently focused Coleridge's attention on the phenomena of imitation. This is not surprising when it is recalled that he was at the same time testing and illustrating his theories by observation of his own children; study of the early growth of the mind is likely to attract attention to its mimetic power. The development of linguistic power in children, particularly, is hard to explain purely in terms of external impressions and associative ideas: it seems necessary to presuppose the presence of an imitative matrix which can, without the intervention of conscious effort, reproduce what is heard and read in its own complexity of form. The continuing presence of that power in later life is associable with the familiar paradox that conscious effort often actively inhibits the process of recall, whereas once the effort has been called off the thing sought may, as Coleridge once put it, start up 'perfectly insulated, without any but the dimmest antecedent connection, as far as ... consciousness extends itself.'[22]

The psychological argument underlying Part Two of *Christabel* seems to involve a further refinement of this theory. When the organic centre of the psyche is disturbed by the penetrative power of strong life-energies, working with daemonic agency, there is a danger that the mimetic power will be drawn to repeat the form under which those powers present themselves. If the organic centre is strong and intact enough in its own inner life, however, the energies encountered will, as it were, simply twine themselves around it, so that its own powers will in due course be strengthened. But if the acting self has lost contact with its own organic centre, it will be at the mercy of the energies that have invaded it, able only to mirror back a reflection of their form.

Geraldine is a daemonic figure who exhibits energy in this latter, uncontrolled mode. She is more likely to be preyed upon by energy therefore (as betrayed in the ravages which Christabel sees when she undresses); when the dominating powers about her are more propitious, on the other hand, she can, as we have seen, rise up in beauty 'like a lady of a far countree'. The same ambiguity invests Sir Leoline, whose bereavement has cut him off from contact with the living world until he inhabits a veritable 'universe of death':

> Each matin bell, the Baron saith,
> Knells us back to a world of death.

This overmastering death-consciousness has made him a figure of
'commanding genius' as defined by Coleridge: strong in energy
but lacking in central insight. His castle witnesses to the need
for the man of commanding genius to define and objectify; it is
another version of Milton's Hell. (The description of the gate-
way to the castle and that of Milton's Hell-gate contain some
striking verbal parallels.[23]) In these circumstances, his energies
fall into ready complicity with those of Geraldine, whose face
reminds him of her father Sir Roland de Vaux, a former friend
from whom he became alienated, and whose daemonic powers
make her sympathetically attractive. As a result he is easily
blinded to the subtlety of the processes involved in Christabel's
behaviour and eventually turns from her.

Christabel herself, by contrast, belongs firmly to the world of
life. She is still a child in the world of energy, however, and
finds it hard to deal with Geraldine's daemonic powers. In spite
of this, she remains unviolated – and seems indeed to be partly
strengthened – by the encounter, for the fears created by her
strange discovery and by the sight of Geraldine's hidden deformity are set off (in a natural reaction, as it were) by the sense
of her mother – which comes as the blood flows back freely into
her veins:

> And, if she move unquietly,
> Perchance, 'tis but the blood so free
> Comes back and tingles in her feet.
> No doubt, she hath a vision sweet.

Her encounter with her father next day involves a similar process: her imitative recreation of the moment of horror is followed
by a revisiting of the subsequent visionary pleasure: the recreation of the vision of fear which occurs when she sees
Geraldine in her father's arms makes her shrink, snakelike, and
draw in her breath with a hissing sound, but when her father
looks round he sees only the complementary moment of her
dilatation into vision:

> The touch, the sight, had passed away,
> And in its stead that vision blest,
> Which comforted her after-rest
> While in the lady's arms she lay,

> Had put a rapture in her breast,
> And on her lips and o'er her eyes
> Spread smiles like light!

Dominated as he is by the vision of death, her father cannot respond to this side of her: his commanding genius seizes rather on her serpentine behaviour – which was in fact no more than the means by which her imitative powers relieved the pressure of remembered fear. He is cut off from the order of life which would enable him to value her embracing life-consciousness and remember her mother's equal powers – indeed,

> Within the Baron's heart and brain
> If thoughts, like these, had any share,
> They only swelled his rage and pain,
> And did but work confusion there.

In the same way he lacks the proper equipment to interpret Bracy's dream, which is cast essentially in the vital/organic pattern – another ordering of the serpent-encircled organism. In this sinister version the dove is constricted from all free animated movement by the windings of a small, attractive snake which insidiously mimes her own movements. There is danger here, but of a subtle kind. Bracy (whose genius as an artist is nearer to the 'absolute' form) proposes to meet it by charming the energies involved with 'music strong and saintly song'. Leoline, however, simply misinterprets the situation, believing the danger to the dove to refer to Geraldine, not (as is the case) to Christabel, and vowing simple physical destruction to the snake, rather than the 'charming' which is Bracy's natural mode. So the Bard is despatched on his way, Sir Leoline leads out Geraldine and Christabel is left isolated in the cold world of death that is embodied in the castle.

Although Coleridge later said that he had hoped in *Christabel* to 'more nearly realize [his] ideal' than he had done in *The Ancient Mariner*,[24] the nature of his new enterprise may be seen to have brought him sharply against questions which the form of the earlier poem had enabled him to circumvent. The problem of how the child of living nature could redeem the death-obsessed father was one that he had already approached in 'The Wanderings of Cain'; could the innocent life-principle ever reinfuse itself into a nature that had become wasted and ravaged by the force of its own warring energies? Coleridge, it seems, could find no firm solution – partly because of his own insistence that innocence and purity were of the same order. Christabel cannot be allowed to face the energies of love in her own conscious experience; she can only meet them in the obscurity of her nocturnal sleep with Geraldine. A Freudian barrier rears itself in the poem, inhibiting Coleridge from succeeding with his larger plan, which, if completed, would presumably have left Christabel ready to meet her lover with a personality strengthened and reintegrated.[25]

There is also something of the old presupposition that the energies of wrath and the energies of love are in necessary connection. Coleridge's aim was evidently to show that those energies, properly understood, could be seen to be springing from the same source. All such energies were related to the desire which should unite the human being with God, but which, through failure of connection, turns back to ravage it under forms of wrathful destruction. That this was Coleridge's idea, and that it remained potent for the remainder of his life, is supported by an unpublished letter to him from W. G. Kirkpatrick,[26] seeking to clarify certain points. He asked about the relationship between human desire and the Good which was God and enquired, "Is it that . . . by a Desire there-after given to wed us to it [i.e. that good], we being made our absolute self divorced from that same good & left to the Worm of that Desire, to that Hunger as of fire, can only in its nature be a Want a Pain & a Rage (?)" To this he added a further marginal note: "(comes seldom save from want & pain) The Love rage & the Wrath rage in Christabel at the Conclusion—why is not Christabel finished?" The phrasing ('wed us to it', 'absolute self') is strongly Coleridgean; Kirkpatrick had evidently either heard Coleridge expounding Christabel directly, or seen the relevance of his more general ideas to the events at the end of Part Two.

An understanding of Coleridge's failure to complete the poem takes us far towards comprehension of the larger contradictions with which he struggled for the rest of his life. 'The reason for my not finishing Christabel', he said later, 'is not, that I don't know how to do it – for I have, as I always had, the whole plan entire from beginning to end in my mind; but I fear I could not carry on with equal success the execution of the idea, an extremely subtle and difficult one.'[27] It will have become clear that the difficulty of 'the idea' springs partly from the fact that Coleridge is running together at least three elements: acute psychological observations, further theories about the common energies that relate wrath and love and the possible light that both might throw upon a metaphysical understanding of the relationship between the human and the divine.

Although the last, metaphysical implications are not universally acceptable, to have an awareness of them is important, since it helps to throw into relief and isolate the straightforward psychological investigations which Coleridge was currently carrying out, investigations which he was to continue during the lapse of his larger poetic powers. As his children developed, for example, their behaviour sometimes seemed to offer dramatic support to his theories. 'Hartley seemed to learn to talk by touching his Mother', he noted in November 1800. On the same occasion he observed that Derwent had had tears in his eyes for the first time when he cried; Dorothy Wordsworth had touched him with cold hands.[28] In each case an important link between touch, vital warmth (or its absence) and the stimulation of some feature of organic growth is being suggested and explored. The relationship between adult and infant consciousnesses is also a fruitful theme: some lines about Hartley which were eventually printed as the 'Conclusion' to the second book of *Christabel* continue the themes discussed above:

> A little child, a limber Elf
> Singing, dancing to itself;
> A faery Thing with red round Cheeks,
> That always *finds*, and never *seeks*—
> Doth make a Vision to the Sight,
> Which fills a Father's Eyes with Light!
> And Pleasures flow in so thick & fast
> Upon his Heart, that he at last
> Must needs express his Love's Excess
> In Words of Wrong and Bitterness.
> Perhaps 'tis pretty to force together
> Thoughts so all unlike each other;
> To mutter and mock a broken charm;

To dally with Wrong, that does no Harm—
Perhaps, 'tis tender too & pretty
At each wild Word to feel within
A sweet Recoil of Love & Pity;
And what if in a World of Sin
(O sorrow & shame! should this be true)
Such Giddiness of Heart & Brain
Comes seldom, save from Rage & Pain,
So talks, as it's most us'd to do.—   (CL II 728)

The ideas, like those embodied in 'Dejection', spring from
reflection on an apparent problem raised by his philosophy. In
its more impulsive behaviour, at least, the child is an incarnation
of the life-spirit at the primary level. Why is it, then, that very
often the father's response to such manifestations is not the
responsive joy which one might expect, but words of 'wrong
and bitterness'? Is it simply a kind of dramatic propriety on his
part, bringing into the charm of the scene a discordant note
which he knows will at once be harmonised by it? Or is the
reason more subtle – is it that the primary consciousness is so
unused to expressing its own inward joy spontaneously that
when it is finally evoked it still expresses itself more naturally
by repeating the language of the wrath that has brought it more
frequently into play in the past?

It is not clear whether Coleridge originally intended these
lines for *Christabel*; if not, he must later have come to see their
aptness to Sir Leoline's 'death-consciousness'; – which makes it
still less possible for him to respond adequately to the dominant
life-consciousness of his child.

While Coleridge produced writings during the subsequent
period such as his letters to the Wedgwoods arguing against the
fashionable 'idolatry' of Locke, Hobbes and Hume,[29] a good deal
of his intellectual energy was being devoted to the collection of
materials, both from books and from life, for a work which
would bring together more positively the fruits of his psychological speculations. Early in 1801 he mentioned his plan to
write

a work on the originality & merits of Locke, Hobbes & Hume/
which work I mean as a *Pioneer* to my greater work, and as
exhibiting a proof that I have not formed opinions without an

attentive Perusal of the works of my Predecessors from
Aristotle to Kant. (CL II 707)

Further light seems to be thrown on this 'greater work' by his
earlier description (in a rare unguarded moment) of his projected
essay on Poetry and the pleasures derived from it, as a work
which would

> supersede all the Books of Metaphysics hitherto written/and
> all the Books of Morals too ... (CL II 671)

One of his tasks was evidently to collect any instances showing the workings of primary or secondary constituents of
consciousness in a pure form. Abnormal psychology was one
obvious possible source. Some years before, he had made a notebook entry concerning

> An ideot whose whole amusement consisted in looking at,
> & talking to a clock, which he supposed to be alive—/the
> Clock was removed—/he supposed that it had walked off—
> & he went away to seek it—was absent nine days—at last,
> they found, almost famish'd in a field—He asked where it was
> buried—for he was sure it was dead—/he was brought home
> & the clock in its place—his Joy—&c He used to put part of
> every thing, he liked, into the clock-case. (CN I 212)

This anecdote provided a natural illustration of the implicit
power of the life-consciousness: the idiot, lacking full development of his secondary powers, endows the clock (which would
normally be used by those powers as a key-instrument for dealing
with the world of objects) with a life of its own and attaches his
affections to it. He has some of the same qualities as Wordsworth's Idiot Boy – who may well have been conceived as a
result of discussions on the subject with Coleridge. (Some years
later, Wordsworth wrote that he had always applied to idiots
that part of a famous biblical text which runs 'Their life is
hidden with God'.[30])

Now, in the spring of 1801, Coleridge came across a story in
the letters of St Augustine which he transcribed, partly in Latin,
into a notebook:

> I knew a person who during imperfect sleep or dozing as we
> say, listened to the clock as it was striking four, and as it

struck, he counted the four, one, one, one, one; and then he exclaimed, why, the clock is out of its wits: it has struck one four times over.   (CN I 915n)

The story was to remain for him a good example of the necessary co-presence of his two perceptual elements in all mental activity: he published it in *Omniana* some years later[31] as an example of

a confusion of (what the Schoolmen would have called) Objectivity with Subjectivity, in plain English, the impression of a thing as it exists in itself and extrinsically, with the idea which the mind abstracts from the impression.

He also applied the anecdote, transferring it now to an idiot, in an attempt to distinguish between the 'common strength' of a nation from the weakness of the individuals taken separately:

A million of men united by common Confidence and free intercourse of Thoughts, form one power, and this is as much a Real Thing as a Steam Engine; but a million of insulated individuals is only an abstraction of the mind, and but one told so many times over without addition, as an Idiot would tell the Clock at noon—one, one, one &c.   (Friend II 98)

Meanwhile his complementary reflection that an idiot would see the clock simply as an organism remained with him for many years. Planning to include him in a later work, he thought of associating him with a waterfall:

The Sopha of Sods.—Lackwit, & the Clock—find him at last in the Yorkshire Cave where the waterfall is— (CN I 1242)

This sense that an idiot would naturally be drawn by the power of his life-sense to some such great natural force was then unexpectedly reinforced, ten years later, when he read in Gilbert White's *Selborne* an account of the 'bee-idiot' from which he extracted the following note:

The Bee-Ideot—with a beelike humming as his only voice— dosed all winter, but all summer out & alert among the meadows & garden, like the Merops apiaster/ = with the Clock Ideot—   (CN III 3961)

The last addition makes explicit the link in his mind between the pure life-consciousness of this figure and that of his original 'clock-idiot'.

While abnormal psychology offered such materials for elaborating his distinction, he could also study it in the growth of his own children. Whereas earlier, the development of the motor senses had seemed to inhibit the growth of the primary language powers in Hartley, the primary symbol-making power once in play outstripped the analytical sense.

> It seems to elucidate the Theory of Language, Hartley, just able to speak a few words, making a fire-place of stones, with stones for fire.—four stones—fire-place—two stones—fire—/ arbitrary symbols in Imagination/ /Hartley walked remarkably soon/ & *therefore* learnt to talk rem. late./   (CN I 918)

The first observation carries on where Augustine's anecdote left off: it suggests the power of shaping imagination in action – and so strongly that it can use even simple difference in number to symbolise the difference between objects as different as stones and fire. But it is the afterthought that shows the larger range of Coleridge's speculation. For the natural impulse would be to associate intelligence of this kind with unusual facility of speech; what Coleridge is suggesting, however, is subtler: it is that the symbol-making faculty is to be associated with a power so central to the psyche that *all* development requires its central participation. The activity of learning either to walk, or to talk, therefore, draws on its powers so fully as to make the alternative learning for the time being impossible. On this assumption (which is closely related to those underlying the philosophy of growth in *The Prelude*), a child's prime need is to have its energies associated harmoniously with those of nature, and thus develop its basic imaginative powers: speech, the faculty of expressing those powers, may easily come later.

The speculation brings Coleridge back to his central preoccupation, for if there is a central area of the human being which is creative yet anterior to the development of speech, it would also seem to be inaccessible to consciousness. The analysing consciousness can hardly help acknowledging the presence of a mystery; as Coleridge goes on to say in his next but one note:

> Materialists unwilling to admit the mysterious of our nature make it all mysterious—nothing mysterious in nerves, eyes,

&c: but that nerves think &c!!—Stir up the sediment into the transparent water, & so make all opaque.   (CN I 920)

This leads him to meditate on the nature of life itself and of central identity – that part in the human being which says 'I'. He leads in by quoting Wordsworth's lines from *Tintern Abbey* and then develops an image which he probably gained from Fichte:[32]

> —and the deep power of Joy
> We see into the *Life* of Things—
> i.e.—By deep feeling we make our *Ideas dim*—& this is what
> we mean by our Life—ourselves. I think of the Wall—it is
> before me, a distinct Image—here. I necessarily think of the
> *Idea* & the Thinking I as two distinct & opposite Things. Now
> let me think of *myself*—of the thinking Being—the Idea
> becomes dim whatever it be—so dim that I know not what it
> is—but the Feeling is deep & steady—and this I call I—
> identifying the Percipient & the Perceived—.   (CN I 921)

A week later Coleridge returns to the subject, reflecting on the manner in which babies learn to come to terms with the world of sense through the varying processes of touch. The baby begins by existing in a total rapport with its mother, whose self is, in important respects, identical with its own. The touch-sense which is centrally important is therefore that of the tongue. It is only when the hand comes into play, providing a countercheck to what has been tasted, that one has the beginnings of 'double touch', followed by adjustment to and control of the larger world of objects:

> Babies touch *by taste* at first—then about 5 months old
> they go from the Palate to the hand—& are fond of feeling
> what they have taste—/Association of the Hand with the
> Taste—till the latter by itself recalls the former—& of course,
> with volition. March 24, 1801.   (CN I 924)

Next day, Coleridge was lying in bed unwell. He observed the prismatic colours in a tumbler and then, after some conversation with Wordsworth shut his eyes. Now he saw

> beauteous spectra of two colors, orange and violet—then of
> green, which immediately changed to Peagreen, & then

actually *grew* to my eye into a beautiful moss, the same as is on the mantle-piece at Grasmere.—abstract Ideas—& unconscious Links!! (CN I 925)

The feature of this experience which drew his underlining pen was the fact that the ocular spectra which had developed colours of its own should then have actually been seen to *grow* into a moss before his inward eye. This could be regarded as evidence of a bias to the organic in the unconscious; next day he followed this by a 'fantastic analogue & similitude' in which he likened Wordsworth's creative mind to the description, in Bartram's *Travels*, of huge exotic plants growing in a rich dark soil on tenacious clay.[33]

With these lines of speculation in his mind it was natural that Coleridge should have sought to fulfil a long-standing ambition by reading the works of Giordano Bruno, where he might have hoped to find some key-statements for the general line of thought he was pursuing. At a first trial he was disappointed, for he found the *De Monade* 'too numeral, lineal, & Pythagorean for my Comprehension'.[34] As for his hopes of finding some secret wisdom which had been made available by Bruno to the great English Renaissance writers he met, this work, at least, suggested the contrary:

Sir P. Sidney, & Fulk Greville shut their doors at their philos. conferences with Bruno—if his Conversation resembled this book, I should have thought, he [could have] talked with a trumpet. (CN I 928)

Elsewhere in Bruno, however, he found passages more akin to what he was seeking. In the *de Immenso et Innumerabilibus*, for example, he was delighted to discover Bruno talking familiarly of the circulation of the blood, twenty-five years before William Harvey expounded his theory at Padua. 'I am inclined to think that this, like many things, was *known* before it was *discovered*,' he wrote later; the Latin quotations from Bruno in the notebooks show that it was not merely the anticipation that excited him, but the indications that Bruno's conception of the circulation was linked to a larger metaphysical idea (like that which we have argued Coleridge himself to have entertained) that the circulation of blood in the human body corresponded to circulation in the universe at large:

> Just as the blood in our bodies *courses around* the whole body and flows back again, so it is in the whole world, in a star, in the earth . . .
>
> And so (it works) just like the blood in our bodies; passes back and forth, flows to the lower parts, and surges back from the feet to the higher parts with equal force . . .
>
> What would happen if everything in nature did not return by a sort of circuit to its own source again; if the sea drank up all the water, if the whole were not restored by an abiding order, who could endure the life of things? It would be as though all the blood were to run to one place and stay there and not return to its starting-point to take up its ancient course again . . .   (CN I 927n)

Bruno's description of the divinity as a great fountain, which had been quoted in Priestley's *Disquisitions*,[35] was here being filled out in a manner congenial to his own mind. Coleridge went on to transcribe some more passages of Latin, in which Bruno skirts pantheism as he describes the intercourse of the earth with the sun and compares it with the sexual intercourse of lesser creatures, characterising the 'fire of Life' as superior to the 'orders of simple air', and asserting that the body receives its spirit and life from the 'maternal fountain' which is 'Soul, a reverenceable spirit, a happy star, glittering inhabitant of the sky singing praises to its author and worshipping him.' 'This', remarks Bruno, 'comes about in an incredible manner which is inconceivable to those who have understanding without insight.' His last line runs: 'Therefore, do not hesitate to call the world a living world.'

A little later, Coleridge concludes his transcriptions with a Latin poem which was to become a favourite of his, quoted both in *The Friend* and in the *Philosophical Lectures*.[36] Bruno's ode on Genius supersedes the sentiments in his own Greek Ode or in Davy's 'Sons of Genius', by declaring that there is no need for the Genius to soar above, since he already knows the truth which images itself in the sun or speaks through nature:

> Let others lust to bind to naked shoulders
> Daedalus's wings, to fly with the clouds' strength
> And seek the buffeting impulse of the winds—

Hunger to be hurled, like Pegasus, beyond
The hollow confines of the flaming world.

For we have known the gift of Genius
And gazed undaunted on our shadowy fate
Lest, being blind to light of the sun, or deaf
To Nature's universal voices, we
Receive the gifts of God ungraciously . . .

The combination of sublime assertion with humility of stance and refusal of hubristic flight was calculated to appeal to Coleridge's own position. He followed this gratifying discovery by a note reminding him to use a poem by Engel (describing the need for an acorn to be vitalised before it could become an oak) as introduction to his planned essay on Locke[37] (asserting, one assumes, the interplay of organic and vitalist, as against a simple mechanistic view).

Throughout these entries in the spring of 1801, there moves a spirit of restless search and speculation, associated with the nexus of ideas which relate the heart and blood to the workings of the universe and which see in the perception of a fountainous nature, when coupled with fountainous response from a heart that is enlightened by the same intuition, a key to human knowledge, teaching man to desist from false aspiration and to cultivate humbly the light and health of his own being.

In April, he borrowed a number of books from Carlisle Cathedral Library.[38*] A number of these were books bearing on physiology – and more particularly on the phenomena of imagination – such as Malebranche's *Search after Truth,* Hobbes's *De Corpore* and Kenelm Digby's *Two Treatises.* It may be significant, in view of Coleridge's known habits, that some of the books borrowed contain pencil markings, and that some of those in Digby's treatises appear by accounts of the power of imagination and the imitative power. Digby stresses the primacy of the heart in each generated creature; he also (in a marked passage) dwells on the relationship between dilatation of the nerves and pleasure on the one hand and contraction of the nerves and pain on the other. In another marked passage he talks about the strange power of imitation in some people, instancing the case of a man who[39]

seeing a rosted pigge, after our English fashion with the mouth
gaping, could not shutt his owne mouth as long as he looked
upon the pigge's.

He also offers a possible explanation for the phenomenon of
birthmarks on the grounds that the fantasy of the child is 'as it
were well tuned to the fantasy of the mother'. For this reason,
the child might blush in unison with its mother, but with more
lasting effects: 'the like happening to the childe, the violence of
that suddaine motion, dyeth the marke or print of the thing in
the tender skinne of it.'[40] Observations and suggestions such as
these run close to Coleridge's speculations concerning the power
of the imaginative force; an idea from Digby which he actually
recorded in one of his notebooks bears on a cognate phenomenon:[41]

Every passion, say the Physicians, hath a distinct Pulse.

Meanwhile, however, physiological questions were also pressing
on Coleridge in a less detached and pleasurable manner. About
this time there appear signs of increasing dependence on the
opium which he had been taking for some years.

The question of Coleridge's addiction has been much discussed.[42] On the one hand it has been pointed out that his
recourse to opium was consistent with current medical practice:
the fashionable Brunonian theory divided diseases into those
supposedly caused by over-stimulation or under-stimulation and
encouraged the administration of spirits or opium as common
remedies.[43] Yet the suspicion has lingered among critics that to
some extent he enjoyed and fostered the habit.[44] In an early
letter to his brother, for example, he had written:

Laudanum gave me repose, not sleep: but YOU, I believe, know
how divine that repose is—what a spot of inchantment, a
green spot of fountains, & flowers & trees, in the very heart
of a waste of Sands!   (CL I 394)

There is also evidence that Coleridge interested himself in other
drugs such as Indian hemp, or 'Bang', which he acquired from
Samuel Purkis. To Thomas Wedgwood, a fellow invalid who
shared his experiments in medication, he wrote (not, one suspects,

without a touch of exhilaration) 'We will have a fair trial of *Bang*'.[45]

Investigation of the question is partly hindered by the fact that most of the evidence comes from Coleridge himself, and drug-users are notoriously bad witnesses in their own behalf. Yet it should be observed that it is by no means impossible to reconcile Coleridge's general account with the facts so far as they are known. 'My sole sensuality was *not* to be in pain!' he insisted.[46] If we read this as a plea that he never took laudanum simply in order to induce luxurious sensations, it is not an unreasonable one, since he suffered from enough pains during the period to warrant regular recourse on medical grounds (– even if the 'pains' were what would now be recognised as 'withdrawal symptoms'). Such usage is still compatible with strong interest in, and even enjoyment of the effects, once administered.

Further light may be thrown on the question by our earlier suggestion that Coleridge was particularly drawn to laudanum as a distillation of vegetative powers. Such an attraction would set his drug-taking in the realm of his intellectual interests – and even offer it a possible moral support. The comment in his letter to his brother is more readily understandable if the 'divine . . . repose' which he speaks of at the centre of his being was regarded as resort to a vegetative centre (not altogether unlike that of the god on the lotus-leaf in the passage quoted earlier[47]) which might be identifiable with the location of the very soul itself.

There is another piece of evidence from this time which suggests that Coleridge's experiments with the drug had implications beyond the medical relief which they gave him. An experience described to Cottle some years later dates from this period:

> I had been almost bed-ridden for many months with swellings in my knees—in a medical Journal I unhappily met with an account of a cure performed in a similar case (or what to me appeared so) by rubbing in of Laudanum, at the same time taking a given dose internally—It acted like a charm, like a miracle! I recovered the use of my Limbs, of my appetite, of my Spirits—& this continued for near a fortnight . . .
>
> (CL III 476)

Coleridge's delight at his temporary cure is all the more explicable in view of its harmonisation with the theory of double-touch. To apply laudanum both externally to the skin and internally in the stomach could be regarded as an unusually efficacious way of dealing with a disease of the nervous system, by ministering to it at once through the agency of touch and at a crucial centre of the organic.

Despite Coleridge's reticence on the further implications of his opium-taking, moreover, there is one later notebook entry which suggests that he had for a time associated it closely with his own psychological and metaphysical investigations. He discusses the case of a man

> whom a *pernicious Drug* shall make capable of conceiving & bringing forth Thoughts, hidden in him before, which shall call forth the deepest feelings of his best, greatest, & sanest Contemporaries.   (CN III 3320)

A possible explanation for the strange paradox, he continues, is that 'the dire poison for a delusive time has made the body, i.e. the *organization*, not the articulation (or instruments of motion) the unknown somewhat, a fitter Instrument for the all-powerful Soul'.

The implication is that by dulling the vital spirits (and so the instruments of motion) opium had allowed a more direct rôle to the organic centre, the natural instrument of the soul – and so, paradoxically, enabled that soul to express itself more directly. But there is also in the tone of the entry a suggestion that Coleridge may both recognise that his interest in such phenomena had assisted his growing addiction and feel a bitterness towards Wordsworth for turning against him after originally showing interest in his observations and researches.

One experience during these years was particularly striking: it is referred to in a note concerning

> ... the curious phænomenon experienced the X^tmas of 1801 at Mr Howel's, N° 10, King S^t, Covent Garden, my Skin deadened, the effect of violent Diarrhœa ...   (CN I 1827)

This, he says, caused him to speculate on 'the intimate connection of Volition, and of the Feeling & Consciousness of Volition, on the state of the Skin'. Although he refers to a former Pocket-book, there is no clear account of such an experience elsewhere. Kathleen Coburn suggests that it might refer to a brief discussion of ocular spectra which concludes with a reference to

> motion communicated to the object by any motion in any part of the body. ex.gr. of the hand moving to & fro the flesh of the Leg.—This important. (CN I 1039)

If so, however, it does not contain enough interpretative content to help us understand the importance he had attached to the phenomenon.

Another important experience (it may possibly have been the one referred to) is described in a letter written in 1817. Discussing animal magnetism, and the theory that the power was transmitted by a special magnetic fluid, Coleridge points out that the 'luminousness' of which the magnetisers speak can easily be a symptom of diseased nerves, and goes on,

> I have myself once seen (i.e. appeared to see) my own body under the Bed cloaths flashing silver Light from whatever part I prest it—and the same proceed from the tips of my fingers. I have thus written, as it were, my name, Greek words, cyphers &c on my Thigh: and instantly seen them together with the Thigh in brilliant Letters of silver Light.—It was some 15 or 16 years ago—I had left a jovial party, after much and very animated conversation, at a Mr Bellew's (an Irish Barrister) and had drank two large Tumblers of very strong Punch. I deduced from the Phaenomenon the existence of an imitative sympathy in the nerves, so that those of the Eye copied instantaneously the impressions made on those of the Limbs.— (CL IV 731)

Coleridge is here suggesting that the nerves ministering to the various senses contain an imitative power so strong that they can 'produce' phenomena indistinguishable from those of actual perception. (He would presumably attribute the extraordinary sharpness of perception gained by some blind people, such as Fowell of Temple Sowerby,[48] to a continuing ability to use the optic *nerves*, so as to register the impressions of other senses as 'sight'.)

At the same time he was also aware of a deadening of his emotions – foreshadowed first, perhaps, in the reference to an 'extinction of *Light* in [his] mind . . . as if the *organs* of Life had

been dried up' quoted earlier.[49] This sense of flatness (it may or
may not have been an effect of opium) was also depriving him of
his vividness of imagination. One may catch Coleridge on the
very brink of his new state in a letter of March 1801, describing
his difficulties in creating new poetry.

> The Poet is dead in me—my imagination (or rather the
> Somewhat that had been imaginative) lies, like a Cold Snuff
> on the circular Rim of a Brass Candle-stick, without even a
> stink of Tallow to remind you that it was once cloathed &
> mitred with Flame. That is past by!—I was once a Volume of
> Gold Leaf, rising & riding on every breath of Fancy—but I
> have beaten myself back into weight & density, & now I sink
> in quicksilver, yea, remain squat and square on the earth amid
> the hurricane, that makes Oaks and Straws join in one Dance,
> fifty yards high in the Element.   (CL II 714)

The choice of 'quicksilver' as an image for the primary consciousness in this state is brilliant, suggesting that the mercurial
quality of his primary consciousness had retired from its more
expansive state, that of the living 'Mercury' with intertwined
snakes on his winged staff, to the dull substance which, while
still magical in its power of instant cohesion, remains essentially
lifeless and semi-poisonous.[50*] Meanwhile, however, the very
power that he has lost is figured by the external energies which
create the dance of the hurricane above his head. Later, returning
to the image, Coleridge was to speak of himself as having delved
in the 'unwholesome quicksilver mines of metaphysical depths.'[51*]
In a further ramification of the idea he says:

> Metaphysics make all one's thoughts equally corrosive on
> the Body by the habit of making momently & common
> thought the subjects of uncommon interest & intellectual
> energy.   (CN I 1313)

The classic statement of his condition is, of course, in the
'Letter to Sara Hutchinson'. Recognising that the life of nature
may not always speak to the life within, that the 'genial spirits'
may 'fail', he considers several possible reasons. including his
'coarse domestic life', which, he suggests, has inhibited the life
of those human and emotional centres that might have enabled

him to share even the sadness of Sara Hutchinson in a manner
that was vital rather than dreary –

> Whence when I mourn'd for you, my Heart might borrow
> Fair forms & living Motions for it's Sorrow.   (CL II 797)

For the same reason, his researches into the human subconscious, which in a happier context would have been undertaken within a context of joyful apperception, have become,
used as a refuge from dull grief, corrosive:

> But to be still & patient all I can;
> And haply by abstruse Research to steal
> From my own Nature all the Natural Man—
> This was my sole Resource, my wisest plan!
> And that, which suits a part, infects the whole,
> And now is almost grown the Temper of my Soul.

In this mood there is no scope for the old image of soft breeze
and harp, with their suggestions of a perfectly attuned sensibility.
The wind-noise that he can hear, with its curiously sinister note,
offers an apt enough comment on that condition. Instead, the
best he can hope for is a visitation from the full storm-blast,
which might at least offer external stimulus to vital powers
which are not stirred from within. Later in the poem, by an
involuting twist, the storm *is* heard – but only after having
raged for a long time 'unnoticed'; and it does not then have a
direct effect upon his feelings. It does, however, operate indirectly, for it provokes an effect of sublimity followed by pathos
through the human associations of its intervening gentler note
(''Tis of a little Child . . .') – and this humanising process seems
subtly to affect the mood of the whole poem, which is now
carried along on a growing tide of hope for Sara, culminating
with the vision of her reaching what he can no longer achieve:
the sense of a vital relationship between her life and that of
nature, through realisation of 'Light & Impulse from above'.

To any comment that, for an apparent elegy to his 'shaping
spirit of imagination', the 'Letter' is disconcertingly imaginative,
Coleridge might have replied that suspension of that spirit did
not inhibit him from writing a poem of the secondary powers –
a poem in which the vital powers of his poetic genius struggle
towards unity but in which there is no attempt to offer the

flowering of a large idea into ramified expression. The fact that he did not think of his 'shaping spirit' as dead but 'suspended' meant that his poem was less elegy than sad commentary.

The fact of that suspension, nevertheless, coupled with his general unhappiness, discouraged further large-scale ventures into poetry. Instead he turned back to his 'researches' – including less 'abstruse' varieties, such as the observations of his own children mentioned above in connection with Hartley. In Derwent, too, the spirit of life flourished strongly: by studying the very earliest processes of his growth and learning as a baby, moreover, it was possible to explore the theory of primary consciousness in a still purer experimental situation. The tongue invited further attention, as the sense which lay closest to the primary and organic, and which also manifested the earliest stirrings into vital life. 'Exceeding Expressiveness of the motion of the Tongue of Toothless Infants', he had written in a note-book of 1801.[52] The key issue, however, was still the learning of language. Did it not seem to be the case that the growth of linguistic ability was in essence an *organic* rather than a vital process? On one occasion, when Derwent was nearly three years old, Coleridge tried to explain to him what his senses were for, and found that he did not as yet associate his sense-organs with their respective perceptual functions. In order to teach him about his tongue, Coleridge held it, and found him quite un-moved. A little later Coleridge told him to hold his tongue and try to say, 'Papa':

> ... he did, & finding that he could not speak, he turned pale
> as death and in the reaction from fear flushed red, & gave me
> a blow in the face/   (CN I 1400)

The implication, in terms of Coleridge's larger theory, is that Derwent's use of the tongue in speech was at one and the same time so basic and so unconscious that the inhibition of that use was greeted immediately by primary passional movements of fear and anger. Three days later, Derwent had another experience of a similar kind, running round and round the kitchen until for the first time in his experience he became giddy. Seeing the result he again became pale with fright, pawing with his hands to try and stop the kitchen moving away from him; next day he was 'fever-hot'.[53] Again a disturbance of the central relationship with the external world had set up a reaction at the primary level, a process of contraction in fear followed by dilation into fever.

At times Coleridge could rise to bolder exposition of his theories and their implication. In the August letter to Southey discussed earlier, for example, where he mentioned an ocular spectrum, a flashback to their Bristol days,[54] he went on to discuss the phenomena of memory and to argue that the manner of their operation ran counter to Hartley's theories. Recollection, he believed, was far more dependent on the recurrence of states of emotion from the past than on any processes of active association. And he went on to outline his own view of the matter by invoking his old imagery of organism and breeze. The ideas in the mind are seen in organic terms: they are like leaves on the trees in a forest. In themselves, therefore, they cannot affect one another: it is only through the operation of vital spirits (imaged as a breeze running through the forest) that they are brought into relationships with each other.

It argues, I am persuaded, a particular state of general feeling —& I hold, that association depends in a much greater degree on the recurrence of resembling states of Feeling, than on Trains of Idea/that the recollection of early childhood in latest old age depends on, & is explicable by this—& if this be true, Hartley's System totters.—If I were asked, how it is that very old People remember *visually* only the events of early childhood—& remember the intervening Spaces either not at all, or only verbally—I should think it a perfectly philosophical answer/that old age remembers childhood by becoming 'a second childhood.' This explanation will derive some additional value if you would look into Hartley's solution of the phænomena/how flat, how wretched!—Believe me, Southey! a metaphysical Solution, that does not instantly *tell* for something in the Heart, is grievously to be suspected as apocryphal. I almost think that Ideas *never* recall Ideas, as far as they are Ideas—any more than Leaves in a forest create each other's motion—the Breeze it is that runs thro' them/ it is the Soul, the state of Feeling—. If I had said, no *one* Idea ever recalls another, I am confident that I could support the assertion. (CL II 961)

At a moment such as this, facing a mystery of human nature that would continue to fascinate artists and find its most extended treatment in Proust's great novel, Coleridge gives his reader a tantalising glimpse of what he might have been able to achieve in happier circumstances.

Even while he continued to apply and extend his theories, however, he was aware that some of the hopes which he had based upon them were not being borne out by experience. The satisfaction that he had hoped to find through hard work and limited association with the Wordsworth household had not materialised, while the central joy which he looked for in his platonic relationship with Sara was missing. Sometimes he could salvage a muted reassurance:

> Why we two made to be a Joy to each other, should for so many years constitute each other's melancholy—O! but the melancholy is Joy—   (CN I 1394)

It was a desperate comfort, however, and soon he was driven to sharper expression of his bewilderment:

> O Σαρα Σαρα why am I not happy! why have I not an unencumbered Heart! these beloved Books still before me, this noble Room, the very centre to which a whole world of beauty converges, the deep reservoir into which all these streams & currents of lovely Forms flow—my own mind so populous, so active, so full of noble schemes, so capable of realizing them/ this heart so loving, so filled with noble affections—O Aσρα! wherefore am I not happy! why for years have I not enjoyed one pure & sincere pleasure!—one full Joy!—one genuine Delight, that rings sharp to the Beat of the Finger!—all cracked, & dull with base Alloy!   (CN I 1577)

The conditions for joy and creativity were present: the place, with its constant influx of light and images, his mind, with its good impulses. Yet the joy which ought by his theories to spring up naturally in these circumstances was missing. Where then was the flaw?

Further reflection led him to diagnose the root of his affliction in the state of his health. In the autumn of 1803, particularly, he shows signs of a growing valetudinarianism. His periods of greatest pleasure, when he is alone with his thoughts, are characterised by the remembered image of the flocking star-lings,[55*] now wistfully internalised but still conveying the old sense of energies shaping themselves delightedly:

My Spirit with a fixed yet leisurely gaze
Following its ever yet quietly changing Clusters of Thoughts,
As the outward Eye of a happy Traveller a flock of Starlings.

(CN I 1779)

He also continues to examine the state of his health by way of categories derived from his general theory, seeking now for relief through some strong and continuous stimulus that might replace the insidious opium by a powerful impact from the central energies of nature, battering its way to the seat of his malaise so violently as to provoke a sanative eruption at the very centre. His awareness of the strange power exerted over the skin by disturbance at that centre (as when a rash paints itself on the skin without direct local stimulus) led him to hope that he might be able to provoke a purgative process of the kind:

The exquisite Affectibility of my Skin, & the instant Sympathy of my Stomach and mesenteries with the Affections of the Skin, exemplified in the shocking Effect of wearing the black Pantaloons next to my Skin, & in my miserable baro-metrical Dependence of my Stomach Sensations on the *weather*, especially damp & wet-stormy weather, forms a specific distinction between my Complaint, & William Wordsworth's Hypochondriasis.—Item, my almost never, on any occasion, even after Intoxication, having the Headach. What shall I say?—A cutaneous Disease *driven in*?—That some philosophical meaning is attachable to this phrase, the Nettle Rash sufficiently proves.—But assuredly, I may at least build hereupon the probability of essential Benefit from a hot Climate. What if it brought out a deforming Eruption on my Face & Body, leaving my inner Life sound & full of faculty?— O I should rejoice. My Soul she would always love, the faith-fully Beloved!—and I could more than pardon her aversion from my bodily Presence.—

Whether Gout and Rheumatism—or, to speak more guardedly, whether certain Diseases at least, which are now classed under Gout & Rheumatism, are not mainly & primarily *cutaneous?* And whether the Skin be not a Terra Incognita in Medicine? And whether this Ignorance, if it exist, does not imply broad fundamental Error in the Theory of Medicine, and probabilize (WHOO!! render probable the existence of) pernicious Mistakes in the Practice?—That this has been and is the case with Metaphysicians, I KNOW—they at least, whatever may be the Fact with regard to Physicians, are not even *skin-deep.*—To end a very serious note playfully, or rather serio-comically, let me remark that our good Forefathers in pronouncing Beauty to be but skin-deep, payed it a higher Compliment than they were aware those words could be construed into. Jan. 9. 1804. past 10 *night.* Grasmere.

(CN I 1826)

Two days after this note Coleridge wrote to Southey, elaborating on some of the arguments developed in it and re-affirming his belief that his disease was not gout or rheumatism specifically, but a disease of the skin, so that a hot climate might bring on a violent eruption which would cure him.[56] On 13 January he wrote again, commenting on the curious phenomena of nettlerash, the overt appearance of which alternated with distressful sensations in the stomach, but never with both present together; he also reported that opium in sufficient doses could produce a truce between the two manifestations 'by the Equipoise of hostile Forces'. Although he knew that damp air was partly to blame he felt that the real reason must be the absence of 'electrical, or other imponderable fluid instrumental to vital action', since the damp could affect him even when he was in a warm room under several blankets with a warm fire. This became another argument for spending time in a warm climate.

Considerations of this kind were leading him steadily towards his decision to spend a period in Malta. In the meantime, however, he elaborated on his speculations concerning the significance of the state of the skin – and was now led, through many of the phenomena mentioned earlier, into his most explicit exposition of the theory of single and double touch, as it had developed during these years.

Of the intimate connection of Volition, and of the Feeling & Consciousness of Volition, on the state of the Skin, I have noticed long ago in a former Pocket-book, occasioned by the curious phænomenon experienced the Xᵗmas of 1801 at Mʳ Howel's, Nº 10, King Sᵗ, Covent Garden, my Skin deadened, the effect of violent Diarrhœa/My Speculations thence on double Touch—the generation of the Sense of Reality & Life out of us, from the Impersonation effected by a certain phantasm of double Touch, &c &c &c, and thence my Hope of making out a radical distinction between this Volition & Free Will or Arbitrement, & the detection of the Sophistry of the Necessitarians/as having arisen from confounding the two.—Sea sickness, the Eye on the Stomach, the Stomach on the Eye/—Eye+Stomach+Skin—Scratching & ever after in certain affections of the Skin, milder than those which provoke Scratching a restlessness for double Touch/Dalliance, & at its height, necessity of Fruition.—Fruition the intensest single Touch, &c &c &c; but I am bound to trace the Ministery of the Lowest to the Highest, of all things to Good/and the presence of a certain Abstract or Generical Idea, in the Top, Bottom, & Middle of each Genus. Λιβιδινοσιτᾶτ των Ιδιωτων [The libidousness of idiots]—this must be explained in the first instance—then of brutal men. (Sensatio urinæ [The sensation of urine], when gratified at any pressing want, wherein it differs &c) Rutting-time of Brutes &c &c &c &c &c &c &c— *An Ocean* (CN I 1827)

His old idea that the sense of reality and life is to some degree phantasmal, being conditional upon the reassuring presence of double touch, is still being pressed: for the first time, however, Coleridge writes openly of certain further physiological implications of his theory. In sea-sickness a disruption between two of the great organic centres of the body, the stomach and the eye, leads to nausea, single touch in one of its great rejecting versions. In love-making, by a different but not altogether unrelated process, the intensification of double touch set up by repeated caresses leads to an overpowering necessity for sexual fruition, an act of single touch in its intensest and most positive form. An intimate connection is presupposed between the operation of the primary consciousness and extreme bodily experiences – nightmare, nausea, orgasm – where the sense of double touch is momentarily submerged.

Coleridge's final flourish: '*An Ocean*', may indicate a sense both of endless possibilities and of intricate problems lying in wait as he tries, for example, to relate the erotic to the metaphysical. At any rate, his thinking now takes a familiar course, turning back to children and their development. Following a train of thought started, perhaps, by his reference to the 'libidinousness of idiots' (a neat illustration of the relationship between the erotic and the primary consciousness, both seen in unfettered form in the idiot according to his theory) he considers the phenomenon of remembering in children, who seem to exhibit the power of primary consciousness in a less controversial form, and then relates the point back to idiots again:

> Important Distinction between the Memory, or reminiscent Faculty, of Sensations—which young Children seem to possess in so small a degree from their perpetual Desire of having a Tale repeated, & the Memory of words & images which the very same young Child manifestly possess in an unusual degree—even to sealing wax accuracy of retention & representation.—Idiots probably the same/perhaps defective in both; but in the latter less so.—   (CN I 1828)

Coleridge's discussion throws into focus a phenomenon familiar to all who have to do with young children and offers a plausible explanation in terms of his theory. The fact that they live so powerfully at the organic level is seen as responsible for their very retentive memories of verbal and visual forms, while their need for repetition of stories betrays a bewilderment at the concurrently incessant and disorganised play of their own vital spirits, on which narrative imposes a welcome temporary organisation.

Finally he sailed for Malta. Continued application of his theory was still helping him organise his responses to nature as he did so: with something of his old Stowey alertness he commented at Malta on the difficulty of distinguishing between the movements of live sea-gulls and those of the spots of foam that 'peopled the *alive* Sea';[57] he also contemplated the sky, 'that soft blue mighty Arch' and closely analysed its 'aweful adorable omneity in unity', seeing it, one assumes, as an effect brought about by co-operation between the primary powers that see it as a 'sapphire Bason' and the secondary which know its true immensity.[58] At other times he had been able to relax from the

strenuousness of such observations to passive contemplation of
what 'the night-side of Nature' revealed directly, as when, on
his voyage, he watched the moonlit water by the ship,

> thickly swarming with insect life, *all* busy-swarming in the
> path, their swarming makes—but within the Shadow of the
> Ship it was—scattered at distances—scattered Os, rapidly un-
> coiling into serpent spirals—O how slow a word is rapidly to
> express the Life and time-mocking Motion of that Change,
> always Os before, always Spirals, coiling, uncoiling, *being* . . .
>
> (CN II 2070)

The visionary core of *The Ancient Mariner* here quietly reasserts
itself through a direct repetition, in the realm of the actual, of
the darting vivid energies that the Mariner had seen 'within the
Shadow of the Ship' – the play of which, Coleridge evidently
thinks, might still be central to an understanding of the nature
of *'being'*. Such moments, however rare, encouraged the hope
that his theories might after all be about to justify themselves in
their entirety, enabling him among other things to return to
England repossessed of 'Pleasure and elastic Health'.[59]

Other Relays

In the event, Coleridge's stay in Malta not only failed to fulfil his larger hopes but proved of little value to his health. Cut off from his friends, often sick and yearning for sympathy, he found the heat and noise of Valetta oppressive rather than stimulating. The hoped-for crisis did not happen; instead, his dependency on laudanum grew stronger. When he finally returned to England his friends were shocked by the change. Dorothy Wordsworth wrote:

> ... never never did I feel such a shock as at first sight of him. We all felt exactly in the same way—as if he were different from what we have expected to see; almost as much as a person of whom we have thought much and of whom we had formed an image in our own minds, without having any personal knowledge of him ...   (WL (1806–11) 86)

Only sometimes, when he was 'animated in conversation concerning things removed from him' did she catch a glimpse of his former self. Worst of all, the 'divine expression of his countenance' was gone except for an occasional 'shadow' or 'gleam'.[1]

Coleridge was in fact now embarking upon the darkest phase of his career, during which the separation from his wife, his desperate love for Sara Hutchinson, his ill-health and his increasing slavery to opium would inflict experiences of misery which culminated in the bitter quarrel with Wordsworth. When he finally emerged from the trough of those years he would refer to the experience as his 'first death'.[2]

It was by no means the end of his career, however. Even while he was passing into the shadows he managed to give some

fine lectures and produce *The Friend*: not long afterwards there
ensued the extraordinary resuscitation of his powers which
enabled him to produce, in the course of a few years, *Biographia
Literaria, Sibylline Leaves*, the *Lay Sermons*, the drama *Zapolya*
and the revised *Friend*, along with various literary and philosophical lectures and the manuscript *Theory of Life*. Afterwards
he passed to the more serene prose and poetry of his last years.
A proper consideration of his later career requires a separate
study, therefore, for it has a shape of its own and merits consideration as a further body of achievement.

Despite the importance of his later works, however, any full
study of them would need to take account of the extent to
which they still reflect the central intellectual concerns of the
years we have been discussing. Although his disillusionment with
opium and his despair at the outcome of his love for Sara
Hutchinson prised him from his former deep involvement, he
could not altogether leave these ideas behind, for they were too
closely intertwined with the very life of his mind, ministering
to what had been most distinctive in his thinking. Again and
again in his later works he can be found trying to find a place
(even if sometimes only in a footnote or appendix) for ideas
which continue to fascinate him and which he evidently still
feels might offer a key to the problems he is discussing.

Nor did his retreat from his more venturesome speculations
involve a simple reassertion of allegiance to old forms and ways.
A constant feature in his whole career (all the more remarkable
in view of the weakness that he sometimes showed in other
matters) is his maintenance of a determined independence –
including an unwillingness to undertake a permanent career or
profession – even if this sometimes resulted in a need to fall back
on others for support in the successive crises to which such
independence led.

In his brief study of Coleridge as poet, Sir Arthur Quiller-
Couch produced a colourful image for the process by which
Coleridge was enabled to survive. Applying to him De Quincey's
comment on Wordsworth, 'Providence set perpetual relays along
his path through life', he went on:[3]

We pursue the man and come up with group after group
of his friends: and each, as we demand 'What have you done

with Coleridge?' answers 'Coleridge? That wonderful fellow?
. . . He was here just now, and we helped him forward a little
way.'

To anyone who has read accounts of Coleridge's life, the comment is a fair one. It does justice to the extraordinary number
of people who at one time or another gave Coleridge temporary
help, and to the attractiveness which they clearly felt – even if,
as Quiller-Couch also remarks, there was a natural exasperation
at his frequent failures of responsibility and ineptitudes in
practical matters.

Extended too far, however, the idea produces a picture of
Coleridge as an over-dependent and anxious figure, continually
demanding consolation from his friends whilst absent-mindedly
consuming their sympathy and financial aid. Such a concept is
not only unjust to Coleridge; when further extended into denial
of his originality, it distorts the literary and intellectual history
of the time.

What emerges from a dispassionate study of the evidence is
rather that Coleridge – and more particularly in his youth – gave
to his friends intellectually in a lavish way. If Quiller-Couch's
image is faithful to our picture of Coleridge stumbling down the
road of his later life and sometimes needing a helping hand to
get to the next stage, the image which serves the early period
best is that of a figure moving with a vitality all its own and
setting off relays of another kind – touching a succession of
persons with an excitement that started them into new modes
of thought and creation.

It is not always easy, of course, to separate an excitement set
off by Coleridge from one which might belong to the currents of
the age. When we look into Blake's ideas, for instance, we find
some extraordinary parallels with Coleridge. Coleridge's delight
in energy is matched and surpassed in Blake's affirmation that
'everything that lives is holy'; his belief in the importance of
imagination, similarly, seems almost cautious at the side of
Blake's insistence on the centrality of 'Vision'.

The parallels run still closer: not only in their common preoccupation with the issue of innocence, but in their fascination
at the interplay between growing forms and free-ranging
energies. One need only turn to the illustrations of the Songs of

Innocence and of Experience to discover many designs in which
a tree-trunk is surrounded by spirals of growing leaf; later this
motif is matched by others in which the serpentine spirals round
a human figure represent the ambiguous workings of his own
energetic selfhood. When Blake wishes to express his sense of
human inspiration, moreover, he, like Coleridge in the Two
Voices section of *The Ancient Mariner*, thinks of two forces, the
one an aspiring and yearning exertion of animal spirits, the other
a quiet and revelatory expansiveness at the heart of vegetation.
First he pictures a bird that puts forth its energies at dawn –
rising from cold earth into an expanse of light which it is thus
enabled to picture as the inside of a great shell:[4]

Thou hearest the Nightingale begin the Song of Spring
The Lark sitting upon his earthy bed, just as the morn
Appears, listens silent; then springing from the waving
/Cornfield, loud
He leads the Choir of Day: trill, trill, trill, trill,
Mounting upon the wings of light into the Great Expanse,
Reechoing against the lovely blue & shining heavenly Shell . . .

At the opposite extreme he sets the sensory-possessing power of
the scent from a wild flower:

Thou perceivest the Flowers put forth their precious Odours,
And none can tell how from so small a center comes such
Sweets,
Forgetting that within that Center Eternity expands
Its ever during doors . . .

Blake, like Coleridge, knew that the road charted by such
perceptions could in other circumstances turn into a fearful one,
carrying the mental traveller away from familiar landmarks of
the eighteenth-century intellectual scene. Nevertheless, he was
willing to travel further and more boldly along it, extending
some elements also to be found in Coleridge's vision, as with his
blending of delight and terror in 'The Tyger' or the fearful
presentation of the poetic act at the end of *Milton*.

We cannot, in the face of such striking parallels, rule out the
possibility of some direct influence. It is not impossible that
Blake was one of those who heard Coleridge discoursing as a

brilliant schoolboy, or that Coleridge heard some of Blake's ideas reported. It is conceivable, in view of the comparative smallness of the contemporary artistic and literary scene, that they had access to each other's ideas through some common circle of acquaintance, such as that which flourished for a time round Joseph Johnson the publisher. Or they may have come to the same paradigms independently. All that we know for certain is that Coleridge annotated *Songs of Innocence and of Experience* many years later and that when they met they discoursed, according to an observer, 'like congenial beings of another sphere'.[5]

In this case, we do not know whether or not direct early influence was involved; in others, where we do know it to have been at work, what then comes to light calls for a re-examination of the phenomenon itself. Traditionally, 'influences' have been, for scholars, largely a matter of discovering precise echoes of language or detail. The conventional picture of the influenced artist is of a man with a model before him, which he brings into the service of his own work; and we judge the quality of the later work by the degree of successful transformation.

As certain critics have pointed out, however, to investigate simply by comparing texts may be to ignore certain important aspects of the process. Harold Bloom, for example, argues that the major ingredient in a poet's relationship with his predecessors is a considerable anxiety, a fear of finding his creative powers completely taken over by some powerful sensibility from the past.[6]

The point is an important one for an understanding of the romantic writers: we need think only of Keats's explicit comments on his relationship to Milton[7a] to see the force of it. And Coleridge and Wordsworth, seeking to create a basis for new poetical creation in the 1790s, were clearly at risk. But we do not do full justice to the situation unless we see that subtle relationships of another kind may also be at work. The presence of an original and ranging intelligence in a generation may produce influence of a positive and welcome kind – though still less easily measurable through resemblances of language or meaning. Such influences may work largely through stimulation, assisting other writers to find their own particular form. At its best, the effect may be like that exercised by Shakespeare's Cleopatra:

> vilest things
> Become themselves in her, that the holy priests
> Bless her, when she is riggish.

– and such influences are obviously harder to track than the conventional kind. Yet the task is not impossible. Bloom has drawn attention to the fact that the relationship between an artist and his 'strong' predecessor is often one of 'misprision': whether deliberately or otherwise, he misreads the other's work to produce a new version of his own, and thus escapes bondage to the past. In the case of a predecessor such as Coleridge, on the other hand, the relationship is less fearful. The next generation may be aware rather of a multi-faceted personality, progressing through many states and conditions and so offering various fresh nuclei of possible organisation to their own experience. To describe influence of this kind we need a metaphor more like that of Krishna at the dance, as described in a passage which Coleridge himself knew:[8]

> A number of virgins having assembled to celebrate in mirth and sport the descent of Kissen (Creeshna) in the height of their joy the god himself appeared among them, and proposed *a dance* to the jocund fair. They objected the want of partners with whom to form that dance: but Creeshna obviated the objection by dividing himself (his rays) into as many portions as there were virgins, and thus every nymph had a Creeshna to attend her in the circular dance.

Allowing for the extravagance of the parallel and transposing the circular dance into a series of relays through time, we may argue that something of the kind was true of Coleridge's relationship to his contemporaries. A succession of young men came along at particular moments of his career, each to be deeply affected by the aspect of Coleridge's personality and thought that was then in the ascendant and stimulated to make a dance-figure of his own from the interplay.

Lamb, for example, knew Coleridge at school, when, we have suggested, Coleridge was first devising the language of the 'heart's imagination' which he moulded upon his reading of Boehme and the Neoplatonists; a similar fusion of the affectionate and the imaginative gives life to Lamb's prose in his *Essays* of *Elia*, over twenty years later. Sometimes the resemblances are surprisingly close. Over the years Coleridge's favourite language of the heart's affections extended itself from the simple images of stream, breeze, green fields and candle-flame to be found also in Boehme, to cover specific experiences that he associated with his love for Sara Hutchinson. In a memorable notebook passage he brought together a list of images 'which never fail instantly to awake into vivider flame the for ever and ever Feeling of you', beginning as follows:

> The fire/Mary, you, & I at Gallow-Hill/—or if flamy, reflected in children's round faces—ah whose children?—a dog—that dog whose restless eyes oft catching the light of the fire used to watch your face, as you leaned with your head on your hand and arm, & your feet on the *fender*/the fender thence/— Fowls at Table—the last dinner at Gallow Hill, when you drest the two fowls in that delicious white Sauce which when very ill is the only idea of food that does not make me *sicker*/all natural Scenery—ten thousand links, and if it please me, the very spasm & drawing-back of a pleasure which is half-pain you not being there—Cheese—at Middleham, too salt/horses, my ride to Scarborough—asses, to that large living 2 or 3 miles from Middleham/All Books—my Study at Keswick/— the Ceiling or Head of a Bed—the green watered Mazarine!— A Candle in it's socket, with its alternate fits & dying flashes of lingering Light—O *God*; O *God!*—Books of abstruse Knowlege—the Thomas Aquinas & Suarez from the Durham Library/   (CN III 3708)

We may compare with this a passage from Lamb's 'New Year's Eve', describing the pleasures of life which he was most loth to abandon:

> Sun, and sky, and breeze, and solitary walks, and summer holidays, and the greenness of fields, and the delicious juices of meats and fishes, and society, and the cheerful glass, and candle-light, and fire-side conversations, and innocent vanities, and jests, and *irony itself*—do these things go out with life?
>
> Can a ghost laugh, or shake his gaunt sides, when you are pleasant with him?
>
> And you, my midnight darlings, my Folios! must I part with the intense delight of having you (huge armfuls) in my

embraces? Must knowledge come to me, if it come at all, by some awkward experiment of intuition, and no longer by this familiar process of reading?

Shall I enjoy friendships there, wanting the smiling indications which point to them here,—the recognisable face—the "sweet assurance of a look"—? (LW II 29–30)

When one has compared Lamb's poised, amused posture – essentially sociable, and offering a climactic gesture to 'irony itself' – with Coleridge's more yearning, despairing evocation, there remains an extraordinarily high content of shared imagery; and if one further compares the description of the children with the fire reflected in their faces ('ah whose children?') with the conclusion of Lamb's 'Dream Children',[9*] one is led to ask whether the contents of this notebook entry might not have been known to Lamb in some form.[10*]

Other elements in his *Essays of Elia* include various amused reflections upon the tricks played by accidents of consciousness or circumstance for which Coleridge's speculations provide an obvious possible source. The discussion of nightmares in 'Witches and Other Night-fears' includes quotations from *The Ancient Mariner* and *Kubla Khan*; in the same essay he laments the poverty of his dream-life compared with Coleridge's.[11] In 'The Convalescent' he describes how 'the sick man swells in the sole contemplation of his single sufferings, till he becomes a Tityus to himself'; in describing 'Captain Jackson' and his 'magnificent self-delusion' he comments: 'There was no resisting the vortex of his temperament'.[12] In 'New Year's Eve', (the essay quoted from above,) there are various further parallels, including a comment on the strange disparity between attitudes to death in summer and winter which employs a snake-imagery markedly Coleridgean:

> In winter this intolerable disinclination to dying—to give it its mildest name—does more especially haunt and beset me. In a genial August noon, beneath a sweltering sky, death is almost problematic. At those times do such poor snakes as myself enjoy an immortality. Then we expand and burgeon. Then are we as strong again, as valiant again, as wise again, and a great deal taller. The blast that nips and shrinks me, puts me in thoughts of death . . . (LW II 30)

Phenomena of consciousness which were for Coleridge portentous with potential metaphysical significance are in Lamb matter rather for ironic contemplation. In the same way, Lamb had early learned not to expect too much from his friend, with the result that, despite one period of coolness, the relationship between the two men remained constant. Remembering the radiance of Coleridge at school he could still, however, twenty-five years later, see him as an 'Archangel a little damaged' and report that 'his face when he reads his verses hath its ancient glory'.[13] Coleridge was aware of a complementary quality in his friend: 'Lamb every now and then eradiates', he wrote, '& the beam, tho' single & fine as a hair, yet is rich with colours, & I both see & feel it.'[14] For Lamb, as we said at the outset, there was always a touch of magic about Coleridge.

While Lamb, through long acquaintance, could continue to see and value the unique quality of his friend's intelligence, men who came later under Coleridge's spell were subject to more decisive disillusionment. Southey soon fell into a semi-amused, semi-exasperated scepticism concerning his friend which remained with him for the rest of his life. It may be questioned, nevertheless, whether he would have found his way to the exotic Eastern topics of his long poems without Coleridge's enthusiasm, which surfaced vividly in *Kubla Khan* and could still prompt him in 1799 to propose a poetic collaboration on the topic of 'Mahomet'.[15] At the height of their collaboration in 1795, indeed, Southey had included in *Joan of Arc* lines which showed him pursuing an interest in dreams similar to Coleridge's (and perhaps reflecting a joint reading of Andrew Baxter):

> Soon she closed
> Her heavy eye-lids; not reposing then,
> For busy Phantasy, in other scenes
> Awakened: whether that superior powers,
> By wise permission, prompt the midnight dream,
> Or that the soul, escaped its fleshly clog,
> Flies free, and soars amid the invisible world,
> And all things *are* that seem . . .   (ix 3–10)

Southey omitted the whole passage from later editions and never again allowed himself so full an entry into that world of speculation; but he was able (again after a period of estrangement) to remain on friendly terms with Coleridge.

To others, still more profoundly affected, disenchantment brought with it a sense of betrayal. Foremost was Hazlitt. As we saw at the outset, his enthusiasm for Coleridge had first been kindled during the period of Godwinian enthusiasm in England; it was also his fortune to have made personal contact with him when he was still at the height of his eloquence. What he could not know was that Coleridge's acceptance of the Wedgwoods' offer of a pension (which actually took place during the visit to Shrewsbury) marked a watershed in his career by allowing him freedom for independent study and writing. Hazlitt encountered Coleridge as a man preaching a social and religious message to his generation: he did not fully appreciate the presence of other intellectual undercurrents which would lead Coleridge, once the suppression of the Swiss cantons had induced a final disillusionment concerning the French Revolution, to take up the more independent political and religious positions which would lead him eventually into the conservatism of his later years.

In further respects, Hazlitt is the figure of the time who most nearly fits Bloom's paradigm of the artist as fearing the insidious possessive power of a great predecessor. For it was not simply that in the early encounters he thought himself to be in the presence of a great prophet, his sights set on political aims which he himself felt he could share; there was also in him a private self which, beneath his forcefulness of self-presentation, was very like Coleridge's. We need only compare his confessions of un-requited love in *Liber Amoris* with Coleridge's long and desperate yearning for Sara Hutchinson, or think of the self-criticism for having loitered his life away 'reading books, looking at pictures, going to plays, hearing, thinking, writing on what pleased me best' which concludes 'I have wanted only one thing to make me happy; but wanting that have wanted everything!'[16] to feel the force of the resemblance. If Hazlitt's later bitterness towards Coleridge is partly explicable as a reaction against an influence which he felt to have been detrimental to his own success, it is also exacerbated by a sense of entanglement at the roots of his being. When he is trying to write a piece of dramatic criticism many years later, he finds that for a mode which will deal with the disparate pieces involved he must explicitly invoke the persona of Coleridge, which enables him to speak in judgement on the triviality of current pieces with accents remembered from long ago:

> The principle of the imagination resembles the emblem of the serpent, by which the ancients typified wisdom and the universe, with undulating folds, for ever varying and for ever flowing into itself,—circular, and without beginning or end. The definite, the fixed, is death: the principle of life is the indefinite, the growing, the moving, the continuous.
>
> (HW XVIII 371)

For Hazlitt, the staider sentiments of the *Lay Sermons* were a severe disappointment and Coleridge's political journalism a betrayal.[17] Nor did it help matters that Coleridge's suspicions concerning Napoleon had later been backed by thoughtful men in the country at large. Yet he could not forget the excitement of his early encounters with Coleridge, or the tantalising range of possibilities, intellectual and social, which had then been opened up to him – indeed his very attempts to deal with the situation in retrospect involved him in a psychological analysis employing terms similar to Coleridge's own. Having described the state of mind that had flourished for a time just after the French Revolution ('The mind opened and a softness might be perceived coming over the heart of individuals, beneath "the scales that fence" our self-interest') he moved to the following disillusioned commentary:

> In the outset of life (and particularly at this time I felt it so) our imagination has a body to it. We are in a state between sleeping and waking, and have indistinct but glorious glimpses of strange shapes, and there is always something to come better than what we see. As in our dreams the fulness of the blood gives warmth and reality to the coinage of the brain, so in youth our ideas are clothed, and fed, and pampered with our good spirits; we breathe thick with thoughtless happiness, the weight of future years presses on the strong pulses of the heart, and we repose with undisturbed faith in truth and good.
>
> (HW XVII 116–17)

Coleridge himself could be fully dealt with, even at that late date, only by creative misprision of his achievement. His great intellectual quest must be reinterpreted as the flights and wanderings of a man losing himself in an endless pursuit of novelties. The passage mentioned earlier, presenting Coleridge as a romantically endowed, if also slightly absurd version of Milton's Satan, winging his way through Chaos, culminates with the following picture of his progress:

> [he] now "laughed with Rabelais in his easy chair" or pointed to Hogarth, or afterwards dwelt on Claude's classic scenes, or spoke with rapture of Raphael, and compared the women at Rome to figures that had walked out of his pictures, or visited the Oratory of Pisa, and described the works of Giotto and Ghirlandaio and Massaccio, and gave the moral of the picture of the Triumph of Death, where the beggars and the wretched invoke his dreadful dart, but the rich and mighty of the earth quail and shrink before it; and in that land of siren sights and sounds, saw a dance of peasant girls, and was charmed with lutes and gondolas,—or wandered into Germany and lost himself in the labyrinths of the Hartz Forest and of the Kantean philosophy, and amongst the cabalistic names of Fichtè and Schelling and Lessing, and God knows who.   (HW XI 33–4)

The stage, it will be noticed, has been carefully prepared, so that Kant, Fichte, Schelling and Lessing can make their appearance in a context of rambling, half-wanton dillettantism, necessary to the implication (developed immediately afterwards) that Coleridge had lost all the sympathy for mankind which had characterised his early enthusiasm for radical politics.

This reduction of Coleridge to a creature of infinite impressibility was not, as it happens, to be without an influence of its own upon later nineteenth-century aestheticism, thus obscuring his original situation further. By a strange reversal, Walter Pater's account of Coleridge praised him for the very features which Hazlitt distrusted. Man, the most complex of the products of nature, he urged, 'is so receptive, all the influences of nature and of society ceaselessly playing upon him, so that every hour in his life is unique, changed altogether by a stray word, or glance, or touch.' Coleridge, so far as he had indulged his 'passion for the absolute' had erred against his own spirit.[18] It is hardly surprising then, that when we read Pater's famous account, in his essay on Leonardo da Vinci,[19] of a sensibility endlessly enriched by beautiful impressions, we recognise an apparent debt to the very syntax, rhythms and imagery of Hazlitt's Coleridge:

> She is older than the rocks among which she sits; like the vampire, she has been dead many times, and learned the secrets of the grave; and has been a diver in deep seas and keeps their fallen day about her; and trafficked for strange webs with Eastern merchants; and, as Leda, was the mother of Helen of Troy, and as Saint Anne, the mother of Mary; and all this has been to her as the sounds of lyres and flutes, and lives only in the delicacy with which it has moulded the changing lineaments, and tinged the eyelids and the hands.

Wordsworth, who knew Coleridge better than did Hazlitt in 1798, could not afterwards disprize his achievement with such facility. For him any disappointment was mingled with an awareness of the extraordinary subtlety and intricacy of Coleridge's intelligence, which he believed to have been revealed all too briefly. Coleridge, he once said to Henry Taylor, had been 'in blossom' only for four years – from 1796 to 1800. The plant, he went on, was perennial, but the flowers were few.[20]

Something of what he meant may be seen from the evidences of influence in the writings of the Wordsworths. While Dorothy showed little sign of having been affected by his ideas in their more philosophical form, there are indications that she was touched by his feeling for magical lights and mysterious energies actually manifesting themselves in nature, as when, on the completion of *The Ancient Mariner*, she wrote in her journal simply, 'A beautiful evening, very starry. The horned moon'; or again, four years later, 'The moon came out suddenly when we were at John's Grove, and a star or two besides.'[21] In the same way, one suspects something more than a fortuitous connection between the successive sentences of an entry in June 1800:

> I sate a long time to watch the hurrying waves, and to hear the regularly irregular sound of the dashing waters. The waves round about the little Island seemed like a dance of spirits that rose out of the water, round its small circumference of shore. Inquired about lodgings for Coleridge ...   (DWJ I 44)

– and even more between those of another, in the following year:[22]

The wind drove and eddied about and about, and the hills looked large and swelling through the storm. We thought of Coleridge...

A full account of the influence of Coleridge on Wordsworth himself would argue that the 'correspondent breeze' of *The Prelude* is a natural successor to the breeze that blew in *The Eolian Harp*; that the very springs and streams of his poetry owe something to his friend's speculations; and that his larger efforts to discover centres of peace in nature owed much to Coleridge's belief that under certain aspects the central powers of nature might be discovered to be in correspondence with similar powers in man. It would also suggest that Coleridge's presence was vital to the activity of Wordsworth's creative powers by reasons of his ability, by vivid speculations, to create an aura of possible magic about the natural world and prompt new ways of looking back at his earlier experience. When, for example, Wordsworth tried to explain the origin and significance of his early lines for *The Prelude* concerning the boy who blew 'mimic hootings' to the owls, he chose terms which were strongly Coleridgean:

> Guided by one of my own primary consciousnesses, I have represented a commutation and transfer of internal feelings, co-operating with external accidents to plant, for immortality, images of sound and sight, in the celestial soil of the Imagina-tion. (W Prel 547)

He speaks of 'primary consciousnesses' rather than 'primary consciousness', it is true, giving a twist of his own to the concept; but he then moves no less surely to Coleridge's 'organic' image of the imagination by his reference to 'celestial soil'. In the same way, Wordsworth's tribute to Coleridge's intelligence in Book Two brings together an imagery of seeds and fountains with a sense of two levels in the consciousness, a 'secondary', by which we make distinctions, and a deeper, unifying power:

> Who knows the individual hour in which
> His habits were first sown, even as a seed,
> Who that shall point as with a wand and say
> 'This portion of the river of my mind
> Came from yon fountain?' Thou, my Friend! art one
> More deeply read in thy own thoughts; to thee

Science appears but what in truth she is,
Not as our glory and our absolute boast,
But as a succedaneum, and a prop
To our infirmity. Thou art no slave
Of that false secondary power by which,
In weakness, we create distinctions, then
Deem that our puny boundaries are things
Which we perceive, and not which we have made.
To thee, unblinded by these outward shows,
The unity of all has been reveal'd . . .

(Prel. (1805) II 211–26)

For Wordsworth, the riddle of Coleridge's powers ran very deep. Only when his friend died, thirty years later, could he afford to acknowledge his qualities openly ('the most *wonderful* man that he had ever known');[28] then, however, the imagery of ice and spring rose up in his mind to produce an elegiac statement of marvellous ambiguity. Two years had not passed, he said,

Since every mortal power of Coleridge
Was frozen at its marvellous source.   (WP IV 277)

Previously he had been bemused by the fate of a friendship, the major phase of which had begun so promisingly yet ended with a love-sick, drug-dependent Coleridge as a burdensome presence in his house, reading all night and then sleeping for most of the day. The very change which he saw taking place had been described at the time in imagery which Coleridge's speculations had charged with new significance:

There is a change—and I am poor;
Your Love hath been, nor long ago,
A Fountain at my fond Heart's door.
Whose only business was to flow;
And flow it did; not taking heed
Of its own bounty, or my need.

What happy moments did I count!
Bless'd was I then all bliss above!
Now, for this consecrated Fount
Of murmuring, sparkling, living love,

What have I? shall I dare to tell?
A comfortless and hidden *well.*

A well of love—it may be deep—
I trust it is, and never dry:
What matter? if the Waters sleep
In silence and obscurity.
—Such change, and at the very door
Of my fond Heart, hath made me poor.

(WP II 34)

Shortly after Wordsworth wrote these lines, De Quincey met
Coleridge for the first time. As one might expect from them, the
Coleridge whom he came to know was different from the ebullient young man who had impressed Hazlitt. The point can be
made very simply by comparing their first impressions. In
Hazlitt's circle Coleridge first broke on the scene as a man who
had travelled up in the coach to Shrewsbury talking at a great
rate with his fellow-passengers: 'He did not cease while he stayed;
nor has he since, that I know of.'[24] De Quincey, by contrast,
first encountered Coleridge standing under a gate at Bridgwater:

I examined him steadfastly for a minute or more; and it struck
me that he saw neither myself nor any other object in the
street. He was in a deep reverie; for I had dismounted, made
two or three trifling arrangements at an inn-door, and
advanced close to him, before he had apparently become
conscious of my presence. The sound of my voice, announcing
my own name, first awoke him; he started, and for a moment
seemed at a loss to understand my purpose or his own situation; for he repeated rapidly a number of words which had no
relation to either of us. There was no *mauvaise honte* in his
manner, but simple perplexity, and an apparent difficulty in
recovering his position amongst daylight realities.

(DQW II 150)

The Coleridge whom he was trying to greet had passed in a
few years from the high spirits of 1798 to the characteristic lassi-
tude of the immediate post-Malta years. Ill-health, opium and
unfulfilled love had taken their full toll; delighted observation of
the energies of nature and the potentialities of humanity had
given place to more abstract patient investigation, including

detailed introspection. In these circumstances it is not surprising that, where Hazlitt's later attitude to Coleridge was still touched somewhere by a delight in expressive energy and in 'gusto', De Quincey's attitudes took on a correspondingly darker colouring. The Grasmere in which he took up residence was a place of less sparkle than in happier days: the Coleridge who had once abounded in enthusiasm for new ideas now often sat brooding in his room for hours on end; much of his attention, when it was not devoted to his own unhappy situation, was focused upon the intellectual implications of his new despondency.

That is not to suggest, of course, that Coleridge had lost all his intellectual powers. De Quincey himself goes on to recall that at the first meeting, once Coleridge had taken him to the house where he was staying and had settled the formalities of reception, he swept, like some great river that had been momentarily checked,

> into a continuous strain of eloquent dissertation, certainly the
> most novel, the most finely illustrated, and traversing the
> most spacious fields of thought by transitions the most just
> and logical, that it was possible to conceive.   (DQW II 152)

The fitting metaphor for Coleridge now, however, is that of a stream rather than an ebullience; a typical conversation with him, in the same way, has a different quality from the excited and exploratory remarks recorded by Hazlitt, as is shown by a reminiscence in the *Confessions*:

> Many years ago, when I was looking over Piranesi's "Anti-
> quities of Rome," Coleridge, then standing by, described to me
> a set of plates from that artist, called his "Dreams," and which
> record the scenery of his own visions during the delirium of a
> fever. Some of these (I describe only from memory of
> Coleridge's account) represented vast Gothic halls; on the
> floor of which stood mighty engines and machinery, wheels,
> cables, catapults, &c., expressive of enormous power put forth,
> or resistance overcome. Creeping along the sides of the walls,
> you perceived a staircase; and upon this groping his way
> upwards, was Piranesi himself. Follow the stairs a little farther,
> and you perceive them reaching an abrupt termination, with-
> out any balustrade, and allowing no step onwards to him who

should reach the extremity, except into the depths below. Whatever is to become of poor Piranesi, at least you suppose that his labours must now in some way terminate. But raise your eyes, and behold a second flight of stairs still higher, on which again Piranesi is perceived, by this time standing on the very brink of the abyss. Once again elevate your eye, and a still more aerial flight of stairs is descried; and there, again, is the delirious Piranesi, busy on his aspiring labours; and so on, until the unfinished stairs and the hopeless Piranesi both are lost in the upper gloom of the hall. With the same power of endless growth and self-reproduction did my architecture proceed in dreams. (DQW III 438–9)

This passage has been commented on by more than one critic. Hillis Miller, who has explored its relevance to De Quincey's own writings, describes what he calls the 'Piranesi effect' in his later visions.[25a] Alethea Hayter has pointed out that such an effect seems to be commonly associated with opium-taking.[26]

For Coleridge, it will be seen, the 'Piranesi' of such a conception is a figure darkly complementary to his original figure of inspired genius. That genius presided over a fountain of self-diversifying forms, rising up for ever in abundance; now the creative genius is seen imprisoned in a circular set of images of his own making. In Coleridge's own nightmares, as related in 'The Pains of Sleep', his imagination had often turned back upon itself to oppress him with the threats of horrifying shapes, or to raise structures which were no longer sunny pleasure-domes overlooking mazy streams but labyrinths in which the dreamer was himself lost.

It was perhaps De Quincey's special vocation to live in the penumbra of great emotions, to find his most vivid utterances in the recollection of former intensity during a period of shadow. In the *Autobiography* his childhood emotions after the death of his sister are recorded in similar terms,[27] and he would seem to have been almost naturally drawn to similar brooding landscapes in later life. But this does not mean that his insights were false: if there is a dark quality to his descriptions of Wordsworth and Coleridge at this time, it is no doubt faithful to an intangible sense, in their presence, of passions spent and intensities surviving without adequate fuel.

The Coleridge he knew was also, as we have seen, a haunted figure, who perhaps found himself stimulated to an unwonted degree by the eagerness of this young man. Certainly some elements of Coleridge's earlier speculations seem to have drifted by some means into De Quincey's mind, making him more conscious of the power of subliminal processes. The concept of a dark magnetism, for example, worked strongly on his imagination at times, as when he focused his impression of London in the imagery of 'vast droves of cattle, suppose upon the great north road, all with their heads directed to London, and expounding the size of the attracting body, together with the forces of its attractive power, by the never-ending succession of these droves, and the remoteness from the capital of the lines upon which they were moving'.[28] Later he describes the attraction as one of an increasing 'blind sympathy with a mighty but unseen object, some vast magnetic range of Alps in your neighbourhood' and then changes the image into that of slow entry into a maelstrom.[29]

Another passage, this time in the *Confessions of an English Opium-Eater*, shows De Quincey exploring further implications of the theme. He speaks of the way in which a water-diviner can 'by some magnetic sympathy between his rod and the object of his divination' indicate the spot at which to look for water or metals, and goes on:

> Not otherwise has the marvellous magnetism of Christianity called up from darkness sentiments the most august, previously inconceivable, formless, and without life; for previously there had been no religious philosophy equal to the task of ripening such sentiments; but also, at the same time, by incarnating these sentiments in images of corresponding grandeur, it has so exalted their character as to lodge them eternally in human hearts.   (DQW III 291–2)

In these dark asseverations we recognise a correspondence with the Coleridge who was still trying to salvage religious significance from his former speculations, and who would continue to insist that the importance of Christianity lay in its continuous presentation of 'truths that find a man'. Devoid of the possibilities presented by his former belief in its physiological validity, however, magnetism could be no more than a metaphor of attraction for Coleridge, as for De Quincey, and as such had largely disappeared from his writings.

As fortune would have it, however, there came a further twist to the affair. We suggested earlier that Blumenbach's deep scepticism on the subject of animal magnetism had been the main cause of the withdrawal of his own, still tentative assent and interest. In 1817, however, a translation of Blumenbach's *Institutions of Physiology* was published in which the author retracted his former scepticism. 'Compelled by my own experience,' he wrote, 'where the Patients were selected by myself and I was myself the sole Agent, I must avow that the facts are as undeniable as they at present are inexplicable.' Copying this statement into the margins of a copy of *The Friend*, Coleridge commented: '. . . since *Hufeland*, Stieglitz, above all, *Blumenbach*, the for so many years zealous Opponents & almost Persecutors of Animal Magnetism, have openly retracted their verdict, surely, I need not be ashamed to join in the recantation.' A similar comment was made in two other copies.[30]

This change of front by the great physiologists seems to have reawakened Coleridge's interest in the whole matter. Their recantations, coupled with his growing awareness of the development of *naturphilosophie* in Germany, may be regarded as responsible for a number of developments in Coleridge's writing, including the last-minute inclusion in *Sibylline Leaves* of a well-known addition to *The Eolian Harp*:[31]

> O! the one Life within us and abroad,
> Which meets all motion and becomes its soul,
> A light in sound, a sound-like power in light,
> Rhythm in all thought, and joyance every where . . .

It probably prompted the long marginal note in which Coleridge argued that faith, as a 'unifying energy', was most likely to exist in 'weak & credulous but sincere, sensitive and warm-hearted Men' and expressed his opinion that Animal Magnetism would be found to be connected with a Warmth-sense, thus confirming his 'long long ago theory of Volition as a mode of *double Touch*'.[32] He wrote a long memorandum on animal magnetism and read all the literature he could lay hands on.[33]

There are also signs that he became for a time more willing to move into old currents of thought – particularly in the presence

of a receptive audience. For this reason, considerable interest
attaches to one particular encounter of his later years: that
occasion in April 1819 when, while walking with his disciple
J. H. Green in a lane near Caen Wood, he was approached by a
young man who 'after enquiring by a look whether it would be
agreeable' joined them. John Keats has left us an account of the
topics which were then broached by Coleridge:[34]

> I walked with him at his alderman-after dinner pace for near
> two miles I suppose In those two miles he broached a thousand
> things—let me see if I can give you a list—Nightingales,
> Poetry—on Poetical sensation—Metaphysics—Different gen-
> era and species of dreams—Nightmare—a Dream accompanied
> by a sense of touch—single and double touch—a dream
> related—First and second consciousness—the difference ex-
> plained between will and Volition—so many metaphysicians
> from a want of smoking the second consciousness—Monsters
> —the Kraken—Mermaids—southey believes in them—
> southeys belief too much diluted—A Ghost story—Good
> morning—I heard his voice as he came towards me—I heard it
> as he moved away—I had heard it all the interval—if it may
> be called so.

This catalogue has usually been read as indicating the diffuseness
and tangentiality of Coleridge's mind. Reading it in the light of
our previous chapters, on the other hand, it is hard to resist the
conclusion that it records an orderly presentation of theories
that had long been revolving in Coleridge's mind: that he began
by commenting on the song of the nightingale (mentioning perhaps his delight in the nightingales in Caen Wood and his
feeling that 'death at such a time would be a reward for life')
and then associated its attractiveness with the particular level of
consciousness to which poetry made its appeal, illustrating his
argument by reference to the phenomena of dreams – and in
particular his theory that nightmare was a condition in which
through some derangement, double touch was transmitted as
single touch – 'to which the Imagination therefore, the true
inward Creatix, instantly out of the chaos of the elements or
shattered fragments of Memory puts together some form to fit
it.'[35] This led naturally to a distinction between the primary and
secondary levels of consciousness, and an assertion that the true

will belonged to the primary level while volition (the state with which human beings are more readily familiar) was largely a function of the secondary. So he was able to move into a critique of metaphysicians who failed to distinguish the two levels of consciousness and of poets who paid too little attention to superstitions and fictitious marvels which appealed to the primary level.

Keats had no more than an hour's conversation; yet the consequences of that encounter for Romantic poetry may have had a significance disproportionate to its length. For it is distinctly possible that this conversation left Keats thinking in a new way about his own experiences, contemplating, for example, the contrast between the warm sensuous moments in which it is hard for human beings to believe in death and the bleak contemplation of frozen forms which reminds them inexorably of death's inevitable intervention. And so, we may reason, Keats was set on the path which would lead him, not long after, to compose an ode to a nightingale in which that riddling contrast would be a central theme.

For Keats, nevertheless, the effect of hearing these topics expounded by Coleridge in 1819 was far different from what it might have been for Wordsworth in 1797. Instead of a bright-eyed eager young man, from whom such ideas issued in continuous bursts, he was listening to a stately, rather sad figure, walking at his alderman-after-dinner pace. Yet still from the darkling depths of that consciousness there proceeded a flow of ideas which struck home to the imagination. What then was the status of this surprising discourse? Was it a vision or a waking dream? Later, Keats was to write further poems, such as the second *Hyperion*, which explored the status of the artist's vision in similar vein. It is hard to resist the conclusion that his encounter with Coleridge, and his recognition, in this portly, dreamy figure, of an inner being who was quite other, was itself the occasion of reflection on the paradoxes involved in poetic activity, and that, by throwing into relief the problems concerned, it helped further to stimulate the achievements of his final phase.

In that generation, poets were responding mainly to Coleridge's early poems – including some which were only just coming forward for publication. Before meeting Coleridge, at least, Keats would seem to have learnt most from the informal sensuousness of his conversation poems. Byron admired *Remorse*, found himself unconsciously plagiarising *Christabel* after hearing Scott recite it, and heard Coleridge himself read *Kubla Khan*; he encouraged the publication of his work and would seem to have found stimulus for his own exotic writing in it.[36] Shelley drew most on the poems up to 1798: just as some of his odes can be seen to follow in a line from Coleridge's 'France: An Ode', so his whole scientific endeavour – his attempt to provide a coherent link between the new facts of science and the growth of democratic vision in the Europe of his day by establishing a convincing metaphysic which should embrace both – falls in with certain radical implications of Coleridge's early thinking which Coleridge himself had not pursued.[37] Although Shelley, like Coleridge, was drawn to the idea of a universal magnetism, on the other hand, his doubts concerning the physical status of such a force were reflected in his tendency to express the idea primarily in metaphorical form, as when he came to voice it in the *Defence of Poetry*:[38]

> The sacred links of that chain have never been entirely disjoined, which descending through the minds of many men is attached to those great minds, whence as from a magnet the invisible effluence is sent forth, which at once connects, animates and sustains the life of all.

After this, it becomes increasingly difficult to distinguish Coleridge's influence from currents that might have found their springs elsewhere. We may simply draw attention to the fact that subsequent preoccupations with the effects of industrialism, and the development of science, were often accompanied by a recognition, if only in imagery and rhetoric, that the energies of life need not be confined within totally mechanistic terms. We come across the phrase 'the magic impulse which has been felt in every department of national energy', for instance, and are surprised to find it being used not by a poetically-minded visionary but by a Manchester business man, seeking to defend the expansion of industry and commerce and the growth of the great Victorian cities.[39] Or we turn the pages of Humphry Davy's works and find that at the end of his life, in 1828–9, he turned away from the strictly scientific treatises that had made him famous and produced a more visionary work, entitled *Consolations in Travel.* In the first chapter, the narrator, sitting in the Colosseum at twilight and meditating on the decay wrought by time there, is visited by a strange experience:

> ...my reverie became deeper, the ruins surrounding me appeared to vanish from my sight, the light of the moon became more intense, and the orb itself seemed to expand in a flood of splendour. At the same time that my visual organs appeared so singularly affected, the most melodious sounds filled my ear; softer, yet at the same time deeper and fuller, than I had ever heard in the most harmonious and perfect concert. (DW IX 222-3)

In the vision, conveyed by a 'superior intelligence', that follows, the narrator is given a total view of the universe, ranging from a picture of man's progress in scientific knowledge through history on to a sense of all intelligence as essentially progressive through the various spheres of the universe. The guide, now called 'the Genius', tries to explain these successive states in a long passage which reminds one of Coleridge's 'monads of the infinite Mind' and his unusual picture of Newton in the Greek *Astronomy Ode*:

> Spiritual natures are eternal and indivisible, but their modes of being are as infinitely varied as the forms of matter. They have no relation to space, and, in their transitions, no dependence upon time, so that they can pass from one part of the universe to another by laws entirely independent of their motion. The quantity or the number of spiritual essences, like the quantity or number of the atoms of the material world, are always the same; but their arrangements, like those of the materials which they are destined to guide or govern, are infinitely diversified; they are, in fact, parts more or less inferior of the infinite Mind, and in the planetary systems,—to one of which this globe you inhabit belongs,—are in a state of probation, continually aiming at, and generally rising to, a higher state of existence. Were it permitted me to extend your vision to the fates of individual existences, I could show you the same spirit, which, in the form of Socrates, developed the foundations of moral and social virtue, in the Czar Peter

possessed of supreme power and enjoying exalted felicity in improving a rude people. I could show you the monad or spirit, which, with the organs of Newton, displayed an intelligence almost above humanity, now in a higher and better state of planetary existence drinking intellectual light from a purer source and approaching nearer to the infinite and divine Mind.   (DW IX 238–9)

The whole section in which this appears is worth reading as another version of speculations that we saw Coleridge entertaining as a young man. Throughout the book Davy makes no mention of him (they saw little or nothing of each other during the last twenty years of his life[40*]) but the book itself is dedicated to Coleridge's friend Tom Poole of Nether Stowey. A reading of it reminds one constantly that this is the Davy who had once written a poem called 'The Sons of Genius', hailed Coleridge as one destined to create 'the new world of intellectual form' and told him that 'thoughts which you have nursed, have been to me an eternal source of consolation.'[41*] Questions of influence or confluence here shade into one another bewilderingly.

The literary generation that followed the Romantic poets, meanwhile, was reacting against their poetry, arguing that it encouraged self-indulgence, sensuousness and introspectiveness at a time when the true need of society was for strong-minded attention to the problems being created by industrialisation. Hence the appearance of many novels and dissertations concerned with 'the condition of England'. When such writers sought the grounds of their own protest, on the other hand, they were driven back, time and again, to the needs and potentialities of the human spirit; and at such moments the earlier Coleridge remained a powerful presence. When we read A Christmas Carol, for example, we remember Godwin's urge to write, in Caleb Williams, a story that should 'constitute an epoch in the mind of the reader', and recognise a kinship of purpose between Dickens's tale and The Ancient Mariner. Marley's ghost, we notice, travels 'on the wings of the wind' – and does so because his spirit did not travel abroad in sympathetic imagination during life:

    ... if that spirit goes not forth in life, it is condemned to do so after death. It is doomed to wander through the world—oh, woe is me!—and witness what it cannot share, but might have shared on earth, and turned to happiness! (Stave i)

It is a more pointed version of the Mariner's restless fate; we may legitimately ask whether Dickens would have found that form for what he had to say had Coleridge's poem not been there to assist the conception.[42a]

When we turn to *Adam Bede*, similarly, we find that George Eliot indicates the mingled susceptibilities and obtuseness of her gentleman-seducer Arthur Donnithorne by his judgement of a book which has just come down from London and which he proposes to lend his godmother:

It's a volume of poems, 'Lyrical Ballads': most of them seem to me twaddling stuff; but the first is in a different style— 'The Ancient Mariner' is the title. I can hardly make head or tail of it as a story, but it's a strange, striking thing ... (ch. v)

Eleven years before, Mrs Gaskell had produced *Mary Barton*, in which she had brought herself to handle the matter – delicate for a Victorian audience – of a woman turned prostitute visiting the house of her innocent niece. The difficult task of portraying her state of mind was assisted by references to the 'witches' cauldron of her imagination' and, when she reached the door, by a direct reference to Coleridge:

She had felt as if some holy spell would prevent her (even as the unholy Lady Geraldine was prevented, in the abode of Christabel) from crossing the threshold of that home of her holy innocence ... (ch. xxi)

When she finally had her interview with Mary, her niece, there was an effect of telepathy between them at one moment, 'As if, according to the believers in mesmerism, the intenseness of her wish gave her power over another.'

Such were the contexts in which Coleridge's supernatural poetry came most naturally to the Victorian mind.

As for mesmerism itself, it enjoyed a considerable revival in England just after Coleridge's death. A public demonstration at University College Hospital in 1838 was attended by Charles Dickens, who retained a lifelong fascination for the phenomenon; Browning, Tennyson, Clough, Collins, Thackeray, Trollope and the Carlyles all interested themselves in its effects.[43] Mesmerism was to occupy an important place in the medical repertoire for the rest of the century (Freud, it will be recalled, employed its methods at the outset of his career[44]), and is still practised by some doctors. The different, but not altogether unrelated question of the rôle of electro-magnetism in healing also remains a live issue, and has been the subject of some interesting recent experiments.[45] During Coleridge's lifetime, however, as we have seen, the topic had for the time being passed out of the public view and survived in his own mind only as an esoteric (if obsessive) current.

In general, Coleridge's importance for his generation during the last years of his life had been of another order, and would require a study of a different kind from the present one to do it full justice. Men such as Julius Hare, John Sterling and F. D. Maurice acknowledged the virtues of his theological ideas, which, as is well known, had an important influence on the Broad Church movement in England[46] and on Transcendentalism in North America.

There were certain respects, however, in which the enthusiasms of Coleridge's youth bore at least indirectly upon that influence also. He believed that the true function of any religion must be, literally, to 'bind' human beings together, and that to be effective it must therefore manifest its congruency with the needs and powers of human nature itself.[47] It was a Christianised version of the 'one Life' concept. And there can be little doubt that the impact of his discourse upon his hearers was itself assisted by a compulsiveness of manner that gave him an air of earnest authority, impressing them with the sense that they were listening to the outpourings of a restless, relentless, inquiring spirit which had found the best solutions it could to the strange contradictory urges that had racked its bodily frame. John Sterling remarked:[48]

> It is painful to observe in Coleridge that with all the kindness and glorious far-seeing intelligence of his eye there is a glare in it, a light half unearthly, half morbid. It is the glittering eye of the Ancient Mariner.

It would be quite wrong to associate the glare in Coleridge's eye with any total lapse into fixity, of course. For Carlyle, indeed, impatient at Coleridge's 'flood of utterance', even the metaphor that had been employed for his conversation by Wordsworth and De Quincey, that of a mighty river, would not serve:

> ... it was talk not flowing anywhither like a river, but spreading everywhither in inextricable currents and regurgitations like a lake or sea. (Carlyle 72)

Others, who had known Coleridge longer, were aware of a surviving ebullience beneath that oceanic flood, and knew that the true virtue of his intelligence had little necessary connection with the topics to which it sometimes committed itself. 'What', asked Leigh Hunt of Lamb as they were walking home one evening after an evening during which Coleridge had delivered a long theological monologue, 'makes Coleridge talk in that way about heavenly grace, and the holy church, and that sort of thing?'. 'Ah!' replied Lamb, 'there's a great deal of fun in Coleridge.'[49]

The fuller implications of Lamb's remark are worth considering: they may help to indicate why so many of Coleridge's hearers insisted that his published works did not represent the fullness of his discourse. They also suggest that what his younger hearers took away from Highgate was less a body of theological ideas than a stimulus to spontaneous powers in their own mind which had little to do with the adoption of formal doctrines – and that in that sense the young Coleridge whose natural eagerness had been to ask questions rather than answer them and to see in the play of mind itself one of the most important and characteristic human activities could still be discerned in the features and accents of the aging talker. Certainly, when Julius Hare heard of Coleridge's death and tried to express his sense of loss, the imagery which came to his mind was striking – and bears on all that has been said in these pages. 'The light of his eye is quenched', he wrote; and he went on to speak of those who would no longer be able to listen to Coleridge's voice and, as they did so, 'feel their souls teem and burst as beneath the breath of spring.'[50]

Notes

(The suffix x to a note indicator in the text signifies that the note contains extra information, as opposed to simple references and cross-references)

Chapter 1

1x. HW XI 18. This is a further instance of the 'Was it for this . . . ?' trope which was used by Wordsworth for the opening of *The Prelude* in its earliest form (and as ll.272–304 for the 1805 version). A correspondence initiated by Jonathan Wordsworth in the *Times Literary Supplement* in 1975 (see e.g. issues of 18 April, 9 May, 6 June, 11 July) brought out a number of previous instances, including Milton's *Samson Agonistes*, Pope's 'Rape of the Lock' iv and Shenstone's Elegy xviii; nevertheless, Hazlitt's unusually sustained version suggests that he may have known the (then unpublished) *Prelude* passage directly from Wordsworth.

2. MS letter of 12 Nov 1827 in Victoria University Library, Toronto.
3. Carlyle 73–4.
4. Ibid. 71.
5. LL II 191.
6. W Pr (Gr) III 469.
7. LL I 197 (Marrs I 217).
8. Leigh Hunt, *Lord Byron and some of his Contemporaries* (1828) p. 300.
9. Gillman 14; and cf my article 'Coleridge's Great Circulating Library' in N & Q June 1956, CCI 264.
10. For a good and wide-ranging discussion of Coleridge's interest in magic see Anya Taylor, 'Magic in Coleridge's Poetry', *Wordsworth Circle* (1972) III 76–84.
11. J. S. Mill, *Dissertations and Discussions* (1859) I 394.
12. See below, pp. 36–8.
13. CL I 184.
14. Note to Boehme (BM) I, leaf facing p. iii.
15. Andrew Tooke, *Pantheon*, plate 4 (1798 ed.). Cf my discussion in *Coleridge the Visionary* (1959) 65 and n.
16. See below, p. 211 (and cf CL V 348–9).
17. A. Tooke, *Pantheon* (1733) pp. 69–73.
18. Exodus 7:10; Numbers 17:8 and 21:8–9.

19. LW II 21.
20. LL II 190.
21. BL II 92–3.
22. TT 23 July 1832.
23. Quoted in letter to Southey, Oct 1794: CL I 112.
24. CL I 93.
25. *Coleridge on Shakespeare* . . . ed. R. A. Foakes (1972) p. 72 (Cf Sh C II 142–5 and Owen Barfield's discussion in C Variety 206).
26. Cf. my discussions in *Coleridge the Visionary*, 69–70 and *Blake's Visionary Universe* (Manchester, 1969) pp. 17–23 and plates 22–40.
27. PL 175–7.
28. CL II 1014 (14 Oct 1803) and 1046–7 (30 Jan 1804).
29. CN II 2196 (11 Oct 1804). Cf. my *Coleridge the Visionary*, pp. 40–1.
30. W. J. Bate, *Coleridge* (1968) 31–3, 137, 186–7; Thomas McFarland, *Coleridge and the Pantheistic Tradition* (Oxford, 1969) *passim*.
31. Note to Herder, *Kalligone*, III, 61 (BM copy C 43. a. 11).

Chapter 2

1x. A later collection, H. W. Weber's *Tales of the East* (3 vols, Edinburgh, 1812), which brings together most, if not all of them in a convenient form, was used by Keats (KL II 130n).
2. *Tales of the Genii* (1766) I 51–2.
3. Ibid. 77, 81.
4. Ibid. 135–6.
5. CL I 355.
6. See above, p. 288, note 9.
7. Leapidge Smith, 'Reminiscences of an Octogenarian', *Leisure Hour* (1860) IX 633–4. Reprinted in C Variety 61–3.
8x. For a modern instance see Richard Humphry as reported in *Observer Magazine*, 12 Sept 1971 (quoted, C Variety, 57).
9. See below, p. 60.
10. CL IV 937n; Gillman 23.
11. Gillman 23.
12. CL IV 750–1.
13. See Samuel Butler, *Hudibras*, ed. John Wilders (Oxford, 1967) I i 536 and II iii 643.
14. G. C. Cell, *The Rediscovery of John Wesley* (N.Y., 1935) p. 117 (cited Stoudt, see below); E. J. Abbey and J. H. Overton, *The English Church in The Eighteenth Century* (1902) pp. 253–64.
15. J. J. Stoudt, *Sunrise to Eternity, a Study in Jacob Boehme's Life and Thought* (Philadelphia, 1957) p. 20 and nn.
16x. 'Hegel believed that Boehme was a pantheist idealist. Franz von

Baader believed that Boehme's realism earned him his reputation as *the* Christian philosopher. Baur reproached Boehme for his gnostic Manicheanism. Bréhier links Boehme with Weigel in introducing his chapter on Leibnitz' (Ibid. and nn).

17. Gray's *Elegy*, II 101–8; W. Prel (1805) iv 109–20.
18. See my essay 'Ice and Spring: Coleridge's Imaginative Education', C Variety 61–5.
19. See, e.g., *The Way to Divine Knowledge* (1762) pp. 238–44.
20. *Aurora*, iii 24.
21. Thomas Taylor, *Concerning the Beautiful* (1787) pp. xiii and xvi.
22. Thomas Taylor, *Philosophical and Mathematical Commentaries of Proclus* (1788) II 246.
23. Ibid. II 312.
24. Morton Paley's *Energy and the Imagination* (Oxford, 1970) gives a good account of the contemporary history of both terms as a background to Blake.
25x. *Ennead*, VI vii 12 (tr. McKenna) 1956, pp. 570–1. I owe this reference to Professor Frank Kermode, who also drew my attention to the parallel with 'Dejection', ll.74–5 ('All melodies the echoes of that voice, / All colours a suffusion from that light').
26. See, e.g., *Coleridge the Visionary*, 262–4.
27x. See, e.g., Akenside's *Pleasures of the Imagination* (1744) I 109–124:

> As Memnon's marble harp, renown'd of old
> By fabling Nilus, to the quivering touch
> Of Titan's ray, with each repulsive string
> Consenting, sounded thro' the warbling air
> Unbidden strains; ev'n so did nature's hand
> To certain species of external things,
> Attune the finer organs of the mind:
> So the glad impulse of congenial pow'rs
> Or of sweet sound, or fair-proportioned forms
> The grace of motion, or the blur of light,
> Thinks thro' imagination's tender frame,
> From nerve to nerve: all naked and alive
> They catch the spreading rays: till now the soul
> At length discloses every tuneful spring,
> To that harmonious movement from without
> Responsive . . .

The whole of Akenside's poem should be read, as presenting the most attractive kind of combined poetic and intellectual expression that was available as model to the young Coleridge. Cf. also Darwin, 'The Economy of Vegetation' (*Botanic Garden*, 1791) p. 18 and Note viii, p. 17; CL I 155; see also below, pp. 52, 98.

28x. *Disquisitions on Matter and Spirit* (1777) pp. 9–10; quoted in part, H. W. Piper, *The Active Universe* (1962) p. 36. Cf. also

Joseph Fawcett, *Sermons* (1795) I 32–3, on God as 'the great spring and impulse that actuates all things'. Fawcett was another radical Unitarian. For Bruno see further below, pp. 243–245.

29. 'Conversation', l.503.
30. 'Table-Talk', ll.380–3.
31x. *Anatomical Dissertation upon the Movement of the Heart and Blood in Animals*, ch. viii (Facs. ed. Canterbury 1894 (ii) 50). Cf. Harvey's dedication to King Charles as 'the Sun of his World, the heart of the Commonwealth' (ibid. (II) p. iii).
32. CN I 1233 (cf. I 467).
33. Marginal annotations to Boehme (BM) I 43 and I 250.
34. Christopher Wordsworth, *Social Life at the English Universities in the Eighteenth Century* (Cambridge, 1894) p. 589 (diary entry for Nov 1793).
35. *Complete Poetical Works of Robert Southey* (1837) II 170–4. Reprinted in my *Coleridge the Visionary* (1959) 297–300.
36. CL I 80.
37. CL I 330.
38. CL I 61 and PW I 55.
39. Letter of 22 Nov 1817, KL I 184.
40. See his letters to Southey (13 Nov 1795, CL I 173) and Poole (6 May 1799, CL I 491).
41. LW II 21 (cf. my *Coleridge the Visionary* (1959) pp. 95–7, 268–9).
42. See above, p. 289 (note 7).
43. DQW V 213–14.

Chapter 3

1. HW XI 16.
2. J. Hucks, *Pedestrian Tour through North Wales* (1795) p. 29.
3. Ibid. 31.
4. H. McLachlan, *Warrington Academy* (Manchester, 1943) p. 63, gives a typical timetable which shows this. See also his *The Unitarian movement in . . . England*, I (1934) pp. 71–140.
5. H. W. Piper, *The Active Universe* (1962). This important study contains much more that is relevant to the present discussion.
6. See my essay, 'Blake, Coleridge and Wordsworth, Some Cross-currents and Parallels 1789–1805' in *William Blake: Essays in Honour of Sir Geoffrey Keynes*, ed. M. D. Paley and M. Phillips (Oxford, 1973) pp. 238–9 and nn.
7x. E.g. Burnet on Mountains (I 35–7, cf. CN I 61 [where the correct reading, as agreed by the editor, is 'Burnet's Mountains']); waterspouts (II 43–6, cf. below, p. 112); a glory round the head (II 56, cf. CN I 258); serpent-worship (II 280); the soul as an Eolus' harp (IV 156) etc. etc.
8. Sulivan I 167 (see also II 441–2 on Epicurus).

9. Lucretius, *De Rerum Natura* (tr. T. Creech) 1743, II 165 (Bk V, 546–600) (Coleridge refers jokingly to this translation in 1801: CL II 674).
10x. This is the conception to be inferred by putting together a long extended image of the sun-rise for falling in love (CL III 304–5) and a reference to the 'fiat' of the uprising sun (Sh C I 126). 'Fiat' is a favourite word of Boehme's in *Aurora*, normally printed in very large type. Cf. *Coleridge the Visionary*, pp. 62, 264.
11. Letter of 2 Dec 1796 (LL I 60).
12. TT 24 Sept 1830.
13. PL 217n, quoting from NB 25.
14. Sulivan III 319.
15. Ibid. 310–20.
16. Cudworth, *Intellectual System of the Universe* (1743) I 77 (page headed 'Atheists make knowledge junior to the World') and II 726–38.
17. J. H. Muirhead, *Coleridge as Philosopher* (1930) p. 270.
18. CL I 137.
19. Godwin, *Political Justice* (1796) i 139. See also my essay (note 6 above) pp. 233–4.
20. E. Darwin, *The Loves of the Plants* (1790) p. 183n (IV, ll.467–8); and cf. D. S. King-Hele, *Erasmus Darwin* (1963) pp. 112–15.
21. E. Darwin, 'The Economy of Vegetation', *Botanic Garden* (1791) (i) 123 (and note xxxi, notes pp. 76–7); 126–8; 128–9.
22. CL I 216.
23x. BL I 12. See also his later claim that in the whole 'there were not to be found 20 images which were described as they would be described by a man in a state of excitement.' *Coleridge on Shakespeare* . . . ed. R. Foakes (1971) p. 55.
24. *The Task*, v 379–445.
25. CL I 396, citing *The Task*, v 496–508.
26. E. Darwin, 'Economy of Vegetation' I i 189–208, in *Botanic Garden* (1791) i (i) 18–20.
27. Note to 'Lines Written at Shurton Bars . . .' (PW I 97n).
28. 'The Economy of Vegetation' I i 193–4 (*Botanic Garden* 1791 (i) 19).
29. PW I 99–100 and nn.
30. RX 18–19 et passim; H. W. Piper, *The Active Universe* (1962) pp. 40–3 et passim; D. S. King-Hele, *Erasmus Darwin* (1963) pp. 140–2.
31. CL I 305.
32x. In the *Philosophical Lectures*, Coleridge tells how Darwin (it is to be assumed) told him that he wished 'to employ a young man of a metaphysical turn to read all former philosophers to him and to give him a syllabus of their opinions which he was not acquainted with' so that he could confute them in his great forthcoming work (PL 213–14 and n).

33. *Zoönomia*, 1794–6, I, 101–7.
34ˣ. Ibid. 105. Cf. his statement, 'I am acquainted with a philosopher, who . . . thinks it not impossible that the first insects were the anthers or stigmas of flowers'. 'Economy of Vegetation', *Botanic Garden* (1791) (i) 109.
35ˣ. I have elsewhere suggested that Coleridge might have made the connection between the Nile and the snake with the tail in its mouth both through the traditional identification of the Nile with Osiris (for whom that emblem would be a natural image) and through his awareness of other rivers, such as the Alpheus, which supposedly rose up in the Arethusa fountain, and Milton's river of Paradise, which returned in part to its own springs (*Coleridge the Visionary*, p. 211). For Coleridge's later use of the emblem, see below, p. 179.
36. Cf. *Coleridge the Visionary*, 241 and CN I 1706n.
37. CL I 144.
38. Lectures (1795) 83.
39. Cf., e.g., his 1796 scheme for teaching young men (CL I 209) and the group to which he dictated some of his philosophical ideas (see J. D. Campbell, *Samuel Taylor Coleridge: A Narrative of the Events of his Life*, 1894, pp. 250–1).
40. Lectures (1795) 208.
41. J. Priestley, *Disquisitions relating to Matter and Spirit*, 1777, Section xvii, pp. 224–33.
42. CL I 192–3. For Priestley's opinion (*Matter and Spirit*, 1792 ed. p. 42) see H. W. Piper, op. cit. 36–7nn.
43. PW I 131–48. For the lines originally written in 1795 see Southey's *Joan of Arc* (1796) (cited in the app. cr. of the PW version).
44. Hartley, *Observations on Man* (1791 ed.) I 13–16.
45. PW II 1112–13.
46. CL I 172.
47ˣ. Enfield's *History of Philosophy* (1791) has a discussion of Leibnitz in volume II, pp. 561–5. Coleridge borrowed only the first volume from the Bristol Library in 1795, but it is clear that at this time he was reading widely in the Library itself. (The references to Leemius, for example, (PW I 133–5nn) were almost certainly taken from the copy of Leemius which is still there, but Coleridge did not borrow them.) There is also a discussion of Monads in Euler's *Letters to a German Princess* (1795) II 42–71, which there is reason to believe that Coleridge read (see below, pp. 82 ff.). Though hostile, this might have led Coleridge on to Wolff and Leibnitz. (Cf. his late statement that 'all the elements, the *differentials* as the Algebraists say, of my present Opinions existed for me before I had even seen a book of German Metaphysics, later than Wolff and Leibnitz, or could have read it, if I had' (Letter of 1825, CL V 421–2) – which could be taken as

suggesting that he *had* read or known Wolff and Leibnitz in early years).
48. Enfield, op. cit. I 393.
49. Ibid. I 384.
50. BM Add MS 34225 f 5v (PW II 1025, ll.56–8).
51. Cf. 'Religious Musings', l.415. The word occurs in all three drafts for the opening of 'The Destiny of Nations': i, l.47, ii, l.9, iii, l.10. (PW I 124; II 1025–7).
52. BM Add MS 34225 f6 (correcting PW II 1026, ll.14–17).
53. Ibid. (correcting PW II 1026 at many points).
54. PW I 100–2 (for the version in *Poems on Various Subjects* (1796) see my Everyman ed. of the *Poems* (rev. 1974) pp. 52–3.
55. James Ridley, *Tales of the Genii* (1766) I 70. See also my essay 'Poems of the Supernatural' in *S. T. Coleridge*, ed. R. L. Brett (1971) p. 48.
56. *Paradise Lost*, iv 771.
57. 1796 version (Poems (Ev.) 53).
58. Annotation to Kant, *Kritik der Reinen Vernunft* (1799) reported by H. Nidecker, *Revue de Littérature Comparée* (1927) VII, 529. (Cited R. Wellek, *Kant in England, 1793–1838* (Princeton, N.J., 1931, p. 83).
59. See, e.g., PW I 412, BL I 57 and n, CL VI 797.
60. CL III 101.
61. Sulivan III 210.

Chapter 4

1. See above, p. 60 (and p. 23).
2. See my *Coleridge the Visionary*, pp. 106–10, 143–5. Coleridge borrowed the relevant volume of Berkeley from the Bristol Library in March 1796 (BB 122).
3. William Law, *Demonstration of the Gross and Fundamental Errors of a Late Book* (&c) (1769) p. 209.
4. Robert Darnton, *Mesmerism and the End of the Enlightenment in France* (Cambridge, Mass., 1968) pp. 10–11, 18 (and index, s.v. Newton).
5. Ibid. 19–25.
6x. Lane Cooper, 'The Power of the Eye in Coleridge' (in his *Late Harvest* (Ithaca, N.Y., 1952) p. 75), quoting C. Mackay, *Memoirs of Extraordinary Popular Delusions* (1869) I 287–8. Cooper's essay (first published in 1910) contains much valuable information on the subject.
7. Hartley, *Observations on Man* (1791 ed.) I 58–80. For Coleridge's later criticisms of Hartley see BL I ch. vi–vii.
8. Ibid. I 16–33.
9. Coleridge's phrase of 1794. See CL I 78.

10. *Zoönomia*, I 6.
11. Ibid. I ch. xl.
12. Ibid. I 110; 122.
13. Ibid. I ch. xviii.
14. Ibid. I 417.
15. Ibid. I 432.
16. See below, pp. 152–3.
17. *Zoönomia*, I 510.
18. Ibid. I 519.
19. LW v 286.
20. *Zoönomia*, I 416.
21. 'Among School Children'; Yeats, *Collected Poems* (1950) pp. 242–5.
22. Andrew Baxter, *Enquiry into the Nature of the Human Soul wherein the Immateriality of the Soul is evinced (etc.)* (1737) II 72–85, etc.
23. See NB 35 ff. 35v–36.
24. Baxter, op. cit. II 182–3.
25. Ibid. II 146.
26. Annotation to K. C. Wolfart, *Mesmerismus* (Berlin, 1814) vol. II flyleaf. Printed in PL 423–4.
27. *Conjuror's Magazine* (June–July, 1792) pp. 458–60, 490–1.
28. *Discourse on Method*, Part V. For Coleridge's early knowledge of the *Meditations*, see J. D. Gutteridge's article, 'Coleridge and Descartes' Meditations', N & Q 1973, CCXVIII 45–6.
29. AR (1825) 171n.
30. L. Euler, *Letters to a German Princess* (1795) II 490.
31. Ibid. I 332–6 and II 42–71; I 296; I 76; I 351.
32. Ibid. II 508–9.
33. Lucretius, *De Rerum Natura* (tr. T. Creech) 1743, II, Bk iv, ll.402–5, 438–44, 449–54 (pp. 38–41).
34. See his marginal note to John Webster, *Displaying of Supposed Witchcraft*, 1667 (BM copy C. 126.1.10) p. 248.
35. Euler, op. cit. II 292–302.
36. BL II 6.
37. See above, pp. 80–2.
38. CN II 2583; Sh C 20–1.
39. *The Life of Monsieur DesCartes (&c)*, Translated ... by S.R., 1693, p. 30.
40. For further discussion and identification of the sources in *Aurora*, see my article, 'Coleridge and Boehme's *Aurora*', N & Q, 1963, CCVII 183–7.
41. See Crabb Robinson's Diary for 14 July 1816: HCR I 185.
42. Darwin, *Zoönomia* (1794–6) I 16.
43. Ibid. I 534–66.
44. Darwin, *Zoönomia*, I 20.
45. Carlyle 79.
46. AR (1825) 228 (Spiritual Aphorism IV).

Chapter 5

1. _Paradise Lost_, ix 445–66.
2. John Cornwell, _Coleridge: Poet and Revolutionary_ (1973) pp. 118–21.
3. Lectures (1795) 277–318.
4. See Coleridge's anecdote, CL I 179.
5. CL I 157–8, 165–6.
6. CL I 177 (and see above, p. 96 (and nn).
7. LL I 39 (Marrs I 44).
8. CL I 238; LL I 49 (Marrs I 53–4).
9. Watchman, 168–72; 350–1.
10. Cottle, _Reminiscences of Samuel Taylor Coleridge and Robert Southey_ (1847) p. 43.
11. Ibid. 42–6; cf. _New Letters of R. Southey_, ed. K. Curry (1965) II 442 and n; and DNB Supplement I (Gilbert).
12. Notes to Excursion iii 931 (WP V 422–3) and 'The Brothers' 1.65 (WP II 2n).
13. W. Gilbert, _The Hurricane: a Theological and Western Eclogue_ (1796) p. 61.
14. Ibid. Preface, iv.
15. Ibid. 53, 57–8.
16. Ibid. 62, 85.
17. Ibid. 77–8.
18. Ibid. 87.
19. See Watchman, 350–1nn.
20. See _Coleridge the Visionary_ (1959) pp. 107–9 and nn.
21. Ibid., and see below, p. 202.
22. CN I 165.
23. See _Coleridge the Visionary_, pp. 109, 213, 241, 322.
24. CL I 261, 246. See also Irene Chayes, 'Coleridge, metempsychosis and 'almost all the followers of Fénelon', ELH (1958) XXV 290–315.
25x. See, e.g., CN I 272(d) ('Rolls round his dreary eye'); 239 ('the high and lofty One'); 182 ('Our quaint metaphysical opinions . . . child deadly sick'); 259(a) ('Deep inward stillness & a bowed Soul') and cf. PW I 160, l.6).
26. Unpublished Ph.D. thesis, _Literature and Natural Philosophy 1770–1800_, for the University of Cambridge (1972) pp. 178–9.
27x. See above, p. 102 and cf. letter to Sotheby in Sep 1802 (CL II 866) where this formula (from Acts 17 28) is given more fully and related to that of the 'one Life'.
28. John Ferriar, 'Observations concerning the Vital Principle'. _Memoirs of the Literary and Philosophical Society of Manchester_ (Warrington, 1790) III 222, is evidently Coleridge's source for the opinions of Monro and Hunter.
29x. I have not been able to discover a copy of this, but from a review

in the *Analytical Review* (1794, XIX 266) it is clear that it related the principle of life to 'specific organization' and 'specific stimulus', the latter being 'something . . . contained in the atmosphere, and probably the electrical fluid'. The role of the blood was also discussed.

30.   Genesis 7:11.
31.   PW I 169–71. First published in *Morning Post*, 10 March 1798, but referred to earlier by Lamb in letter of 5 Feb 1797 (LL I 94).
32.   PW I 170.
33x. R. Watters, *Coleridge* (Literature in Perspective Series) (1971) pp. 47–8. I am not convinced, however, by his statement that the rook (though 'winging the dusky air') is 'ominous', since 'rooky' in Shakespeare's text could be read rather as an image of gregariousness and the 'one Life' from which Macbeth (in Coleridge's words) has torn himself 'live asunder' (Sh C I 76). It is the rook's lack of immediate charm which would seem to be paramount in the first impression.
34.   I Kings 17:2–6 (and cf. *Paradise Regained* ii, 266–9).
35.   Carlyon I 144.
36.   HW XVII 120.
37.   See RX 255–8 and nn.
38.   PW I 287.
39.   RX 237; 257–60.
40.   In an unpublished B. Litt. thesis for the University of Oxford.
41x. BM E.g. MS 2800 ff. l–lv (reprinted *variatim* in PW I 285–6). From the MS version it seems that the separate paragraphs form two draft fragments, not necessarily in order.
42.   CN I 172, 174 and nn; *Coleridge the Visionary*, 126, 190, 235.
43.   PW I 289.
44.   See M. L. Reed, *Wordsworth: the Chronology of the Early Years, 1770–99* (Cambridge, Mass., 1967) 208–9nn, and my article on Coleridge's 'Poems of the Supernatural' in S. T. *Coleridge*, ed. R. L. Brett (1971) 53–60 and nn.
45.   *Coleridge the Visionary*, 218.
46.   Ibid. 217–22.
47x. In the Crewe holograph manuscript they seem to run on continuously from the second stanza, but careful examination of the original manuscript in the BM suggests that this may be an accidental effect. In all published versions they form a separate unit. It should be observed, incidentally, that this is not necessarily the original manuscript: indeed the description at the end suggests rather that it was a later transcription or reconstruction. It is reproduced in *A Review of English Literature* (1966) VII (between pp. 32–3) along with an article by John Shelton, and in the BM *Quarterly* (1962–3) XXVI, pp. 77–83, with an article by T. C. Skeat.
48x. See also the incident in *Tales of the Genii*, cited above, p. 19.
49.   See *Coleridge the Visionary*, 253–4 and nn.

50. For further discussion of the poem see *Coleridge the Visionary*, 199–276, and my essay on the Poems of the Supernatural in *S. T. Coleridge*, ed. R. L. Brett (1971) (esp. pp. 53–70), which both summarises and extends the earlier discussion.

Chapter 6

1. CL I 319–20.
2. CL I 320–1.
3. CL I 325.
4. CL I 334.
5. In the Crewe MS. See *Coleridge the Visionary*, 200, and above, p. 29, n. 47.
6. WP II 511.
7. Jonathan Wordsworth, *The Music of Humanity* (1969) p. 179, ll.216–22 (cf. WP V 385).
8. See the discussion of 'This Lime Tree Bower' in his unpublished D.Phil. thesis on the Conversation Poems for the University of Oxford (1976).
9. WP I 236–8.
10. WP I 360.
11. WP I 361–2.
12. PW I 5.
13. WP II 263.
14. PW I 215–20.
15. 'The Idiot Boy', WP II 67–80.
16. 'Old Man Travelling', WP IV 247 and app. cr.
17. Humphry House, *Coleridge* (1953) pp. 78–9 gives the classic account; Norman Fruman, *Coleridge: the Damaged Archangel* (1972) pp. 305–9 has picked out one or two further parallels.
18x. Letter to Sara Hutchinson, CL II 791. The phrase 'ecstatic fit', which is from Milton's 'The Passion', gives a further suggestion of Coleridge's early poetic aspirations.
19. PW I 20.
20x. Hans Christian Andersen's 'The Snow Queen' gives one classic version of this idea. Coleridge preferred the image of the snake-constricted heart: see below, p. 217.
21. For further discussion, see my essay in C Variety, 69–78.
22. W. Prel (1805) vi 274–326.
23. Carlyon I 183 (and cf. CL II 864, quoted above, p. 126).
24. House, op. cit., 82.
25. Note of c. 1807–8: see B. Ifor Evans, 'Coleridge's Copy of "Fears in Solitude" ', TLS 18 April 1935, p. 255.
26. HW XVII 112n.
27x. The phrases are Robert Penn Warren's – see his essay 'A Poem of Pure Imagination', reprinted in his *Selected Essays* (N.Y. 1958) p. 214. In many respects this is one of the most suggestive

essays ever written on the poem, but it does not take sufficient account of the full subtlety involved in Coleridge's symbolism (cf. *Coleridge the Visionary*, pp. 167–72) and it tends to use phrases such as those quoted which, while adequate to the immediate context, lie open to objections such as those of E. E. Bostetter (see below, p. 149 and note 7) and William Empson (Preface to *Coleridge's Verse: a Selection* (1972) pp. 40–42).

Chapter 7

1. See RX, e.g., pp. 75–6, 229 and 33 and *Coleridge the Visionary*, 101–4.
2. DQW II 153.
3. *Hours in a Library* (1892) III 359.
4. William Empson, *Coleridge's Verse: a Selection*, ed. Empson and Pirie (1972) p. 78.
5x. Abe Delson, 'The Symbolism of the Sun and Moon in *The Rime of the Ancient Mariner*', *Texas Studies in Lit. and Lang.* (1974) XV 707–20. For an interesting interpretation of the poem as a basically sceptical document, reflecting Coleridge's awareness of epistemological problems raised by scientific theory, see D. M. Robbins, *Literature and Natural Philosophy, 1770–1800*, unpublished Ph.D. thesis for the University of Cambridge (1972) esp. pp. 227–66. For a brief and spirited outline of the idea that Coleridge wrote the poem deliberately as a study in rationalisation, see Lionel Stevenson, ' "The Ancient Mariner" as a Dramatic Monologue', *The Personalist* (1949) XXX 34–44.
6. See *Coleridge the Visionary*, ch. V, and above, p. 298, n. 27x.
7. E. E. Bostetter, 'The Nightmare World of *The Ancient Mariner*', *Studies in Romanticism* (1961–2) I 241–54. Reprinted in *Coleridge* (Twentieth Century Views) ed. K. Coburn (Englewood Cliffs, N.J., 1967).
8. From the preface to the 1832 edition, cited by R. H. Wells in his unpublished B.Litt. thesis for the University of Oxford.
9. PW II 551.
10. R. Darnton, *Mesmerism and the End of the Enlightenment in France* (Cambridge, Mass., 1968) p. 8.
11. See above, p. 113.
12. See R. A. Knox, *Enthusiasm* (1950) ch. xxi, esp. pp. 520–2.
13. See above, p. 89 (and cf. 82 and n.).
14. Bernard Martin, '*The Ancient Mariner*' and the '*Authentic Narrative*' (1949) pp. 37–41.
15. John Newton, *Authentic Narrative*, Letters viii–x (1782) pp. 87–97, 113–15.
16. For a scientific account on these lines see William Oliver's Letter, *Transactions of the Royal Society* (1704) XXIV, 1562–4.
17. DQW II 145.

18.   *Blake, Coleridge, Wordsworth, Lamb, etc.,* . . . *Selections from* . . . *H. C. Robinson,* ed. E. J. Morley (Manchester, 1922) pp. 31–2.
19.   1798 version, ll.57–60, 396–434. PW II 1032; 1039–40.
20.   W. Schrickx, 'Coleridge and the Cambridge Platonists', REL (1966) VII 71–91.
21.   Cudworth, *Intellectual System of the Universe* (1743) II 647–8, (quoted Schrickx (op. cit. 81) from 1678 ed.).
22x. LL I 95 (Marrs I 97). It may be noted that the 'five motives' (sensation, imagination, ambition, sympathy, Theopathy) do in fact correspond to the 'stages of prayer' formulated by Coleridge (see pp. 153–4 above).
23.   1800 Preface to *Lyrical Ballads,* W Pr I 122–4.
24.   Letter by Alexander Dyce, quoted in Coleridge's *Poems,* ed. H. N. Coleridge (1852) pp. 383–4.
25.   WP I 329.
26.   ll.364–5 (PW II 1040).
27.   PW I 40–4.
28.   HW XVII 117.
29.   *The Pilgrim's Progress* (1678) pp. 35–6.
30x. 'I should almost despair of that Man, who could peruse the Life of John Woolman without an amelioration of Heart.' To Poole, CL I 302 (cf. III 156 and CN III 3440). In the same month Lamb mentioned Coleridge's liking for Woolman (LL I 94–5; Marrs I 96–7).
31.   John Woolman, *Journal* (Dublin, 1776) pp. 3–4, 12, 22 and 28.
32.   Jerome, Comm. in *Epistolam ad Galatas,* vi, 10.
33.   W. Prel (1805) x 901.
34.   CL I 350. The image of the God on the lotus seems to have been drawn from several sources, as I hope to show in a subsequent study.
35.   CL I 334 (For J. D. Gutteridge's unpublished thesis see p. 298 (note 8) above).
36x. It is possible that this curious phrase was prompted by an observation recorded by his companion Joseph Hucks when they visited Cader Idris together: 'The whole mountain is apparently composed of a huge mass of stones, thrown together as a heap of rubbish without order or design; for wherever you turn up the sod or turf . . . you come to these stones. . . Near the summit of the mountain there is no turf, and what is remarkable, these stones are smaller there. . .' J. Hucks, *Pedestrian Tour through North Wales* (1795) pp. 113–15. The idea of a sublime mountain which was really a heap of little things was one which was calculated to capture Coleridge's sense of paradox.
37.   'The Pedlar', ll.126–8: J. Wordsworth, *The Music of Humanity,* p. 176 (cf. WP v 383).
38.   For this and another later version, see W Prel 525.

39. *Critical Review* (Oct 1798) p. 201. (For an earlier version in a letter see J. W. Robberds, *Memoir of William Taylor* (1843) I 223.)
40. See my article, 'Coleridge and Lamb: the Central Themes', *Charles Lamb Bulletin* (1976), N.S., No. 14, pp. 119–20. Southey also discusses Dutch painting in his review, however.
41. See *Coleridge the Visionary*, 147–8. Norman Fruman's discussion (*Coleridge, the Damaged Archangel* (1972) pp. 311–12) misses the special characteristics of the German ballads.
42. G. Bürger, *The Chase, and William and Helen*, tr. W. Scott (1796) p. 14.
43. See above, p. 59.
44. Letter of 7 Mar 1815, CL IV 545.
45. B. Ifor Evans, 'Coleridge's copy of "Fears in Solitude" ', TLS (18 April 1953) p. 255. (See above, pp. 142–3.)
46. BL I 18n.
47. *Lyrical Ballads*, 1800, unnumbered pages (214–15). Quoted RX 520.
48. LL I 136–7 (Marrs I 142).
49. T. Allsop, *Letters, Conversations and Recollections of S. T. Coleridge*, 1836, I 95.

Chapter 8

1x. CL I 425–6. (When re-edited for *Biographia Literaria* (BL II 134) 'a sort of wild dance' turned into 'a set of dances', followed by a pun on 'reels'.) For a comment on the incident by Wallace Stevens see his essay 'The Figure of the Youth as Virile Poet', *The Necessary Angel* (1960) pp. 40–1. This is taken up by M. H. Abrams in 'Coleridge and the Romantic Vision of the World', C Variety 133.
2x. The invasion took place in December 1797. For a critical account of the 'symbolic' significance of this event for English romantics, see C. Cestre, *La Révolution Française et les Poètes Anglais* (Paris, 1906) pp. 357–67.
3. See *Coleridge the Visionary* (1959) 191 and n.
4. See above, pp. 82–4.
5. E. P. Thompson, 'Disenchantment or Default? A Lay Sermon', in *Power and Consciousness*, ed. C. C. O'Brien and W. D. Vanech (1969) pp. 167–70.
6x. Letter to Poole, May 1796, CL I 209. For further important light on Coleridge's interest in Germany, including the significance of his friendship with Thomas Beddoes, see E. S. Shaffer, *'Kubla Khan' and the Fall of Jerusalem* (Cambridge 1975) esp. pp. 23–33.
7. For Bürger, see above, p. 178 and n. 41; for Coleridge's reaction to Schiller in 1794 see CL I 122 and PW I 72.
8. BL I 138; CL I 861.

9. BL I 138; CL I 494, etc.
10. Edith J. Morley (ed.), *Crabb Robinson in Germany, 1800–05*, p. 74.
11. WPr (Gr) III 469, from R. P. Graves, *Memoirs*, pp. 288–90.
12. Reported by Mrs Davy, WP (Gr) III 441–2.
13. *Recollections of the Table-Talk of Samuel Rogers* (1856) p. 203n.
14. Carlyon I 138–41.
15. I hope to develop this point elsewhere.
16. See, e.g., below, p. 227.
17x. '... the great rocky fragments which jut out from the Hills both here & at Porlock & which alas! we have not at dear Stowey!' CL I 498. Later he hunted for a house at Porlock: CL II 591.
18. See, e.g., G. Yarlott, *Coleridge and the Abyssinian Maid* (1967) pp. 31, 223–6.
19. CL I 542.
20. CL I 547.
21. DW I 23–7.
22. *Life and Correspondence of Robert Southey*, ed. C. C. Southey (1849–50) II 21.
23. CL I 588.
24. 22 Apr, 24 Apr 1802. DWJ I 136–8.
25. CL I 638.
26x. See below, pp. 230, 255. In what seems to be an original observation, Norman Fruman (*Coleridge the Damaged Archangel* (1972) p. 496, n. 43) notes that the bustard image probably derives from a similar description by Wordsworth in 'Guilt and Sorrow', st. xii (cf. WP I 99).
27. Marginal Note to Boehme (BM) I (i) 40.
28. Richard Haven, *Patterns of Consciousness* (Amherst, Mass., 1969) p. 135.
29. Ibid. p. 138, quoting marginal note to Boehme (BM) I (i) 42.
30. J. Cottle, *Reminiscences of S. T. Coleridge and R. Southey* (1847) p. 329.
31x. Plates 4 and 25 (in 1798 ed.). For a further mention of this paradigm in 1812 see HCR I 61.
32. Letter to Poole, *Fragmentary Remains of Sir Humphry Davy*, ed. J. Davy (1858) p. 74.
33. Marginal note to Boehme (BM) I 127.
34. See above, p. 50 and n.
35. Letter to Coleridge, *Memorials of Coleorton*, ed. William Knight (Edinburgh, 1887) II 58.
36. CL III 266.
37. CL IV 975.
38. CN III 4417.
39. *Friend* II 146.
40. Ibid. II 258.
41. Annotation (dated 1821) to copy of Swedenborg, *Pars Prima de*

Cultu et Amore Dei, in Houghton Library, Harvard, quoted
by Richard Haven, unpublished B.Litt. dissertation on Coleridge
and Boehme, University of Oxford (1953) p. 239.

42. CN II 2546.
43. To Tulk, CL IV 769.
44ˣ. C & S 219–21. See also the rest of the discussion, culminating in
     the statement that 'evolution is implied in the conception of
     life'.
45. CL VI 551.
46. CN III 4243. Cited by Kathleen Coburn, *The Self-Conscious
     Imagination* (1974) pp. 15, 51.
47. Ibid. 49, citing Folio Notebook f. 46.
48. Ibid. 12, citing Folio Notebook f. 7v.
49. See, e.g., E. L. Grant Watson, *The Mystery of Physical Life*
     (1964) esp. pp. 40–5. I am grateful to Owen Barfield for this
     reference.
50. Goethe, 'Über die spiral-Tendenz der Vegetation' (1831) *Goethes
     Werke* (Weimar, 1887–1918) II, vii, 37–68. For a brief account
     in English, see G. Adams and O. Whicher, *The Living Plant*
     (Clent, Worcs., 1949) pp. 11–12.
51. See J. D. Watson and F. H. C. Crick, 'A Structure for Deoxy-
     ribose Nucleic Acid', *Nature* (25 Apr 1954) CLIIX 737–8 and
     associated papers on following pp.

Chapter 9

1.   See PW I 267–84, WP I 308–12 and nn.
2.   HW XVII 117.
3.   ll.532–3, PW I 284.
4.   Friend I 59n.
5.   Friend II 51 (cf. I 59 and nn).
6.   BL II 5. The phrase 'known and familiar' also turns up in a
     discussion of dreams by Sulivan (Sulivan III 109). It may well
     be of wider provenance, but I have not come across it elsewhere.
7.   HW XVII 118.
8.   Above, p. 217.
9.   BL I 202.
10. Note of Mar 1811, CN III 4056.
11. CL I 491–3.
12. *King John*, III iv, 92–7. See Sh C II 61–2 (cf. R. A. Foakes,
     Coleridge on Shakespeare (1971) p. 49).
13. CN I 563; CL I 556–7 (cited CN I 563n).
14. NB 25 ff. 2–1 (cf. *Coleridge the Visionary* (1959) p. 247 and
     Anima Poetae, ed. E. H. Coleridge (1895) pp. 290–1; also (for
     the last idea) Friend II 31.
15. CL II 876, 796.
16. CL II 832.

17x. CN II 2389n. See also the important evidence from Martha Fricker about Mrs Coleridge's temper cited by Miss Coburn in this note, and the parallel passage of 1804, CN I 1816: 'Mrs C is all *strange*, & the Terra incognita always lies near to or under the frozen Poles.' For Coleridge's knowledge of Geysers from Darwin, see above, p. 50.

18. CN I 1575, William and Mary may be referred to.

19. CN I 1589.

20x. James Alban Finch argued that the preamble to *The Prelude* (W. Prel (1805) I 1–54) was composed on 18 Nov 1799, when Wordsworth had left Coleridge after the Sockburn tour: 'Wordsworth's Two-Handed Engine' in *Bicentenary Wordsworth Studies*, ed. Jonathan Wordsworth (1970) p. 12 and n. If Wordsworth's ideas had been assisted by his discussions with Coleridge, it is possible that Coleridge also found his future purposes clarified on the same occasion.

21. See the review attributed to him in *Quarterly Review* (Aug 1834) III 1–38; reprinted in *Coleridge: The Critical Heritage*, ed. J. R. de J. Jackson (1970) pp. 620–51, where the phrase is on p. 645.

22. IS 3, quoting NB 44.

23. See my essay on Coleridge's 'Poems of the Supernatural' in *S. T. Coleridge*, ed. R. L. Brett (1971) p. 82.

24. BL II 6.

25. See my discussion in *Coleridge the Visionary* (1959) pp. 194–8.

26. See above, pp. 3–4 and n.

27. TT 6 July 1833.

28. CN I 838.

29. Feb 1801, CL II 677–703.

30. WL (1787–1805) 357. Cf. Colossians 3:3, 'For ye are dead, and your life is hid with Christ in God.'

31. *Omniana*, ed. Southey (1812) I 219–21.

32. See G. N. G. Orsini, *Coleridge and German Idealism* (Carbondale, Ill., 1969) pp. 178–83.

33. CN I 926.

34. CN I 928.

35. See above, p. 33.

36. *Omniana*, ed. R. Southey (1812) I 241–2. Translated by George Whalley: see PL 324–7, 450–2 and Friend II 282.

37. CN I 930 and n.

38x. CN I 937. The books are listed in George Whalley, *Samuel Taylor Coleridge: Library Cormorant*, unpublished Ph.D. thesis University of London, 1950, Appendix B. Through the kindness of the Carlisle Cathedral Librarian I have been enabled to examine some of them personally there.

39. Kenelm Digby, 'A Treatise of Bodies': *Two Treatises* (Paris, 1644) p. 335.

40. Ibid. 336.

41. CN I 1005. From Digby, op. cit., 299. The editor's note cites the 1645 edition of Digby, page 377 (which should be 365). It was the 1644 edition that Coleridge in fact borrowed from Carlisle.

42. See, e.g., Griggs, CL III xxx–xli and C Variety 37–44; E. Schneider, *Coleridge, Opium and 'Kubla Khan'* (Chicago, 1953); Alethea Hayter, *Opium and the Romantic Imagination* (1968) pp. 191–8, etc.; and Molly Lefebure, *Samuel Taylor Coleridge: A Bondage of Opium* (1974) (but see note 44 below).

43ˣ. John Brown's *Elementa Medicinae*, first published in 1780, was translated with a prefatory biography by Thomas Beddoes in 1795, at about the time when Coleridge came to know him. Brown's key-concept was that of 'excitability', which he regarded as the chief, and perhaps identifying, characteristic of life, and closely related to 'vitality'. He classified diseases into those which were due to understimulation and those due to overstimulation, and argued (in opposition to remedies involving 'reducing') that most were due to the former.

   It is of some interest that a translation of Brown's work appeared at Göttingen in 1799 (the year that Coleridge left there) and led to several years of acrid and even violent dispute on the subject (see DNB, entry John Brown).

44ˣ. Notably by Molly Lefebure (op. cit. 185, 196, etc.). Evidence is handled in a rather cavalier fashion in this book, however (see my review, TLS (6 Sept 1974) p. 949) and the opinions expressed concerning the exact dates of his growing addiction should not be accepted without careful examination.

45. Feb 1803, CL II 933–4.

46. CN II 2368.

47. See above, p. 163.

48. See CN I 572 and n.

49. See above, p. 198.

50ˣ. Blake seems to have explored the same range of symbolism, particularly in 'Tiriel' (Tiriel being the intelligence of Mercury). See my *Blake's Visionary Universe* (Manchester, 1969) p. 367, note 9.

51ˣ. BL I 10 (cf. letter of Aug 1806, CL II 1178). In the *Transactions of the Royal Society* there is an account by Dr W. Pope of a quicksilver mine in Friuli, where deleterious effects on health and the short expectation of life among the labourers are described. *Transactions*, 1665, I 21.

52. CN I 960.

53. CN I 1401.

54. See above, p. 91.

55. See above, p. 230. For the full run of images, which was first noted by George Whalley, see his essay, 'Coleridge's Poetic Sensibility' in C Variety 10–11.

56. CL II 1028–9.

57. CN II 2345.

58. CN II 2346.
59. CL II 1028.

Chapter 10

1. WL (1806–11) 86–7.
2. See, e.g., the note at the beginning of his last 1819 lecture: PL 395.
3. Preface to *Poems* (World's Classics) (Oxford, 1907) p.v. Reprinted in his *Studies in Literature* (1918) I, 213.
4. *Milton* 31 (*Complete Writings*, ed. G. Keynes (Oxford, 1966) p. 520).
5. *London University Magazine* (1830) II 318 (cf. *Coleridge the Visionary* (1959) pp. 29–31.
6. Harold Bloom, *The Anxiety of Influence* (New York, 1973) and *A Map of Misreading* (New York, 1975).
7. 'Life to him would be death to me' (&c). Letter of 24 Sept 1819, KL II 212.
8. Thomas Maurice *History of Hindostan* (1795–8) I 107–8. See *Coleridge the Visionary* (1959) pp. 263–4.
9. 'We are not of Alice, nor of thee. . .' LW II 103.
10. For an extended discussion of this and related issues see my article 'Coleridge and Lamb: the Central Themes', *Charles Lamb Bulletin* (1976) N.S. No. 14, 109–23.
11. LW II 69.
12. LW II 186–7, 192.
13. LL II 190 (see also above, p. 4).
14. To Godwin, CL I 588.
15. 'The Flight and Return of Mahomet'. See CL I 531 and above, pp. 227–8. Passages from the projected poem may be found in PW I 329 and Southey, *Oliver Newman* (1845) p. 113.
16. HW XVII 116.
17. See, e.g., HW VII 114–18, 119–28; XVI 99–114; XI 34.
18. Walter Pater, 'Coleridge's Writings', *Westminster Review* (1866) n.s. XXIX 106–32. Article revised for *Appreciations* (1889).
19. Pater, *The Renaissance: Studies in Art and Poetry* (1873) (Revd ed. 1888) p. 130.
20. *Autobiography of Sir Henry Taylor* (1885) I 188.
21. 23 Mar 1798, DWJ I 13; 8 Feb 1802, Ibid. 109. Cf. *The Ancient Mariner* (1798) lines 202 and 205; 258 (PW II 1036–7).
22. 29 Dec 1801 (DWJ I 97). Cf. *Ancient Mariner* (1798) l.123 and Coleridge's 1803 letter quoted above, pp. 207–8).
23. W Pr (Gr) III 469 (from R. P. Graves); cf. 492.
24. HW XVII 107.
25x. J. Hillis Miller, *The Disappearance of God; five nineteenth-century writers* (Cambridge, Mass., 1963) pp. 66–7, 77. He points out (p. 69n) that there is no exact design corresponding to the

description, but argues that it 'contains in essence the effect of Piranesi's whole series'.

26. Alethea Hayter, *Opium and the Romantic Imagination* (1968) pp. 93–8 and plate iv (also index, s.v. Piranesi).
27. DQW I 33–49.
28. Ibid. I 178.
29. Ibid., I 180–1. For the Maelstrom, see above, pp. 213–14.
30. Friend I 59n, quoting J. F. Blumenbach, *The Institutions of Physiology*, tr. J. Elliotson (1817) 127–8.
31. PW I 101 and n.
32. See above, p. 81
33. BM Add MS 36532: published IS 45–50; note to TT 30 Apr 1830.
34x. KL II 88–9. For an extended discussion see my essay 'A Stream by Glimpses' in C Variety 223–40.
35. See above, p. 87.
36. See Leslie Marchand, *Byron: a Biography* (1957) II 528, 542–3, 568, 597, etc., and refs.
37. See, e.g., A. M. D. Hughes, *The Nascent Mind of Shelley* (Oxford, 1947); Joseph Barrell, *Shelley and the Thought of his Time* (New Haven, Conn., 1947); D. King-Hele, *Shelley, his thought and work*, 2nd ed. (1971).
38. Shelley, *Works*, ed. R. Ingpen and W. E. Peck (1926–30) VII 124. I owe this reference to Mr P. M. S. Dawson.
39. W. R. Greg (apparently), quoted by Asa Briggs, *Victorian Cities* (1963) pp. 96–7.
40x. De Quincey's essay on Davy suggests that a coolness may have been setting in an early as 1808–9 (DQW III 16, 21–2). Cf. Davy's 1808 characterisation of him to Poole, *Fragmentary Remains of Sir Humphry Davy*, ed. J. Davy (1858) p. 75: 'His mind is a wilderness, in which the cedar and the oak, which might aspire to the skies, are stunted in their growth by underwood, thorns, briars and parasitic plants.' The two men met and apparently dined together in 1823, however (ibid. 114).
41x. CL II 1103n. Just before Coleridge left for Malta he planned a work to be entitled 'Consolations and Comforts', which eventually became *The Friend*: see, e.g., CN I 1646 and n, CL II 1036.
42. For Dickens's reading of Coleridge five years before, in 1839, see *Letters of Charles Dickens*, ed. M. House and G. Storey (Oxford, 1965–) I 597.
43. F. Kaplan, *Dickens and Mesmerism* (Princeton, N.J., 1975) pp. 15–21, 26, etc. For a further good account see Jonathan Miller, 'Mesmerism', *The Listener* (22 Nov 1973) XC 685–90.
44. S. Freud, *An Autobiographical Study*, tr. J. Strachey, 2nd ed. (1946) pp. 27–30.
45. See R. Bentall, 'Healing by Electromagnetism – fact or fiction?' *New Scientist* (22 Apr 1976) LXX 166–7.

46. C. R. Sanders, *Coleridge and the Broad Church Movement* (Durham, N.C., 1942).
47. For the former, see, e.g., letter to Cottle, 1814, CL III 479 and cf. his note to Leighton's *Expository Works* (1748) I 83, to be published in my edition of the Leighton annotations for the Collected Coleridge *Marginalia*; for the latter see his projected work 'The Mysteries of Religion grounded in or relative to the Mysteries of Human Nature' (letter of 1810, CL III 279) – and cf. CL VI 895 for a significant discussion in 1832.
48. John Sterling, *Essays and Tales* (1848) I xxv.
49. Leigh Hunt, *Autobiography*, ed. R. Ingpen (1903) II 54 (interpolation by T. L. Hunt). Discussed by Owen Barfield in his essay, 'Coleridge's Enjoyment of Words', C Variety 218.
50. Quoted, Augustus J. C. Hare, *Memorials of a Quiet Life* (1873) II 87.

Index

(*Page-references in bold type indicate central discussions;*
(*sel.*) *indicates selected references on a pervasive topic*)

Aaron, 10
Abrams, M. H., 301
Absolute genius, 115–18, 170
Abyssinia, 98, 117
'Active universe', 49, **231**. See
     also Piper, H. W.
Aeolian harp, 251, 291. See also
     Eolian Harp, The
Aesculapius, 9, 206, 211
Aether, 60, 71f
Aids to Reflection, 82, 94
Air, 25, 32, 45, 123–4
Akenside, M., 33 and n
Albatross, 108, 156, 167–8
Alchemy, 24
Alice (*Through the Looking-
     Glass*), 22
Allegory, 58, 215
America, 97–8
*Ancient Mariner, The Rime of
     the*, ix, 84, 90, 107–8, 113,
     124, 143–6, ch. 7, 186ff, 193,
     195, 215, 220, 222, 235, 259,
     263, 267, 272, 284f
Ancient of Days, 182
Andersen, H. C., 298
Angels, 90, 204, 268
Animal life, animation, 42, 49f,
     53–6, 105–6, 139–40, 159, 230.
     See also Suspended animation
Animal magnetism, **73**, 81, 85,
     151, 158, 171, **220–3**, 225, 228,
     232, 247–9, 279, 285–6
Apollo, 33, 98, 117
Apples, 25, 141
Aquinas, 266

Arabian Nights' Entertainments,
     18, 20–1
Arch, 82, 258
Archimage, 4
Aristotle, 210, 239
Aspasia, 14
Associationism, 13, 60, 76
Atomism, 70
Augustine, St, 239–40
'*Autumnal Moon, Sonnet to
     the*', 132

Bacchus, 10
'Bang', 246–7
Barfield, O., 289, 303, 308
Bars, 139
Bartram, W., *Travels*, 243
Bastille, 51
Bate, W. J., x, 14
Baxter, A., 60, **79–81**, 268
Beanfield, 64–9, 79, 95
Beddoes, T., 105, 199, 301, 305
Bees, 79, 214. See also Honey,
     swarm, insects
Bee-idiot, 240
Being, 98–9, 196–7, 198, 205, 215,
     222, 259. See also 'I myself I'
Belisarius, 18
Berkeley, 71, 122
Biographia Literaria, 6–7, 11f, 50,
     106–7, 119, 123, 261
Blake, W., 23, 38, 262–4, 305
Blood, 31, 33, 44–5, 105, 188f,
     221, 227, 234, 243, 270,
     297
Bloom, H., 264–5, 269

Blumenbach, J. F., 193, 221–2, 279
Boehme, J., 9, 15, **23–32**, 36, 122, 139, 174, 265; *Aurora*, 23, 24–31, 35, 38, 89–90, 123–5, 154, 176, 178
Bostetter, E. E., 149
Bowles, W. L., 47
Bowles the Surgeon, 105
Brahmans, 163, 204
Braun, A., 218
Breeze, 25, **64–8**, 137, 140f, 168, 172, 174, 196, 203, 209, 211, 231, 251, **253**, 266, 273
Bristol, 41ff, 198f
Bristol Library, **62 and n**, 71n
Brown, John, 305
Browning, R., 286
Bruno, Giordano, 33, 243
Brunonian theory, 246 and n
Bunyan, J., 160
Bürger, G., 178 and n, 181, 193
Burnet, T., 291
Butler, S., 23
Butterfly, 68
Byron, Lord, 282

Caduceus, 9
Calenture, 97, 152
Candle, 25, 266
Carlisle Library, 245
Carlyle, T., 4, 94, 286
Carlyon, C., 194–5, 225
Casimir, 48
Cato's Letters, 23
Ceres, 99
Charm, charms, 87, 112, 235, 238, 247
Chaucer, 39
Chayes, I., 296
Cheapside Library, 6, 19f
Chemistry, 5, 24, 74. *See also* Davy, H.
Child-labour, 137
'Child of Nature', 132–4, 136–7, 186
Children, 75, 129–30, 181–2, 202–4, 233, 241–2, 252–3, 257, 267
Christabel, 134, 146, 186–92, 195, 220, 231–8, 282, 285
Christianity, (sel.), 102–4, 278, 286–7 and n. *See also* God, Sons of God
Christ's Hospital, 4, 9, **20–1**, 23, 28–9, 37, 43, 138–9, 263–4
Circles, 6, 9, 55–6, 60, 108, 116, 179–80, 214–18, 270, 277
Circulation, 44–5, 74, 243–4
Cleopatra, 264–5
Coleridge, Anne (sister), 138
Coleridge, Berkeley, 195–7
Coleridge, Derwent, 203–4, 237, 252–3
Coleridge, George (brother), 180
Coleridge, Hartley, 132, 136–43, 202–4, 217, 237–8, 241
Coleridge, H. N., 232
Coleridge, James (Brother), 11
Coleridge, John (father), 18, 20
Coleridge, Sara (wife), 41, 53, 66, 95, 199, 203, **229 and n**
Coleridge, S. T., Life (sel.): Childhood at Ottery, 1772–82, 18–20; schooldays at Christ's Hospital, 1782–91: *See* Christ's Hospital; at Jesus College, Cambridge, 1791–3, 36f, 43, 67; enlistment as a dragoon, 1793–4, 2, 37; Welsh tour, 1794, 11, 42–3, 300; Cambridge and London, *late 1794*, 41–3, etc.; Pantisocratic scheme, 1794–5: *See* Pantisocracy; public lecturer at Bristol, 1795, 57–9, 79, 268–9 and chs. 2–4 *passim*; marriage to Sara Fricker, *October 1795*, 95; at Clevedon and Bristol, 1795–6, 95–101; at Nether Stowey as writer and preacher, 1796–8, 106–7, 269, 275 and chs. 5–7 *passim*; in Germany, 1798–9, 193–8, 214, 220, 221–2, 225–6, 305; at Nether Stowey, 1799, 198–9; in Lake District and

London, 1799–1804, chs. 8–9 *passim*; love for Sara Hutchinson, 1799–1810: *See* Hutchinson, S.; in Malta and Italy, 1804–6, 11, 210, 256, 258–60, 271; return to Lake District and London, 1806–16, 213, 260–1, 273–4, 275–9; residence at Highgate, 1816–34, 3–4 216, 279–81. *See also Table Talk*
Colours, 27, 32 and n, **90–1**, 242
'Commanding genius', 115–17, 188, 234
'*Concerning Poetry* . . .', 13
Conjuror's Magazine, 81
Consciousness, (sel.) 59, chs. 4 and 7 *passim*, 188–9, 197, 215, 223–5, 256, 273–4, 280
Constitution of the Church and State, On the, 217 and n
Conversion, 151–8, 160–1
Cook, T., 218
Cooper, Lane, 294
Cornwell, J., 95
Cottle, J., 41, 97, 120, 199, 247
'Counterfeit infinity', 155, 162, 164, 167f, 208
Cowper, William, 33, 51, 138, 152
Crabb Robinson, H., 152, 193
Creech, T., 292
Crick, F. H. C., 218
Cudworth, R., 49, 57, 155
Curse, 169, 220–2

Dance, 7, 150, 176, 185, 265, 272
'*Dark Ladie, The*', 187
Darnton, R., 72–3, 151n
Darwin, E., 33, **50–7**, 65, 69, **74–7**, 81f, 86, 90, 96, 105, 152, 213, 292
Darwin, R. W., 75, 91
Davy, H., 13, **199–203**, 204f, 210–12, 226–7, 244, 282–4, 307
Death, 20, 123, 139–40, 143–6, 157, 163, 196–7, **207–8**, 227, 267, 270f, 280f
Death of Abel, 113, 151

Déjà vu, 100–1
'*Dejection*', 290. *See also* 'Letter to Sara Hutchinson'
Delirium, 76, 152–3, 155, 277
Delson, A., 148 and n
De Quincey, T., 5, 39, 147, 152f, 261, 275–9, 287, 307
Descartes, 82, 89, 107, 151
Destiny of Nations, See Joan of Arc
Dickens, 284–5
Digby, K., 245–6
Double Touch, 81–8, 190, 201, 242–3, 247–8, **256–7**, 279, 280
Doves, 206, 235
Dreams, 75, 79–81, 100–1, 115–17, 156f, 183, 196, 267f, 270, 276–7, 280. *See also Kubla Khan*, Nightmare
Dulcimer, 117
'Dungeon, The', 151
Dupuis, C. F., 100
Durham Library, 266
Dyer, G., 41, 48

Eagle, 68, 213
Eastern Tales, 18–21
Ebullience, 8, 13, 192, 275–6
Echo, 137
Eddyings, 9, 56, 62, 203, 206, 207, **214–17**, 273
Egyptian symbols, 15, 33
Eichhorn, J. G., 193
Electricity, 5, 24, 32, 50, 72, 210, 256, 297
Eleusis, 99
Elijah, 110
Eliot, George, 285
Empson, W., 67, 148, 299
Energy (sel.), 8, 29, 45, 52–3, 63, 80f, 115–18, 139–41, 143, 150, 166–7, 187–8, 202, **204**, 211–12, 235–8, 250, 282
Enfield, W., 62 and n
Engel, J. J., 245
Enthusiasm, 63, 80
'*Eolian Harp, The*', 63–9, 79, 95, 105, 120, 126, 132, 182

Epicurus, 48–9, 291
Eternity, 14
Euler, L., 82–6, 293
Evans, Mary, 11, 46, 57
Evolution, 217 and n
Evolvent, 217
Exeter, Society at, 50–1 and n
Expansion, 56, 139, 142f, 170, 172, 273
Eye, (sel.) 29, 39, 80, 91–2, 101, 120, 129, 131f, 142, 171f, 195, 231, 237, 240, 257, 287. See also Animal magnetism

'Facts of Mind', 100, 201
Faculties, 128, 165, 180
Faith, 22, 81, 158, 226, 279
Fall, 26
Fanaticism, 6, 63
Fancy, 15, 152, 158, 160, 215, 225
Fawcett, J., 291
Fear, 171–2, 177, 188, 234, 252–3. See also Nightmare
Fénelon, 100
Ferriar, J., 105
Fiat, 46–7 and n, 99, 182
Fibonacci series, 218
Fichte, 271
Finch, J. A., 304
Fire (sel.), 30, 45, 64, 97f, 113, 244
'Fixities and definites', 8, 84, 141, 166–73, 194, 225, 270, 286
Flashes, 52, 90, 162, 196
Flood, 106–7
Flower, B., 101
'Foster-Mother's Tale, The', 133
Fountain, see Springs
Fowell, 249
Fragrance, 19, 27, 32, 64–5, 68–9, 95, 263
'France: an Ode', 186, 282
French Revolution, 1, 103, 149, 161, 175, 186, 217, 269, 270
Frend, W., 41, 48
Freud, S., 286

Friend, The, 6, 53–4, 82, 214–15, 222, 244, 261, 279
'Frost at Midnight', 136–43
Fruman, N., xi–xii, 298, 301, 302

Gaskell, Mrs, 285
Genesis, 15, 46–7
'Genial', 46, 62, 63f, 93, 206, 229, 250, 267
Genius, 19, 67, 92, 97f, 115–18, 178, 182, 200, 208–9, 211f, 224f, 244f, 277, 283
Gessner, S., 113
Geysers, 50, 229
Ghosts, 89, 280
Gilbert, W., 96–9
Gillman, Anne, 68
Gillman, J., 4
Glass harmonica, 151
Glow-worm, 52
God (sel.), 13, 42, 53, 59, 62–3, 67–8, 102, 106, 141, 156, 179, 192, 196, 207
Godwin, W., 1–2, 42, 50, 74, 143, 149f, 201, 224, 269, 284
Goethe, 218
Göttingen, 193f, 214, 305
Gravitation, 36, 50, 74, 83, 210, 231
Gray, T., 24
'Greek Ode on Astronomy', 36, 244, 283
Green, J. H., 280
Greg, W. R., 282
Greville, Fulke, 243
Grief, 197, 226
Growth, 46, 75, 143, 217, 219, 241–3, 252, 270, 277. See also Children, Organic
Guilt, 114, 120
Gutteridge, J. D., 127, 165, 295

Haggern, M., 52–3
Hamlet, 89
Hare, Julius, 286, 287
Hartley, D., 13, 50, 58, 60, 71, 73–4, 76, 92, 156, 210, 253, 294

Harvey, William, 33 and n, 45, 243
Haven, R., xi, 210
Hayter, A., 277
Hazlitt, W., 1–3, 4, 42, 113, 135, 143, 158, 222, 269–72, 275
Heart, (sel.) 30, 33–8, 44–5, 82, 110, 123, 138, 151, 158, 169, 217, 221, 238, 245, 251, 253, 265–6, 270, 275, 278
'Heart of hearts', 30
Heat, 30, 35–6. *See also* Warmth-sense
Hegel, 23 and n
Herder, *Kalligone*, 14
Hermes, 9
Hermit, 145
Hesperides, 9
Hieroglyphics, *See* Egyptian
Hobbes, 238, 245
Home, J., *Douglas*, 77
Homer, 29
Honey, honey-dew, 65, 170. *See also* Bees
Horse-hair, 216
House, H., 142, 298
Hucks, J., 42, 300
Hufeland, C. W., 279
Hume, David, 80, 82, 88f, 201, 238
Humphry, R., 289
Hunt, L., 5, 287
Hunter, J., 105
Hutchinson, J., 229
Hutchinson, Mary, 229n, 266, 304
Hutchinson, Sara, 92, 199, 201, 205–8, 228–9, 251, 254, 260f, 266
Hutton, J., 53
Hypnosis, *see* Animal magnetism

'I myself I', 105–6f, 242
Iamblichus, 28–9
Ice, 28, 100, 112, 125, 139–42, 153, 167, 274
Iceland, 50, 229

Idealize, 202
'Idea-pot', 8
Ideas, 78, 201, 208, 224, 229, 243, 253
Identity, 197, 224. *See also* Being
Idiots, 53, 134, 239–41, 257–8
Illusion, 83–9, 152, 267
Imagination, 22, 38, 76f, 87, 93, 104, 152, 159–60, 180, 187, 207, 212, 225, 241, 245–6, 250f, 262, 269, 273, 280
Imitation, 232–5, 245–6, 249
Immortality, 102, 197, 225–6, 229, 267, 273
Incomprehensibility, 66f, 101, 179
Indian thought, 32–3. *See also* Brahmans
Infinity, 62, 107, 154–6, 164, 169
Influence, 232, 264–5, 269–70, 284
Innocence, (sel.) 65–9, 134, 190, 285
Insects, 55–6, 65–6, 77–9, 203–4, 228, 259. *See also* Bees
Instinct, 58, 71, 199, 203–4
Intelligence, 12–13, 15–16, 49, 100, 179, 283, 286
Irradiation, 91, 231, 268
Irritability, 231

Jasmine, 65, 68, 95
Jena, 193
Joan of Arc, 59–64, 79, 99, 102, 120, 158, 213, 293
John, St, 107, 161
Johnson, J., 264

Kant, I., 107, 193f, 239, 271, 294
Kaplan, F., 307
Keats, 38, 131, 183, 264, 280–2, 289
Kermode, J. F., 290
Kinglake, Dr, 201
Kirkpatrick, W. G., 3, 236
'Known and familiar', 303
Krishna, 33, 265

Kubla Khan, ix, 7, 19–20, **115–18**, 125, 146, 154, 187, 198, 202, 267f, 282

Lamb, C., 4f, 10, 21, 28, 39, 49, 77, 96, 102, 107, ch. 6 *passim*, 156, 183, 265–8
Lamb, Mary, 96
Lapland, 112
Lark, 174, 263
Laudanum, *see* Opium
Lavater, J. C., 69
Law, W., 23, 26, 71, 85
Lay Sermons, 261, 270
Lectures (1795), 57, 96
Leemius, 293
Lefebure, M., 305
Leibnitz, 62, 290, 293
Lessing, 271
'Letter to Sara Hutchinson', 139, 205–7, 208, 250–2
Liberty, 51–2, 98, 144–5, 169, **186**, 188
Life, (sel.) 14, 71, **105–6**, 110–11, ch. 6 *passim*, 157, 188, 197f, **207f**, 234–6, 242, 270. *See also* Theory of Life
Light, (sel.) 29, **32–7**, 46, 52–3, 55, 83, 97ff, 104, 198, 207, 212, 222, 237, 249, 254, 272, 279, 287. *See also* Sun and Moon
'Littleness', 52, 162, **164–6**, 175, 183, 300
Lloyd, Charles, 224
Locke, 73, 76, 238, 245
Logos, 59, 217
Louis XVI, 85
Love (sel.), 12, **47**, 64–9, 94, 160, 169, 236–8
'Love-fires', 28, 154
Lowes, J. L., 147
Lucifer, 25, 28
Lucretius, 32, 45, 48–50, 84
Lyrical Ballads, 113, 119, 134, 151, 175, 186–7, 285

Macbeth, 109
Macrobius, 45

Madness, 76, 96f
Maelstrom, 50, 213–14, 278
Magic, 5–10, 20, 65–6, 112–13, 268, 273
Magnetism, 50, 71, 82–7, 98, 132, 278, 282. *See also* Animal magnetism
Mahomet, *see* Mohammedanism
Malebranche, T., 245
Manchester Memoirs, 106
Mania, 152, 155
Martin, B., 152
Materialism, 13, 43, 60–2, 105, 241
Mathematics, 5, 218–19
Maurice, F. D., 286
Maximus Tyrius, 36
McFarland, T., x–xi, 14
McLachlan, H., 291
Memnon, 33, 52, 98
Memory, 42–3, 197, 229, 233, 253, 258
Mercury, 9, 11, 211
Mesmer, A., 72–3, 85. *See also* Animal magnetism
Metaphysics (sel.), 13, 23, 48, 100f, 119, **194–5** 207, 210, 239, 250, 253, 256, 280
Methodism, 35, 151
Michelangelo, 10
Mill, J. S., 7
Miller, J. Hillis, 277 and n
Miller, Jonathan, 307
Milton, J., 3, 32, 51, 65, 95, 104, 119, 181, 234, 264, 271, 288, 293, 298
Mimosa, 55
Mind, 12f, 47, 62, 98, 122, 283–4
Mirror, 8, 137, 141, 202, 211
Mohammedanism, 109–11, 227–8, 268
Monads, 61–2 and n, 83, 111, 283–4
Monro, 105
Moon, 11, 99–100, 122, 132f, 149, 169, 171f, 174, 181, 188, 206, 217, 222, 232, 272, 283

Moral ideas, 13, 106–7, 147–8, 179f, 214, 224, 239
Moritz's Magazine, 227
Moses, 10, 39
Mother-child relationship, 58, 187–92, 195, 231, 246
Motion (sel.) 197, 259
Myrtle, 64f, 68, 95
Mystics, 10
Myth, 15. See also Allegory
Mythology, 99, 103, 116

Napoleon, 270
Necessitarianism, 13, 23, 50, 76, 257
Neoplatonists, see Platonism
Newton, Isaac, 13–14, 23, 27, 34, 36–7, 43, 60, 71f, 74, 76, 283f
Newton, J., 152f
'Nightingale, The', 130–2, 182, 220f
Nightingales, 65, 68, 194, 214, 263, 280
Nightmare, 75, 86–7, 94, 144, 149, 183, 257, 280
Nile, 50, 293
Nitrous Oxide, 200–3, 226–7
Novalis, 23

Objective, 82, 240
Ocular spectra, 75, 91, 242–3, 253
Okenism, 228
Omniana, 240
'Omnific', 63 and n
'One Life', 125–43, 145, 166, 203–8, 279, 286, 296
Opium, 213, 246–9, 256, 260f, 274f, 277
Organic, 15–16, ch. 3 passim, 66, 78, 198, 205, 209, 211, 212–13, 217, 223, 243, 249, 252, 258. See also Vegetation
Organisation, 5, 248
Orgasm, 257
Osorio, 109–13, 125, 133, 150, 163–4
Oxygen, 59, 72

'Pains of Sleep, The', 277
Paley, M. D., 290
Pantheism, 213
Pantisocracy, 2, 7, 41, 43, 96
Paradise, 26, 65–6, 95, 116–18, 173
Passions, 7, 226, 246
Pater, W., 272
Paul, St., 15, 107
Penn Warren, R., 148, 298–9
Percy, Thomas, 178
Perfectibility, 74
Philosophical Lectures, 6, 49, 244, 292
Phoebus, 98
Phyllotaxis, 218
Pindar, 29
Piper, H. W., 43 and n, 290, 292
Piranesi, G. B., 276–7
'Plastic', 45–8, 66, 105
Plato, 12, 14, 58, 100, 105, 217, 228
Platonism, 9, 12, 23, 28, 43, 103, 265
Plotinus, 28–9, 32
Poole, T., 106, 119, 196–7, 198, 284
Pope, A., 2, 26, 65, 288
'Populousness', 135–6, 254, 258
Prayer, 153
Priestley, J., 33, 43, 57, 59, 196, 244
Primary consciousness, see Consciousness
Prospero, 2
Proust, 254
Psyche, 68
Psychology, 54–5, 79ff, 111, 198, ch. 9 passim
Pulse, 169, 246, 270
Purkis, S., 246
'Pye, To Mr', 179–80
Pythagoras, 62, 217, 243

Quarll, P., 18
Quicksilver mines, 250 and n. See also Mercury
Quiller-Couch, Arthur, 261–2

'Raven, The', 107–9, 162f
Ravens, 107–10
Reason (sel.), 47, 87, 159, 225
'Recantation', 186, 282
Recognition, 70ff
'Reflections on having left a Place of Retirement', 95
Religious Musings, 1, 153, 195
Remorse, 282. See also Osorio
'Revealed Religion . . .', 57
Reverie, 75, 196, 283
Revolution, 216–17
'Riddle of the World', 94, 179–82
Ridley, J., 19–20, 65, 117n
Robbins, D. M., 104, 299
Robinson Crusoe, 18, 21
Rod, 6, 10, 278
Roland, Mme, 68
Roman Catholicism, 110, 154, 191
Romance, 17–22, 87, 115, 131
Rooke, B., 54, 82
Roscoe, W., 97
Rose, 68, 95
Rousseau, 26–7, 34
Russian palace of ice, 51

'Sabbaths of the soul', 214
Salitter, 27, 36
'Salutation and Cat', 48
Sambuca, 117
Satan, 3, 95, 271. See Lucifer
Saumarez, R., 43
Schelling, 23, 271
Schiller, 193 and n. See Wallenstein
Schimper, W. P., 218
Schrickx, W., 155
Scott, W., 178–282
Sea-sickness, 257
Seeds, 49–50, 99, 273
'Semina rerum', 49
Sensibility, 24, 74, 120, 217
Series, 202, 224
Serpents, 9–10, 14, 55–6, 205–6, 211, 213, 259, 270, 291
Shaffer, E., xi, 301

Shakespeare, 183, 226, 264–5
Shakespearean Criticism, 6, 216
Shaping spirit, 230, 251–2
Shelley, 282
Shelvocke, G., 156
Shrewsbury, 4
'Shurton Bars, Lines written at', 52–3, 161–2
Sibylline Leaves, 108, 261, 279
Sidney, Philip, 243
Single touch, see Double Touch
Skin, 248–9, 255–7
Sky, 82–4, 139, 186, 190–1, 258, 263
Smith, Leapidge, 39
Snakes, 217, 234–5; with tail in mouth, 56 and n, 179–80. See also Circles, Serpents, Watersnakes
Sockburn, 199, 201, 228
Socrates, 58, 283
Somnambulism, 82, 85
'Songs of the Pixies', 158
Sons of God, 99, 202
Soul, 79, 105, 122, 231, 244, 247f, 255
Southey, R., 1, 36, 41, 59, 60, 79–80, 90f, 96, 114, 117f, 165, 177–8, 183, 198, 200, 215, 253, 268–9, 280
Spectre-ship, 143–4
Spinoza, 107, 193–4, 198, 228
Spirals, 9, 55f, 217–19, 259, 277. See also Serpents
Spirit (sel.), 105, 121, 137, 140, 195, 231, 255
Springs, 8, 30–7, 44–5, 56, 62, 67, 83, 89–90, 98–100, 106–7, 122–4, 154, 160, 169, 183, 230, 244, 246, 273f, 287
Starlings, 230, 255
Statius, 48
Stephen, L., 147
Sterling, J., 286
Sterne, L., 34
Stevens, Wallace, 301
Stieglitz, J., 279
Stoudt, J. J., 23–4 and n

Suarez, 266
'Subjective', 82, 240
Sublimity, 14, 35, 37, 162, 178
Sulivan, R., 44–6, 49, 58, 64
Sun, 2, 11f, 14, 18, **31–7**, 44–5, 83, 99–100, 116, 121f, 139–42, 149, 168, 181, 196, 203, 211f, 222
Supernatural, 22, 88–9, 97, 148, 187, 193, 280
Superstition, 22, 92, 138, 145, 158–60, 281
Surinam toads, 216
Surprise, 75
Suspended animation, 49
Suspension, 88, 142, 187, 207, 251–2
Swarm, 197–8, 259
Swedenborg, E., 35, 80, 97–8, 100, 217
Swift, J., 183
Swiss cantons, 186, 269
Swoon, 170–1
Symbol, 148–9, 241, 299. *See also* allegory, myth

Table Talk, 152, 184, 236
Tales of the Genii, 19
Tartar Tales, 19
Taylor, J., 90
Taylor, T., 29, 100
Tennyson, 286
'The Hour when we . . .', 129
Thelwall, J., 101–6, 162, 193
Theory of Life, 216, 261
'This Lime Tree Bower', 110, 120–2, 127, 162, 164, 214
Thompson, E. P., 193
Thoth, 100
'Three Graves, The', 220–1
Tieck, L., 23, 85
Tillotson, J., 80
Time (and Space), 13, 75, 283
Tobit, 113
Tooke, A., *Pantheon*, 9–10, 211
Touch, 75, 242. *See also* Double Touch
Trance, 153, 170–1, 189–90

Transcendentalism, 286
Trees, 9, 15, 124, 145, 186, 187–8, 203f, 208f, 212, 219, 245, 307
Trinitarianism, 12, 40, 45–6, 58, 59–60, 103
Two Voices, 153, 170–1
Typhoon, 111–12

Unitarianism, 12, 35, 41, 43, 103, 147, 153–4, 185, 291
Unity, 59, 139, 166, 210–11, **227–30**, 240, 258, 274
'Universe of Death', 8, 233–4 and n
'Universe of Life', 8, 234–6. *See also* Life, One Life
'Unrealize', 215

Valley of Rocks, 113, 115
Vegetation, vegetative, 8, 42, 45, 47, 49f, 53–6, 77, 108, 127–40 *passim*, 145, 159, 187–9, 216, 230, 247, 263, 272
Vines, 55, 205
Vishnu, 163
Vital force, 197, 201, 204, 209, 211, 217, 223, 248, 251–2, 305
Volition, 55, 75–8, 85, 87, 230, 242, 248, 256–7, 279f
Voltaire, 23
Vortex, 57, 112, 166, **213–14**, 267

Wakefield, G., 41, 48
Wallenstein, 5, 192
Wand, 9
Wandering Jew, 113
'Wanderings of Cain', 113–15, 133–4, 151, 165, 235
Warmth-sense, 55, 75, 81–9, 139, 144–6, 151, 189, 200, 206, 221, 225ff, 229, 267, 270, 279
Watchman, The, 48, 96
Water, *see* Springs
Waterfalls, 162, 208, 228, 240
Water-snakes, 169, 179, 259
Waterspouts, 57, 112, 291

Watson, J. D., 218
Watters, R., 110
Webster, J., 295
Wedding-guest, 176–7
Wedgwood family, 238, 269
Wedgwood, T., 246–7
Wells, R. H., 113, 149
Wesley, J., 23, 151
Whalley, G., 304
Whirlpool, see Vortex
White, Gilbert, 240
Will, 12, 46, 55, 71–2, 78, 257, 280. See also Volition
Wolfart, Mesmerismus, 81n, 85
Wolff, 294
Wonder, 94, 274
Woolman, J., 160–1 and n
Wordsworth, C., 36n
Wordsworth, Dorothy, ch. 6 passim, 174, 185, 238, 260, 272; Journals, 135, 204, 272–3
Wordsworth, John, 199
Wordsworth, Jonathan, 288
Wordsworth, W., 4, 24, 38, 52, 97, 113, ch. 6 passim, 149–52, 156–7, 163f, 174f, 182–3, 185,

192, 199, 201, 210, 213, 217, 220–1ff, 224, 232, 243, 248, 255, 260, 261, 264, 272–5, 278, 287; 'A slumber . . .', 198; 'Castle of Indolence' stanzas, 204; 'Expostulation and Reply', 129; 'Goody Blake and Harry Gill', 220f; 'Lines . . . in Early Spring', 129; 'Lines left . . . in a Yew-tree', 156–7; 'The Brothers', 97; 'The Convict', 157; 'The Excursion', 97, 175; 'The Idiot Boy', 132, 239; 'The Pedlar', 126; 'The Prelude', 140, 161, 165–6, 217, 230–1, 241, 288; 'The Tables Turned', 128; 'The Thorn', 126, 145, 159–60; 'Tintern Abbey', 124, 132, 182, 242. 'We Are Seven', 130
Wrath-fires, 28, 155

Yeats, W. B., 78

Zapolya, 261
'Zoödynamic Method', 14